WITHDRAWN

China's Relations with Japan, 1945–83:
The Role of Liao Chengzhi

STUDIES ON EAST ASIA

Editorial Board

Sean Breslin, University of Newcastle upon Tyne
James Cotton, Australian National University
Gordon Daniels, University of Sheffield
Delia Davin, University of Leeds
Reinhard Drifte, University of Newcastle upon Tyne
David S. G. Goodman, Murdoch University
Ian Neary, University of Essex
Don Starr, University of Durham

CHINA'S RELATIONS WITH JAPAN, 1945–83:

The role of Liao Chengzhi

Kurt Werner Radtke

Studies on East Asia

MANCHESTER
UNIVERSITY PRESS
Manchester and New York
Distributed exclusively in the USA and Canada by St. Martin's Press

Copyright © Kurt Werner Radtke 1990

Published by Manchester University Press
Oxford Road, Manchester M13 9PL, UK
and Room 400, 175 Fifth Avenue,
New York, NY 10010, USA

*Distributed exclusively in the USA and Canada
by* St. Martin's Press, Inc.,
175 Fifth Avenue, New York, NY 10010, USA

Editorial responsibility for *Studies on East Asia* rests with the Northumbrian Universities' East Asia Centre, University of Newcastle upon Tyne and University of Durham, England, which promotes publications on the individual countries and cultures of East Asia, as well as on the region as a whole.

All rights reserved. No part of this publication may be reproduced, stored in a retrieval system or transmitted, in any form or by any means, electronic, mechanical, photocopying, recording or otherwise without the prior permission of the Publishers

British Library cataloguing in publication data
Radtke, Kurt Werner
 China's relations with Japan, 1945–83: the role of Liao Chengzhi.——(Studies on East Asia).
 1. China. Foreign relations with Japan. Role of Chengzhi, Liao 2. Japan. Foreign relations with China. Role of Chengzhi, Liao
 I. Title II. Series
 327.51052′092′4

Library of Congress cataloging in publication data
Radtke, Kurt W. (Kurt Werner), 1945–
 China's relations with Japan, 1945–83 : the role of Liao Chengzhi / Kurt Werner Radtke.
   p.   cm.—(Studies on East Asia)
 Includes bibliographical references and index.
 ISBN 0–7190–2795–0
 1. China—Relations—Japan. 2. Japan—Relations—China.
 3. China—History—1949– 4. Japan—History—1945– 5. Liao, Ch'eng-chih, 1908–1983.
 I. Liao, Ch'eng-chiah, 1908–1983. II. Title. III. Series: Studies on East Asia (Manchester, England)
 DS740.5.JSR33 1990
 303.48′251052—dc20   90-36569
 ISBN 0 7190 2795 0 *hardback*

Printed in Great Britain
by Billings of Worcester

Contents

Acknowledgements		1
Preface		2
Introduction		4
1	Between China and Japan, 1908-1937	23
2	The War	63
3	The Foundations of the PRC's Japan Policy	92
4	Economic and Political Relations, 1955-1963	116
5	Friends and Foes: 1963-71	158
6	Enemies Become Friends 1971-1978	192
Eventide		243
China, Japan and Liao Chengzhi, Conclusions		255
Bibliography		266
Index		289

Acknowledgements

I would like to express my gratitude to the Netherlands Organisation for the Advancement of Pure Research (ZWO) for financial support for field trips to Japan (1979) and Taiwan (1982). I should also like to thank the Foundation for the Promotion of Cultural Relations between the Kingdom of the Netherlands and China and the Isaac Alfred Ailion Foundation for financial grants to cover typing and correction expenses. I am also grateful to the Institute of Developing Economies (*Ajia keizai kenkyusho*), Tokyo, and to Peking University, Department of History, for accepting me as a Visiting Research Fellow in 1979 and 1984 respectively, and to the Institute of International Relations, Taipei, for assistance during my research in Taiwanese archives (1982), and the staff of these archives. I should like to thank the American Consulate-General in Hong Kong for permission to use their bibliographical file on Liao Chengzhi, and Mr W van Kemenade for his assistance in making the file available to me. I am greatly obliged to Mrs R L Robson for improving the English usage in this manuscript.

I am greatly indebted to the published research of four scholars in particular: Lee Chae-Jin (*Japan Faces China*), Gilbert Fook-lam Chan (*A Chinese Revolutionary*), Alexander Ching-an Yang (*The Policy-Making Process in Japan's Policy Toward the People's Republic of China*), Haruhiro Fukui (esp *Party in Power* and *'Tanaka Goes to Peking'*), as well as the compilers of the series *Nihon Chugoku koryu nenshi* without whose pioneering efforts my research would have been virtually impossible.

The list of politicians, journalists, academics and others - mainly in China and Japan - prepared to share their knowledge with me is too long to be mentioned exhaustively. A few names stand out, however. I am particularly grateful to Professor Hama Kazuhiko of the Institute for Developing Economies (Tokyo) and Professor Liu Jiaquan of the Beijing Institute of Foreign Languages (of which Liao Chengzhi was Chairman for many years), Mr Tagawa Goro (*Yomiuri shinbun*), and also to Mr Akatsu Masuzo, Mrs Chen Choumei, Mrs Anna Chennault, Professor Cynthia L Chennault, Professor Eto Shunkichi, Mr Fujiyama Aiichiro, Mr Hagiwara Teiji, Professor Ichikawa Kenjiro, Mr Ichiko Kenji, Professor Ishikawa Tadao, Mr Warren Kuo, Mr Kawakami Toichi, Mr Kawamura Toichiro, Mr Lu Zhenji, Mr Miyazaki Seimin, The Royal Netherlands Embassy, Tokyo, Mr Saionji Kinkazu, Mr Sakumoto Naoyuki, Mr Shirato Norio, Professor Takeuchi Minoru, Mr Tan Juezhen, Professor Karl A Wittfogel, Professor Yamaguchi Ichiro and Mr Yoshizaki Kozo. Last but not least I should like to thank Mr Hayakawa Tadashi, Mr Kawakami Koichi and Mr Chuang Chen-yan for their hospitality during my stays in Tokyo and Taipei. While I was a Visiting Fellow at Peking University in 1984 I was unable to interview Mrs Jing Puchun (Liao Chengzhi's widow), but I am grateful for publications concerning Liao which were kindly given to me then.

Preface

In more than one sense a biography - even a political one - can never be a scientific construct; it deals with an individual human being, linked to his human fellows and his physical and social surroundings in innumerable ways. A biographer attempts to impose a certain order on the chaotic multitude of facts available. There can be no absolute truth in the order he creates; as a human being grows older, memories of his own past gain a life of their own, change, and eventually grow into a series of myths about his own identity which in turn give rise to new dreams and aspirations. Out of the clash between these dreams and 'reality', actions and new dreams arise, in a never ending stream. It clearly needs a poet and a poet's imagination to create a biography - in this sense, describing the career of a politician on the basis of fragmentary evidence in faded newspaper clippings and eulogies is hopelessly inadequate as a biography. A well-edited collection of photos of Liao's life, including reproductions of some of his paintings, drawings and cartoons, has been published in Chinese and Japanese and provides interesting glimpses, but has only a fraction of the material available on the mainland.[1] Moreover, it is to be expected that substantial evidence yet unknown will be published in years to come.[2]

My aim is much more modest. By tracing the fate of China's most prominent Japan specialist I have attempted to present a picture of Chinese politics towards Japan that shows how the Chinese political situation influenced both the policy makers and their policies. It is a picture that is perhaps more influenced by my own subjective feelings and ideas than by preferences for a particular scientific model of Chinese politics. Not surprisingly, the greatest obstacle to any such study is the closed nature of the Chinese political system. The actors on this stage wear masks, and we do not know the playwright(s). The façade is very simple: in the main roles, the sage-king Mao Zedong and his assistant, Prime Minister Zhou Enlai.[3] But in this play, the puppeteers are also puppets, and there is no omniscient master-playwright. Liao Chengzhi usually appears in interludes and sideshows; a good-humoured heavyweight meeting countless foreign visitors, Overseas Chinese, and Japanese businessmen and politicians. One moment he is a Communist revolutionary; but he already turns his head to address a joke to a businessman eager to conquer the China market.

What was Liao Chengzhi's true face? What is the true face of Chinese politics? I will not dare to attempt an answer. Perhaps the question itself is wrong. China's defeat in the Opium War (1839-1842) did not only mark the beginning of the end of the Chinese Empire and its traditional culture. The adoption of an alien ideology - Communism - did not provide a miraculous cure for China's ills; it was also responsible for catastrophic events such as the 'Great Leap Forward' and the 'Great Proletarian Cultural Revolution' (GPCR). What were Liao's true beliefs? Communism? Or did he 'believe in China'? What were his dreams for the future? There seems no answer to these questions. And yet, by presenting diverse facets of

Preface

Liao's life story we may perhaps gain some understanding of an issue vital to China's future: China's future relations with its past enemy Japan.

Notes to Preface

1   Lu Xuezhi et al comp *Liao Chengzhi de yisheng*, (Xinhua, 1984) (distributor: Kodansha). See also *[Shashinshu] Ryo Shoshi no shogai*, (Tokyo: Xinhuashe, 1984) and the special issue of *China Reconstructs* (in Chinese), 'Liao Chengzhi - yige weida de aiguozhe gemingjia', *Zhongguo jianshe* (tekan) (September 1983).

2   On 9 February 1984 a notice in the PRC press asked for material on Liao's life to be sent to the Liao Zhongkai-He Xiangning Memorial Hall in Canton.

3   The difficulty of evaluating Liao's political achievements is apparent from the fact that some of his initiatives were long known under different names: 'Accepting Liao's ideas the Central Committee [of the CCP] promulgated the following regulations in the name of Chairman Mao: "Rules and Regulations Concerning Requests by Overseas Chinese to Use State-owned Wasteland"'; in the name of [Prime Minister] Zhou: 'The Handling of Overseas Chinese Contributions for the Running of Schools'; and 'Preferential Treatment of Overseas Chinese Investments Companies Owned by the State'. (*Liaogong zai renjian*, Zhongguo xinwenshe, comp Hong Kong, 1983), pp 83-4.

Introduction

Braving the howling northerly he takes vigorous strides, deep in the forested mountains that seem limitless. He is looking for fragrant plum blossoms that keep falling, fighting frost and snow. 'Looking for plum blossoms in the snow' is the title of that painting. It is an allegory of a man imbued with revolutionary ideals. He needs courage to break through the realm of evil to find the flower of his ideals. That painting was jointly created by a mother and her son, by Liao Chengzhi and his mother He Xiangning.[1]

We cannot be sure that Liao Chengzhi - the central figure of this book - ever found the 'flowers of his ideals'. On the other hand, he was appointed to one of the highest organs of the Chinese Communist Party (CCP), the Politburo in 1982. It was a more powerful position than that of vice-president of the People's Republic of China (PRC), which would have accorded him one of the highest-ranking formal positions in the state structure. He was destined to die a few days before his appointment to this largely ceremonial position. For most of his political career his highest published position within the party was member of the Central Committee. Within the government of the PRC he occupied the cabinet post of head of the Overseas Chinese Affairs Commission (OCAC), in addition to having been mentioned occasionally as an 'adviser' to the Foreign Ministry, and a number of lesser appointments. A formal analysis of his career pattern based on published records would hardly lead to the conclusion that Liao Chengzhi was the leading PRC Japan specialist. This is not to say that he 'determined' PRC policy towards Japan. To a large extent this policy also depended and depends on the general direction of PRC foreign policy. There seems no doubt, however, that Liao was uniquely important in shaping the implementation of PRC Japan policy. Between 1952 and his death in 1983, for a period of more than thirty years, he met almost all leading Japanese politicians and businessmen, and took part in most important negotiations either as a leading negotiator himself or in the background, second only to politicians like Zhou Enlai or Deng Xiaoping (while Mao acted so as to be seen as the great chessplayer moving his pieces from a distance). Born in Japan, Liao spoke the local dialect of Tokyo better than many Japanese from outside the capital. His humour and informality won him many friends in Japan, where he was not automatically classified as one of the 'Communist cadres' from behind the bamboo curtain. While Liao did not belong to the small echelon of CCP top leaders like Zhou, Deng, Ye Jianying or Li Xiannian it seems beyond doubt that he did not merely execute party policy towards Japan, but that his advice played an important role in the decision-making process in Peking. His personal involvement in the development of PRC relations with Japan was so vital that, in a sense, he was irreplaceable, and it is interesting to note that with his death there was nobody to take his place as an *eminence grise* in policy-making towards Japan, often acting as

Introduction

personal representative of Prime Minister Zhou, with less formal but higher political authority than that possessed by members of the PRC foreign ministry.

Liao Chengzhi owed his importance not only to his personal qualities as a shrewd negotiator and tactician, but to personal links with several top leaders, Zhou Enlai in particular, and his family background in general. He was the only male offspring of a famous revolutionary couple active in China's Republican Party, the Guomindang (Kuomintang, KMT). His father was Liao Zhongkai, close comrade-in-arms of Sun Yatsen, father of the Chinese Republican Revolution. His mother, He Xiangning, came from a family of rich Hong Kong merchants. She too had joined the revolutionary movement that led to the overthrow of the last Chinese dynasty in 1911. She and Sun's wife, Song Qingling, became close friends, a friendship that may have become even stronger after the death of their husbands in the mid-twenties. Sun died in March 1925, followed a few months later by Liao Zhongkai who fell at the hands of an assassin. Leftists and Communists alleged that the 'right-wing' of Sun's party, the KMT, had been involved in Liao's murder. He Xiangning apparently shared such suspicions, and although both she and Sun's widow remained prominent KMT members throughout the thirties and forties when the party was led by Chiang Kaishek, they continued to sympathise with leftists and Communists. The fact that both ladies represented a living link with two of the most prominent Republican revolutionary leaders of the KMT made them almost unassailable politically, even for the right-wing of the KMT. To some extent, Liao had similar protection which saved his life more than once when a member of a 'lesser' family would have obtained the distinction of revolutionary martyrdom.

Born in 1908, Liao Chengzhi was seventeen when his father was assassinated. Before this he had already been involved in student politics. Barely three years later, in 1928, he joined the Communist Party, then an anti-government subversive movement with little or no apparent chance of success. What was it that made Liao relinquish the option of a fairly comfortable life as a member of the ruling élite? Was it the thought of revenge for his father's assassination, for which leftists held rightist members of the KMT responsible? There was a strong emotional bond between Liao and his mother, even before his father's death.[2] Perhaps this bond was a natural consequence of the fact that, due to his father's extremely active political life, he saw little of him. One would suspect that He Xiangning must have worried about her only son's leftist activities since his involvement in an uncertain revolutionary movement put the continuation of the family line at risk. We do not know that she tried to persuade her son to leave the Communist Party but there is also little proof that she encouraged him.[3] As it turned out Liao had not chosen an easy path: during the next twenty years or so, before the Communist takeover in 1949, his life was often in danger: he was arrested in Shanghai in 1933 and released only due to the intervention by He Xiangning, Sun's widow, Song Qingling, and others, while other revolutionaries arrested at the same time were executed. Soon afterwards Liao fled towards a guerrilla base, from where he shortly afterwards started on the long flight from government troops that was later glorified by the Communists as the 'Long March'. According to various reports he nearly fell victim to one of the numerous bloody purges characteristic of the early history of the CCP. Liao's persecutor was Zhang Guotao, then a top CCP army commander, and it was apparently due to Zhou's intervention that Liao did not share the fate of others killed in this internecine strife. His hour of revenge came when Zhang himself was purged in 1937 in Yanan, the small town in one of the poorest parts of northwest China which became the legendary centre of Communist guerrilla activity during the war against Japan and was never occupied by the Japanese. Liao did not stay there, but was soon sent southward, where he was active for the Communist party in areas not yet under Japanese occupation, trying to strengthen anti-Japanese resistance in Guangdong province and adjoining areas. When Hong Kong was finally conquered by the Japanese following the outbreak of the Pacific War in December 1941 Liao managed to escape to the northern part of Canton province, where he was arrested by the Chinese government. He spent the rest of the war in government custody in various provinces not under Japanese control, until his release in January 1946 in Chongqing (Chungking), the seat of the Chinese government during the final years of the war against Japan. While in prison, he refused to obtain his release by renouncing his CCP membership, and was rewarded by the party with alternate membership of the Central Committee, granted *in absentia* in 1945. Despite his release in January 1946 nearly four long, difficult years lay before Liao; years of civil war, flight from Yanan, underground work in Hong Kong and elsewhere, until the Communist takeover in October 1949. To him it must have seemed the end of a long fight.

The search had not been in vain - or so it seemed. He must have been certain that with the Communist conquest of virtually all of China (except Taiwan) the foundation had been laid for the realisation of at least some of the ideals for which he had suffered. The reality of Communist Party life before 1949 may have shaken his belief in Communist ideals at times, but if so there is no record of such doubts. The euphoria of Communist victory may have brushed aside any doubts he held. After all, would victory not also mean that 'revolutionary excesses' were a thing of the past? And that the land reform of the early fifties would be the last of the bloody upheavals that had shaken China so many times in the past centuries? Who at that time could imagine that, in 1958, only nine years after coming to power, Mao would unleash the 'Great Leap Forward' to be followed by the nightmare of the 'Cultural Revolution', which brought untold suffering to the Chinese people and virtually wrought complete havoc among the established Communist élite?

During the Cultural Revolution Liao also came under attack and was placed under house arrest for some years. Like some other members of the Communist élite he apparently escaped a worse fate due to some limited protection afforded by a few high-ranking politicians (like Zhou Enlai) who had been able to survive. Liao's career reached a low ebb when he lost his membership of the Central Committee in 1969, when Lin Biao was presented to the people as Mao Zedong's successor. Later accounts seem to confirm that Liao's firm belief in the eventual victory of his Communist ideals was not shaken even then. Then at last he must have realised that the coming to power of the Communist Party did not mean that

Introduction

the fight for his ideals had ended. Two years later Mao Zedong's successor first became a non-person and was then called a traitor and blamed for all the miseries of the past years. Lin Biao's fall marked the beginning of rehabilitation for numerous members of the Communist élite, including Liao Chengzhi, although like many others he still had to face occasional attacks by 'leftists' that only ceased when the death of Mao Zedong in late summer 1976 put an end to a whole era.

It was some two years before the succession struggle was decided in favour of the traditional Communist élite, symbolised by the third rise to power of Deng Xiaoping. It also meant a further rise for Liao who shortly before he died achieved membership in the powerful Politburo. In a way his career thus reached a happy end. But did Liao believe that the ideals that made him join the Communist movement in his youth had come closer to realisation? During the last years of his life he must have been aware that China's youth was in the grip of a deep crisis about (Communist) beliefs. Likewise in 1978 he must have been saddened to see that, when the political turmoil of Mao's late years had ended, the authorities received a wave of applications for exit permits from Overseas Chinese living in the PRC. We can only speculate on his innermost feelings. According to the record he rarely lost his 'revolutionary optimism' and confidence in the future, and perhaps his well-known *joie de vivre* was at least as much due to his basic character as to his convictions. His humour and optimism also helped considerably when his health, uncertain since the sixties, deteriorated towards the end of the seventies. He had been suffering from heart disease, among other things, and by 1979 seemed to be dying. He made a remarkable recovery after a heart bypass operation carried out in the United States in 1980, but he knew he had little time left. Three years, perhaps, the doctors had told him. The party also knew, but his career seemed unaffected: in September 1982 he was appointed member of the powerful Politburo at the age of 74 at a time when the CCP called for the replacement of aged leaders by the younger generation. But then, his appointment was more a recognition of his contribution in the past than the beginning of a new stage in his career.

Although extremely active during those years he must also have spent time on reflection and looking back. Liao's mother had died in the early seventies when his complete rehabilitation had not yet been assured, and Liao must have deeply regretted that he had not been in a position to look after her adequately during her last years. When Liao returned to China after his successful operation in the United States Song Qingling, Sun's widow, the longtime friend of Liao's mother and the Liao family in general, fell ill.

> (Before Song Qingling died on 29 May 1981) For more than half a month I was all the time at the side of her sickbed or pacing along the corridors ... Song Qingling whom I had first got to know more than 65 years before ... On the twentieth of May, at nine o'clock in the morning, auntie - I usually addressed Chairman Song in that way - had quite a long conversation with me ... She was often not able to understand my Peking (standard) dialect because of my [thick] Cantonese accent. Her Peking dialect with its Shanghai accent was

also a rather laborious affair. And we just had to converse in English, that had been the language of our conversations for a long time. ...4

Liao Chengzhi emphasised Song Qingling's wish expressed in her will

to have the statue of Sun Yatsen at the Sun Yatsen Mausoleum changed, and to have Sun wear a 'Sun Yatsen uniform' instead of the traditional long scholar's garment... On that occasion he also mentioned that he would like to have a joint statue of Sun Yatsen and Song Qingling.5

It was the Central Committee of the CCP which had charged Liao with the execution of Song Qingling's will, and he was also appointed an adviser to the Song Qingling Foundation.6 Essentially Liao behaved towards Song Qingling as a traditional filial Chinese son should behave towards his own parents. Loyalty and service should not end with death, and it was a sacred duty to preserve the honourable memory of the deceased for generations to come.

In August 1982 Liao travelled to Canton for the opening ceremony of the Memorial Hall to his parents, Liao Zhongkai and He Xiangning. Sitting in a wheelchair because of a fractured leg he was now able to present himself before his parents as having done his utmost to restore their name to the glory they deserved. Liao Zhongkai had been an important collaborator of Sun Yatsen, but he had never been a Communist.7 Since 1981 the CCP, however, had increased its attempts to present itself as willing to 'co-operate' with KMT leaders on Taiwan in order to extend Communist authority over the whole of China. As part of this campaign the CCP stressed the importance of leaders such as Sun Yatsen, Liao Zhongkai, He Xiangning, Song Qingling and others in order to underline the 'seriousness' of its overtures. Although part of a political campaign, Liao must have been deeply satisfied with these moves which at the same time enhanced the status of his own family in Communist China. Yet, even at the time of his mother's death in 1972, in the aftermath of the Cultural Revolution, her funeral had not been a small affair. She had been granted the privilege of burial rather than the more usual cremation,8 and at the time Liao had escorted her body to Nanjing where she was buried next to her husband. It was Liao himself who wrote the inscription 'The Tomb of Liao Zhongkai and He Xiangning'.9 According to Jing Puchun, Liao's wife, Liao had always been very filial towards his mother. He did not omit to pray for his parents on Remembrance Day (Qingming), and for several years went in person to visit the grave on that day.10 In May 1983, only a few weeks before his own death, Liao visited the grave for the last time, and wrote a poem to commemorate his parents:11

Nanjing is unsurpassed.
I arrived exactly on Remembrance Day.
I let the pen record what's in my mind.
Fresh flowers grieve at my parents' grave.

We can only guess what these lines meant to Liao, particularly the last line: the silent grief of the flowers lamenting his parents' death may perhaps be taken as an expression of his private sorrow. In the public sphere, Liao Chengzhi compiled a book entitled *Huiyi yu huainian* ('Memories') in honour of both his parents.12

Introduction

When Liao himself left this world he had also fulfilled another duty of a traditional filial Chinese son: he left behind several children and grandchildren, some of whom were embarked already on careers of their own. His son, Liao Hui, was in fact appointed one of the vice-heads of the Overseas Chinese Affairs Commission under the State Council (an office headed previously by He Xiangning and Liao Chengzhi).13 Liao Zhongkai had been actively engaged himself in the first two decades of this century in obtaining financial assistance to support the Republican revolution among Overseas Chinese. Liao had thus been able to follow up a tradition begun by his father, and had assisted his son to commence a career in the same field.

It is tempting to assume that throughout his life, Liao strove to carry out the tasks his father had left unfinished. However, the ideals cherished by his father had been very different from the goals pursued by his son. During the shooting of a film on Liao Zhongkai's life, Liao himself emphasised that 'Liao Zhongkai was a revolutionary of the twenties, and should not be presented like a present day Communist party member'.14 To some extent this is of course merely a reflection of the fact that father and son grew up in completely different surroundings and lived in different historical periods. It would be wrong to impute Communist ideals to a Republican revolutionary like Liao Zhongkai who, although leftist, seems to have retained his reservations about Communism. And yet, in many ways, the image of his father as a revolutionary may have been a source of inspiration for Liao, all the more so since Liao Zhongkai died at the hands of an assassin, ostensibly a martyr in China's fight against foreign imperialism and capitalism, the declared enemies of the Communist party.

Life seems so often dominated by chance happenings. Often we do not even realise that we are constantly making choices, while we assume that we are acting in accordance with common sense. But behind the choices we make lie our dreams, visions, thoughts of which we are not always conscious ourselves. At times it may be difficult to uncover and describe them even in persons with whom we are thoroughly familiar, yet without discovering them our understanding of others will always be superficial. Throughout this study we will be confronted with a wealth of material: data concerning Liao as a politician, an official and a 'public person', and at times we may be in danger of forgetting the person behind the mask. The main task of this study is, in fact, not so much to describe Liao Chengzhi as a human being as to delineate his political role in the development of relations between the PRC and Japan since 1949. Moreover, I was not able to acquaint myself with his private life to the extent that I could presume to try to create an image of Liao with a fair resemblance to the impression he left behind in the hearts and minds of people who knew him well. I should like to limit myself to mentioning a few episodes from Liao's life which may have proved to be of particular importance when he became the PRC's leading Japan specialist.

Liao Chengzhi was born in Tokyo and spent a number of years at a very impressionable age in Japan.

> I think that the place where I was born was the Okubo district in Tokyo ...15 Mr Wu Qiongshi who was a personal friend of my mother ... testified with a solemn expression on his face that my nurse was a Japanese lady called Obasan, with a white oval-shaped face that evoked trust ... Therefore it is a fact that I was born in Okubo and raised at the breast of a Japanese lady. Half my blood in my infant years was the gift of a Japanese lady. It was perhaps fate, if I am not mistaken, that later in life I was labelled 'pro-Japanese', and just as there is the saying 'where there is fire there must be smoke' it is an unshakable fact that I was born in Japan and raised at the breast of a Japanese lady.16

Liao's first playmates apparently were mostly Japanese children. The primary school Liao attended in Tokyo was Roman Catholic,

> where I was the only Chinese boy among thirty Japanese. My grandfather had been a good Christian, but my father was not. There was very little of the Christian spirit in this school and I learned to hate the Japanese Catholic teacher who looked down on me as an inferior being. Whenever I could not answer questions in class he would say: 'As a little Chinese pig of course you don't know anything'. Then when I was offended and stubbornly refused to try to answer questions, he would announce loudly: 'I'm not surprised to find a Chinese acting like a pig. No Japanese would act this way'. I often had to fight with the Japanese pupils to maintain my dignity, but the majority were not unkind to me. I had several good school friends and one special pal who once beat up another boy for insulting me.17

Despite some occasional problems he seemingly did not suffer much discrimination. In many ways he grew up just like the Japanese children around him. His parents were nationalistically minded Chinese revolutionaries, but in those days, before the Japanese invasion of the Chinese mainland, Japan was often seen as an example of successful modernisation, demonstrating the ability of an Asian nation to resist Western colonisation. Many Chinese revolutionaries who had come to Japan at that time had found much support there for their activities and had made friends with Japanese like Miyazaki Toten, whose son, Miyazaki Seimin, was later to play a prominent role in the Japanese movement for friendship with the PRC. After several years of primary school in Japan Liao returned to China and was enrolled in a Catholic high school in Canton. By that time Japan had started to compete with other powers for influence in China and was therefore increasingly resented by Chinese nationalists. Just because of his Japanese background Liao may have stressed his own anti-Japanese patriotism more than other students, although there seems to be little evidence of this. In fact, Liao did return to Tokyo (for a short period in the late twenties) after the assassination of his father. During this stay he took part in leftist and Communist political activities, as well as demonstrations against Japan's increasing involvement in China. There is no doubt about the genuineness of Liao's patriotism, and yet, he must have had mixed feelings when, as a result of his activities, he was expelled from Japan in early

Introduction

summer 1928. After all, Japan had been like a second home for him. He may not have realised then how long it would be before he could revisit the country of his birth. According to the records it took him until December 1954, more than 26 years. Japan's large-scale encroachment on China started with the establishment of a puppet regime in China's northeastern province, Manchuria, followed by a gradual advance into North China that erupted into full-scale war in the summer of 1937. Between 1932 and 1937 Liao had taken part in the Communist movement directed toward the overthrow of the Chinese government. With the establishment of a common resistance front against Japan Liao was sent to South China where apparently he was not involved personally in fighting Japanese troops, although he was engaged in resistance support work. When the Japanese occupied Hong Kong he was able to escape, only to be arrested shortly afterwards by the government, spending the rest of the war in government prisons. By that time the common anti-Japanese front had long given way to a continuation of the old struggle between the Communists and the government. During all these years Liao devoted himself to the Chinese cause, and there is no reason to cast doubt on his loyalty to China. Nevertheless, it was perhaps a happy coincidence that his fate prevented him from being involved in physically fighting Japanese or from becoming a prisoner-of-war in a Japanese camp.

After the war anti-Japanese feeling ran so high that the CCP repeatedly faced serious problems (for political as well as economic reasons) in trying to re-establish links with Japan. Throughout the war years Liao had never been one of the CCP's traditional 'Japan specialists' but, after the establishment of the PRC in 1949, he would soon be promoted to head the CCP's Japan policy group. It is not difficult to imagine that he must have felt deeply involved personally. Despite the general hatred towards Japan he may have felt personal sorrow over the estrangement that separated Japan and China, all the more since post-war Japan was set on a course that joined it in a quasi-alliance with Communist China's most hostile enemy, the United States. Yet it was not only Japan's link with the United States that prevented an early thaw in relations with the PRC. It is most likely that intra-party discussions often saw severe differences on policy towards Japan, in particular during the time of the Great Leap Forward, when the PRC decided to break off all relations with Japan in 1958, and even more so during the so-called GPCR. It would be naive to assume that in those debates Liao would have consistently represented a 'pro-Japanese' wing among policy advisers. I would think it quite likely, however, that he was genuinely concerned to reduce the effects of emotionally based anti-Japanese feelings among policy-makers.

Throughout the fifties and sixties one of the main aims of PRC policy towards Japan was to weaken Japan's link with the United States. Who at that stage could have foreseen that, during the seventies, relations between the PRC and Japan would improve to such an extent that politicians and observers outside the PRC were talking about a possible axis Peking-Tokyo-Washington? Even in his wildest dreams Liao could hardly have imagined that he would eventually visit the country of his father's birth, the United States, for a life-saving heart operation in 1980.

China's Relations with Japan

Although Liao Zhongkai devoted almost all his time to politics as one of Sun Yatsen's most trusted aides and the children did not see much of him, he certainly took care that they received a good education. Having grown up in the United States it is not surprising that he should stress the need to study English, and Liao recalls that 'Father sometimes taught English to me when he returned to Japan in the summers'.[18]

It seems quite likely that Liao's fluency in English - spoken with an American accent - was due to his father's influence. Just as Liao's father had emphasised the importance of studying English, so Liao, in his turn, urged his children and grandchildren to study English properly. One of his grandchildren, Yu Yanwen recalls that:

> In spring 1981, when I went to Nanjing to visit the family grave, on the train grandfather started to ask me about my study of foreign languages. When he heard that I had made some progress and was preparing to major in foreign languages he was very happy. He asked me what difficulties I had in learning English. I told him that my pronunciation was not sufficiently standard. He ... told me sternly that pronunciation was the most basic barrier; he asked for my exercise books, pulled his glasses from his pocket, and had me pronounce the words he pointed to, and corrected me over and again ... Then I sang the 'Straw Hat Song' in English. Grandfather listened with great relish.[19]

It seems only natural to expect that Liao's concern for and interest in English derived from his father's education, and that Liao Zhongkai must have told his children about the United States, the country of his birth. We know little about Liao's changing image of the United States, and it is difficult to assess his emotional attitudes towards it and Westerners in general. Perhaps it was the same mixture of admiration for a strong and powerful country with a natural antipathy for a power that seemed to symbolise the rule of a foreign race over a large part of Asia (so common among his contemporaries). Yet his background made him realise the undeniable importance of being open-minded:

> He (Liao) used to say that small children should not only master
> Chinese and arithmetic, but also foreign languages. A foreign language
> is a means of social communication, and the practical use of English is
> even wider.[20]

Before the Communist take over, the US had supported the Chinese government against the insurgents. In the period after 1949 the co-operation and alliance between the US and the Republic of China (ROC) on Taiwan became in Communist eyes the most obvious example of continued American domination of a part of China. To some extent policy towards Taiwan was deeply linked with the PRC's policy towards Overseas Chinese in general, an area in which Liao played a major role. Ye Jianying had been the PRC's most important spokesman on Taiwan until 1981; he gradually retreated from this position, and Liao came to the fore. In July 1982 Liao addressed a public letter to Jiang Jingguo, President of the ROC.

Introduction

Here he mentioned that he had met Jiang fifty years earlier during their stay in the Soviet Union, and appealed to Jiang's patriotism for co-operation in achieving early reunification of China under PRC sovereignty. A few days later when Liao met his daughter Liao Jian and other family members:
> Conversation turned to the letter to Jiang Jingguo, and my younger brother said that the letter had brought about widespread reactions all over China. He asked father whether there really was any hope for reunification of the fatherland. Father answered in a very assertive manner: 'Of course there is hope, after all we are all descendants of the Chinese race. We don't have red hair and blue eyes, and what enmity is there that could not be overcome? In my view, solidarity and unification is the [general] trend, and I hope that I will be able to see the fatherland reunited during my lifetime. Should Jiang Jingguo give his approval at this very minute I would fly to Taiwan straight away ...'[21]

It seems only natural that Liao perhaps could never feel the affinity towards Westerners that he felt towards Japanese. Nevertheless, he may have felt a certain fascination for the US, his father's birthplace.

Liao did have first-hand experience of several European countries having travelled in the late twenties, in particular to Germany and Holland. His talent for languages showed itself again when he was able to pick up not only some German, but a few Dutch phrases. Very little is known about his personal impression of these countries. He revisited Europe numerous times as a delegate to Communist international front conferences during the fifties, and made friends among European sympathisers. Liao had also visited the Soviet Union some time between 1928 and 1932, and spoke some Russian. But, just as there is some doubt about the nature of his stay in the Soviet Union at that time, there is little unambiguous evidence about his personal attitude towards that country. In the fifties like so many other Communist politicians, Liao was also a member of the Sino-Soviet Friendship Society, and it is not difficult to find remarks sympathetic to the Soviet Union, just as it is easy to point to critical remarks made at a later stage.

Liao had been raised bilingual, being fluent in Chinese and Japanese. He had learned French at school in Japan, and he was also very good at English. In addition to Russian he knew some German. His personal experiences had acquainted him with a wide variety of cultures, political traditions and points of view. Liao most likely had absorbed these impressions in an intuitive artistic way, quite differently from some of his more intellectual contemporaries. To give an example, Zhang Xiangshan, another PRC Japan expert, had gone to Japan before the war and fallen in love with Japanese literature, studying and admiring modern novelists like Natsume Soseki and Kikuchi Kan, and classics like the *Makurasoshi* and *Tsurezuregusa*.[22] Liao's interest in the literary tradition was limited. He seems to have preferred Japanese detective novels and bestsellers,[23] but according to another source also showed interest in modern writers such as Ishikawa Takuboku, Kunikida Doppo and Akutagawa Ryunosuke.[24] It would be wrong, in my view, to call Liao a traditional scholar-politician. His temperament was much more that of an artist, sizing people up intuitively.25 Rather than writing classical poetry Liao preferred to draw cartoons, and he is also known for his calligraphy. He does not seem to have fallen for theories and 'isms' which apparently bored him. His well-known wittiness testifies to a keen intellect mixed with great natural curiosity for people and their individual personalities. It is hardly surprising, then, that he should have hated dead bureaucratic routine. A small incident related by Ma Wanqi may illustrate this point.

> In 1955 I went to Peking to attend a meeting. He Xiangning invited myself and my wife to go to Southern China on a tourist trip. At that time Liao full of humour said: 'The scenery there is so beautiful, you go and spend your honeymoon there'. I'm not sure whether he had put a message through, or whether it was due to a misunderstanding by the people who received us in the south, but when we reached Suzhou and Wuxi they thought we were on a honeymoon trip, while in fact we were at that time already parents of five boys and two daughters.26

Liao's informality also extended to his private life. In the words of his cook:
> Liao had a very busy life, but when he returned home he always used to chat and laughed together with us. When we played *go* he also joined in the game. When we played bridge he participated. When we practised shooting he would challenge us to compete with him. He was a man of the older generation, and he was also a man of high standing while we were low class (sic!). He, however, would not pay attention [to such differences]...27

Nonetheless it would be an over-simple assumption that Liao was prepared to disregard social distinctions as a result of his Communist ideological convictions. Liao was doubtless aware of the fact that he belonged to one of China's 'good' families, and his apparent lack of airs is perhaps at least partially attributable to the luxury that genuine members of the upper classes can afford to indulge in: pretending to ignore their status - of which everybody is well aware, anyway.

The first impression of Liao indicates that he does not quite fit the standard image of a leading Communist politician, well versed in party ideology and ready to pounce without mercy on opponents at home and abroad. Nevertheless, it seems highly unlikely that even an individual like Liao was able completely to withstand the influence of 'party life'. According to most accounts he seems to have tried to separate his political life from his private, family life to a considerable degree. Throughout most of this book Liao appears hidden by the mask of the party-man who emerges in official speeches and writings; and as a politician attempting to sway the Japanese and other foreigners during negotiations. In order to describe Liao's career against the background of the development of Japan's relations with the PRC it is often impossible to go into detail about Liao the individual, and there will be little room also to dwell on his private life. It is only towards the end of the study, when we come to the final days of Liao's life, that it is possible to present a few glimpses of him as an individual and the head of a large extended family. To

Introduction

understand Liao's success in dealing with, often, non-Communist foreigners - or Overseas Chinese -, however, it is vital to keep in mind that he could afford to interpret 'politics' in a broad sense, rather differently from Communist politicians of lower rank who had to take care not to offer any reason for ideological attacks. A good example of this was related by Chen Fuli, a well-known landscape photographer, who was elected to the 5th National People's Consultative Conference. Lacking political experience Chen felt that he:

> was unable to carry such a heavy responsibility ... When Liao learned of my feelings he immediately told me smilingly and in a relaxed tone: 'All right, you say you don't understand politics. But I can tell you, [just] by taking pictures with your camera of our fatherland's immense and beautiful rivers and mountains, its economic construction and the people whose spiritual and material life becomes increasingly rich day by day, [by taking pictures] in a realistic and aesthetic way you rouse the hearts of the people and encourage their fighting spirit. That is precisely the greatest, the best of all politics.'[28]

If anything, this passage illustrates Liao's willingness to understand 'politics' in a sense wider than in its usual ideological context, where the term is loaded with ideas such as 'struggle against class enemies' and 'party dictatorship'. In fact, following accepted united front practice Liao was in favour of co-operating with persons whose ideological point of view might differ from the current party line:

> Some years ago a progressive cineast from the United States ... discussed co-operation with us. After more than six months the script had been completed, but it could not be used. Some among us argued that kind of co-operation was very difficult to bring to fruition, and that it was a lot of work for nothing. When I asked Liao for advice he said: 'The education and environment where such friends live are completely different from ours, and their ideological approach shows some difference as a matter of course. But we also should recognise sincerely the strong points in what others do, and it is very likely that these ... are understood by foreign audiences and accepted. That is different from our way which is premised on general conceptions which appear normal to those who understand them (ie Communist ideology), but which cannot be fathomed by those who are not acquainted with them.'[29]

The problems touched upon in this passage are similar to those that tend to encumber so many joint ventures between foreigners and Communist Chinese, but it will take a great deal of time before Liao's relatively conciliatory approach becomes generally accepted. This flexibility notwithstanding, it would be wrong to conclude that he paid no attention to ideology. Rather it shows Liao's understanding of modern psychological warfare which makes conscious use of opinions and statements differing from one's own convictions in order to undermine and soften up the position of one's counterpart. In this vein Liao also showed an unusual tendency to break loose from the entrenched habits of many other Communist cadres who reject any association with 'ideological impurities'. At the beginning of 1978 the Royal British Radiology Academy awarded the Chinese scientist Wu Hengxing honorary membership of the Academy.

> There were some people who said that 'we don't want an honour bestowed on us by the capitalist class'. I did not know what to do, and decided to dare ask Liao for advice. When he heard my story he said categorically: 'What's that, "capitalist class", that's just nonsense. Chairman Song Qingling in the past has received honours from abroad, why should we refuse them? It's nothing to do with "capitalist class", it is an acknowledgement of the standard of science in our country. How many people in the world are there qualified to receive this kind of honour?'30

Since such an award might serve to improve the PRC's image abroad Liao saw nothing wrong with it. In an age where images influence economic transactions and affect a country's political standing Liao's course of action indeed seems a sensible one, certainly from the point of view of foreign policy. It might also serve domestically to enhance national pride. As it is, anti-foreign 'exclusionists' may well increase their influence again in the future, but for the time being (1984) appeals to national pride and patriotism did not necessarily foster xenophobia.

> In 1978 there was a wave of emigration in [our] society. Due to 'leftist' (ie exclusionist) influence policy towards Overseas Chinese could not be carried out properly, and many Overseas Chinese and their dependents who had settled in China were also affected. At the Xinglong farm (one of the many farms for Overseas Chinese) more than 800 people wanted to emigrate. When Liao learned about the situation he boldly demanded that the farm leadership get rid of 'left' interference (referring to its overly 'ideological' approach). ... What has hurt Overseas Chinese and their dependents most was that we have neither respected nor trusted them, and quite a few well educated people have had no way of putting their knowledge into practice. If we do not get rid of 'leftist' things, and a [correct] policy towards Overseas Chinese cannot be implemented, it is hardly surprising that they want to leave. We also have to explain ... that the state's problems are temporary, and that prospects are bright. [After all], the fatherland still remains their father even if it were poorer than it is now.31

Appeals to patriotism have frequently replaced ideological slogans in other countries, also to some extent in the Soviet Union. One may even assume - although it remains difficult to prove - that Communist politicians like Liao Chengzhi themselves become disenchanted with the need to maintain an often changing and inconsistent ideological approach, and many perhaps would not undermine the power monopoly of the Communist Party. However, formal identification with the system remains a necessity, and accommodation becomes a habit, so much so that someone like Liao may have been hard put to identify 'personal' beliefs as opposed to 'public' views. The 'system' referred to is,

Introduction

however not an abstract ideological edifice. It also consists of the human network of party members who organise themselves into numerous (informal) factions, whose membership tends to vary with the passing of time and is determined at least as much by personal friendships and loyalties as by ideological convictions. By tracing the composition of the group of politicians with whom Liao preferred to associate we may gain an important additional clue about Liao's 'personal' stance on a number of issues. The present writer has prepared such a study, which is however too voluminous to be included here and will be published separately.

There is only one period when Liao - like so many others - was clearly in opposition: during the period of the GPCR. Following the death of Mao the Chinese Communist media tried to create a new myth (they are perhaps the only genuine mythologists of our time) claiming that, during the period from 1966 up to Mao's death in 1976, 'leftist radicals' had temporarily usurped the party. Despite general and widespread opposition to these radicals, policies throughout the period were determined by the usurpers. The truth is, however, different. For example, foreign policy clearly was not determined solely by xenophobic radicals, as is shown by the *rapprochement* towards the United States and other non-Communist countries during the early seventies. In all fields of domestic and foreign policy there was constant struggle between various factions, as shown for example in the resurrection of Deng Xiaoping in 1973, shortly before Liao's much publicised trip to Japan and Deng's fall in early 1976. The general condemnation of pre-1976 policies by virtually all Chinese politicians following the rise of the pro-Deng group around mid-1978 should be seen rather as an expression of triumph over the vanquished 'leftist' factions than an attempt to set the historical record straight. There seems to be little doubt that Liao genuinely and bitterly opposed many policies adopted in the field of Overseas Chinese policy between 1966 and 1969 and thereafter. There may have been aspects of PRC policy towards Japan, even after the establishment of diplomatic relations in 1972, with which he disagreed. It is however inadmissible to regard all post-1978 statements by Liao - or any other Communist politician - as revelations of truth, or as statements that reveal Liao's genuine *personal* viewpoints, once his own faction was back in power. Now as in the past expressions of 'individual' convictions by Chinese Communist leaders are carefully tailored to fit the current ideological 'wind'. By the same token, there has been no lessening of attempts to conceal the exact role of any individual Chinese politician in the decision-making process, or his factional affiliations which more often than not can be best deduced by studying appointment and career patterns. This concealment usually continues after a politician's death, but published eulogies may include incidents of a more or less anecdotal nature providing some pertinent clues. Perhaps the most dramatic account of Liao's personal links with Communist China's élite is that portraying him as protector of Marshall He Long's children during the Cultural Revolution, when Liao himself was under attack.[32]

Eulogies such as those published after Liao's death also provide vivid glimpses of characteristic aspects of Chinese political culture. Like other leading Communist politicians Liao had adopted a 'pet project' enjoying his personal and individual protection, one of the favourite status symbols of Chinese Communist leaders such as Zhou Enlai. One of Liao's pet projects was the above-mentioned Xinglong state farm for Overseas Chinese. Of course the fate of a pet project varies with the political fortunes of the patron.

> Due to the Communistic wind and serious natural disasters ... Xinglong was facing all sorts of difficulties in 1959. Liao sent comrade Zhang Fen of the Overseas Chinese Affairs Committee under the State Council to Xinglong farm as secretary of the party committee in order to strengthen it, so as to help the Overseas Chinese and their dependents overcome these difficulties. During the ten years of trouble (ie from the beginning of the Cultural Revolution until the death of Mao) Xinglong met with serious disasters. As a result of the extremely leftist production policy ... more than 4,000 *mou* planted with coffee shrubs were all cut down, and the whole farm presented the appearance of wasteland. Difficulties on the farm were relatively great towards the end of 1976. When I came to Peking to report on the situation Liao not only provided us with ideological lessons and very great encouragement, he also approved delivery of 100 tons of steel, five large lorries and gave tractors to our farm ... When the trucks and tractors drove onto the farm staff and workers surrounded them ... and many were moved to tears.[33]

Liao is shown here personally intervening in the bureaucratic process affecting an individual or a small community, a privilege reserved particularly for high-ranking politicians. To give but one example, there are numerous accounts of how Zhou Enlai intervened and thus successfully saved people from the clutches of 'wicked and corrupt' officials.

Another incident again showing Liao as a compassionate leader, was when he helped two Overseas Chinese who had come to the PRC from Malaysia and had settled in Canton in 1954.

> Later their children came to Hong Kong, and from 1970 they had asked for exit permits three times in the hope of being reunited with their children in Hong Kong, but never received an answer. Last year (ie 1982) after Ju Jiu had become acquainted with the case he wrote to Liao stating the circumstances ... The result was that, before two weeks had passed, the Public Security Office of Canton received a document from the authority concerned requesting them to obtain detailed information about both applications. According to what I learned both have most recently received approval to go to Hong Kong to be reunited with their families.[34]

For the outside observer such stories tell perhaps more about the workings of the PRC system than about the individual politician concerned. They clearly belong to a centuries-old tradition found in eulogies of popular 'good' officials in official and unofficial works of history. It goes without saying that such eulogies provide us with a convenient catalogue of traditional Chinese virtues, hard work, love of learning, frugality, modesty and incorruptibility, and it is often hard to tell whether praise is genuine or part of an inveterate ritual. Despite repeated emphasis on Liao's frugal lifestyle - also mentioned by his wife, Jing Puchun - it is fairly clear that Liao did indulge in several luxuries.[35] Perhaps best known is his love of abundant good food and drink - which were partly responsible for his considerable weight despite his short stature of not much more than 160 cm, and which of course also contributed to the severity of his heart ailment.[36]

> Once, while leading a delegation of Chinese officials to Africa he stopped the convoy of official cars that was touring the countryside in order to capture a large rat that had run across the road. ... he had the creature cooked and served for dinner.[37]

This penchant of Liao's perhaps does not wholly concur with either traditional ethics or austere Communist ideals, but it may seem excusable in a country that has always prized food as one of life's most precious material possessions. Not surprisingly this habit was repeatedly used in attacks on Liao during the Cultural Revolution. Occasionally he was also attacked for nepotism, and several accounts by family members seem specifically designed to counter this, such as in the following by his daughter Liao Jian:

> We have many relatives abroad, both on our grandmother's and our grandfather's sides. Grandmother was born and raised in Hong Kong, and there were eleven brothers and sisters ...; now there is already a fourth generation. Father once said that the in-laws of his generation abroad were enough to fill ten tables. In recent years our country has pursued an 'open-door-policy', and when our relatives came to China to visit us they suggested to father that they might assist us to study abroad, and they also invited us abroad to visit relatives. Whenever such an offer was made father would always express his gratitude and refuse politely. Up until now none of us six children has ever been abroad for study, and ... to visit relatives. I was born ... and went to primary school in Hong Kong until the fourth grade, being looked after by numerous relatives. The year before last, a relative took the trouble to send us a written invitation to ... Hong Kong, and when that relative came to Peking he repeated the same suggestion in person to father. Subsequently I brought the invitation to the attention of my unit as prescribed by procedure. Somehow the request reached the hands of my father where it got stuck. When the same relative saw father in Canton in spring this year and brought the matter up again father gave his agreement. But when I went to ask father he only retorted if China was not good (enough), what would I want to go to Hong Kong for, wasting other people's money at the same time. In this way my hope of visiting my Hong Kong relatives came to nothing. We have some understanding for father's attitude. In the past there were some people who made use of the open-door-policy, kept their eyes fixed on foreign countries and tried to move heaven and earth ... to go abroad. My

father did not approve of this and he did not wish his children to follow that example, and we therefore acceded to his wishes. My younger brother Doudou graduated from Jinan University last year. His girlfriend wanted to go to the States to study, and Doudou himself also wanted to go, but, in the end, father did not let him go. After their marriage Doudou was happy to stay and work in China.[38]

The very fact that Liao's son, Liao Hui, became increasingly involved in politics, travelling to Japan in 1979 and being appointed one of the deputy-heads of the Overseas Chinese Affairs Commission under the State Council, would of course fuel rumours about nepotism.

Before his death Liao was able to look back on considerable personal achievements both by himself and his family, and it would be easy to forget that these years of fulfilment came only after many years of deprivation and suffering. There is no doubt that he enjoyed the good years in his life, and yet he did abandon the prospect of a relatively comfortable and easy life after his father's assassination in 1925. He became heavily involved in student politics and joined the Communist Party in 1928. Liao himself decided to join a rebel movement, a choice hardly motivated by hopes of a rapid and brilliant career befitting the son of a prominent politician. Was it the thought of revenge for his father's assassination that made him choose this course? If so we should take into account that, at least after 1949, Liao repeatedly discounted revenge as a guiding motif for PRC policy towards the KMT.[39] We know very little about the *individual* motivation that made Liao join the Communist movement. Like so many other well-educated young Chinese of his day he may have been fascinated by the Marxist promise that the movement would be able to help China regain a place among the great and powerful nations on earth. Once a member of the CCP he was of course subject to party discipline. While he would be able to express his preferences, ultimately his party superiors would decide where to post him. Liao's personal ability was the basic reason for his later success. The high reputation of his parents among Overseas Chinese of various political shades was probably the main reason for his appointment to top positions in the area of Overseas Chinese policy, and even now he is perhaps best known abroad as an Overseas Chinese leader. Liao's most important contribution to politics however lies in the area of relations with Japan, an achievement which was officially acknowledged by Japan with the posthumous award of one of the highest distinctions of the Japanese Empire for his contribution to the development of Sino-Japanese relations.[40] Indeed it is the basic aim of this study to demonstrate how and why Liao came to be the PRC's foremost Japan specialist, and to present some assessment of his personal contribution in that area of policy-making. Through his background, his work in Overseas Chinese affairs and his personal knowledge of Japan Liao was perhaps better aware than many other leading Communist politicians of the difficulties China would have to face on the road to genuine modernisation and an easier life for all Chinese.

Introduction

Notes to Introduction

1. Zhu Zha, a well known medical worker, and the wife of Wang Jiaxiang, former ambassador to Moscow, in *Liaogong zai renjian*, p 59. Most human figures appearing in He Xiangning's paintings are Liao's work, Yu Feng, 'He Xiangning Zhongguohua yizuo zhanlan suibi', *Huiyi yu huainian - jinian geming laoren He Xiangning shishi shi zhounian*, pp 247-54 (reprinted from *Wenhuibao*, 15 March 1979). See also Hu Lanqi, 'Huiyi He Xiangning xiansheng', *Huiyi yu huainian - jinian geming laoren He Xiangning shishi shi zhounian*, pp 189-200.
2. 'He Xiangning loved Liao Chengzhi very much - and Liao, too, adored his mother.' Hu Lanqi, 'Huiyi He Xiangning xiansheng', p 196.
3. Interviews conducted on the mainland and in Taiwan revealed widely differing opinions concerning He Xiangning's political views. Yi Wen (pseud) disputes the common view that He Xiangning consistently opposed Chiang Kaishek, saying that she accepted Chiang's offer to move into lodgings at the Whampoa Military Academy after the her husband's assassination, where both families stayed next to each other for some time. This would mean that Liao Chengzhi and Jiang Jingguo were 17 and 15 respectively when they first got to know each other. Yi Wen does not accept the common view that He's subsequent opposition to the marriage between Chiang Kaishek and Song Meiling was political. According to him she opposed the marriage simply because she thought it morally reprehensible for Chiang to abandon his former wife - the mother of Jiang Jingguo - in favour of Song Meiling, Yi Wen (pseud), 'Jingguo Chengzhi', (ie Jiang Jingguo and Liao Chengzhi) *Zhanwang*, (Hong Kong) 493, pp 6-7. The roles of both Song Qingling and He Xiangning are in need of future detailed study.
4. Liao Chengzhi 'Wode diaoyan', *Zhongguo jianshe. Jinian Song Qingling tekan* (August 1981), p 14. Liao also mentions that 'during the early 60s I had once visited London where we (ie including Song Qingling) went straight to the grave of Marx to pay our respects.' (*ibid*, p 15).
5. *Ibid*, p 72.
6. *Ibid*, p 71. 'On the proposal of Deng Xiaoping and some other leading comrades of the old guard a "Song Qingling Foundation" was set up ... Liao checked and personally revised its draft regulations on several occasions while he was in hospital.'
7. Liao Chengzhi stressed this point in commenting on the shooting of the film 'Liao Zhongkai'. See Tang Xiaodan, in *Liaogong zai renjian*, p 98.
8. Lu Dingyi recalls that He Xiangning had told Prime Minister Zhou that she wished to be buried together with Liao Zhongkai. Liao, however, did not want to claim special privileges and advocated cremation. Only after Zhou's repeated persuasion did Liao agree to the traditional burial (*PD*, 19 June 1983). Clearly, in those egalitarian days Liao wanted to avoid any impression of asking for special privileges.
9. Jing Puchun, in *Liaogong zai renjian*, p 7.
10. *Ibid*.
11. *Ibid*. For a reproduction of Liao's manuscript of this, his last poem, see *Liao Chengzhi de yisheng*, p 161, which also contains a picture of Liao Chengzhi and Jing Puchun bowing in front of his parents.
12. *Jingji ribao*, (24 June 1983).
13. *Ouzhou shibao*, (11 November 1983).
14. Tang Yaodan, in *Liaogong zai renjian*, p 97.

15 According to Ikeda Daisaku, *Wasureenu deai*, (1979) p 57, Liao was born in Tokyo, Koishikawa; see also *Yomiuri shinbun*, (11 June 1983). Lu Dingyi, *PD*, (19 June 1983), 'Liao was two years younger than I.'
16 Liao Chengzhi, *Waga seishun no Nippon - Chugoku chishikijin no Nippon kaiso*, (1982), pp 3, 5.
17 Wales, *Red Dust. Autobiographies of Chinese Communists as Told to Nym Wales*, (Stanford, 1952), pp 26-7.
18 *Ibid*, p 27.
19 Yu Yanwen (one of Liao's grandchildren), in *Liaogong zai renjian*, pp 164-5.
20 *Ibid*, p 164.
21 Liao Jian, in *Liaogong zai renjian*, p 156.
22 Zhang Xiangshan, in *Waga seishun no Nippon*, pp 157-9.
23 *Liaogong zai renjian*, p 129; he also loved all kinds of sport, Japanese *sumo*, but also baseball, *Yomiuri shinbun*, (11 June 1983).
24 Tan Juezhen, 'Ryo Shoshi o kataru', *Ekonomisuto*, (28 March 1953), pp 28-9.
25 Shimakura Tamio, *Pekin nikki*, (1972), p 105.
26 Ma Wanqi, in *Liaogong zai renjian*, p 124.
27 Xu Fu, in *Liaogong zai renjian*, p 102.
28 Chen Fuli, in *Liaogong zai renjian*, p 116.
29 Sita Huimin, in *Liaogong zai renjian*, p 28.
30 Wu Huanxing, in *Liaogong zai renjian*, p 91.
31 *Zhongguo nongmin bao*, 28 June 1983. He Xiangning also wrote a letter to Overseas Chinese at Xinglong farm, published in *Qiaowubao* 8 (1958). The farm was established in 1951 (*Zhongguo nongmin bao*, 28 June 1983).
32 *Liaogong zai renjian*, pp 156 f, 172 f.
33 *Zhongguo nongmin bao*, (28 June 1983).
34 Weng Huiling, in *Liaogong zai renjian*, p 120.
35 Jing Puchun, in *Liaogong zai renjian*, p 7. See also Lu Zhenji, 'Feiwei qiaoweihui zhuxi Liao Chengzhi beikou zhi mi', *Feiwei qiaowu jianbao*, (1 May 1968), pp 4a-b.
36 See for example *Liaogong zai renjian*, p 53.
37 Letter from Professor Cynthia Chennault of 15 May 1985.
38 Liao Jian, in *Liaogong zai renjian*, p 155.
39 'We who belong to the Liao family have never thought of revenge.' Miyazaki Seimin, in *Liaogong zai renjian*, p 143. A similar remark was reported by Gong Ping [Jiangxisheng zhengfu wenshiguan] 'Xiangqi le Liao Chengzhi de yifu hua', *Liaowang*, (November 1982), p 33.
40 *Liao Chengzhi de yisheng*, p 164.

CHAPTER ONE
Between China and Japan 1908-1937

Liao Chengzhi's grandfather, Liao Zhubin, was a native of Canton and, like Liao himself, was educated at a Christian school.[1] Liao Zhubin obtained a position with the Hong Kong and Shanghai Banking Corporation which in the 1860s sent him to its Branch Office in San Francisco.[2] This sets his grandfather clearly apart from the mass of poor Chinese migrants to the American west coast:

> Unlike most Chinese immigrants, Liao Chu-pin (Liao Zhubin) did not migrate to America because of economic hardship at home. In fact, his brother, Liao Tzu-san, was an official in the Manchu government, while the family as a whole was one of means, and ... commercial ties in Hong Kong.[3]

It is perhaps not surprising that Liao Chengzhi's sister Liao Mengxing found it inappropriate to emphasise her grandfather's 'bourgeois' background, and she is 'definitely incorrect in claiming that her grandfather sold himself as a "contract slave" in order to help his poverty-stricken family'.[4]

Before migrating to America Liao Zhubin had fathered a son, Liao Entao, born in the family's native district, Huiyang in Guangdong province.[5] Liao Entao later became an imperial official at the embassy in Tokyo.[6] Liao Chengzhi's father, Liao Zhongkai, was born in San Francisco in 1877 or 1878.[7] There were other children, but only the names of Liao Langru and Liao Bingyun are known.[8] Liao Zhongkai spent his youth in the United States, and was sixteen or seventeen before he went to China. He never claimed American citizenship but identified himself with China.[9] It is questionable whether he grew up bilingual in the United States, but his later command of written Chinese suggests that he must have learned Chinese as well as English.[10] Later accounts suggest that Liao Zhongkai was imbued with the kind of proud nationalism so common among expatriates anywhere. It is quite likely that Liao Zhongkai, as mentioned by his daughter Liao Mengxing, experienced anti-Chinese discrimination in the United States.[11] He also received a more classically oriented, traditional Chinese education, as evinced by literary pastimes such as writing poems in the classical style.[12] According to Liao Chengzhi, 'He was a Confucian scholar like most of his friends, (but) the only classics he ever quoted were obscure ones that sanctioned revolt'.[13]

Like so many Chinese revolutionaries Liao Zhongkai was motivated first and foremost by a desire to make China a strong and prosperous country, able to resist further encroachment by foreign powers but his nationalism was not associated with xenophobia.[14] His personal knowledge of the United States and his later experience in Hong Kong, Canton and Japan greatly contributed to his understanding of the difficulties in the path of modernisation. Like Sun Yatsen to whom he was connected by bonds of friendship and close co-operation in the cause of the Republican revolution Liao Zhongkai remained convinced that China's modernisation would be impossible without aid from abroad.15 His exposure to socialist thought was largely limited to those Western and Japanese works popular in Japan during the first decade of the present century. The Russian revolution of 1905 attracted attention in Asia, but did not make Liao Zhongkai embrace the Marxist concept of class struggle. Even his association with Anarchism and Nihilism - probably due to Russian influence - ended after the overthrow of the Qing dynasty.16 Liao Zhongkai remained a broad-minded man. Although severely critical of Christianity when it became a tool of foreign imperialism, he did not object to the Christian religion as such. In fact he sent his own son Liao Chengzhi to Christian schools in Japan and China.17 When Liao Zhongkai left the United States he returned to China in the company of his ailing mother who died some months later. Liao Zhubin stayed on with the Huifeng Bank in San Francisco, where he later died. Before his death Liao Zhubin stayed at the house of his uncle, who, like Liao Entao, was an imperial official.18

In 1897, three years after arriving in China Liao Zhongkai married He Xiangning, Liao Chengzhi's mother.19 She was born in Hong Kong in 1880.20 Her father came from a poor family but had made a fortune in the tea business. Referring to the number of officials the Liao family had produced a Japanese scholar bluntly denounced the marriage as a camouflaged union 'between rich merchants of Hong Kong and bureaucrats of Canton'.21 The marriage was arranged by He Xiangning's father who was favourably impressed with Liao Zhongkai's reputation as a diligent and good man.22 To all appearances it was a successful marriage, although the revolutionary activities of Liao Zhongkai left little room for family life.23 In the eyes of her daughter, Liao Mengxing, He Xiangning was a:

> kind of rebel against conservative customs and outlook. She had bitterly and successfully resisted having her feet bound ... and managed to educate herself by keeping in touch with the lessons a private tutor gave the boys in the family (girls were not taught in those days because there was a superstition that 'they would take away the boys' wisdom').24

Liao Mengxing also mentioned that her mother was inspired by the nineteenth century anti-imperial rebel movement, the Taiping.25

Like so many other Chinese students Liao Zhongkai soon fell under the influence of Japan's modernisation efforts. Japan turned out to be the first Asian nation able to build a modern nation-state with a strong economic base, a nation that successfully resisted encroachment by Western powers. There was a tremendous increase in the number of Chinese students going to Japan in the wake of the Chinese Reform Movement of 1898 led by Kang Youwei and Liang Qichao, and Liao Zhongkai soon prepared to leave for Japan accompanied by his wife.26 (Exactly eighty years later, in 1978, the PRC once again decided to send large numbers of students to Japan.) The idea apparently was not supported by the Liao and He families, partly since Chinese custom discouraged women from going abroad.27 Although Liao Zhongkai's elder brother, Liao Entao, was at that time a diplomat for the Chinese Imperial Government, he is said to have refused his brother financial support.28 Liao recalls that her mother:

> insisted on supplying (the necessary funds for going to Japan) by selling jewellery and furniture from her dowry. She had to do that in the face of opposition from both families because such a thing used to be considered disgraceful.29

Later, when Liao's uncle and brother refused to support them in Japan,30 He Xiangning succeeded in persuading her parents to help financially. Liao Zhongkai and his wife arrived in Tokyo in 1902. While he enrolled in economics at Waseda University, his wife studied painting and the arts at the Tokyo Girls Art School.31

These were years of rapidly developing student radicalism, a direct consequence of the humiliations that China underwent in the wake of the failure of the Boxer uprising.32 Liao and He were sympathetic to the anti-Manchu movement headed by Sun Yatsen. They met Sun in the summer of 1903 and soon became active supporters of his movement.33 In the same year He returned to her parents' home in China and gave birth to a daughter, Liao Mengxing, in 1904.34 Soon afterwards she left her daughter in the care of her parents and returned to Japan.35 At that time Japan was embroiled in a war with Tsarist Russia and the Japanese victory in 1905 gave further impetus to revolutionary sentiments among Chinese at home and abroad, not least because it was the first victory by an Asian power over a European imperialist state. In the wake of these developments various revolutionary groups in Japan were reorganised into the so-called Revolutionary Alliance (*Tongmenghui*), with its headquarters in Tokyo. The Alliance became one of the leading organisations working for the overthrow of the Chinese imperial dynasty. In 1905 Liao Zhongkai and his wife joined the Revolutionary Alliance, and He Xiangning was either the first or second woman member.36 When Liao later travelled to China he returned to Japan with their daughter Mengxing.37 Their friends in Tokyo included Zhu Zhixin and Hu Hanmin, later accused of involvement in Liao Zhongkai's assassination.38 Liao again left Japan for China in 1906 on a mission for Sun Yatsen, only to return towards the end of 1907.39 Shortly after his return to Tokyo Liao Zhongkai enrolled in political economics at Chuo (Central) University where he graduated in the following year.40 On 25 September 1908 He Xiangning gave birth to a son, Liao Chengzhi.41

Early Life

During the spring and summer of 1907 Sun Yatsen and his friends had attempted to take advantage of local unrest in Guangdong province to foment a number of local uprisings. Government troops crushed insurrections near Shantou (Swatow) in May and Huizhou (Waichow) in June. The latter was the native area of the Liao family, a place which enjoyed a certain fame as a seat of 'trouble' in Canton province. This was also the area in which the relatively small Communist guerrilla movement in Canton province was active during the late thirties and forties. With the failure of the 1907 uprisings and increasing police repression in Japan, support for the Revolutionary Alliance among Overseas Chinese had fallen drastically.[42] It seems that Liao Zhongkai and He Xiangning had not been too conspicuous in the eyes of the Japanese police for revolutionary activities, since their Tokyo home became a meeting place for revolutionaries 'who thus avoided the attention of the Japanese police',[43] and it also served as a postal address for Sun Yatsen's mail.[44] For security reasons they 'dismissed domestic help and did all the cooking and cleaning themselves', rather unusual for a lady from a well-to-do family.[45] Nevertheless it seems they were able to lead a reasonably comfortable life with the financial support of He's parents from whom their daughter's revolutionary activities, according to Liao Mengxing, remained hidden.[46] During that period Liao Zhongkai, He Xiangning and Zhu Zhixin wrote many letters soliciting funds from Overseas Chinese for the Republican revolution, and their activities among Overseas Chinese made them well-known in such circles.[47] This began the involvement of the Liao family in the field of Overseas Chinese politics which was finally crowned with the successive appointments of He Xiangning and Liao Chengzhi to chairmanship of the Overseas Chinese Affairs Commission after 1949, as well as Liao Chengzhi's son Liao Hui to the same office.[48]

After the failure of the 1907 uprisings revolutionary activities were at a low ebb. In 1909 Liao Zhongkai returned to China.[49] Both He Xiangning and Liao Mengxing insisted that he went to China on a mission for Sun Yatsen. Liao's biographer, Chan, reports that he had taken the imperial examination for students returned from abroad and obtained a position in the imperial government in the northeastern province of Jilin. He was still there when, on 10 October, the uprising took place in Wuchang in south-central China, that led to the downfall of the last Chinese dynasty a few months later. Chan would not dismiss the possibility that He Xiangning's and Liao Mengxing's reference to a mission for Sun Yatsen was to exonerate Liao Zhongkai from the blemish of collaboration with the imperial dynasty.[50] In the wake of the Wuchang uprising Canton province declared itself independent of Manchu rule, and Hu Hanmin asked Liao Zhongkai to assume responsibility for the financial administration of the province. Liao accepted the offer but despite his enthusiasm he met with little success.[51] Liao Zhongkai was now in a position to have his family return to China; the year was 1911. He Xiangning, accompanied by her seven year old daughter, Liao Mengxing, and the toddler Liao Chengzhi went to live in Canton.[52] The Republican revolution soon came under threat from Yuan Shikai who attempted a restoration of imperial rule. Due to the danger of arrest Liao Zhongkai boarded a ship and left Canton for Hong Kong. To ensure the safety of his family he instructed He Xiangning to travel to Hong Kong by train. The British authorities in the colony refused to grant them permission to stay prompting He Xiangning to comment that this conduct of the Hong Kong government symbolised 'the hostility of British imperialism to the revolutionary movement of the Chinese people'.[53] In the same year the Liao family fled to Japan, and went to live in the Shibuya area of Tokyo (Aoyama 7-chome),[54] where they shared a house with Hu Hanmin. Their frugal lifestyle is said to have surprised their Japanese friends who had expected something different from an ex-military governor and former commissioner of finance.[55]

Following events in China in 1914, Sun Yatsen reorganised the Republican party into the China Revolutionary Party (*Zhonghua gemingdang*) to work to overthrow Yuan Shikai. For a short period Liao Zhongkai remained mostly in Tokyo assisting Sun Yatsen by managing the party's finances and organisation.[56]

By the time the Liao family returned to Japan, Liao Chengzhi was approximately five years old; he had been three when they left Japan for Canton:

> I did not stay there (in Japan) for long. In my memory has remained the picture of a small monkey given by my father, and lying in bed together with him. Since I was born in the year of the monkey it must have been due to this very deep link that we shared our bed for half a year. However, the link was soon broken. Flight from China as a refugee. What (also) remains in memory to some extent is my childhood in the Setagaya district of Tokyo. I think it happened after my fifth birthday. Mother had dressed me in a small Japanese coat (a *haori*) with a splashed pattern in the Satsuma style in dark blue, and a kimono as well as small pattens (*geta*). Setagaya in those years was all fields. I was dancing madly like a bat. But what was most charming for me were Asakusa and the twelve storey *Panorama*. It was an absurdly tall building, but for a child of five its contents posed a difficult problem. The zoo was more interesting. Most charming, however, were toy shops. Mother bought me a long spear. ... I was completely walking on air, wielding my spear wherever I went and soon got scolded. Before arriving back home in Setagaya I inadvertently had dropped this important and famous weapon into the wheels of a rickshaw which wrecked it completely. I screamed like a monkey; I ended up having my behind thoroughly spanked and finally returned to my senses. The next thing I can remember is the girl O-ume. Her father who was the boss of a rickshaw shop, lived next door, and she was my best friend during my Setagaya years. We were playmates living next door to each other. It would be an exaggeration to say she was my first girlfriend. Yet in fact, she was my only close friend among the girls. I can still remember her black hair that was all combed upwards onto the top of her head, into the shape of a split peach. A pair of large shining black eyes, and a smile constantly playing around her mouth: she sat well-behaved at the dinner table like a princess. Two or three times a week she would have dinner at our place. When something was funny she would nudge my elbow, giggle, pout her small mouth; like a pair of young swallows we would fly around, jump, and when tired devote ourselves to all sorts of games. The high point was playing doctors. She was stronger than me. It was always I who got pushed over, coming down with a thud like the

proverbial frog in the pond. Our departure for China (1918) put an end to the Setagaya romance.[57]

When Liao returned to Japan in 1927 he attempted to trace her. She had seemingly survived the Great Kanto Earthquake of 1923, but all he was told was that she had become a geisha:

> When I had convinced myself that O-ume had become a geisha, and moreover settled in the area where geishas of the highest class lived, I collapsed like a balloon from which all the air had escaped. And so, in the end, I have never met her again up to the present day, although I would have liked to. Should she be alive and well, I should like to pray fervently for her happiness.[58]

Later the family moved to Shibuya, where they were within five minutes walk of Sun Yatsen's residence (Aoyama 6-chome):[59]

> In the new house mother and father gave me a strict education. When Zhu Zhixin had time he would come and check my arithmetic. My father would watch the movement of my small hand holding the pencil without letting his glance wander. For a naughty boy of five or six there was nothing so disagreeable as arithmetic. When my mouth opened for a yawn father's eyes would flash like fire. They were just like the eyes of the tiger in the zoo. Frightened, I would suppress my yawn. I would recall O-ume. I wonder how long this went on; anyway, eventually fate made me enter primary school. Accompanied by mother the three of us entered a large building next to Kudanzaka. It was a wooden building. In the middle of the massive two-storey school building with two wings was a large exercise yard. The ground was not earth but covered with marvellous pebbles the colour of tiles, and in those days it was a most modern exercise yard. Later I learned that this was Akatsuki primary school. Guided by my mother I was led into a large room, and presently three teachers appeared. One was a foreigner who sported a goatee that looked like the mane of a horse and whose bald head was glittering like an electric light bulb. He spoke in fluent Japanese. Heavens, I thought, confused. But the bearded Frenchman did not give me a break and fired a volley of questions. I still remember what they were about.
>
> 'What time did you get up this morning?'
> 'At six.'
> 'Do you have lunch on your own?'
> 'No, together with my father, mother and my elder sister.'
> 'What sorts of games do you like?'
>
> I did not know what to answer. Even a child like me realised that I could hardly answer 'playing doctors'. Mumbling something I tried to avoid a straight answer. Suddenly he fired his next question.
>
> 'The swing?'

> The new house in Shibuya had a large garden and I remembered that there was a swing.
>
> 'Yes, the swing.'
>
> Mr Beard smiled.
>
> 'Right. And in addition?'
>
> ... And next there was the Japanese teacher. His hair was peppered with grey and he sported a small moustache. Sharp eyes behind glasses. He asked me a question on ciphering. No problems with plus and minus. I did not understand his next question. Mr Moustache smiled.
>
> 'Right, well, how about the second class?'
>
> Like a victorious general I returned to the Shibuya home ... When I stretched out my hands to take off my shoes, a soft white hand suddenly emerged, and deftly took my shoes off. I turned my head in utter amazement. My eyes saw the white and round face of a Japanese lady, her hair bound in Japanese fashion. Of course, unlike O-ume, it was the mature body of an adult.
>
> 'The young lord had no problems with the entrance exam, I suppose?'
>
> Mother gave the answer.
>
> 'That has all been arranged. He's put into second grade.'
>
> 'Well, my congratulations.'
>
> The maid's name was Otsuru and she was our newly-arrived help in the household. Otsuru was unmarried and really treated me with love.[60]

These were happy childhood years for Liao Chengzhi:

> Obasan (his nurse) - O-ume-chan (his playmate) - Otsurusan: they remain in my memory like sweet-smelling flowers that I can never forget as long as I live.[61]

Of course, there was the occasional incident of anti-Chinese discrimination, but Liao had several good friends at school, and the majority were not unkind to him:[62]

> Before leaving Japan I had wanted to be in the navy. In Japan all the boys wanted to join the navy. I hoped to help build up China's rotten navy some day.[63]

Liao never made it into the navy - but he must have remembered his boyhood dreams when, about fifteen years later, he travelled from Shanghai to Europe on a mission for the CCP, carrying out organisational work among Chinese seamen.

Liao Chengzhi completed the fourth grade at Akatsuki primary school,[6] earning much praise from fellow students for his drawings painted on the wall of the classroom:[65]

> I was always fond of drawing, like my mother. I remember that one day one of father's Japanese friends came to see us and asked me to draw something for him. We knew he was connected with the secret service and I had been told to be careful, but I decided to give him

> something to think about. I drew a cartoon showing France and China together beating up Japan. His face turned red and he was furious.66

It was the action of a naughty, mischievous boy, and irresponsible at that, but apparently remained without serious consequences:

> When I was a child I knew that my father's profession was 'patriotic work', but I did not know the nature of it, except that it was dangerous and that my mother was constantly worried about his safety.67

Liao was a bright boy, but of course at about the age of eight too young to see the matter in perspective. Some time in 1916 Liao Zhongkai left Japan for China. After the death of Yuan Shikai in June 1916, Sun Yatsen sent Liao Zhongkai and Hu Hanmin to Peking to discuss further developments. The following year Sun and Liao moved to Canton, where Liao was again charged with financial affairs of the party and the province. There is conflicting evidence concerning Liao Chengzhi's travels during this period; it seems that he joined his father in China in 1918, while his mother and sister stayed in Japan which they left just before the Great Kanto Earthquake in 1923.68 Liao Chengzhi and his father first went to north China, but since the son could not speak the northern dialects, having learned the Cantonese of his parents, he did not attend school. It is said that his father taught him English 'two hours a day', but perhaps we should not take this too literally in view of Liao Zhongkai's extremely busy life as a politician.69

Canton

In the autumn of 1919 Liao Chengzhi left for the south to become a student at the Canton Christian College, an institution under the management of American missionaries:70

> Canton Christian College was one of the most conservative schools in all China. We had to listen to the idiotic preaching of the missionaries for two hours every day and during the whole of Sunday morning, as well as two hours a week of bible lessons. Most of the students hated this compulsory religionising, and it had the opposite effect from that desired by the preachers. Practically the only students who really liked Christianity were the girls.71

Despite the emphasis on 'religionising' the College enjoyed a high reputation in China, as did a number of Christian colleges. Liao was sent to Christian schools, first in Japan (Akatsuki was a Catholic primary school) and then in Canton primarily because of their generally high standard. Although Liao Zhongkai's father had been Christian, Liao Zhongkai himself was not. It seems that his outspoken attacks on some aspects of this foreign religion were not a sufficient reason for him to have his son leave the Canton Christian College. Despite Liao's open attacks on Christian hypocrisy it has been claimed by one of his fellow students in Japan that he used to read the Bible in English.72

During this period Liao Zhongkai's political activities must have left little time to look after his son. One of his main tasks was to raise sufficient funds for Sun's military campaigns, but he soon became involved in the conflict between Sun Yatsen and Chen Qiongming, then governor of Canton province. Chen Qiongming's supporters carried out a coup in June 1922, and Chen attempted to force Sun Yatsen's resignation. Liao Zhongkai was arrested by Chen. He Xiangning must have returned to China some time before the spring of 1922.[73] Her first move after her husband's arrest was to bring Liao Chengzhi and his sister, Liao Mengxing, to safety in Hong Kong.[74] Subsequently she succeeded in meeting Liao Zhongkai who realised that his life was in danger. Liao wrote two poems, one addressed to his wife and one to his children in which he expressed his last thoughts and wishes to them:

Farewell, My Daughter Xing, Farewell, My Son Cheng
Don't grieve, my daughter, don't weep, my son
Father has left, he won't say 'I'll return.'
My joy it would be, my son, my daughter,
to know you are safe.
My pleasure it would be, my daughter, my son,
if you study hard.
There is no change in what grieves me, what pleases me -
it's only my body that won't be there.
My body - what is it but a stinking bag of bones,

Human life - what counts is the human soul,
As the soul advances, so does virtue.
There's one more thing I'd like you not to forget:
Remember me, and be filial to mother.

Two months later Liao Zhongkai was released, partly due to He Xiangning's personal efforts,[76] anticipating her attempts to free her son in the early thirties and again during the forties. The whole affair must have deeply impressed Liao Chengzhi, by then thirteen years old, and he must have read and reread the poem after his father's assassination two years later. It is noteworthy that the poem does not enjoin his children to avenge their father's death. Liao Zhongkai in fact even cautions them not to put their own lives at risk.

Was it a premonition that made Liao Zhongkai write these lines? Perhaps he guessed that his children would become involved in political movements just like himself. Liao Chengzhi was still a teenager, but we can imagine that his father's role must have made a deep impression on him; and little may he have guessed that his brief and casual glimpse of a man called Zhou Enlai in 1924 had brought him face to face with the number two leader of a future Communist China.[77]

Only in 1923 was Chen Qiongming driven out of Canton. In March of that year Liao Zhongkai, He Xiangning and Liao Mengxing returned to Canton.[78] It is not clear when exactly Liao Chengzhi left Hong Kong but by the time the rest of the family returned to Canton he apparently was attending Canton Christian College.

After his release towards the end of August 1922 Liao Zhongkai and his wife first left for Hong Kong, and then Shanghai.[79] In September the Soviet emissary Joffe travelled to Japan where he was soon joined by Liao Zhongkai who had taken his wife and his daughter with him. The official reason for Liao's journey was the marriage of his cousin on his father's side, Liao Liuwei to Shao Xuchong. Liao Entao received them in Tokyo in the most friendly fashion, having no idea that the real purpose of Liao Zhongkai's visit was secret talks with Joffe.[80] These talks were concluded with the Sun-Joffe Manifesto in January 1923 which laid the formal basis for entente between the KMT and the Soviet Union.[81] This is not the place to deal in detail with developments preceding and following the Manifesto. According to Liao Chengzhi his father's:

> political position was further to the left than Sun Yatsen's. Sun's third book, *National Democracy*, criticised Marxism in a nonsensical way, but my father never did. He sympathised with the new Communist party from the beginning and talked of Lenin constantly. Sun Yatsen never reached the point where he wanted to follow in Lenin's footsteps. Father was loyal to the Kuomintang, but saw clearly that a true democracy must lead to Socialism in the end. I think I can say that he had become a real socialist by the time he died. He was firmly convinced that co-operation with the Communist Party and with Soviet Russia was fundamental to the realisation of the national-bourgeois-democratic revolution. Mao Tse-tung, Chou En-lai, Lin Po-chü, and other Communists were his close friends, and Cheng Ken was his student.[82]

Liao Zhongkai's leftist stance resulted in a rumour that he himself had joined the Communist Party, and some newspapers in the British colony of Hong Kong labelled him a Communist. Yet, despite his involvement in leftist politics and the labour movement, it is highly doubtful whether he ever accepted basic Communist concepts like 'class struggle'.[83] Within the KMT there was increasing opposition to the alliance with Moscow and co-operation with the CCP, as well as to KMT reorganisation, but for the moment Liao Zhongkai emerged as the leader of the more radical, leftist faction and the most important collaborator of Sun Yatsen. By this time he had come to outrank other politicians such as Hu Hanmin or Wang Jingwei.[84] Liao's strong anti-imperialist stand became particularly pronounced after the beginning of the collaboration between the KMT and the Soviet Union in 1924, as shown for example by Liao Zhongkai's speech on 14 February 1924.[85] Dissent against the leftist course continued within the KMT, but the support and authority of Sun Yatsen, father of the Republican revolution, did much to render opposition ineffective. Sun died on 12 March. The day before his death he had signed both his political and personal will. In his political will he defended the current party course and the alliance with the Soviet Union in a document drafted by Eugene Chen. His testament was witnessed by He Xiangning among others.[86] Anti-Communist members of the KMT have since claimed that Sun was too ill to study the documents he signed. Following Sun's death Liao Zhongkai was one of the most likely contenders for leadership of the KMT.

While polarisation within the KMT continued, tensions increased in Southern China where strike action by Chinese workers in Canton was watched with apprehension by the British, the more so since these actions were accompanied by strong anti-foreign sentiments. The strike wave itself had been sparked off on 30 May when British police fired on demonstrators, and was seen by the British as 'essentially a political move and a direct challenge of British authority in the Far East'.[87] The event proved a catalyst for leftist student activities in which Liao Chengzhi and his friends also took part. Liao himself had become a member of the KMT in August 1924.[88]

At Canton Christian College Liao had made friends with quite a few youngsters, some of whom were to become lifelong friends. Situ Huimin, a prominent Overseas Chinese recalls that:

> we got to know each other when we were fifteen or sixteen ... Using the language of today Chengzhi was a 'child of a high-ranking cadre', but he did not assume airs *vis-à-vis* us children of overseas Chinese, members of the Communist Youth League or members of the New Student Society, and he had quite a few good friends. At times, the old residence of Mr Zhongkai (ie Liao Chengzhi's father) at Dongshan, Baizi Road, no 11 became a gathering place for us young people.[89]

Another friend was Si Mu, later to become one of the directors of the China News Agency (*Zhongguo xinwenshe*):

> As many as sixty years ago I made the acquaintance of Chengzhi when I was studying literature at Lingnan University in Canton (to which the Canton Christian College was attached). Chengzhi's elder sister Mengxing and I were in the same grade, and 'little Liao', who was several years younger than I was had just enrolled in the third year of the college attached to Lingnan University. In the next year I taught several history lessons to college students, and frequently met 'little Liao'. My first impression was that he was intelligent, lively, humorous, and that he loved to tell jokes. During the lessons he loved to bring up some questions which were not easy to answer, and also aired divergent opinions (quite unusual for a Chinese student at that time ...). It showed that he used his brains and did not believe tradition blindly. At that time there was a Japanese student called Kusano Shimpei who also taught Japanese at Lingnan University. Since Chengzhi had been brought up in Japan and had attended primary school there, he spoke fluent Japanese, and got along very well with Kusano who was an uninhibited romantic. At that time I was running the Canton Society for the Study of Literature at Lingnan University, studying the writing of modern (ie vernacular) poetry which we loved more than anything else, and Kusano, who was absolutely enraptured

by poetry, was frequently in touch with us. So it came about that there were even more opportunities to have chats with Liao on long walks.[90]

Kusano Shimpei and Liao Mengxing were fellow students at that time:

> Liao was six years younger than I, and had just enrolled in the first class of the Middle School. In those days he was not as massive as later on. His skin was dark, and he had a strong individual character.[91]

Kusano Shimpei later became a well known Japanese writer. Among numerous other friends still alive when Liao Chengzhi's died were Huang Dingchen, who became chairman of one of the so-called 'democratic parties' under Communist domination,[92] and Xu Zhang who later became a professor of Microbiology at Columbia University.[93] Liao's sister, Liao Mengxing, showed great interest in politics.[94] Her brother seems to have joined the KMT in 1924 or 1925 (perhaps one of its youth organisations, since he was then only 16 years old), and was active in left-wing student groups.[95] It has also been claimed that he became a Marxist during his student days although there is little evidence for this:[96]

> After the rise of the anti-imperialist patriotic wave of the 30th May Movement Lingnan was also drawn into it, and the Liaos as well as Mengxing's later husband, Li Shaoshi, were at the centre. Students, academic and other staff became members of a 'cell' of the left-wing of the KMT which was led by Liao Zhongkai. I (Si Mu) also became a member. In this way we, who had been student friends, became comrades-in-arms. At times we also went to Chengzhi's place in order to receive guidance from Liao Zhongkai and his wife Xiangning. Following the Shaji (Shakee) massacre of 23 June anti-imperialist demonstrations were held in Canton, and demonstrating workers, peasants and students were fired upon by British troops in Shamen, with a number of fatal casualties...[97]

Liao Chengzhi himself also took part in the demonstration and was an eyewitness of the massacre.[98]

At that time Liao Zhongkai who was also head of the KMT's workers' department, was one of the leading figures in the strike and the boycott, which was instrumental in consolidating the KMT power base in Canton province.[99] Until now Liao Zhongkai had been Minister of Finance, Governor and Financial Commissioner of Canton province, head of the KMT Workers' Department, and party representative to the Whampoa Military Academy. In July 1925 he also became a member of the government and military councils. His increase in power led to the supplanting of Hu Hanmin - leader of a separate faction - by Wang Jingwei. Liao Zhongkai also attacked other members of Hu's faction. He continued a leftist course, was in close touch with the Soviet agent Borodin and maintained relations with CCP members. Small wonder, then, that Liao Zhongkai had made himself many enemies, both within the KMT and among foreign representatives.[100] Several assassination attempts did not deter Liao Zhongkai from continuing his course, until he was felled by bullets one day in August 1925, as described by his daughter Liao Mengxing:

Father's assassins hid behind the pillars of the building of the Central Executive Committee of the Kuomintang, where he went with Mother to attend a meeting on 20 August 1925. It was no coincidence that very few of its members were on hand that day. Obviously they had been warned beforehand. Mother was walking ahead, talking with another member of the Women's Department when she heard the shot. She ran back towards my father and stooped down where he had fallen. Another shot rang out, but it flew over her head. By this time one of my father's bodyguards had shot down the assassin who fired it. The other bodyguard was wounded. My father died on his way to the hospital. When the news reached me, I was in college, taking a summer course in sericulture. On reaching the hospital, I found him already cold and stiff.[101]

The assassin was arrested, and before dying in hospital made a confession implicating a relative of Hu Hanmin.[102] For the time being Liao's opponents were unable to turn his death to their own advantage. Despite the work of a special investigation committee there was a cover-up and the full story never came to light. One can hardly blame He Xiangning for accusing Liao's political opponents of having masterminded the assassination, although definitive proof seems to be lacking. She blamed 'the imperialists' for having paid 'the reactionaries' to murder Liao Zhongkai in order to sabotage the Canton-Hong Kong strike. According to her, one of the assassins confessed that 'Hong Kong had offered a sum of two million *yuan* for the assassination of the Communists in Canton'.[104] In the eyes of many Liao Zhongkai became a martyr and a symbol. He Xiangning called upon her fellow Chinese to emulate her husband's revolutionary zeal in their fight for national freedom.[105] Some Hong Kong newspapers started a sordid counter-attack accusing Liao Zhongkai of corruption, and reported that he had deposited a sum of over three hundred thousand *yuan* in a certain unidentified bank in the colony. On 9 November Liao Mengxing and Liao Chengzhi made a public denial of the charge. In an open letter published in *Minguo Daily* they offered to donate the money to labour organisations in Canton if any person could furnish evidence that their father had actually placed any amount in excess of ten thousand *yuan* in a bank.[106] It is not quite clear to what extent, and whether, Chiang Kaishek had taken sides. According to one report, he had invited mother and children to stay at the Official Lodge of Whampoa Military Academy, and so it happened that Jiang Jingguo - many decades later to become the leader of the anti-communist ROC - and Liao Chengzhi, then fifteen and seventeen respectively, spent some time together. If this is correct, Chiang Kaishek acted in this way out of gratitude to Liao Zhongkai for his achievements in the area of KMT finance. According to the same source, He Xiangning first supported the pro-Chiang Kaishek forces during the split between leftists and rightists in the Kuomintang as a token of her gratitude to Jiang for having looked after them after Liao Zhongkai's assassination. This, of course, is at variance with Communist historiography which used to depict Chiang Kaishek as the arch criminal *par excellence*.[107]

Liao Chengzhi had not yet turned seventeen when his father was assassinated. Afflicted by grief and sorrow he seems to have become more intent than ever on continuing his involvement in politics, fighting for a cause which had claimed his father's life:

> Just after my father's assassination, I organised a strike of all the workmen at Canton Christian College, and at the same time my sister's future husband led a supporting student movement. We demanded better wages for the workers, the abolition of compulsory Sunday sermons, and the lifting of the ban on cigarette-smoking. The strike was the first the workmen had ever tried, and it was victorious. They were surprised and delighted. The teachers tried to force Li (Liao Mengxing's future husband) and me to leave school but they dared not expel me because of my father's influential position in Canton.[108]

To tell the truth Liao and his friends did not succeed in mobilising large numbers of their fellow students:

> The college was a truly colonial school for the sons and daughters of the comprador-bourgeoisie, and did its work well. Most of the students were ignorant of political affairs and had little common sense. I intensely disliked the type of young comprador that I found there. These students, true to their comprador origins - dependent on foreign imperialists - , attacked our revolutionary students saying that the struggle against imperialism was nonsense.[109]

In his farewell poem written in 1922 Liao Zhongkai had urged his children not to put their lives at risk. At the same time, however, he had enjoined them to be faithful to their mother. Like Sun Yatsen's wife, Song Qingling, He Xiangning also entered politics after her husband's death, and it does not seem far-fetched that her example further inspired Liao Chengzhi to continue the fight. Perhaps his continued involvement in student politics was also one way of coping with the shock of his father's assassination. At the Second National Congress of the KMT in January 1926 both Song Qingling and He Xiangning were elected to the party's Central Executive Committee. The leftist members saw their position weakened, and Hu Hanmin was able to make a comeback.[110] Intraparty strife became more intense, culminating in the expulsion and persecution of Communists and leftists from the KMT in 1927. The changing situation had also affected Canton Christian College, with leftist students leaving one after the other.[111] Despite these developments Liao Chengzhi did not give up his involvement in student politics, and when a new anti-Communist government was set up in Nanking in opposition to the leftists in Hankou (Wuhan) a second strike was attempted at the College:

> Our strike had the support of progressive forces outside, so we were able to take a strong stand. The school closed down and most of the pickets and strikers had to go into Canton city. The school asked the police to come ... and guided them in their attempt to make arrests. Three of the worker leaders were executed. Such is Christianity in China! Fortunately, the leftist students escaped before the secret-

service agents made their search. Twenty of these were Communists. I was only a Kuomintang (KMT) Leftist, but sympathetic to the Communists. After a while the school reopened... During the arrests, I left the school and went to Japan ...[112]

One of Liao's friends, Situ Huimin, reports how Liao helped other students to escape arrest, and many went to Shanghai.[113] These were very difficult months for the Liao family. In summer 1926 Liao Mengxing had become so ill that 'mother worried that Liao Zhongkai's favourite child might pass away'.[114] He Xiangning continued her political activities, also in the face of mounting tensions which erupted in the anti-Communist purge of April 1927. Thereafter He Xiangning and her children moved to Shanghai.[118] Liao Chengzhi left the KMT, in the following year becoming a formal member of the CCP.[116] A close friend of Liao in those days, Tan Juezhen, insists that Liao did not become a member of the CCP during his stay in Tokyo; according to him, the CCP showed no understanding of Liao's humour, - on the contrary, it made him appear flippant, which seems to have been one of the reasons to refuse him party membership.[117]

CCP Membership and Return to Japan

Liao's leaving the KMT may not imply a major change in his convictions, since until that time there was a wide spectrum of opinion within it. He Xiangning remained a member of the KMT, and one may wonder whether she approved of Liao's move.[118] In the same year Liao went to Japan, probably in June or July 1927.[119] In Tokyo he met some of his friends from Canton, such as Xia Yan, Huang Dingchen and Situ Huimin. According to Huang:

The Tokyo 'Special Branch' of the CCP in Japan organised a 'Society for the Study of Social Science' in order to unite an even greater number of the masses to study Marxism-Leninism and to develop revolutionary activities. (Liao) Chengzhi was an activist of the society, and participated actively with great enthusiasm, whether it concerned study or social activities, and showed himself to be a very courageous fighter.[120]

Liao Chengzhi entered a high school attached to Waseda University[121] but admits that he:

didn't do much studying there, and instead organised a 'League for the Investigation of Social Science'. In 1927 there were about four thousand Chinese students in all of Japan. They had a general student association with headquarters in Tokyo. The leftist students also had a separate organisation, including both Chinese and Japanese. This leftist society numbered three hundred Chinese and two hundred Japanese members in Tokyo, of whom there were seven or eight at Waseda. Most of the Chinese members of this group spoke Japanese well. It was necessary to spend a year or so studying Japanese, because no classes were held in Chinese. I stayed in Japan for ten months, then was kicked out after the Tsinan (Jinan) Incident on 3 May 1928. We had organised an anti-Japanese demonstration in Tokyo, and the police ordered us to leave the country. Some were arrested and tortured, and about forty of us ran away.123

According to Tan Juezhen, the famous Japanese philosopher Kawakami Hajime stimulated Liao's interest in Social Science.124 During his stay in Tokyo Liao had also been involved in an organisation of students from Canton.125

Liao Chengzhi had been about ten years old when he left Japan for Canton. Now nineteen years old, many of his childhood memories must have grown rather faint. His trip also became an opportunity to trace his childhood years with the aid of a personal friend of his mother, Mr Wu Qiongshi, who lived in Tokyo.126 But even Mr Wu could not tell him the whereabouts and the fate of his nurse. According to Mr Wu his former playmate O-ume had become a geisha, but either he did not know her address or did not wish to tell Liao. Mr Wu was Liao's guardian, and apparently informed his mother in detail about his life.127 It is difficult to say whether he approved of Liao's political activities which certainly had a negative effect on his scholarly efforts. At school Liao also became a member of the *Bunka shicho kenkyukai* of which some members are still alive. Kawamura Toichiro - who later became a company director in Tokyo - recalls:

> In about 1928-29 we were together at the school's club called *Bunka shicho kenkyukai* and frequently went to have *nabemono* (a dish served in a pan) or *sushi* .. in the vicinity of Nihonbashi (in downtown Tokyo). Liao had an excellent physique, and his head was closely cropped. He was quite outgoing, and his way of talking was lively and casual.128

Liao seems to have enjoyed his return to Japan but we can only guess as to whether he ever considered remaining there for an extended period. The situation in Japan had by now changed considerably with strong pressure to eradicate Communist influence altogether. Any open involvement in the movement carried the risk of arrest and deportation and Liao Chengzhi was not prepared to renounce politics. He took a very active part in the rivalry and factional wars between students loyal to the Chinese government under Chiang Kaishek and leftists and Communists. It seems that he was arrested twice during his stay in Japan.129 One of his friends, Huang Dingchen, describes such a clash in detail:

> On 12 March 1928 that bunch of reactionaries conducted anti-Communist activities under the guise of commemorating the anniversary of Sun Yatsen's death. In order to unmask the sinister enemy the Tokyo Special Branch (of the CCP) issued two statements entitled 'Statement Concerning the Current Situation' and the 'Letter to Shiguang Sheng' which opposed the collaboration between Jiang (Chiang Kaishek) and Wang (Jingwei) ... Both statements were distributed at the 'Commemorative Meeting' in the form of leaflets. Chengzhi actively participated in handing them out. When the cultural programme started and the lights went out we made use of the

> opportunity to scatter the leaflets like snowflakes among the participants ... This activity frightened the enemy, and also attracted the attention of the Japanese police. After the incident these reactionaries and the Japanese police banded together and conducted searches everywhere. On 18 March a meeting was called under the leadership of the Tokyo Special Branch (of the CCP) to commemorate the founding of the Paris Commune as well as the patriotic incident on Tiananmen Square (in Peking) on 18 March. Before the meeting we had anticipated that the reactionaries would certainly try to disrupt it, and we therefore had taken appropriate measures. The meeting was held according to plan, watched over - as expected - by the enemy. However, it was conducted successfully, and the speeches proceeded without a hitch. A cadet, who had come to watch drew his knife in an attempt to attack the chairman of the meeting, but was intercepted by our comrades, using folding chairs as weapons. It came to straight blows, the attacker was struck unconscious and fell to the ground. Liao Chengzhi boldly took part. The masses who had participated in the meeting got up and pasted slogans on walls, distributed leaflets and chanted slogans. The meeting ended victoriously, and the troublemakers who had arrived only then failed miserably. During the whole fight Chengzhi displayed quickwittedness and courage, and received the praise of the comrades.[130]

Huang Dingchen reports these events with the obvious pride of a participant, and the wording betrays the ideological language of the day. On a broader perspective such clashes hardly served to win new supporters, being perhaps more important as a reaffirmation of one's loyalty to the group to which one belonged. The effect on the Japanese public was negligible and it seems doubtful whether activities went much beyond preaching to the converted.

Student activities took on a different dimension in the wake of the Jinan Incident when a military clash between Japanese troops and Chinese government forces in Jinan (Shandong province) led to a massacre among the local population. Chinese students in Japan were indignant, and the incident stirred patriotic feelings against the Japanese:

> On 3 May 1928, after the Jinan massacre, the Tokyo Special Branch (of the CCP) set up a conference of Chinese students in Japan opposing Japanese aggression in China, the massacre of our fellow countrymen and the (Japanese) occupation of Jinan. At the conference we decided to establish a Great Anti-Japan Alliance in order to continue activities against Japanese militarism. Liao Chengzhi actively participated in this work. He was a backbone cadre of the provincial association of Cantonese students in Japan, and carried out much work in that capacity.[131]

Soon afterwards Liao was arrested by Japanese police for a short period, and expelled from Waseda High School, the reason apparently being 'non-payment of fees and absence over a long period'.132 Soon Liao was forced to leave Japan.133 Before his departure he met his friend Kawamura Toichiro again.

A CCP Activist in China and Europe

On leaving Japan Liao must have wondered whether it would be farewell forever. He had become *persona non grata* in Japan which seemed firmly set on confrontation with China. Also, anti-Communism was growing there, and the government was able to frustrate leftist or Communist attempts to gain an effective foothold. Liao Chengzhi remained firmly committed to his leftist activities, thus making his legal return to Japan virtually impossible. Liao's sister had likewise been expelled from Japan, according to her own account due to her connection with a left-wing friend, at that time not yet a Communist Party Member.134

As in Japan, China under Chiang Kaishek was continuing its anti-Communist course. After the anti-Communist purge of April 1927 He Xiangning had repeatedly attempted to dissuade Chiang from following this line. Chiang would not yield. A last opportunity for He to persuade Chiang came when the latter invited her to act as a witness at his marriage. Having overcome some opposition to his proposed marriage with Song Meiling, the sister of Sun Yatsen's widow, Song Qingling, he had wanted to have Liao Zhongkai's widow attend the wedding. When Chiang did not give in to her attempts at political persuasion she simply refused to attend the wedding which took place on 1 December 1927. Li Dequan, wife of warlord Feng Yuxiang, was then invited to act as witness instead. Li Dequan, it may be remarked, later became increasingly involved in the leftist cause and in 1954 became formal leader of a delegation to Japan, the actual head of which was He Xiangning's son, Liao Chengzhi.

After his expulsion from Japan Liao went first to Shanghai.135 For a short while he worked in the Shanghai branch of the Great Anti-Japan Alliance, where he also again met Huang Dingchen, his old friend from college days, who had also gone to Japan and likewise been expelled.136 Some time in 1928 he is reported to have become a formal member of the CCP in Shanghai, although the dates given differ between spring and August of that year,137 and he is said to have worked in the Propaganda Department of the CCP in the French Concession.138 Briefly the Liao family was reunited, but He Xiangning was very much concerned about the personal safety of her children.139

According to the information quoted so far Liao's departure for Europe thus could not have taken place before the summer of 1928, although there is some contrary evidence.140 Most likely he left China for Europe in November.141 According to his official biography published after his death the CCP sent him to Germany in 1928 where he became a member of the German Communist Party.142 Liu Tiansu recalls that He Xiangning had advised Liu to leave China for security reasons and go abroad to study.143 Huang Dingchen, himself afterwards arrested and imprisoned for a long time, mentions that He Xiangning had wanted Liao to go to Germany to study,144 and it seems reasonable to assume that, although not the initiator of Liao's trip to Europe, she should wholeheartedly agree with it. He Xiangning also left China and went first to the Philippines and Singapore where she raised funds for the establishment of a Liao Zhongkai memorial school.145 Subsequently she went to France, where her daughter also travelled,146 arriving in the autumn of 1929.147

There is little information about Liao Chengzhi's precise movements in Europe, and some contradictory evidence concerning times and places. He is also said to have worked in the International Seamen's Union,148 visiting such ports as Antwerp, Rotterdam and Hamburg, in addition to other places.149 Apparently he studied in Germany for a period.150 Some time between 1928 and 1929 he met Karl August Wittfogel.151 Some of his activities were of a clandestine nature, and he was arrested twice, once in Hamburg and once in The Hague. Having been imprisoned for two weeks for leading strikes in Rotterdam he was deported from Holland, and suffered the same fate in Hamburg.152

In 1929 he was reportedly active in Germany. Lu Dingyi, later a prominent CCP propagandist, and one of the earliest victims of the GPCR, met him in Berlin on the way to the 'Second Congress of the Great International Anti-Imperialist Alliance' held in Frankfurt. It may have been on that occasion that Liao met Professor Wittfogel. According to Lu Dingyi, Liao was then studying in Berlin.153 In the same year he seems to have been sent to Hamburg by Qu Qiubai where he was secretary of the Hamburg party branch committee of the International Seamen's Club.154 Although formally a member of the German Communist Party it seems quite likely that he remained subject to CCP discipline, as indicated by his link with Qu Qiubai.155 Some time around 1930 Liao Chengzhi was arrested in Hamburg and spent a (short) time in prison:156

> At the end of 1930 Liao Chengzhi was released from prison [most likely a reference to his imprisonment in Hamburg] and went to France, intending to join his mother... His stay brightened He Xiangning up... Daily routine was as follows. The lady [ie He Xiangning] did the cooking, [Liao] Chengzhi cleaned and cut the vegetables, I [Liu Tiansu] fried the vegetables, Zeng Qingji was responsible for dishwashing after meals and keeping the kitchen clean. We took our meals in [Zeng] Qingji's room, since it had a small kitchen. It was there that Mrs He [Xiangning] taught me Cantonese soy sauce dishes. I remember, most fascinating was [Liao] Chengzhi's way of cutting beef, he always used to beat a rhythm with his kitchen knife while cutting, making everybody burst out laughing. Whenever the meal was ready, Mrs He would stand next to the study desk and call out laughing: 'Quickly, move the table, dinner's being served!' That was, because our desk was [also] our dining table, when having meals the four of us could only sit at the table after having moved the desk into the middle of the room.157

At some stage Liao had visited the Soviet Union, apparently to attend a Congress in the summer of 1930.158 Probably in 1931 he was also enrolled at the Far Eastern University where he met Chiang Kaishek's son, Jiang Jingguo, then also a student in Moscow.159 Among his other acquaintances was Qu Wu, later to become vice-chairman of the Central Committee of the Minge, one of the 'democratic parties' under Communist control.160 By no means all students in the Soviet Union were Communists or even leftists,161 the most prominent among them being Chiang Kaishek's son. There is little confirmed information about the duration of Liao's stay in the Soviet Union and there is a rumour that he participated in a training programme for secret agents but evidence is lacking. It is obviously of great importance to know more about Liao's individual reaction to his stay in the Soviet Union but there is little conclusive evidence.162

Zhu Ziqi relates that he:

> got to know Liao Chengzhi in the beginning of November 1949 in the house of Ren Bishi ... When he learned that I was going to accompany Ren Bishi to the Soviet Union he enthusiastically said to me: 'That's a good opportunity to study,' and we spoke a few sentences in Russian, hoping that I would not forget to make time after my arrival in the Soviet Union to write something and send it to him.163

Shanghai and Arrest

It is not even clear how and when he left the Soviet Union, but by 1932-33 Liao was back in Shanghai.164 Following his activities in Europe organising Chinese seamen it is not surprising that he became Head of the Propaganda Department of the All-China Trade Union (*Zhonghua quanguo zonggonghui*) in Shanghai as well as secretary of the party branch of the CCP in the All-China Seamen's Union (*Quanguo haiyuan zonggonghui dangtuan*).165 In Shanghai he engaged in underground activities under the name of He Liuhua.166 He apparently met Zhou Enlai during this period, but it is not quite clear how relevant these meeting(s) were.167 In Shanghai he also met his future wife for the first time. He Xiangning had also returned to Shanghai in 1931 and lived next door to Jing Hengyi, a well-known Chinese politician. In the thirties, He Xiangning, Jing Hengyi (Liao Chengzhi's father-in-law) and Sui Shuren also formed an artists' society *Han zhi you she*.168 Jing Hengyi had a daughter called Jing Puchun. She recalls that:

> We lived at number 7, and He Xiangning lived on the upper floor of number 8. My father frequently had me do errands for He Xiangning... Once I saw there a young man wearing a Chinese style gown, and she introduced him to me as her nephew who had come to see her, but he left very soon. I hadn't noticed him at all.169

A few years later Nym Wales (Helen Foster Snow) conducted an interview with Liao Chengzhi in which he is reported to have said that he:

arrived in Shanghai just after the Shanghai fighting in 1932 and was immediately betrayed by a former comrade and arrested by British controlled police in the International Settlement.[170] I had been detained at the Bureau of Public Safety for two weeks when I decided to fool the police by saying I would betray the whereabouts of another comrade in exchange for my own liberty. I led the police to my mother's house, as she happened to be in Shanghai then. Luckily she was at home. When she found that I was a prisoner, she raised heaven and earth and secured my release. Several of us had been arrested at that time (including Cheng Ken, an old friend of Canton days, who was sent to Nanking on the same train with me and was also released) and one of my best comrades was sent to Nanking and executed.[171]

Virtually all other sources place his arrest in Shanghai in March 1933.[172] Liao adds explicitly that he was betrayed immediately after his return to Shanghai. Since nothing is known of two arrests during that period one should conclude that either Liao's memory slipped during the interview or that, in fact, he only arrived in Shanghai in 1933, and that for some reason or other sources (including his 'official biography' in *PD* 17 June 1983) wish us to believe that he spent part of 1932 in Shanghai. On the other hand, the story of this arrest in 1932, which became known to the outside world only after two weeks, differs from his well-publicised arrest in 1933, which was mentioned by a number of sources, and was also witnessed by his future wife, Jing Puchun:

On the evening of 28 March 1933 I had already fallen asleep. A servant of the He Xiangning household knocked at our door. My father woke me up and we arrived together at their house. We saw two French policemen together with a young man in handcuffs dressed in an old Western-style suit. When I had a close look I discovered that it was the 'nephew' who had been introduced to me. Immediately afterwards the young man was led away. Before leaving he whispered something secretly in auntie's ears (ie He Xiangning). When he had left auntie said to my father: 'Please accept my apologies, Mr Jing (Hengyi), for not having told you previously that young man was my son Liao Chengzhi.' The next day auntie called a taxi and drove to the office of the Mayor of Shanghai, Wu Tiecheng, and sat down in his reception room and told him: 'If you don't release Chengzhi you can pick me up, too.' She urged him to give an immediate reply, refusing to leave without having received a clear assurance. Wu Tiecheng had no other choice but to put a call through to Jiang Jieshi (Chiang Kaishek). As a result he told auntie that the matter was now settled, and that she could get him back in a 'few days' time. In this way Chengzhi was released within a few days. Three persons acted as guarantors: my father (Jing Hengyi), Liu Yazi and Song Qingling. This episode was the beginning of my relationship with Chengzhi. I learned only later that Chengzhi was in fact not staying at his mother's place.

He had given the police his mother's address in order to let her know he had been arrested ...173

Contrary to common practice the arrest of Liao Chengzhi was reported in the press:

One day I suddenly saw the news of the arrest of Liao and Luo Dengxian in the *Shenbao*, together with a photo of both of them ... . Arrests of CCP members were (normally) kept secret, and were not reported by journalists. This time journalists reported Liao's arrest. I was worried about their safety.174

Immediately after the arrest the Communist paper *Leninist Life (Liening shenghuo)* of 2 April 1933 carried an appeal for the release of Liao Chengzhi, Luo Dengxian and Yu Wenhua. The arrest was blamed on co-operation between imperialist authorities in Shanghai, the city administration and the KMT authorities. The reason given for the arrest was participation in anti-Japanese, anti-imperialist work and the labour movement. According to this article, Wang Qiliang and Wang Yuncheng had given the authorities information leading to the arrest. The article continued that previous arrests and executions had been protested against, and that it would have been absolutely impossible to maintain silence after Liao's arrest.175 The article also called for the release of other political detainees. In addition readers were urged to call for a conference supporting Liao and the others, for petitions lists, to send a delegation to Nanjing, and to organise visits to the prisoners. On 1 April 1933 Song Qingling published an '[Address] to the Chinese People' (*Gao zhongguo renmin*) in which she protested against the 'illegal arrest of Luo Dengxian, Chen Geng and Liao Chengzhi'.176 It is not clear whether and when Liao was actually sentenced.177

A condition for Liao's speedy release was the promise by the guarantors that henceforth he would refrain from engaging in political activities, and he was released a few days later. Despite a heart ailment He Xiangning immediately called a taxi and drove to the mayor demanding her son's release, just as she had fought for her husband's release a decade earlier.178 She had not been alone in her fight. In addition to the guarantors she had the support of such well known personalities as Cai Yuanpei and Sun Yatsen's widow, Song Qingling, as well as various organisations. It nevertheless seems likely that the standing of He Xiangning and the support of Song Qingling were crucial in having Chiang Kaishek think twice before executing Liao Chengzhi.179 Yu Feng recalls that:

it was father who presided over the court dealing with Liao's case (since his jurisdiction extended over cases concerning the English concession in Shanghai). He Xiangning furiously reproached the Nanking government and requested leftists from among writers and artists in Shanghai to tell my father the true story; in the end, this brought about Liao Chengzhi's release...180

Others arrested with Liao were not so lucky. Luo Dengxian, for instance, died in the same year. After Luo had been seen by a friend on 5 April 1933, nothing was heard of him until August, and he died soon after. When his son Luo

Weiming, studied in Peking after 1949 he lodged in Liao Chengzhi's house, as did several orphans of other comrades.[181] Liao had been saved, at least partly due to his prominent family background but there was another point which may have made Liao Chengzhi feel guilty towards Luo Dengxian and others who were not released. His guarantors had promised that Liao would stay out of politics, and after his release he was in fact placed under house arrest, as Jing Puchun recalls:

> After his release auntie had him confined in her house for more than a month, during which period he was not to leave the house. So it was that we became more familiar with each other, having long talks together. I discovered that he was a man of many talents, a good singer, painter, knowing foreign languages. At that time he painted an oil portrait of me that I have treasured up to the present day, and it now has its place on the wall in my bedroom.[182]

There is no concrete evidence that Liao Chengzhi was fully aware of the conditions of his release, in particular the obligation to abstain from politics, and went along with these conditions. It has been claimed, however, that he, as well as others, in fact did submit statements disavowing Communist affiliation, in contrast to other more steadfast comrades.[183] For some time Liao adhered to the promise made by his guarantors. Then quite suddenly in August 1933 he left Shanghai. At the time Jing Puchun left Shanghai in May 1933[184] it seems that Liao and she had already fallen in love. Liao explained the reason for his flight in letters to his mother and Liu Yazi, one of the guarantors. The letter to Jing Puchun was lost later on, but she writes that:

> He requested me to wait for another two years if I really loved him. After that nearly four years passed during which I did not receive any news ... In fact he did write letters ... but they were all intercepted by my elder brother who opposed my affiliation to Liao.[185]

The letter to Liu Yazi has been preserved and is on display in the Liao Zhongkai-He Xiangning Memorial Hall in Canton. In this letter he asked Liu to look after his mother, and significantly added that he himself was leaving 'on behalf of those many people' (ie to work for the Communist Party), requesting him not to worry.[186]

The Long March

This version of events conflicts with Chang Chuan who claimed that the marriage was arranged between their parents.[187] From Shanghai Liao fled to Communist-held territory and enlisted in the Red Army.[188] In leaving without authorisation he must have risked reprisals against his guarantors, although little is known about any consequences. Judging by Huang Dingchen's recollections his mother approved of his flight[189] which seems not to have been merely a spontaneous individual decision, but to have been prepared following consultations with Communist Party organs. The Central Committee of the CCP had left Shanghai for guerrilla-held territory at the end of 1932,[190] but clandestine channels of communication may have been used to inform Liao of party orders. According to his official biography published after his death, he was then appointed a member of the executive committee of the provincial committee of a Communist base in Central China and also Head of the Propaganda Department of the Trade Union.[191] The same source reports that he was appointed general secretary of the General Political Department of the Red Fourth Front Army, an appointment confirmed by other sources.[192] Starting from the Oyuwan Soviet, a Communist rebel base, he joined the flight of the Communists with Xu Xiangqian, and seems to have served as an artillery officer at one stage.[193] One of the leaders of this column of the 'Long March' was Zhang Guotao who like many other Communist leaders indulged in terrorist purges within his own party.[194] One of Zhang's victims was Liao Chengzhi whom he arrested together with Luo Shiwen and Zhu Guang, apparently in December 1934.[195] From March 1935 until his release in the winter of 1936 he followed the Army 'under escort'.[196] Liao was stripped of his party membership and, according to several later accounts, his life was in acute danger,[197] this in addition to the incredible hardships suffered by the participants on the 'Long March'. Many years later Liao Chengzhi 'good-humouredly recalled his attempt to boil his leather belt for eating during the course of the Long March'.[198]

The date of his arrest is not known, but the danger passed after the merger of the Red First and Fourth Frontal Armies in the province of Sichuan in south-west China in the summer of 1935. The history of the flight of the routed Red Fourth Frontal Army goes back to the autumn of 1932, after the fourth encircling offensive by Chinese government troops. Available information does not allow us to determine Liao's precise movements before June 1935, and it is not clear for how long and under what circumstances he carried out assignments on the basis of his appointments of 1933 and 1934. When arrested Zhang accused Liao of being a traitor. Perhaps Liao's speedy release in the spring of 1933 may have aroused suspicions that he had become a turncoat. Despite the severity of the treason charge Liao escaped execution and death, and his luck held. Liao himself once remarked that it had been his gift as a propaganda artist that made him so indispensable that Zhang Guotao decided to take him on the Great northern trek.[199] One of those defending Liao during that period was Ren Bishi.[200] The decisive event ensuring Liao's eventual release is said to have followed a chance meeting with Zhou Enlai.[201] Zhang Guotao had apparently wished to keep Liao's arrest a secret from Zhou, but:

> it was not long before Zhou Enlai, then already a very important figure in the CCP, heard of Liao's arrest, and was waiting for an opportunity to save him. This opportunity arrived when the Red Fourth Army together with the Red Second Frontal Army advanced in the general direction of Gansu and Ningxia towards Yuwangbao, and Liao had a sudden and unexpected encounter with Zhou Enlai... Liao was constantly under guard, and Liao was concerned whether problems would arise for Zhou if he, Liao, should suddenly address Zhou. Zhou

Enlai, however, had recognised Liao and approached him. Keeping Liao's guards in mind Zhou simply shook Liao's hands without showing any expression on his face. He left (again) without saying a word. The same day Zhou sent a liaison officer to Liao. Accompanied by the officer Liao entered headquarters. Many people were present inside, including Zhang Guotao. When Zhang saw Liao in the company of Zhou's liaison officer he casually asked whether Liao was in fact an old acquaintance of Zhou's, although he was aware of the fact. Without replying to Zhang's question, Zhou turned to Liao Chengzhi and sternly said to him in such a loud voice so that all present could hear it: 'Have you realized and acknowledged your own faults? Well, I suppose you are willing to correct your mistakes?' In front of all the people present Liao answered Zhou's questions in the affirmative. Zhou merely said 'Is that so?' and adding 'All right then', asked him to stay on for a while to have dinner before leaving. Zhang Guotao was unable to thwart Zhou, who at that time was a vice-chairman of the CC Revolutionary Military Commission of the Communist Party. Sitting at the table Zhou Enlai did not bring up the problem of Liao's situation again. This was meant by Zhou to indicate to Zhang Guotao that the matter had now been resolved. Had Zhou Enlai not behaved in the way he did, Zhang may have been able to move first by executing him, since Zhang Guotao had certainly been informed of Zhou's previous handshake with Liao in the presence of Liao's guards. Now, however, Zhang Guotao was forced to improve Liao's treatment until his final release.[202]

Others apart from Zhou Enlai may in fact also have wished to assist Liao but lacked authority and standing to do so. Lu Dingyi virtually apologised for his inaction many years later:

> It goes without saying that I did not believe Liao to be a counter-revolutionary but I had also been attacked by the Wang Ming group, and there was nothing I could do. On the contrary, I had to feign not to know him lest Liao meet with disaster on account of me.[203]

How well did Zhou Enlai know Liao Chengzhi? Zhou of course had known Liao Zhongkai quite well. His meetings with Liao Zhongkai's son however had been rather superficial encounters. Zhou may have wished to save Liao for purely personal reasons, but he also must have realised that Liao Chengzhi's execution by the CCP would have a disastrous effect on the relations with leftist members of the KMT, represented by He Xiangning and Song Qingling.[204]

It seems Liao was finally released some time between late 1935 and early 1936 after about two years under arrest.[205] During this period he had been subjected also to the suffering and agony of the flight from government troops which reduced the Communist guerrilla forces to about one-tenth of their original size before reaching a sanctuary in northwestern China. Liao indeed was lucky to survive both Zhang Guotao's persecution and the 'Long March' itself. His fortunes improved when, somewhere *en route* between Sikang and northern Shaanxi, he was rehabilitated and appointed editor in the new Red China News Agency of which Miss Zhang Jinjiu was the director.[206] Shortly after his release he met Ma Haide, later to become one of the few non-Chinese officially employed by the PRC.[207] At that time Liao Chengzhi was still with the Red Fourth Frontal Army, as confirmed by Lu Dingyi:

> In October 1936 the First Frontal Army moved west from Northern Shaanxi in order to join up with the Second and Fourth Front Armies. I was head of the Propaganda Department of the Army's Political Department. One day I welcomed comrades from the Fourth Frontal Army which had advanced to northern Shaanxi to our camp, and to my surprise saw Liao Chengzhi among them. He had already been released... I was very happy because he had not been murdered by Zhang (Guotao). I went to meet him. The Red Fourth Frontal Army dragged on by Zhang Guotao had crossed over three snow-clad mountain ridges plus the steppe, suffering unimaginable hardships ... All the way Liao had been treated as a criminal ... and his situation had been even worse ... Liao asked me about his mother, and told me that he had not had any contact with her for a long time. I suggested he send her a picture of himself. ... Later I heard that he had not been executed due to (the standing of) his father and mother, and also because of (his ability to) make drawings. Back in the (Communist) base areas Zhang Guotao wanted to print paper notes and needed to make use of Liao's (talents). Liao was only released due to comrade Zhou Enlai's efforts after their arrival at Yuwangbao in Gansu.[208]

Zhang Guotao had been in disagreement with the 'central leadership' of the remaining guerrilla forces over many questions of military tactics, strategy, the location of future Communist-held base areas, etc. Zhang's own units suffered devastating defeats in the winter of 1936-1937, and it is not surprising that on reaching Yanan, the main Communist sanctuary throughout the anti-Japanese war, the 'central leadership' took him to task in March 1937,[209] as told by Warren Guo:

> Following the massive campaign against Chang Kuo-tao in various organisations, training schools and armed units in early 1937, the CCP central leadership convened an enlarged Politburo conference to formalise the anti-Chang Kuo-tao struggle. It was attended by about 40 persons, including members of the Politburo and the Central Committee, and ranking military and government leaders. Chang Kuo-tao himself was present as a Politburo member. Presiding at the meeting, CCP Secretary General Chang Wen-tien announced that discussions would centre on Chang Kuo-tao's errors in review of the split of the Party and its Red Army during the Long March... Many noted Communist big shots made heated attacks on Chang Kuo-tao at the conference... The most dirty and abusive language came from Liao Cheng-chih, who had suffered prolonged imprisonment in the 4th

Frontal Army as a counter-revolutionary suspect. Likewise, he attacked Chang Kuo-tao's policy for suppressing counter-revolutionaries. In particular, he told of the sex-orgies during the counter-revolutionary suppression campaign. According to him, wives and daughters of local despots and gentry, when seized by the 4th Frontal Army, were raped and tortured to death by soldiers. The soldiers punished female prisoners by playing with their vaginas. Liao described these scandals in unspeakable terms, and at last he yelled, 'this is the line of Chang Kuo-tao - a trick for sexual pleasure'.[210]

Liao's attack was certainly not decisive in the downfall of Zhang Guotao who later left the CCP, but at last he had been able to revenge himself and release his pent-up emotions.

After his arrival in Yanan Liao Chengzhi continued to work in the field of Communist propaganda and the news media. He was appointed head of the editorial office of the Central Committee of the CCP as well as general editor of its official organ, *Liberation Weekly (Jiefang zhoukan)*, serving as editor for twenty issues.[211] Another source lists Liao's positions as Secretary of the Liberation Publishing Office, Head of New China (News) Agency, and Deputy Head of the United Front Work Department of the Central Committee.[212] Of course, he also engaged in all kinds of activities, such as acting as interpreter when foreigners came to visit or lecture at the 'Resistance University'.[213] Reading this impressive list of titles one should perhaps recall the harsh realities of those days. In the words of Ma Haide:

In 1937, when only in his twenties, he had been charged with translating cables in German, Japanese, French and English... There were no desks, and Liao therefore put the cable drafts in his pocket, and would take them out again for translating; sometimes he would still keep on translating while we were on the move.[214]

The most likely reason for Liao's appointments in these areas should be sought in the fact that he was actually one of the very few surviving Communist cadres whose intellectual background and knowledge of foreign languages fitted him for such a position. It goes without saying that his family background - in particular the links with the left-wing KMT through his mother and Song Qingling - must also have played an important role. In addition, Liao's bitter attacks on Zhang Guotao must have made him appear a reliable supporter of the current leadership.

Liao was one of the leading Communist figures interviewed by Nym Wales (Helen Foster Snow) in Yanan on 21 May 1937:

Liao was apparently not enthusiastic to let others publish about his life. But I insistently requested an interview with him, since his parents were really too important. He had just been suffering from dysentery quite severely, and was just recovering. He lay on his *kang* (tiled heater) and looked exceedingly emaciated. The living quarters of officers and men of the Red Army were commonly kept spotless. However, in Liao's room there was dust all over the place. On the walls portraits of Gorky and Mao Zedong. Agnes Smedley gave him a hand and started cleaning up his room. She had accompanied me, and also wanted to make use of the opportunity to hear something about his life. He was not keen on having his photograph taken. His face was emaciated and his nose stuck out, but his reactions were fast and he spoke beautiful English with an American accent. I had watched him more than once on the theatrical stage of the Red Army in Yanan. In a play called 'Spy' he had played the role of a Spanish army officer. He severely interrogated an unfortunate Republican (prisoner) in a very overbearing manner, and his portrayal of a cruel and inhuman Franco officer was superb, so much so that we started getting concerned lest the audience might get up and give him a beating. Later, in the play 'Ah Q',[215] he also performed two roles very successfully. He claimed that he could perform any role. I discovered that he was indeed a man of many talents. He could speak German, Japanese, French, Russian, English and Chinese. During our conversation he never stopped smoking; holding a fly swat he would jump off his *kang* and hit at flies. He recalled that when crossing the steppe during the Long March food had been very bad. He had lost his own ration of noodles, and had to resort to making portraits of his comrades in order to get hold of something to eat. Somebody told me that he was a superb journalist, and that he had collaborated in editing two serial publications in a widely acclaimed style. He had written plays, engaged in making stone prints, woodblock prints, cartoons, and oil paintings and water colours. He had made portraits of Xu Teli as well as other leaders. He was not only a superb actor, but also a well known singer and director. He was quite good at table tennis and basketball. His physical condition was consistently good, working fourteen hours every day. He was also a good sailor performing on the stage for which he won very high praise in Yanan...

Yet even here, in the poor Yanan outback, he had not forgotten his appreciation of excellent food:

He had a very long argument with me over ... whether pork or donkey meat tasted better. He appeared to be very westernised, Americanised. He was a fast worker as well as a fast talker. He was not yet married.[216]

Endnote

Liao's career is closely linked with the history of Chinese Communist journalism. Although Miss Zhang was formally the director, this area of party activity was led by Qin Bangxian, head of the Organisation Department. On the topic in general, see *Zhongguo chubanshi* and *Zhongguo baoxueshi*, passim, particularly Wu Huaijiu's review of the story of Xinhuashe in *PD*, (1981.11.5). The history of Communist-owned newspapers began with *Hongse Zhonghua bao* published in Jiangxi in 1932. Attached to it was the newsagency *Hongse Zhonghua she*. Later *Hongse Zhonghua bao* was renamed *Xin Zhonghuabao*; on 1 September 1937 the newsagency was renamed *Xinhua she* becoming independent ('Shei ti gongfei wenxuan kailu', p 26). Further details can be found in two series *Xinwen yanjiu ziliao* and *Xinhua ribao de huiyi*, published in Peking. See also Kuo, *Analytical History*, vol III, p 231: 'After the Sian Incident, the Northeastern Army evacuated to Yenan. The immediately subordinate organisations of the CCP Central leadership then moved into that city in January 1937 ... to strengthen their propaganda, the Communists ... published a newspaper, *Hsin Chung-hua jih-pao* ... and a periodical magazine *Chieh-fang*, as Party organs ... (further) the intra Party periodical *Tang ti kung-tso* ...' See also Eto-Sakano, 'Kokusai seiji', p 279.

Despite declarations of co-operation in the anti-Japanese war effort the struggle between the government and the Communists continued; as early as November 1939 the government attempted to stop the publication of *Jiefang* and arrested its editor Kusano, *Konichi Shina*, p 29. A more serious interruption came with attacks on Communist front organisations in August 1938 (Johnson, *Peasant Nationalism*, p 38). Such incidents continued to be reported in the leftist press (for instance, *Fuxiao bao*, 28 November 1939; 24 June 1940; editorial in *Xin Zhonghua bao*, 19 June 1940). Front organisations and their publications in Hong Kong had a particularly interesting role (for a contemporary report, see Nakayasu, *Saikin Shina kyosanto shi*, p 358).

On Zhou's arrival in Chungking in 1940 he presided over the CCP propaganda apparatus ('Shei ti gongfei wenxuan kailu', p 43). Later, a 'China Youth News Agency' was established (*Xin Zhonghua bao*, 12 December 1940). On 16 May 1941 it amalgamated with *Jinri xinwen* as a central party organ called *Jiefang ribao* to counter anti-Soviet propaganda that became stronger after the agreements between the Soviet Union and Japan (according to *Xinhua ribao*, 21 May 1941). For further details on the problems confronted by Communist journalism, for example *Qiqi bao* on 11 April 1942 and *Xinhua ribao* of 12 December 1942.

Notes to Chapter One

1. Gilbert Chan Fook-lam, *A Chinese Revolutionary: The Career of Liao Chung-k'ai (1878-1925)*, (PhD Columbia University, 1975) (Xerox University Microfilms), pp 28 ff. Much information in this chapter about Liao's parents is based on Professor Chan's dissertation.
2. *Ibid*, pp 30-1.
3. *Ibid*, p 33.
4. *Ibid*.
5. *Ibid*, p 30. Liao Entao died in 1954. See also *ibid*, p 28.
6. Howard Boorman, ed *Biographical Dictionary of Republican China*, (New York and London, vol I, 1967; vol II, 1968; vol III, 1970; vol IV, 1971) vol II, p 366.
7. There is no agreement on the precise date. See Chan, *op cit*, pp 34-5. *Liao Chengzhi de yisheng*, p 15, mentions 23 April 1877 as Liao Zhongkai's date of birth.
8. *Ibid*, p 37.
9. According to Chan, *op cit*, Liao 'maintains that his father did not know any Chinese language when he returned to China for the first time', p 38 and Wales, *Red Dust*, p 26. Liao Mengxing differs: 'Grandfather, ... save[d] enough to build a family. He took care to give his sons some basic knowledge of the Motherland, so that after his death, when my father returned to Canton at 17, he had a good enough grounding in Chinese to continue his studies there.', Liao Mong-sing, 'My Father Liao Chung-kai', *China Reconstructs*, (November 1964), pp 25-9.
10. Chan, *op cit*, pp 38 ff. See also fn 9.
11. 'Father ... witnessed anti-Asian discrimination in the USA and the cruel handling of Chinese seamen ... aboard the ship on which he returned. ... he disembarked in Hong Kong ... [and] he saw British police beating up Chinese coolies ...', Liao Mong-sing, 'My Father Liao Chung-kai', p 25; see also Liao Mengxing, *Wode muqin He Xiangning*, (Hong Kong, 1973), p 3.
12. Chan, *op cit*, p 81.
13. Wales, *op cit*, p 31.
14. Chan, *op cit*, p 440.
15. *Ibid*, pp 20-1.
16. *Ibid*, pp 110-11.
17. *Ibid*, p 440. Liao is said to have completed primary school and one year of middle school at Pui Ching Baptist Academy, Canton, *Biographic Information*, (US Department of State, 3 June 1956).
18. He Xiangning, *Huiyi Sun Zhongshan he Liao Zhongkai*, (Beijing, 1957), p 49.
19. *Ibid*.
20. *Ibid*, pp 57 ff. Chen Cisheng, 'Geming muqin He Xiangning xiansheng', *Huiyi yu huainian - jinian geming laoren He Xiangning shsishi shi zhounian* pp 136-49 (reprinted from *Guangxi ribao*, Xihuangyao ed, early 1945): 'He Xiangning married in 1899, she had just turned 20 (sui).' According to *Liao Chengzhi de yisheng*, p 15 she was born on 27 June 1878 in Hong Kong and died aged 94. According to He, Liao Zhongkai was two years older than her (*Huiyi Liao Zhongkai*, p 49). Liao Mengxing says her mother was 95 when she died (*Wode muqin He Xiangning*, p 1). Also Chen Fengxi, 'Yi He Xiangning laoren', *Huiyi yu huainian - jinian geming laoren He Xiangning shishi shi zhounian*, pp 222-32: 'When He Xiangning died ... she was 94 ...' According to Chen Cisheng, He was born in 1899 ('Geming muqin He Xiangning xiansheng').
21. Chan, *op cit*, pp 57-8.

22 Chan, *op cit*, p 57, quoting Liao Mengxing, 'My Father Liao Chungkai', p 25.
23 Liao Mong-sing, 'My Father Liao Chung-kai', p 25. The second quotation is found on p 60.
24 Ibid, p 25. See also Helen F Snow, *Women in Modern China*, (The Hague, 1967), p 102, and Liao Mengxing, *Wode muqin He Xiangning*, p 2.
25 Chan, *op cit*, p 60, quoting Liao, 'My Father Liao Chung-k'ai', p 25.
26 Jiang Yihua, *Guomindang zuopai de qizhi - Liao Zhongkai*, (Shanghai, 1985), pp 16 ff. On Chinese students in Japan, see Huang Fu-ch'ing, *Chinese Students in Japan in the Late Ch'ing Period*, (1982, trans K Whitaker), passim, and Kamigaito, *Nihon ryugaku to kakumei undo*, (1982), passim.
27 Chan, *op cit*, pp 85-6, and Liao Mong-sing, 'My Father Liao Chung-kai', p 25. He Xiangning says she was influenced by her rich family background and that her husband taught her progressive ideas, *Huiyi Liao Zhongkai*, p 50.
28 Chan, *op cit*, p 37.
29 He Xiangning confirms this, adding that when they had difficulties later her family supported them, *Huiyi Liao Zhongkai*, pp 49-50; Liao Mong-sing, 'My Father Liao Chung-kai, p 25.
30 Chan, *op cit*, pp 85-6.
31 He Xiangning, *Huiyi Liao Zhongkai*, p 50. He entered a preparatory course in economics, then the Department of Politics and Economics of Central University (*Chuo daigaku*). According to Chan, Liao Zhongkai 'reached Tokyo in January 1903 and his wife ... about two months later', *op cit*, pp 66-7. Liao Mengxing says her mother arrived a year later (*Wode muqin He Xiangning*, p 3). Chen Cisheng says: 'Mr Liao went to Japan in November 1901; in February or March of the following year she arrived in Tokyo.' ('Geming muqin He Xiangning xiansheng', p 141). Also Boorman, *op cit*, vol II, p 67. Waseda University was then a hotbed of ideological ferment under the influence of Ookuma Shigenobu's liberalism, greatly emphasising academic independence (Chan, *op cit*, p 73). See *Sodai seikatsu*, (1953), for a brief background history of the University.
32 Huang, *Chinese Students in Japan*, and *Chugokujin Nihon ryugaku shi*, (1970), passim.
33 He Xiangning merely states that they met Sun in 1903 and 'we, first one, then the other, became members of the *Tongmenghui*' (He, *Huiyi Liao Zhongkai*, p 50, and Chan, *op cit*, p 84).
34 According to He Xiangning, Liao Zhongkai left for Tientsin in 1904 on Sun's orders to contact Boucopaix and returned to Japan only after the establishment of the *Tongmenghui*, resuming his studies in the autumn (*Huiyi Liao Zhongkai*, pp 50-1).
35 According to Liao's memoirs in *Renmin Zhongguo*, as quoted in *Kakyoho* of 25 June 1983 He Xiangning followed Liao Zhongkai in 1902 to study in Tokyo, returning to her parents' house in Hong Kong in 1903 to give birth to her daughter Mengxing, born in 1904. She returned to Japan, leaving Mengxing in the care of her parents. Liao Zhongkai brought one-year-old Mengxing to Japan in 1905. She later entered the kindergarten attached to the Futsu-Ei-Wa Primary School in Kanda, Mizakicho. See also Liao Mengxing's contribution to *Waga seishun no Nippon*, pp 13 ff.
36 Chen Cisheng, 'Geming muqin He Xiangning', p 143: 'He Xiangning was the first woman to join the *Tongmenghui*.' Nym Wales reports that Liao told her this in an interview (Wales, *op cit*, p 30). The inaugural meeting of the *Tongmenghui* was on 20 August 1905 which disproves Liao Mengxing's claim that her parents joined in 1904 (*Wode muqin He Xiangning*, p 4). According to Boorman, *op cit*, vol II, p 67, He Xiangning was the 'second woman to join the *T'ung-meng-hui*, the first being Madame Ch'iu Chin ... executed by the Manchus in 1907'. Hummel states that Mrs Ch'iu was 'one of the first to join' (A Hummel, ed *Eminent Chinese of the Ch'ing Period*

China's Relations with Japan

(1644-1912), 2 vols, Washington, 1943, 1944, p 70). According to Chen Xianggong, *Qiu Jin nianpu ji zhuanji ziliao*, (Zhonghua shuji, Peking, 1983) p 25, she joined in August 1905.

37 Chan, *op cit*, pp 94-5; He, *Wode huiyi*, pp 14-15; Liao Mengxing, *Wode muqin He Xiangning*, p 4.
38 See Chan, *op cit*, pp 85-6.
39 Chan, *op cit*, pp 111 ff.
40 According to He Xiangning Liao Zhongkai graduated from Chuo daigaku in 1909. Chan also mentions that according to Saneto Keishu Liao graduated from Hosei University (*op cit*, p 114).
41 *PD*, 17 June 1983. This 'official' date agrees with that in *Biographic Information* of 3 June 1956. According to Chen: 'Liao Chengzhi was born in 1907, which meant the end of her (ie He Xiangning's) studies, since she had now to look after two children (Liao Mengxing had come to Japan in the meantime).' (Chen Cisheng, 'Geming muqin He Xiangning xiansheng', p 142).
Some sources date his birth in 1905 or 1906 (*Gongfei ganbu jiyao*, Taipei, pp 284-5 and *Feiwei huaqiao jianbao*, (periodical), p 56). A Japanese source shown to me by a Foreign Ministry official also gave 1906. A photo of Liao dated April 1916 shows him as eight rather than ten or eleven as far as one can judge (in *Liaogong zai renjian*; the photo is in *Waga seishun no Nippon*, p 10). It also shows Liao Zhongkai, said to have left Japan for China in March 1916 (Boorman, *op cit*, vol II, p 365).
Xia Yan, a friend of Liao's, is also confused about Liao's birthdate. He recollects (*PD*, 15 June 1983) that Liao had just turned twenty in the autumn of 1925, whereas a different version of his recollections published in *Liaogong zai renjian*, p 10, says that Liao was seventeen at the time. He Xiangning suffered a miscarriage before Liao Chengzhi's birth, and it is possible that this previous pregnancy accounts for the confusion. The conflicting evidence concerning Liao's age at the time of his first departure from Japan for China further complicates the verification of his birthdate. Although one should not discount the possibility that for some reason Liao wished to appear younger than he was I decided to accept the 'official' birthdate given in *PD*. See also Lu Dingyi's remark in *PD* of 19 June 1983: 'Liao was two years younger than I.'
42 Chan, *op cit*, p 112.
43 Liao Mong-sing, 'My Father Liao Chung-kai', p 26.
44 Liao Mengxing, *Wode muqin He Xiangning*, p 4.
45 Liao Mong-sing, 'My Father Liao Chung-kai', p 26.
46 Liao Mengxing, *Wode muqin He Xiangning*, p 4, and Chan, *op cit*, p 66.
47 In this period Liao Zhongkai's close friends included Hu Hanmin, Zhu Zhixin, Fang Shengdong and Lin Zhuming. He Xiangning, *Huiyi Liao Zhongkai*, p 50. Zhu Zhixin even coached Liao Chengzhi in arithmetic when he had time (*Waga seishun no Nippon*, p 8).
48 Liao Mengxing, *Wode muqin He Xiangning*, p 5.
49 Chan, *op cit*, p 114. There is considerable disagreement on the date of He Xiangning's graduation and return to China (at the earliest, about six months after Liao Zhongkai, at the latest in 1911; see Wales, *op cit*, p 26; Chan, *op cit*, p 114, and Boorman, *op cit*, vol II, p 67).
50 Chan, *op cit*, pp 115 ff, 150.
51 Boorman, *op cit*, vol II, p 67, and Chan, *op cit*, pp 124 ff.
52 According to Liao Mengxing the family returned to China in 1911 (*Kakyoho*, 23 June 1983); see also Chen Cisheng, 'Geming muqin He Xiangning xiansheng', p 142, and Chan, *op cit*, p 114.
53 Chan, *op cit*, p 158, quoting He Xiangning, 'Wo de huiyi', p 24.

54 Liao Mengxing, in *Kakyoho* of 23 June 1983. Liao Zhongkai and He Xiangning returned to Japan with Sun Yatsen after the failure of the so-called Second Revolution of 1913 (*Kakyoho*, 25 June 1983). He Xiangning adds that Liao Zhongkai had to flee to Japan after the assassination of Song Jiaoren and Yuan Shikai's rebellion on 20 March 1913 (*Huiyi Liao Zhongkai*, p 52).

55 Chan, *op cit*, pp 158-9.

56 Chan, *op cit*, p 158. Boorman, *op cit*, vol II, p 365. The correct Chinese name is *Zhonghua gemingdang*, misspelled *Zhongguo gemingdang* by He Xiangning (*Huiyi Liao Zhongkai*, p 52).

57 Liao Chengzhi, in *Waga seishun no Nippon*, pp 6-8. Liao Mengxing says the family left Japan for China in 1911, to return to Japan in 1913 where they went to live first at Shibuya, Aoyama 7-chome, and *then* Liao entered the second grade of Akatsuki primary school (*Kakyoho*, 23 and 25 June 1983). Later they moved to a different address.

58 *Ibid*, p 7.

59 According to Liao Mengxing the family fled to Japan in 1913 and lived in the Shibuya district of Tokyo. According to Liao he was five when he lived in the house in Setagaya. If he was indeed born in 1908 he seems to confuse the addresses. He remembers correctly that before leaving Japan for the first time they had lived in Setagaya. 'We had to break up our house in Setagaya. Return to China. Father and mother were extremely busy, moving all over [the country], and fled again to Japan.' He continues, 'I was wondering whether we would return to Setagaya, but we went to nearby lodgings in Aoyama.' (*Waga seishun no Nippon*, p 7.) It is unlikely that Liao would have vivid memories of the Setagaya house had he been three years old, conceding even an above-average memory. The most likely explanation is of course that memories of the Setagaya house were kept alive in the family. Otherwise, such a passage might support the argument that Liao was older when he moved to the Setagaya house, and that he was indeed born before 1908.

60 *Waga seishun no Nippon*, pp 7-11.

61 *Ibid*, p 11.

62 Wales, *op cit*, p 27.

63 *Ibid*, p 28.

64 *Yomiuri shinbun*, 12 June 1983.

65 Chen Shunchen, in *Liaogong zai renjian*, p 129.

66 Wales, *op cit*, p 28.

67 *Ibid*, p 27.

68 Boorman, *op cit*, vol II, p 365, says that He Xiangning and the children lived in Tokyo until 1923, but Wales, *op cit*, p 27 states: 'In the summer of 1918 Liao Zhongkai journeyed to the north. During a large portion of the following twenty-seven months, [he] lived in the French concession in Shanghai with his wife and his two children.' According to *Liao Chengzhi de yisheng*, p 18, Liao Chengzhi was in Shanghai in June 1917, travelling to Japan in 1918 with his parents.

69 Wales, *op cit*, p 27.

70 Liao left for Canton Christian College in autumn 1919 (Wales, *op cit*, p 27, and Chan, *op cit*, pp 195-6). On Canton Christian College see J G Lutz, *China and the Christian Colleges, 1850-1950*, (Ithaca, 1971), passim.

71 Wales *op cit*, p 28.

72 Tan Juezhen, 'Ryo Shoshi o kataru', *Ekonomisuto*, p 29. See also Tan Juezhen, 'Ryo Shoshi o kataru', *Yokohama West Rotary Weekly*.

73 Liao Mengxing, *Wode muqin He Xiangning*, p 5. According to *Kakyoho* of 23 June 1983, Liao Mengxing returned to China in 1923.
74 Liao Mengxing, *Wode muqin He Xiangning*, p 5.
75 For the text of the poem, see Liao Mengxing, *Wode muqin He Xiangning*, p 8.
76 One reason for his release was previous co-operation in financing Chen's units, He Xiangning, *Huiyi Liao Zhongkai*, pp 52 and 56; Liao Mengxing, *Wode muqin He Xiangning*, p 10.
77 Arai Takeo, *Shu Onrai no jissen*, p 168.
78 Dieter Heinzig, *Sowjetische Militärberater bei der Kuomintang 1923-1927*, (1978) [Osteuropa und der internationale Kommunismus, Band 1], pp 92 ff, 97-8. Liao Mengxing added: 'Sun Yatsen's talks with the Soviet special emissary Joffe sent by Lenin were interrupted due to the work of secret agents in Shanghai', *Wode muqin He Xiangning*, p 13.
79 Chan, *op cit*, pp 245-56.
80 This contrasts strongly with his earlier attitude related above; see He Xiangning, *Huiyi Liao Zhongkai*, pp 56-7; Liao Liuwei, in *Liaogong zai renjian*, p 176; Liao Mengxing, *Wode muqin He Xiangning*, p 13; He Xiangning, *Huiyi Sun Zhongshan*, pp 16, 30, and Chan, *op cit*, p 276, fn 291.
81 Heinzig, *op cit*, pp 92 ff. Wales, *op cit*, p 30.
82 Wales, *op cit*, p 30.
83 Chan, *op cit*, pp 110, 431.
84 Chan, *op cit*, pp 248 ff.
85 *Ibid*, pp 20-1.
86 Boorman, *op cit*, vol II, p 68.
87 Chan, *op cit*, pp 448-9. According to Liao Mengxing, (*Wode muqin He Xiangning*, p 14) Mao Zedong, Wu Yuzhang, Lin Boju, Deng Yingchao, Nie Rongzhen and many other CCP members and leftists gathered in Canton. See also He Xiangning (*Huiyi Liao Zhongkai*, p 60) who emphasises the importance of the 'peasant movement'.
88 *Liao Chengzhi de yisheng*, p 19.
89 Situ Huimin, in *Liaogong zai renjian*, p 25.
90 *Ibid*, p 17.
91 Kusano, in *Liaogong zai renjian*, p 148.
92 Huang Dingchen, in *Liaogong zai renjian*, pp 14 ff.
93 *PD*, 28 June 1983.
94 Wales, *op cit*, p 27.
95 It seems Liao Chengzhi 'helped plan a sympathy strike in Canton', Boorman, *op cit*, vol II, p 363.
96 *PD*, 17 June 1983.
97 Si Mu, in *Liaogong zai renjian*, p 17.
98 Wales, *op cit*, pp 28-9.
99 Chan, *op cit*, pp 445 f. On KMT involvement in the Hong Kong strike, Deng Zhongxia, *Zhongguo zhigong yundong jianshi (1919-1926)*, (1953, first edn 1949) pp 239-41, Jean Chesneaux, *Le mouvement ouvrier Chinoise de 1919 à 1927*, (Paris-La Haye, 1962), pp 349-50, 429; Mao Chaojun, *Histoire*, N ed, p 287; Liao Mengxing, *Wode muqin He Xiangning*, pp 16-19.
100 Boorman, *op cit*, vol II, pp 366-7.
101 Liao Mong-sing, 'My Father Liao Chung-kai', p 29.
102 This differs from Liao's recollections. He adds: 'the assassin lived for two days in the hospital, and confessed that Hu I-sheng, brother of Hu Han-min had ordered him to kill my father.', Wales,

op cit, p 29. He Xiangning recalls that the arrested assassin confessed acting on Hu Zhuowei's orders, *Huiyi Liao Zhongkai*, p 64. Lu Dingyi's most recent account repeats ritualistic slogans accusing Hu Hanmin of the murder and blaming Chen Duxiu for not struggling against them (*PD*, 19 June 1983). The question of Liao Zhongkai's murder has not been definitely solved; see also Liao's remark on 'KMT slanders' reported by Miyazaki Seimin in *Liaogong zai renjian*, p 143, stressing that Liao Zhongkai's murderers 'were Hu Hanmin, Wu Tiecheng and Deng Zeru', and trying to refute 'slanders', probably reports like that by Yi Wen mentioned below.

103 Heinzig, *op cit*, pp 228-9. See also Chan, *op cit*, pp 403 ff.
104 Chan, *op cit*, p 450.
105 *Ibid*, p 426.
106 *Ibid*, p 427.
107 Yi Wen, 'Jing Guo Chengzhi', p 6.
108 Wales, *op cit*, p 32.
109 *Ibid*.
110 Boorman, *op cit*, vol II, p 68; Chang Kuo-t'ao, *The Rise of the Chinese Communist Party 1921-1927*, (1971), Vol 1, p 482.
111 Si Mu, in *Liaogong zai renjian*, p 18.
112 Wales, *op cit*, p 32.
113 Situ Huimin, in *Guangming ribao*, 25 June 1983.
114 Liao Mengxing, *Wode muqin He Xiangning*, pp 21 ff.
115 *PD*, 15 June 1983. This is also apparent from Xia Yan's recollections (*Liaogong zai renjian*, p 10). This is not the place for detailed discussion of He Xiangning's political role. During interviews conducted in Taiwan I was told that her political understanding was limited. Similarly Yi Wen explained her well known opposition to Chiang Kaishek's marriage with Song Meiling as being due to her disagreement with Chiang who wanted to abandon his former wife, Chiang Chingguo's mother, in favour of Song Meiling (Yi Wen, 'Jingguo Chengzhi', p 7).
116 *PD*, 17 June 1983. According to *Liao Chengzhi de yisheng*, p 22, he entered the CCP in August of that year. *Ibid*, p 20, merely states that he left the KMT and joined the CCP after Chiang Kaishek's anti-Communist purge in April 1927. According to the same source he had joined the KMT in August 1924 (*ibid*, p 19).
117 Tan Juezhen, 'Ryo Shoshi o kataru', *Ekonomisuto*, p 29. During his stay in Japan Tan Juezhen stayed at the same address as Liao Chengzhi (*ibid*, p 28).
118 I was repeatedly told that He Xiangning did not approve of Liao's radicalism at that time, but was unable to obtain independent confirmation. Lu Dingyi says he 'respected He Xiangning all the more for letting her only son "continue revolution"' (*PD*, 19 June 1983), but even if she did not actively oppose Liao's radicalism this would not necessarily imply agreement.
119 Liao mentioned that he had been in Japan for ten months before his expulsion in May 1928 (Wales, *op cit*, p 32). Several sources confirm that he left for Japan in 1927 (for example, *PD*, 17 June 1983). When Situ Huimin went to Japan when the Canton Commune failed he met Liao, then attending Waseda University (*Liaogong zai renjian*, p 25). Chen Peishi says he met Liao in Berlin in 1927 (*Nanfang ribao*, 14 June 1983). Other evidence points strongly to 1927 as the date of his departure for Japan, and 1928 as the date of his expulsion, and one should ascribe the dates given by Chen to a slip of memory.
120 Huang Dingchen, in *Liaogong zai renjian*, p 14.

121 *Guangming ribao*, 17 and 20 June 1983; *Kokusai boeki*, 16 June 1983. In his recollections as told to Nym Wales, he merely said that he 'entered Waseda University', (*op cit*, p 32). Quite a few sources ignore the fact that he was never enrolled in university courses.
122 Liao also confessed to Suegawa Hiroshi whom he met again on his visit to Japan in 1953 that he 'didn't study too much' (*Yomiuri shinbun*, 11 June 1983). It has been claimed that he organised this society ('*Shakai kagaku kenkyukai*') with his friends (*Yomiuri shinbun*, 11 June 1983) but it is unclear whether he was a co-founder (also fn 116). I was often told by Japanese interviewees that at this time he was not conspicuous as a 'Marxist' student. Other sources ascribe the foundation of the society to the Tokyo 'Special Branch' (*tezhi*) of the CCP (Huang Dingchen, *Liaogong zai renjian*, p 14) or simply state that he took part in the society (Situ Huimin, in *ibid*, p 25).
123 Wales, *op cit*, p 32.
124 Tan Juezhen, 'Ryo Shoshi o kataru', *Ekonomisuto*, p 29.
125 Liu Jiaquan and Xiao Xing, 'Liao Chengzhi yu Kangri minzu tongyu zhanxian', *Renmin ribao*, (27 May 1984), p 5.
126 Liao Chengzhi, in *Waga seishun no Nippon*, pp 3-5.
127 *Ibid*, p 8.
128 *Kokusai boeki*, 16 June 1983.
129 Liao later told Xia Yan: 'If I count my two arrests in Japan, my two arrests in Germany for involvement in the seamen's union, then I have been imprisoned seven and a half times, seven times before liberation, and during the disastrous years of the GPCR I was kept under house arrest - [and not worse] for five years thanks to the protection of Zhou, that's half [an arrest] ...', Xia Yan, in *PD*, 15 June 1983.
130 Huang Dingchen, in *Liaogong zai renjian*, pp 14-15. See also *PD*, 16 June 1983.
131 Huang Dingchen, in *Liaogong zai renjian*, p 15 and *PD*, 16 June 1983.
132 *Yomiuri shinbun*, 12 June 1983. I had no access to the Waseda records so cannot confirm this.
133 I have been unable to verify the formal reason for Liao's expulsion from Japan.
134 Liao Mengxing, *Wode muqin He Xiangning*, p 28.
135 Wales, *op cit*, p 32.
136 *Liaogong zai renjian*, p 15.
137 Probably Liao became a formal CCP member *after* returning to China. His official biography merely says that he entered the party in spring (*PD*, 17 June 1983), while Huang Dingchen gives August (*PD*, 16 June 1983); see also *Liao Chengzhi de yisheng*, p 22. Two other sources confirm his membership for 1928 (*Jingji ribao*, 25 June 1983 and *Ouzhou shibao*, 12-13 June 1983). W L Chu, 'Liao Ch'eng-chih - A Maoist "Liberated" Cadre', *Issues and Studies*, (November 1972), pp 86-8 is wrong in stating: 'in 1925 he went to Japan again and entered the Waseda University and concurrently joined the Chinese Communist Party'. According to *Five Hundred Leading Communists (In the Eastern Hemisphere, excluding the USSR)*, (Supplement IV, Report: The Strategy and Tactics of World Communism. Committee on Foreign Affairs, comp, US Congress, 1948 [National and International Movements], p 22 he joined the party in 1927.
138 *PD*, 17 June 1983.
139 Huang Dingchen, in *Liaogong zai renjian*, pp 15 f.
140 See fn 115. According to Huang Dingchen, 'Weida de aiguo zhuiyi zhanshi - He Xiangning', in *PD*, 11 September 1982, Liao must have left Shanghai for Europe after July 1928.
141 *Liao Chengzhi de yisheng*, p 22.

142 *PD*, 17 June 1983. I have been unable to ascertain to what extent his later movements in Europe were directed by the German or Chinese Communist Party, or through Comintern channels.
143 Liu Tiansu, 'Liangshi, cimu - huiyi zai He Xiangning xiansheng bian de rizi', *Huiyi yu huainian - jinian geming laoren He Xiangning shishi shi zhounian*, pp 172-88.
144 Huang Dingchen, 'Weida de aiguo zhuiyi zhanshi - He Xiangning', in *PD*, 11 September 1982. On his arrest, Huang Dingchen, in 'Jinian Song Qingling tekan', p 55.
145 On He Xiangning's travel route, see Liu Tiansu, 'Liangshi, cimu', p 183.
146 Liao Mengxing, *Wode muqin He Xiangning*, p 28.
147 Liu Tiansu, 'Liangshi, cimu', p 182.
148 *Ouzhou shibao*, 12-13 June 1983.
149 Wales, *op cit*, p 34.
150 Chen Peishi, a Hong Kong barrister first met Liao in Berlin while Liao was studying there in 1928, *Nanfang ribao*, 14 June 1983. I could obtain no relevant records. Hamburg University, for instance in a letter of 9 August 1978 informed me that there are no extant records 'da in der Universität Hamburg durch Kriegseinwirkung ein grosser Teil der Archive zerstört wurde. Eine Nachforschung, ob Herr Liao Cheng-chih an der Universität Hamburg immatrikuliert war, ist daher nicht möglich.' *Five Hundred Leading Communists*, p 22 confirms that he studied at Berlin and Hamburg Universities.
151 From a letter of 15 August 1978 addressed to the present writer.
152 Wales, *op cit*, p 33 and Situ Huimin, in *Liaogong zai renjian*, p 27. Also Lu Dingyi's article in *PD*, 19 June 1983 referring to the relatively comfortable Dutch prisons, when compared with Chinese prisons. The Netherlands Ministry of Internal Affairs says there are no records concerning Liao in the relevant government archives (letter of 8 November 1978). *Biographical Dictionary of Republican China* (1967), pp 363-4, says Liao was expelled from Holland in 1929.
153 Lu Dingyi, in *PD*, 19 June 1983 and 17 June 1983. Compare also Chen Peishi's reference to Liao as a student in Berlin (*Nanfang ribao*, 14 June 1983): 'In June 1930 Liao Chengzhi welcomed his mother, who had come from Paris, in Berlin. One reason for this visit was to meet Mrs Sun Yatsen, and secondly, to view the situation in Germany. In Germany she stayed at our place... In the beginning of her stay Liao Chengzhi had her accompanied twice on sightseeing trips. At that time I did not know yet that Liao Chengzhi was a Communist Party member, ... He loved to discuss revolution, to discuss global currents. Judging by his manner of speaking he was an adherent of Communism. At that time I had an aversion against adventurism. Liao Chengzhi explained to me in detail that the Communist Party was likewise opposed to adventurism ... When he returned to Hamburg I submitted my request to join the Party. The party delegated Comrade Cheng Fangwu for coaching and checking [my background].'
154 *PD*, 17 June 1983.
155 This raises the interesting and rather important question whether Chinese Communists operating overseas who, like Liao, had joined a foreign Communist party remained subject to CCP discipline, and to what extent they may have been subject to orders straight from Moscow.
156 Liu Tiansu, 'Liangshi, cimu', p 183.
157 Ibid, pp 187-8.
158 *PD*, 17 June 1983.
159 Weng Shaoqiu, in *Liaogong zai renjian*, p 127 and *PD*, 13 June 1983. See also *Su'e tongjian*, (nd), p 667. According to Yi Wen, Liao and Chiang Chingkuo knew each other as students at the

Sun Yatsen University in Moscow, and both are said to have 'participated' in the Soviet Communist Party ('Jingguo Chengzhi', p 7).

160   Wales, *op cit*, p 34. *PD* 13 June 1983 confirms that Liao visited the Soviet Union at that time. I was told by Kuo Hualun that during conversations with him Liao did not refer to this stay.
161   Saito Takeshi, *Shina - kiko to jinbutsu*, (1937), p 63 ff. Quite a few members of the right wing '*Lanyi* Society' attended Sun Yatsen University.
162   Naka Hosaku, *[kaitei zoho] Saikin Shina kyosantoshi*, (1944, first edition 1940), p 150. Lu Zhenji adds that Liao was trained as a secret agent (*Liao fei Chengzhi beikou zhi mi*, p 2b). A similar report appeared in *Nippon Times*, 12 January 1956: 'He was deported from Japan in 1928 for ... subversive activities, went to study in Europe and wound up with four years of intensive training at the Soviet Secret Police School in Moscow ... and he is part of the loyal Comintern members ... protecting Soviet interests in Red China.' Though it was fashionable during the fifties among some Western observers to make lists of 'pro-Soviet' Chinese Communists such attempts seemed often without firm foundation (Dutt, *op cit*, p 120). I have seen a source claiming a link between Liao Mengxing and Soviet intelligence in the PRC, but this is highly speculative and spurious. On intelligence co-operation between the PRC and the Soviet Union during the early fifties, see *Guojun 'Feiqing yanjiu' youliang xinde xuanji*, Dijiuqi yanjiuyuan guowai kaoxha baogao, June 1961, vol 24, p 112, mentioning Fang Fang and Geng Baiju, both close collaborators of Liao, and *Sinianlai fei Su goujie zhi zongjie yanjiu*, (Taipei, December 1953), [Gongfei junshi congshu, di3ji], pp 43 and 288. Liao also wrote a eulogy on Deng Fa, who is known to have fulfilled an important role in Communist intelligence, but I have been unable to find more specific evidence about his links with Deng Fa, Hua Yingshen comp, *Zhongguo gongchandang lieshi zhuan*, (Hong Kong, 1949), p 190. On Deng Fa, see *Guojun [Feiging yanjiu] youliang xinde xuanji*, p 76.
163   *Liaogong zai renjian*, p 60.
164   *PD*, 17 June 1983.
165   *Ibid*. According to Kuo Hualun, in 1932 (personal communication).
166   *Biographical Information*; *URS Biographical Service* (Union Research Service), Hong Kong.
167   Interview with Kuo Hualun, 1982. According to Kuo Zhou Enlai met Liao in Shanghai when Zhou visited Jiangsu province in 1932.
168   Yu Feng, 'He Xiangning Zhongguohua yizuo zhanlan suibi', p 250.
169   Jing Puchun, in *Liaogong zai renjian*, pp 1 f.
170   According to other sources he engaged at that time in underground activities in Shanghai, Wales, *op cit*, p 34.
171   *Ibid*. The arrest and torture of Chen Geng is described by Edgar Snow, *Random Notes on Red China, 1936-1945*, (Cambridge, Mass: 1968),pp 93, 99.
172   According to Yi Wen, 'Jingguo Chengzhi', p 7, Liao returned to Shanghai as early as 1931. *Five Hundred Leading Communists*, p 2 mentions 1932 as the year of his return.
173   Jing Puchun, in *Liaogong zai renjian*, p 1. See also *Liao Chengzhi de yisheng*, p 9.
174   *PD*, 19 June 1983. Xia Yan says that Liao was arrested together with Luo Dengxian in *June* 1933 in Shanghai (*PD*, 15 June 1983). A partial reproduction of the article in *Shenbao* of 30 March 1933 is found in *Liao Chengzhi de yisheng*, p 22.
175   *Liening shenghuo* of 2 April 1933. See also Warren Kuo, *Analytical History of the Chinese Communist Party*, (4 vols, Taipei, 1968-71), vol 2, p 480: '(after the departure of the Central Committee from Shanghai) the Central Committee left behind a newly-established Central Bureau

in Shanghai. It was composed of Wang Yun-cheng, Lu Fu-tan, and Li Chun-sheng. The trio defected after their arrests by the Kuomintang.'
176 'Jinian Song Qingling tekan', *Zhongguo jianshe*, (August 1981), p 11.
177 According to the summary of issue no 1 of 14 April 1933 of *Gongnong tongxun she texun* contained in Hsüeh Chün-tu, *The Chinese Communist Movement, 1921-1937*, (Stanford University, 1960), p 86 the issue 'also contains (1) a letter by Madame Sun Yat-sen to the Chinese people, dated 1 April 1933, protesting against the sentences given to Lo Teng-hsien, Liao Ch'eng-chih, and three others by the Kiangsu Provincial Supreme Court'.
178 Li Mei, in *PD*, 27 June 1983. See also Huang Dingchen, 'Weida de aiguo zhuiyi zhanshi - He Xiangning', in *PD*, 11 September 1982: 'After He Xiangning had conferred with Liu Yazi she went to Shanghai police headquarters, and succeeded in rescuing Liao Chengzhi.'
179 *PD*, 27 June 1983, 19 June 1983; Xia Yan, in *Liaogong zai renjian*, p 10. According to Cai Jianguo, 'Liao Chengzhi's father and Cai Yuanpei had had frequent social contact, and were joined in deep revolutionary friendship. Then in March 1933 ... he was released thanks to the efforts of Cai Yuanpei, Song Qingling and others.' (*Liaogong zai renjian*, p 30). It has even been argued that Liao's release was due to Chiang himself who still felt obliged to the family for the financial support Liao Zhongkai had provided: 'He was arrested in 1931, and Jiang Kaishek had immediately ... [had] him transferred to Nanking, where he was kept under his own ... supervision ... as a means of protection for Liao before his release.' (Yi Wen 'Jingguo Chengzhi', p 7).
180 Yu Feng, 'He Xiangning Zhongguohua yizuo zhanlan suibi', p 251.
181 Liao Jian, in *Liaogong zai renjian*, pp 155-6. See also *Liao Chengzhi de yisheng*, p 44: 'One of them was Ye Jianmei, child of Ye Ting.'
182 Jing Puchun, in *Liaogong zai renjian*, p 2.
183 Interview with Kuo Hualun, 1982. See also Kuo, *Analytical History of the Chinese Communist Party*, vol 3, p 269: 'He was arrested by the 4th Frontal Army because during his imprisonment in Shanghai he was known to have pledged loyalty to the Kuomintang intelligence organisation and promised to work for the Kuomintang in Communist areas. During the Communist ... March, he was put under surveillance and set free only after his arrival at Paoan in northern Shensi.'
184 Jing Puchun, in *Liaogong zai renjian*, p 2.
185 *Ibid.*
186 *Ibid.* For a reproduction of the letter to Liu Yazi, see *Liao Chengzhi de yisheng*, p 23.
187 Chang Chuan argues that the marriage was arranged between the two families; the Jing family had previously supported Liao Zhongkai financially, creating an obligation for the Liao family. It is unclear when this would have been arranged. See Chang Chuan, 'Liao gong de zuihou shike', *Zhengming* (July 1983), no 69, pp 26-9. The two versions are not necessarily mutually exclusive.
188 *PD*, 17 June 1983. According to Cai Xiaoqian, Bo Gu sent Liao to Zhang who immediately arrested him on suspicion of working for the KMT. If Chiang Kaishek himself took Liao into 'protective custody' such rumours may have reached Communist leaders and led them to doubt his loyalty (interview with Cai Xiaoqian, 1982). Kuo Hualun merely mentioned that Liao left Shanghai for the Fourth Red Army under Xu Xiangqian (interview with Kuo Hualun, 1982).
189 'Not long after he had been released from prison He Xiangning also supported his participation in the 25,000 kilometre "Long March"'. (Huang Dingchen, 'Weida de aiguo zhuiyi zhanshi - He Xiangning').
190 Kuo, *Analytical History*, vol 3, p 480, and vol 2, pp 383, 482.

191 *PD*, 17 June 1983. According to *Liao Chengzhi de yisheng*, p 24, he was a Committee member of the Provincial Committee of the 'Chuan-Shan Soviet Area'.
192 Lu Zhenji, *Liao fei Chengzhi beikou zhi mi*, p 2b; *Jinnianlai gongfei pohai qiaobao*, (1969), [Diqing yanjiu congkan zhi 20], p 8; *Zhonggong ganbu jiyao*, p 20. Liao's appointment in the political department may have mainly concerned 'cultural work'.
193 Wales, *op cit*, p 34. According to Ookubo Yasushi, *Chugoku kyosantoshi*, 2 vols, 1971, 1972, p 851 he was an artillery officer under Lin Biao's command.
194 *Ibid.*
195 *Liao Chengzhi de yisheng*, p 24.
196 *Ibid.*
197 Xu Dixin, in *Liaogong zai renjian*, pp 32-3, and *PD*, 21 June 1953. It is difficult to gain a clear picture of this period. According to J15 he seems to have been involved in an education campaign in the Shangangning area, working with Wu Liangping, Wen Tao, Wang Yiming, Zhu Guang (1934?). According to Kuo Hualun Liao Chengzhi's freedom of movement was curtailed, but he was not a complete prisoner. Kuo met him in Sichuan province after his arrest by Zhang Guotao (interview with Kuo Hualun, 1982).
198 Personal communication from Mrs Anna Sun Ford who met Liao Chengzhi in October 1973.
199 Xia Yan, in *Liaogong zai renjian*, pp 12-13. See also Liao Ming, *ibid*, p 158.
200 Zhu Ziqi, in *Liaogong zai renjian*, pp 60-1.
201 In PRC political mythology Zhou Enlai embodies the *deus ex machina* whose intervention sets wrongs right. In this he fulfils an important function with regard to the legitimacy of a system whose unjust features are well remembered. It is difficult to accept at face value so many reports of acts of redemption by Zhou. Yi Wen questions this episode ('Jingguo Chengzhi', p 7).
202 Arai, *Shu Onrai no jissen*, pp 172-5.
203 Lu Dingyi, in *PD*, 19 June 1983.
204 Ma Haide, in *Liaogong zai renjian*, p 68.
205 *Ibid*, and Lu Dingyi, in *PD*, 19 June 1983. Liao is also said to have claimed that he was locked up by Zhang Guotao for four years (*Feiyou zhongyao jianghua huibian*, (vol 5, 1981-82), p 372).
206 'A "Red China News Agency" was formed with Miss Chang Chin-chiu as director and Liao Cheng-chi as editor.' (Kuo *Analytical History*, vol 3, p 186). See also the endnote to this chapter.
207 Ma Haide, (Adviser, Ministry of Health), in *Liaogong zai renjian*, p 68.
208 *PD*, 19 June 1983.
209 Kuo, *Analytical History*, vol 3, p 237. See also Zhu Ziqi, in *Liaogong zai renjian* p 61 and Snow, *Random Notes on Red China*, pp 7 f referred to in William F Dorrill, 'Transfer of Legitimacy in the Chinese Communist Party: Origins of the Maoist Myth', *China Quarterly*, 36 (October-December 1968), p 53 fn 19.
210 Kuo *Analytical History*, vol 3, p 239, fn 1.
211 See note at end of this chapter.
212 *Ouzhou shibao*, 12-13 June 1983.
213 Interview with Kuo Hualun, 1982.
214 Ma Haide, in *Liaogong zai renjian*, p 68.
215 Based on Lu Xun's short story 'Ah Q'.
216 Helen Snow, *Liaogong zai renjian*, pp 136-7.

CHAPTER TWO

The War

Liao stayed in his new positions in Yanan for several months. On 25 June 1937 Mao addressed a letter to He Xiangning in which he told her about Liao's achievements and added that she should not worry about him.[1] From Yanan he had been able to let his family know that he was alive and well but he was soon to rejoin them in the south.[2] As a result of the ever increasing Japanese pressure on China, culminating in the outbreak of full-scale war in the summer of 1937, the Chinese government had agreed to suspend its campaigns against the Communist guerrillas in order to concentrate all efforts on the fight against Japan. It is not certain whether it was the CCP that sent Liao to the south, or whether Liao himself had volunteered for new assignments closer to his native Canton province. Some time between September and October 1937 Liao left Yanan first for Shanghai and subsequently for South China where he worked in the Hong Kong-Canton area.[3]

Beginning with the establishment of a puppet regime in Manchuria in 1931 Japan had edged southward, bringing an ever larger part of North China under its effective control. Public sentiment against Japanese interference had grown and had risen to a high pitch in November-December 1936.[4] Pressure increased on the government to focus all its military power against the Japanese invaders instead of internal enemies. Military tension between Japanese and Chinese forces continued to heighten until the outbreak of the Sino-Japanese war on 7 July 1937. With an agreement between the government and the Communist guerrillas to co-operate in the defence of China it now became possible for Communist officials to operate publicly in areas under government control. It goes without saying that both sides remained suspicious of each other, and increasing clashes between the parties rendered the co-operation agreement progressively ineffective as the war went on.[5]

When Liao left Yanan a young lady was waiting for him, Jing Puchun:
In the autumn of 1937 Pan Hannian arrived in Shanghai from Yanan, and carried ... a letter from Chengzhi which said that he was going to leave for Hong Kong very soon. I went to see auntie right away, to find that she had also received a letter ... and was just getting ready to leave ... She had already bought a ticket for the steamer ... to leave the next day. She suggested I should act as her nurse, so I wouldn't need a ticket. So it was arranged, and we travelled to Hong Kong in a first class cabin, and I slept on the floor .... I stayed in Hong Kong ... until Liao Chengzhi arrived in January 1938. We married on 11 January ... Our marriage was characterised by feelings of complete trust. Chengzhi was a revolutionary with great responsibility, whose ... activities left him little spare time, and he seldom returned home. Sometimes, when he could not cope, he also asked me to assist.[6]

Hong Kong

It seems that, up to this time, Liao Chengzhi's career within the CCP had rested mainly on his personal talents coupled with his family background which had been rewarded by appointments in the field of propaganda and the media. His tasks in southern China demanded greater personal initiative, and also allowed him to establish links with other Communists with whom he was going to work together closely, in some cases for several decades until his death. Some of his (new) acquaintances were figures who already occupied relatively high positions, such as for example Xu Dixin, one of the best known PRC economists.[7] Pan Hannian (not to be confused with Pan Zinian) carried out underground work in Hong Kong.[8] Lian Guan was later to become a leading official in overseas Chinese affairs under Liao.[9] There were also others as for example Yang Kanghua,[10] Tong Xiaopeng,[11] Situ Huimin[12] and the famous painter Ding Cong.[13] Xu Dixin remembers how he:

> met Liao Chengzhi for the first time in Nanjing in October 1937. ... the Japanese aggressor ... had already landed at Jinshanwei in Zhejiang province. I arrived at the (Communist) Eighth Route Army Office in Fuhougang, Nanjing, having come from Jiaxing which was under ... artillery fire. ... at the office of Pan Zinian Chengzhi was also present. He was dressed in the cotton uniform of the Eighth Route Army ... Finally Pan had us think up a means to leave Nanjing as quickly as possible, and [suggested] reuniting again in Wuhan (Hankou).[14]

Tong Xiaopeng gives a vivid description of their departure from Nanjing:

> At that time the second period of collaboration between the CCP and the KMT had already started ... The Eighth Route Army had set up an office in Nanjing. Chengzhi arrived in Nanjing from Yanan following a decision of the Central Committee of the CCP and was preparing to leave for Hong Kong via Shanghai. (His task was) to develop national united front work as part of the resistance struggle... On arriving at our Nanjing office we gave him a warm welcome ... Towards the end of October the situation in Nanjing became critical, and it was decided to evacuate the office. ... there were only Ye Jianying, Li Kenong, myself and three others persevering in Nanjing (Li Kenong later became one of the most important party intelligence and security specialists in the history of the Communist movement; the famous Ye Jianying was one of the few eminent military leaders whose career was not interrupted during the turmoil of Mao's last years).[15] After many detours the seven of us, ... arrived in Changsha in two small dilapidated cars. Since the cars broke down we boarded a small motor launch, and it was already December by the time we arrived in Hankou. It was a tiring journey beset by hardships, but we were full of confidence of victory in the war of resistance (against Japan). *En route* or during stops it was Chengzhi in particular who performed many brilliant feats. It was due

to him that laughter prevailed in our tiny detachment ... He became in fact our 'club leader'. That was the beginning of our deep friendship.16

There are conflicting reports on the date of Liao's departure for Hong Kong. He most likely left Wuhan at the beginning of 1938,17 arriving in Hong Kong during the first days of January.18 A contemporary Japanese source states that he was charged with transmitting the following order to party members in Hong Kong:

1 To expand and strengthen the National United Front more rapidly than previously on the basis of co-operation between the CCP and the KMT;
2 on condition that the KMT government proceed in a desired direction and moreover support the functioning of a government of national defence, the CCP would co-operate with and assist it, following government leadership in the war against Japan;
3 to make efforts to mobilise, organise and arm the masses of the people, and to make efforts for the liberation of the Chinese nation and its independence;
4 to purge traitors, enemy spies and Trotskyites speedily, and to strengthen the national front.19

Early in 1938 Liao published a book(let) entitled *Shouhuo he jiaoxun* (*Results and Lessons*) in which he argued the case for continued resistance against Japan.20 After his arrival Liao quickly moved to establish an office of the Eighth Route Army in Hong Kong, which doubled as a CCP liaison office.21 One of Liao's closest collaborators Lian Guan reports how it was Zhou Enlai who took the initiative to obtain permission to set up this office in the British colony:

In 1938 ... Song Qingling, Liao Chengzhi's mother He Xiangning, Liao's sister Mengxing and her husband Li Shaoshi as well as Liu Yazi arrived in Hong Kong one after the other. Liao Mengxing and Liu Wugou, Liu Yazi's daughter, acted as secretaries for Song Qingling ... At that time the CCP Central Committee sent Pan Hannian and Liao Chengzhi to Hong Kong to act as representatives of the Eighth Route Army and the New Fourth Army and also as persons in charge of various southern provinces. In this connection Zhou Enlai told the British Ambassador to China, General Carl, that the brave resistance of the Eighth Route Army and the New Fourth Army had won the admiration of large masses of Overseas Chinese who freely contributed material aid and funds, as well as medical aid. For this reason (he said), we need an office in Hong Kong to handle these contributions, and he requested him to forward his request to the Governor ...22

Liao had just married (on 11 January) but it seems unlikely that his urgent tasks left much time for a honeymoon, since he had been appointed a leading member of the Hong Kong branch of the Southern China Communist Party Organisation, and Member of the Party Committee for Guangdong Province at a Party Conference in April 1938.23 His assignments covered almost all aspects of what is commonly called united front work.24 In short, he had to obtain effective support for

Communist policy goals from the greatest possible cross-section of people, with only anti-Communists excluded. The upsurge of resistance to Japan had led to a mushrooming of organisations in support of the war, and leftists and Communists had made skilful use of this situation to increase their contacts and influence within such organisations. Song Qingling was one prominent leftist figure involved in numerous such organisations. Mme Sun had remained a member of leading KMT organs, but it is highly likely that she carried out clandestine tasks for the CCP as early as 1933. After Shanghai fell in November 1937 she also had arrived in Hong Kong where she continued to promote the war effort:[25]

> Liao Chengzhi gave support to the 'Protect China Alliance' led by Song Qingling,[26] and united ... patriotic Overseas Chinese and international friends .. to aid the Chinese war of resistance and speedily forwarded the ambulance cars, medicine and army blankets donated to the Eighth Route Army and the New Fourth Army in Wuhan and Chongqing. Overcoming ... difficulties he aided the Qiongya Column and the Dongjiang Column (two guerrilla organisations in Canton province and on Hainan Island) who ... continued their bitter resistance struggle behind enemy lines. He established many links with foreign friends, making known to them the success booked in the resistance struggle by the policies of the CCP and the Eighth Route Army and the New Fourth Army, exposing the slander[s] ... of reactionaries in and outside China (a reference to rumours about Communist treachery).[27]

It was apparent that the CCP consciously cultivated the image of Liao as successor to his father, thereby claiming an unbroken line of legitimacy from Sun Yatsen through Liao Zhongkai to Liao Chengzhi representing the CCP's united front approach. In 1938 Ye Jianying wrote a commemorative article on the 13th anniversary of Liao Zhongkai's assassination, in which he referred to a visit to Liao Zhongkai's grave with Liao Chengzhi. In this article he pointed out that the way Liao 'inherited and follows the life-aim' (a literal translation of Liao Chengzhi's given name 'Chengzhi') of Liao Zhongkai made him a worthy successor, true to the old Chinese saying 'There is no death when one has a son' (*you zi wei bu si*).[28]

It was during these years in particular that Liao Chengzhi became very adept at working together with people from all walks of life, including anti-Communists, and it is no exaggeration to claim that this experience proved invaluable in the years of the People's Republic when Liao in fact headed united front work operations towards Japan as well as towards Overseas Chinese. Liao seems to have made a very favourable impression on many of his colleagues during these years, as is evident from Qian Junrui's recollections. Qian at that time was working in Wuhan. He had been one of the founders of the Sino-Soviet Friendship Association[29] and was later to become one of the PRC's specialists on Sino-Soviet relations. He had met Liao Chengzhi in January 1938, but had remained in Wuhan when Liao left for Hong Kong a few days later. Qian remembers that:

> we in Wuhan carried on work for the 'All-China Save the Nation Federation'. Whenever somebody came to Wuhan from South China

or Hong Kong they always brought news about Liao's activities ...,
praising his ability to unite people, whether they were compatriots from
Hong Kong or Macao or Overseas Chinese from South-east Asia, in
particular Singapore, Malaya and Indonesia. They said he was busy
day and night, sometimes not (even) finding time to snatch a meal...30

Liao also established links with Overseas Chinese in Thailand and the Philippines,31 and the contacts established during these years stood him in good stead when he became the PRC's leading official dealing with Overseas Chinese after the war. Yi Mei describes how Liao engaged in activities to assist Chinese resistance in Thailand during the early period of the anti-Japanese war:

... Liao was in Hong Kong, guiding our relief activities among
Overseas Chinese. News concerning Yanan and the northward move of
the New Fourth Army in their fight against the Japanese was brought to
us by people Liao sent us. Liao enjoyed a very high prestige among
Overseas Chinese abroad at that time. Everybody believed that one day
he ... would follow his father ... in (his efforts) to help guide China
toward a brighter future ... Material aid and funds collected by us in
Thailand for the war of resistance were channelled through Song
Qingling and her network to the anti-Japanese forces in China.32

When the Burma Route was opened Liao transmitted orders to stop anti-British activities in the area, but it is extremely difficult to ascertain the extent of his own influence in operations in this area.33 Aid given by Overseas Chinese had played a conspicuous role in fostering the Republican revolution, and Liao Zhongkai had been one of the most important KMT leaders involved in securing such funds. Faced with the war against Japan the Chinese government under Chiang Kaishek continued to seek assistance from Overseas Chinese. Back in their Yanan sanctuary the CCP leaders had few opportunities to compete with the government for overseas funds. Yanan in fact did come up with occasional guidelines for policy towards Overseas Chinese, and some activities in this area were carried out in northern China. Liao Chengzhi and his collaborators, Song Qingling above all, were most likely given considerable freedom to develop their own approach and establish a network of links with Overseas Chinese in South-east Asia.34

Liao Chengzhi was also active in the Hong Kong media and related 'united front work' activities.35 He was involved in the first English edition of Mao Zedong's works to be published in Hong Kong, and also distributed overseas.

Situ Huimin, one of Liao's old friends from his days at Canton Christian College also arrived in Hong Kong about this time, and he describes a good example of the often difficult and complex nature of Liao's work:

My deepest impression of Liao Chengzhi's conscientiousness ... dates
back to 29 March 1938, when we arrived in Canton from Hong Kong.
The morning of that day he accompanied Mao Dun, Xia Yan, Pan and
others on a trip to Sun Yatsen University. Subsequently we returned to
Dongshan Baizi Road no 11 ... After a short rest he told me that he
wanted to invite me for lunch at the American Western Restaurant ...

with (Chinese) students who had attended the military academy in Japan during the twenties. When I asked him who would attend I was flabbergasted, since these people were all middle and high ranking military KMT officers. Amongst them was a small number of those who had been close to us during our student days in Japan, and ... influenced by progressive ideas; one or two had even participated in the Society for the Study of Social Science. But by now (1938) they had already served in the KMT army for quite a number of years, and had participated in activities against the Communists and the people. In addition there was also an ... small number who had drawn their knives to attack us at gatherings of progressive students ... How could we sit ... with them at one table? He ... explained to me that those people were all professional officers. '... when we were in Tokyo ... the majority of these people had entered the military academy to obtain a (good) position and become prosperous? But ..., there are amongst them also some who, during their term at the military academy, had tended towards progressive (ideas), such as the cadet Xu Chongshi (the younger brother of warlord Xu Chongzhi), who ... entered the ranks of progressive students before ... joining the CCP. At the beginning of the thirties he went over to the Red Army in Jiangxi. ...such people are not incapable of changing. In the present situation (we all have to strive for) unity in our war of resistance. All those (invited) are old acquaintances. Even if we fought on opposite sides during our "armed struggle" (ie during the factional fights in Tokyo) - today we should join hands. As for those friends who ... had belonged to the progressive students, there is now an ever greater obligation to unite with them ... to make them co-operate ... effectively. You know, in those years, they were called "officer bulls". Since they are bulls they may be used by the reactionary KMT clique, but they can also serve the revolutionary cause under the banner of opposition to aggression and protection of the fatherland. We should try to win them over ... to fight together...'37

Liao was able to persuade Situ Huimin to come along, and he had to admit that later developments proved Liao right:

Some of these people left the camp of the reactionary KMT clique, and after the end of the anti-Japanese war went to Hong Kong to carry on business there rather than wishing to take part in the civil war on the side of the reactionary armies (ie the government forces). When I was in the United States during the final phase of the war of liberation (before 1949) in a NCNA report from China I came across a list of the first batch of KMT officers who had switched sides. The first name on the list, Mai Xiachong, was one of the friends who ... had lunch together with us in the American Restaurant in Canton. When I returned to China Chengzhi told me that this friend had come to see him very soon after his surrender to the Communists to pour out his feelings and hopes for the future. One may (indeed) say that this proved that Liao's persuasive efforts ... had achieved their purpose.[38]

Liao had to act very flexibly, adapting to his surroundings to appear acceptable to people who were not Communist, but whose co-operation was thought desirable and necessary. His lifestyle differed considerably from the media image of the puritan Communist cadre. On the surface he may even have resembled a typical 'bourgeois' to the point of confusing more orthodox 'comrades':[39]

> At the time of the first anti-Communist wave in 1939 Xin Po, Sima Wensen, Shi Pilan and I (Yu Feng) left the Political Department of the Fourth War Area and arrived in Hong Kong from northern Canton province via Dongjiang. First of all we went to see Liao to report to him. When he saw my respectful attitude he drew his eyebrows together in a frown: my hair was as short as that of a boy, and I wore an old uniform. I hastened to present my report to him, but he did not let me speak and first dragged me off to Zhonghuan Road, bought me a white jumperskirt and a white hat, and told me to put them on right away. We then sat down in a coffeeshop and started talking.[40]

Liao's work demanded organisational talent. Living mainly in Hong Kong he had wide access to information concerning not only his own area of activities but also the general military and political situation in Asia and beyond. Now about thirty years old, he had already suffered numerous arrests and harrowing experiences, but had not lost his characteristic streak of humour. Nevertheless he seems to have gained greater maturity:

> ... Liao met Pan Hannian who had arrived in Hong Kong from Shanghai. Chengzhi was as enthusiastic, friendly and approachable as he (always) used to be. The only difference was that he had put on weight. When talking with us and analyzing the domestic and international situation, interpreting CCP policies, his face did not assume the mask of Communist lecturing cadre bandying slogans. His speech evoked interest and was full of sarcastic, ironic remarks that made people laugh, but set them thinking at the same time. The way he talked showed that he was already a revolutionary politician who had gained a more mature understanding of politics and theory.[41]

Liao never lost his dislike of hollow-sounding, dry, formal speeches, a trait that set him apart from some party colleagues and one of the reasons why he was later relatively popular with visitors to China, especially Japanese. His informality had its root in his own character and was not merely assumed; at the same time he will have realised that his approach was more likely to break down the reserve of non-Communist counterparts than the politspeak of many of his colleagues.[42]

Liao Chengzhi however was also able to compose sober analyses of the political situation. As early as October 1937 he published an article in *Jiefang zhoukan* on problems in introducing a compulsory draft system.[43] In an article published in 1939 he commented on problems of the United Front in an age of collaborators such as Wang Jingwei.[44] In a talk with Yin Linping in July 1941 he predicted that the United States and England would be forced by considerations of national interest to face Japan militarily.45 Generally speaking, however Liao did not yet belong to the group of the CCP's Japan experts like Li Fanfu who might be asked to present their analysis of the international situation.46

Japanese Invasion

As the international situation continued to deteriorate the temporary truce between the Chinese government and Communist guerrillas had already broken down on many fronts. The climax was reached in the so-called Anhui Incident. When the government claimed that the Communist New Fourth Army had refused to obey orders government forces annihilated a large part of the New Fourth Army. Some Communist leaders who were able to escape made their way to Hong Kong via south-west China (Yunnan), joined by other Communist refugees. Hong Kong became a haven where the CCP could operate in relative safety for the time being. The influx of newcomers presented an additional task for Liao Chengzhi. He had never been a military figure in the proper sense of that word, but nevertheless became involved in the organisation of guerrilla activities in the south, particularly in Canton province. As early as 1938, when Japanese forces landed in Yawan Bay, Liao had contacted Zeng Sheng, Wu Youheng and Zhou Boming and decided to mobilise sailors from Hong Kong to go to Baoan to organise armed guerrillas to fight the Japanese. This was in fact the beginning of the 'East River Column' resistance forces under the control of the CCP in Canton province. It developed in the home area of the Liao family where, roughly thirty years earlier, uprisings had taken place against the imperial Qing dynasty.47 It is virtually certain however that Liao did not become involved in the guidance of day-to-day military operations.48

Soon Liao had occasion to prove his organisational talent under the threat of Japanese occupation. As he had predicted, the Japanese decided to direct their military strength not against the Soviet Union, but Southeast Asia, the USA and their allies. Hong Kong was also attacked on 8 December 1941 as part of Japan's march to the south. Yu Feng, an editor of the Hong Kong newspaper *Huashangbao* for which Liao was also responsible49 described the first days of the attack:

> under attack by shells ... the colleagues from the *Huashangbao* kept publishing for three or four days. The other Hong Kong newspapers had all stopped publication already. At that time I was the editor of the supplement under the guidance of Xia Yan. When at last we, too, had to stop publishing Xia Yan formally announced Liao Chengzhi's directive to that effect at a meeting of all editors, including the director Fan Changjiang and general editor Hu Zhongchi. He also transmitted specific measures to be taken for the evacuation of our personnel. Everybody was to move to a different place and to receive expenses for two months paid in advance. Except for our contact - different for each

of us - nobody was to be told of our new addresses, and we were to await orders there for our withdrawal from Hong Kong.50

Liao's directive was based on instructions in a secret order from the CCP Central Committee cabled to Hong Kong,51 his task being to evacuate 'comrades and friends' marooned in Hong Kong to the 'great rear' and Communist base areas. Altogether about 800 persons left Hong Kong in this way, including some KMT officials and their relatives, as well as English military personnel. Among those rescued were close colleagues such as Xia Yan, his old friend Situ Huimin, as well as Zhang Wenbing, the famous writer Mao Dun, Hu Sheng, Liang Suming and Hu Feng.52 Liao's mother, his wife Jing Puchun and Liu Yazi also escaped:

> on 8 December ... the Japanese militarists ... attacked Hong Kong. At that time we were staying in Kowloon. At dawn Chengzhi ... returned in a great hurry and told me and my mother-in-law to leave quickly. I asked him what had happened. He answered: 'The Japanese have arrived, and you're still not leaving?' Carrying (our children) Jianjian and Kaisun we left Kowloon and rushed to Hong Kong where we stayed at the house of Cai Tingkai. The Cai family had already left ... Very soon it became impossible to stay on in Hong Kong. My mother-in-law, Liu Yazi and others, including myself, boarded a wooden sailing vessel bound for Haifeng. Normally Dongjiang could be reached in two days, but we hit bad weather and drifted at sea for seven days and nights. (By that time) our food and water were all gone. Just then we ran into a CCP-led guerrilla patrol. When they learned that Liao Zhongkai's wife was on board they immediately sent sweet potatoes, drinking water and milk powder. Thanks to their help we reached Haifeng safely. He Xiangning wrote a (classical style short) poem describing the situation:

The water's gone, no more food as we cross over to Haifeng. We dare to brave the doom of our time...53

Arrest and Imprisonment

Liao himself also boarded a fishing-boat and escaped to the northern part of Canton province.54 On his way he passed through Huiyang, the place of origin of the Liao family, and got caught in a Japanese air bombardment.55 Due to the Japanese attack on Hong Kong, Liao's plans for co-operation with the British against the Japanese were not realised, but these contacts laid the basis for future co-operation with the Dongjiang Guerrilla units.56 He had been able to escape the Japanese, but his presence in government-controlled territory soon became known to the government security service, the *Zhongtong*. There are several accounts of his arrest, which according to his letter to Zhou took place on May 30,57 of which I would like to present first an account from a Communist source:

The *Zhongtong* had learned from a traitor that, at that time, Liao was a committee member of the Southern Bureau of the CCP, and that he was active in the Jiangxi-Guangdong (Canton province) area. Thereupon Feng Qi, the special envoy of the *Zhongtong* stationed in Jiangxi, set a trap for Liao following directives of Xu Enzang, Head of the *Zhongtong*, and Liao was arrested. ... [and] imprisoned in the notorious Majiazhou concentration camp in Taihe in Jiangxi. After his arrest the agents first tried 'shock interrogation' by threatening to kill Liao in order to obtain evidence. Except for admitting his party membership Liao refused to answer ... Once their scheme had failed they tried 'exhausting interrogation' which went on day and night without giving Liao a moment's rest, but, as before, without result. The agents' third plan was to lock Liao up together with a fake 'progressive' who was to gain Liao's confidence ... After two months this (method) produced no results (either). In the fourth place they had the traitor Guo Qianhui try to induce Liao to turn traitor following his own example. When Guo Qianhui came to Chongqing in 1943 to take up a position as special officer in the *Zhongtong* office he referred to this episode during a conversation I had with him. Guo once mentioned that, when he had arrived in Liao's cell Liao didn't pay any attention to him. As soon as he started speaking Liao began to curse him: 'Traitor, you're not fit to talk to, get out, get out.' Guo also added that Liao was 'very tough'. The head of the concentration camp at that time, Shi Jin, also told me later that he had applied 'soft tactics', talking to him in a rather more 'friendly' way. His food and conditions were improved somewhat, and he was given 'preferential treatment'. Several times he tried to 'talk him over', but Liao's stance remained unchanged. Despairing of their inability to persuade Liao they cancelled all his so-called 'preferential treatment', and gave him just enough to live - and not enough to die.59

This account differs from a very intriguing recollection by Gong Ping:

Liao was engaged in leadership of secret (underground) work in northern Canton province. He was arrested by an officer of the government secret service in Jiangxi province, Zhuang Zufang; the plan to arrest him had been reported beforehand to Jiang Jingguo who was than an official in the same province. Only then was he arrested, and brought to Ma Jiazhou concentration camp in Jiangxi.60

I have so far been unable to find corroborating evidence; should Gong Ping's version be basically correct Jiang Jingguo may have become involved not so much to arrest Liao, but perhaps to prevent his possible execution, in a manner reminiscent of reports of Chiang Kaishek protecting Liao Zhongkai's family after his assassination. Kuo Hualun's recollections do not refer to Jiang Jingguo:

Having gained the control of the CCP Kiangsi Provincial Committee's leadership and staff, together with its radio communications, the Nationalist security office in Kiangsi had them working as usual for counter-intelligence purposes. The original radio-communications man was ordered to try resuming contact with the CCP South China Working Committee by using the old code, station designation, and frequencies. This radio contact, finally resumed in November 1941, enabled the Nationalists to feed the CCP South China Working Committee faked reports and requests. ... By this time the Kwangtung Bureau of Investigation and Statistics had also obtained valuable information from Yao Hua, secretariat chief of the South China Working Committee, who had become a counter-intelligence agent. The ensuing raids broke up that Communist Committee and all its clandestine organs scattered from Chukiang to Tapu in eastern Kwangtung. Fang Fang, secretary of the CCP South China Working Committee, made a narrow escape; and Yao Hua was left alone for counter-intelligence needs. Otherwise all members of the secret Communist setup were captured. Included was the well-known Communist, Liao Cheng-chih, arrested at Lochang in northern Kwangtung after his escape from Japanese-occupied Hong Kong early in the Pacific War.[61]

Liao survived the Majiazhou camp to be transferred to a secret prison in Xifeng (Guizhou), and subsequently in 1944 to a prison in the wartime capital Chongqing.[62] During his imprisonment his wife and mother were staying in Shaoguan, where Lian Guan informed them of Liao's arrest. Lian Guan did not know, however, where he was being held.[63] On 3 September 1942 he wrote a letter to his wife[64] which arrived only in 1943:

I think it happened on the evening of a day in 1943 when a stranger knocked at our door. When asked who he was he said he had something to tell us. When he had finished speaking he closed his umbrella, took a letter out of the bamboo handle and passed it to me. Right away I realised that it was a letter by Liao written to me from a prison in Jiangxi. The letter said that he was imprisoned there, and wouldn't mind dying, but he would never do anything which he would have to hide from his parents or the people (meaning that he would never betray the Communist cause), and asked me not to worry. The stranger's family name was Yao. He was employed at the prison where Chengzhi frequently gave him lessons in patriotism. He very much sympathised with Chengzhi's fate, and was determined to go to the CCP (headquarters) in Yanan. Chengzhi had told him to go to Canton province to look up Lian Guan and Qiao Guanhua and establish contact with them ...[65]

On 28 September 1942 Liao wrote a letter to Zhou Enlai.[66]

The prison camp was situated in Majiazhou in the Taihe district of Jiangxi province.[67] Liao survived and even found opportunities to make drawings. He was a very prominent prisoner, and his artistic talent was widely known. He was even asked for a drawing by the head of the *Zhongtong* in Jiangxi province:

'Mr Liao, your traditional-style paintings are full of deep meaning. Would you be so kind to grant me one of your paintings?' With a cold smile Liao grasped a brush and made a painting entitled 'Withered tree: wicked dog' threw down the brush and said 'I'm giving it to you to remember me.' The result was that the scoundrel left red-faced ...68

Liao also dedicated some of his drawings to fellow prisoners, but it goes without saying that these drawings were meant to encourage them.69 It was from this prison camp he sent cartoons and a message in 1944 to the war-time capital Chongqing to the effect that he was in good physical and mental shape:

> One cartoon showed him eating rice, from which he was fishing grains of sand and a cockroach. The other one showed him sitting on a wooden pail which served as his toilet (indicating he was not even permitted to go to the toilet). There were several large mosquitoes on his buttocks.70

According to one source he seems to have passed through the secret prison in Xifeng in Guizhou,71 and was also sighted in Zengjiayan in Chongqing. In the same year (1944) Liao was transferred to a prison at the foot of Mt Geluo in Chongqing where he was kept in the custody of the Military Security Service on Chiang Kai-shek's orders.73 During his period of imprisonment several attempts were made to secure his release, including appeals by Zhou Enlai, but to no avail.74 We do not know whether Liao's survival was due to sheer luck, but it seems likely that, despite his harsh treatment, care was taken not to have this prominent and valuable prisoner killed needlessly. Not all prisoners were so lucky. Zhang Wenbin, who had been vice-secretary of the South-China Work Committee of the CCP, was one of Liao's fellow prisoners at Majiazhou, and he described the following incident after the death of a fellow-inmate:

> Liao requested the prison authorities to see the body of the martyr to pay his last respects, but was refused permission (in the first instance). Liao then conducted an unrelenting struggle with the reactionary authorities until he was finally able to see him ...75

While Liao was still imprisoned he was elected an alternate member of the CCP Central Committee in June-July 1945.76 According to one source he was elected 'with the highest number of votes in recognition of Chengzhi's contribution to the revolution and his heroic struggle in prison.' In addition, this promotion may also have been intended to increase his status for additional protection. Liao himself did not become aware of his new status until after his release in January 1946.

Since her escape from Hong Kong Liao's mother He Xiangning had remained free, at the same time participating in activities in support of leftist politics. She was accompanied by Liao Jian and Liao Jian's younger brother, whom she took to Guilin.78 It was not long before Guilin also fell to the Japanese. He Xiangning's daughter, Liao Mengxing, was in Chongqing at that time, when she received a letter from her mother indicating her intention to travel to Chongqing. Preparations for He Xiangning's return were made with the assistance of the Eighth Route Army Office in Chongqing. Unexpectedly, however, He Xiangning stayed on in Guilin, according to Liao Mengxing as a result of intrigues to keep her away from the wartime capital.[79] In Guilin He Xiangning was in touch with members of a KMT faction opposed to Chiang Kaishek's leadership, and she apparently also established liaison with the Communist underground.[80] When Guilin came under threat of occupation, the CCP assisted He Xiangning to move to a different place close to where Ye Ting, a famous general from the New Fourth Army, was staying.[81] Ye Ting's personal freedom had been restricted by the government, and he was under close guard by government agents. He Xiangning was able to meet him, but Ye Ting was soon transferred to Chongqing by the government.[82] In the summer of 1944 the Japanese carried out an offensive in southern China which also threatened Guilin, and He Xiangning moved to Babu where she was subsequently joined by Chen Shaoxian and others.[83] He Xiangning kept in touch with the CCP underground and attempted to set up an anti-Chiang Kaishek organisation consisting of the KMT-dissenters Chen Cisheng, Li Minxin, Chen Shaoxian, Li Langru and others; she also urged Li Jishen to organise an armed 'self-defence unit'.[84] Following the end of the war against Japan in August 1945, He Xiangning moved back to her native Hong Kong from where she continued her efforts to drive a wedge between dissenting KMT members and the government while maintaining close links with the CCP.[85]

Release

After the war both the government and the Communists realised that a new outbreak of civil war would be met with hostility by a population exhausted by many years of war against Japan. With neither party wishing to appear unconciliatory, talks were held concerning a political solution. These led to an initial agreement on 10 October which also contained a reference to the release of political prisoners. Liao was not yet among those to be released, but his treatment improved, and one day he was even visited in prison by Chiang Kaishek himself:
> Before the meeting the prison authorities had a suit made for him and had given him a haircut.[86]

Liao was then taken to another building in a small car and after about ten minutes Chiang entered:
> Chengzhi remained seated and did not move, glancing at Chiang. It was Chiang who started the conversation: 'You've had a difficult time. If only you would stop working for the Communists I would certainly give you a high position. Don't forget that you are the descendant of Liao Zhongkai and He Xiangning, and you should not do anything you have to be ashamed of.' Chengzhi replied that was exactly why he refused to accept the offer. Chiang retorted 'If that's the way it is don't have regrets later.' Chengzhi did not reply, and there was nothing for Chiang but to leave. Chengzhi was brought back to his prison. Everything remained as before, only the food improved. At first he had

been given two bowls of salted rice per day, mixed with grit and water. He was not allowed to have anything else to drink. Now he also received vegetables and soup for lunch and supper. Chengzhi did wonder whether Chiang might have granted this improvement before having him finished off.[87]

Despite unceasing efforts to have Liao released, it took more than two months before the long-awaited moment came. Following the mediation efforts of General Marshall an agreement on a truce between the government and the Communists, which also facilitated agreements on exchange of prisoners was reached on 10 January 1946. During the first days of January 1946 a high KMT military official, Ma Fawu, had been captured by the Communists, and the KMT agreed to exchange both Liao Chengzhi and General Ye Ting for Ma Fawu and four other prisoners.[88] Liao Chengzhi had not been informed about his impending release until the very last moment. In the afternoon of 22 January 1946, Liao was brought to the office of Shao Lizi, member of the Political Consultative Conference.[89] Liao and Ye Ting were then welcomed by the CCP delegation to the conference.[90]

When the CCP delegation had been informed of the KMT's approval for Liao Chengzhi's release everybody was elated. Somebody was sent to buy him underwear and a Western-style suit, arrange a room for him where he could stay, and an elaborate arrangement of firecrackers was obtained... When Liao arrived ... he received a most enthusiastic welcome... The noise of firecrackers rent the air, causing passengers in buses passing by to put their heads through the windows to watch the scene. Deng Yingchao (Zhou Enlai's wife) walked up to him to give him a friendly welcome. I took a snapshot of both together, as well as a separate shot of Liao alone. The photo recorded traces of Liao's prison past: his hair was uncut, he had grown a small beard, and was holding a small bamboo-pipe ... Liao Chengzhi was free, but as soon as he was released he showed his concern for General Ye Ting and the others still in prison...[91]

Immediately after his release he was looked after by his old friend Huang Dingchen[92] and recuperated from his ordeal in the famous Hongyancun area of Chongqing.[93] In March 1946 Ye Ting was also released. There was also a joint welcome by the CCP for Ye Ting and Liao Chengzhi, and Liao Chengzhi talked about his experiences at a small gathering called by Zhou Enlai.[94] It did not take long for Liao to resume his duties. Soon afterwards he moved on towards Canton.[95] Lin Ping, the political commissar of the East River Column guerrilla forces in Canton province had arrived in Chongqing to participate in talks with the government about the agreed disengagement of forces.[96]

Ye Ting was to meet with a tragic fate soon after he had regained his freedom. He was scheduled to fly to Yanan on 8 April with Deng Fa, Wang Ruofei and Liao Chengzhi. The plane, piloted by an American, crashed in a mountainous area in bad weather, killing all on board.[97] According to his wife's recollections Liao had told her as late as 7 April that:

we were to leave for Yanan the next day. He told me that if I wanted to do any shopping it would have to be done quickly. I bought some daily necessities such as thermos flasks and aluminium rice containers which were lacking in Yanan. In the evening, Chengzhi left to attend a meeting. I packed our hand luggage in an old leather case and went to sleep. Chengzhi did not arrive until about 5 o'clock the next morning. He told me that we wouldn't be leaving that day, and that Zhou Enlai wanted him to go to Canton to deal with the transfer of the East River Column to Shandong. I told him that, after the meeting that had lasted the whole night, he should have a rest now, and that I would go to the airfield to see the others off to Yanan. The rain was falling in thin threads. The plane was an American military aircraft piloted by an American military officer. Qin Bangxian, Ye Ting, Wang Ruofei and Deng Fa boarded the plane. Wang Ruofei's uncle and his nephew boarded the plane instead of Liao and myself. During the afternoon we still had no news of their arrival in Yanan, and a telephone call to Xi'an did not help us to any further information. A search plane sent by the US army discovered that the plane had crashed, and its seventeen passengers and four crew all dead. This incident, which shocked China and the world, became known as the '8 April tragedy'. Chengzhi and I were deeply shocked. Whenever the incident was mentioned Chengzhi used to say that we who are alive must never forget these comrades, that we should carry out their unfinished tasks and redouble our fight for the liberation of the nation.[98]

At the beginning of May Liao flew to Nanjing.[99] Although released in January he had not yet met his mother again, but in Nanjing he met relatives, friends[100] and his sister Liao Mengxing who had been widowed and lived in Nanjing with her little child Li Mei:

Zhou Enlai sent somebody to go to Shanghai to escort my mother, Liao Mengxing, and myself to Nanjing where the CCP delegation was in order to meet Liao Chengzhi. Mother and he had not seen each other for more than four years, since Pearl Harbour in 1941. When uncle was in prison my father Li Shaoshi was killed in Chongqing. When I met Liao he found out that I had not been able to get over my grief and sorrow. He gave me a drawing: he had painted a fat man who was sitting on a chair and laughed, with a naughty expression in his eyes. The caption read: 'The nerves of revolutionaries should not be like thread, they should be like steel wire. Therefore: keep laughing; keep looking forward, and never bury yourself in grief.'[101]

In Nanjing Liao was involved in the work of the truce supervision teams set up on the basis of the January agreement.[102] He was also engaged in propaganda work, writing and editing manuscripts for the *Mass Weekly (Qunzhong zhoukan)*, where Li Weihan was responsible as final editor:

often working until deep into the night. When hungry he would walk down the street to a corner to have a snack and then go back to work. At that time Li Weihan was the final editor. Li once assessed (Liao's workstyle in the following words): 'However much you change Liao's articles, he willingly accepts the alterations, which goes to show Liao's modest attitude.'103

Li Weihan, with whom Liao collaborated, later became one of the most influential figures in the area of 'united front work'. Another prominent propagandist also present in Nanjing and in touch with Liao was Lu Dingyi.104 His official assignment was to negotiate for the withdrawal of the 'East River Column' to the north-eastern province of Shandong, assisted by Lin Ping, whom he had met in Chongqing shortly after his release.105 The withdrawal was only part of a wider strategic movement to the north of all Communist forces in the south. Communist guerrilla forces had been rather weak in Canton province, and their temporary retreat must have been interpreted by many as a sign of military weakness. In a wider perspective the withdrawal facilitated the consolidation of Communist forces in north-east China with the support of Soviet occupation forces who had delayed their departure from China after the end of the war against Japan. In the latter half of 1946 the truce gradually broke down and moves were undertaken in 1947 to re-establish guerrilla forces in Canton province.

Liao's return to Canton must have been an emotional experience, not only because he returned to his native province. It was there that he once more saw his two children who were living in Canton in the care of his mother, He Xiangning. Liao Jian the elder one was now seven years old:106

> One pitch dark evening, when my brother and I were ready to go to sleep, somebody suddenly arrived looking for grandmother. He carried with him a letter. When grandmother saw that letter she put her arms around me and my brother: 'Quickly, get ready to follow this gentleman, and you'll be able to see your daddy.' Grandmother took us to a man whose beard covered his whole face... My brother and I were scared. When we saw him looking at grandmother we rushed away. Grandmother turned her head and called 'stupid children, come here, at once, this is your daddy.' Before we had quite grasped what was going on daddy's large hands already had embraced us tightly. He kissed us, and his beard pricked us so much that we cried out...107

Yanan Days

Following the withdrawal of Communist forces to the north, CCP personnel working in areas under KMT control were withdrawn consecutively to Yanan in the second half of 1946. Liao Chengzhi returned to Yanan in July 1946 with his wife, but without his children.108 A section of those transferred to the north were assigned to work for the New China News Agency (NCNA).109 During and after the Long March in the mid-thirties Liao had occupied important positions in the world of the media and these associations had continued during his stay in South China from 1938 until his imprisonment in 1942. After his release in January 1946 he had co-operated with Lu Dingyi and Li Weihan in Nanjing. Back in Yanan he was now appointed head of the NCNA. When compared to the similar position held in Yanan after the Long March the size and importance of the NCNA clearly outclassed its predecessor, and it may be said that this appointment meant that (for the first time) Liao occupied a leading position in an important CCP organ. This appointment was paralleled by similar positions in the party's propaganda organs, but no dates for these latter appointments are available.110

Qian Junrui who previously had been working in the General Administrative Office of the Central Committee of the CCP was also transferred to the NCNA, as well as to the *Liberation Daily (Jiefang ribao)*:

> This time I worked under the direct guidance of Liao. He had taken over the position of Head of NCNA from Bo Gu, and I was appointed Head of the Editorial Committee. Other leading persons with whom I co-operated were Ai Siqi, Chen Kehan, Wu Lengxi, Hu Jiwei and Liao Gailong... Working under the guidance of Liao encouraged us to work hard and display our creativity. There were three main reasons for this: 1) Liao was able to transmit directives from Chairman Mao of the CCP Central correctly and in good time. Liao also organised discussions, and did not just make do with a brief report. 2) Liao was thoroughly democratic. He was good at listening to other opinions, in particular divergent opinions and criticism of himself. At the same time, he did not go along with opinions that went against Marxist principles - faults he pointed out ruthlessly - and yet, he permitted discussion and argument. 3) Liao was good at making use of the strong points of others... In addition, he was very strict on the point of editorial revisions. I remember that, on one occasion, he revised the draft of an editorial concerning the action against hunger and the civil war in the 'great rear' seven or eight times; when still not satisfied he gave orders to pass it on to Chairman Mao before publication. When the Editorial Committee decided to have him write a draft he invariably set to work himself, and never delegated the task to somebody else. Reports were always written by himself, at least the outline, and he never asked the secretary or somebody else to write them for him.111

There is good reason to believe that Qian Junrui listed these points precisely because Liao was subsequently forced to submit to self-criticism, 'admitting' lack of consultation with Mao Zedong as well as principal political errors. In a way Qian's remarks can be regarded as a posthumous exoneration of accusations made in 1947, and should not just be seen in the context of an ordinary eulogy.

Living conditions in Yanan were still very harsh at that time, and Liao is reported to have shown particular concern for colleagues who fell ill.112 The civil war had flared up again in the second half of 1946 and, in that winter, government forces under Hu Zongnan had massed in preparation for an attack on Yanan. Yanan had remained the sanctuary of the CCP throughout the Japanese war, never occupied by either the government or the Japanese forces. The decision to evacuate Yanan temporarily in March 1947[113] was certainly sound militarily, but must have been disconcerting even for those Communist leaders who realised that the withdrawal was not an indication of a general decline of Communist power. The withdrawal from Yanan also necessitated comprehensive preparations for the transfer of the NCNA so as not to disrupt the news network of the CCP centred in Yanan, and presented a great challenge to Liao. To make things more difficult he was concerned about a very personal matter: his wife Jing Puchun had just given birth to their child, Dudu. As head of the NCNA Liao had been provided with a horse for his personal use but gave it to his wife.[114] This meant, of course, that he himself had to make do without a horse. The continuation of operations during and after the evacuation of Yanan were the topic of discussion at the highest level.[115]

In addition to continued fighting in the civil war Communist forces were engaged in pushing through large-scale land reforms in areas under their control. It is hardly surprising that, in the turmoil of the civil war and the revolution, many of these reforms led to excesses which became so widespread that they seriously undermined popular support in some areas. The leadership of the CCP decided to reverse its previous stance and moderate its approach to land reform. Simultaneously a party purge was initiated. One of its aims was the strengthening of discipline in a party whose membership had rapidly grown in numbers during the preceding years. Mao Zedong also made use of the purge to shift responsibility for these excesses to his political opponents. Recent research has thrown light on events during this period.[116] The NCNA came in for some criticism, as did its head, Liao Chengzhi. He was blamed in particular for having approved the publication of reports on the land reform without having received relevant instructions from Mao Zedong or Zhou Enlai. More specifically the Agency was accused of not having adopted a critical attitude towards those excesses.[117] Liao and other leading cadres were personally criticised by Mao Zedong during a meeting in a village in Pingshan district in Hebei province, where the Central Committee had moved following the withdrawal from northern Shaanxi. Liao had to submit to self-criticism 'in front of the masses.'[118] It seems that his confession was accepted by the party 'gods' since Liao was not 'purged'. This episode however may have contributed to his unexpected transfer back to Canton province where he was appointed secretary of the South China Bureau of the CCP.

Return to South China

Even before the withdrawal of Communist forces from South China in 1946, pressure against Communist activities in Canton had become so great that He Xiangning - who had arrived in Canton in 1945 - soon moved to Hong Kong where Great Britain had re-established its colonial rule after the end of the Japanese occupation.[119] Hong Kong was soon to become one of the major centres in the south from where the Communists, often making use of front organisations and leftist sympathisers, tried to influence both politicians and general public opinion against the Chinese government, and a major centre for underground operations.[120] One of the most important Communist leaders in Hong Kong at the time was Fang Fang, who later made a career in the area of Overseas Chinese affairs.[121] Even before Liao Chengzhi's return to Hong Kong his mother had engaged in liaison between Communists and groups and individuals opposed to the government.[122] For some time her old friend Song Qingling had abstained from public political activities but, with the breakdown of the truce arrangements, Song again openly took part in Chinese politics when she protested publicly in July 1946 against the delivery of US arms to the Chinese government.[123] Co-operation between the CCP and other dissenting groups was, however, not always smooth, despite rather successful Communist attempts to penetrate non-Communist political organisations such as the Democratic Alliance (*Minmeng*).[124] Due to his previous experience in Hong Kong Liao Chengzhi seemed very well qualified indeed to continue this sort of united front work. An important part of CCP activities in Hong Kong included trade union activities under the leadership of Liu Ningyi who was appointed to this task in 1946 after Deng Fa had perished in the fateful air crash on 8 April 1946.[125] After the establishment of the PRC Liu Ningyi remained in the area of trade union work, but also took part in international front organisations, leading missions to a variety of countries, including Japan, in a way that paralleled Liao Chengzhi's activities to some extent, and there may have been not only co-operation, but also a certain rivalry between Liao and Liu Ningyi.[126]

Liao's appointment made him the virtual head of the Hong Kong party apparatus, and his assignment also included Overseas Chinese affairs. As in the past, one of the main aims of Overseas Chinese policy was obtaining financial support, and money transferred by Overseas Chinese became an important source of foreign currency for the PRC.[127] It goes without saying that the CCP also tried to increase its political support among Overseas Chinese. Moreover, Hong Kong became a meeting place for Communist cadres engaged in preparation for the takeover of Taiwan province,[128] and it is fairly clear that Hong Kong was also a base for liaison with pro-Communist organisations throughout South-east Asia.

For the time being military developments in Canton province remained relatively low-key until the arrival of the main Communist field armies that overran China from bases in north and northeastern China from late 1947 until the takeover in October 1949. After the evacuation of the East River Column in the summer and autumn of 1946 the South China Bureau of the CCP first focused its activities on Hong Kong itself.[129] With the renewed onset of the civil war the CCP called for the establishment of a 'People's Armed Liberation Committee in Canton province' which would also invite a delegate from the Democratic Alliance as adviser. The funding of these operations depended to some extent on Overseas Chinese contributions.[130] The re-establishment of Communist guerrilla forces in Canton province on the basis of the former East River Column was a difficult and arduous task. Not only did the government suppress these attempts by force, it seems that popular support was relatively limited. (See endnote to this chapter.) According to existing estimates guerrilla forces in southern Canton province, as well as the northern part of the province, did not exceed a total of 10,000. The formal announcement of the establishment of a united force of Guangdong and Guangxi provinces had to wait until August 1947.[131] While Liao played a certain role in the organisation and (financial) support operation for these forces, he was mainly:

> engaged in painstaking work of uniting various groups within the highly complicated context of Hong Kong society, comprising compatriots in Hong Kong and Macao, Overseas Chinese, democratic parties, intellectuals, and ordinary workers as well as such great leaders among Overseas Chinese as Chen Jiakang.[132]

It goes without saying that a good deal of Liao's activities such as possible links with Vietnam described by Chen Shixiang for which I have not been able to find corroborating evidence, were of a clandestine nature:

> Chinese Communist relations with the Viet Minh gained momentum after 1947. In the spring of that year Liao Ch'eng-chih, then chief of the CCP's South China Bureau, visited Viet Minh bases in Viet-Bac. In June Fang Fang, a major general in Mao's army, came to Viet-Bac. Liao Ch'eng-chih and Fang Fang had been active in Canton during the KMT-CCP negotiation period from early 1946 to early 1947 ... Liao ... was very active in Canton in 1946-47. In calling Chang Fa-k'uei 'Uncle Hua' (Chang's other name is Chang Hsiang-hua) he seemed to be able to use his father's name and influence 29 years earlier in the same city to get along very well with the Kuomintang leaders in Canton. Fang Fang was an able aide to Liao... After the negotiations failed, they visited Hong Kong, Kwangsi, and Ho Chi Minh's Vietnam. Liao and Fang attended the cadre conference in Soc-Giang on 1 August 1947, convened by the Viet Minh. The South-west Democratic United Army, now renamed the 'Yueh-Kwei Border Democratic United Army', stationed in the Hundred-Thousand Hills, was placed temporarily under Liao's command to co-operate with the Viet Minh. At that time, Gen Hsiang Ying, former deputy-commander of the Communist New Fourth Army, was in Siam (Hsiang went there in the late spring of 1946), responsible for Chinese Communist activities in all of Indo-China, and in touch with the Communists in Siam, Malaya, and Indonesia. During his stay in Siam Hsiang was reported to have helped the Viet Minh arrange the purchase and shipment of arms to Viet-Bac. He was transferred to the China-Vietnam border area in the autumn of 1947 where he presumably took over the command of the Democratic United Army from Liao.[133]

There is little published information about Liao's whereabouts and activities in 1948; a picture apparently taken in 1948 shows him with his wife and a child in Shijiazhuang.[134]

Endnote

Unfortunately I was unable to obtain some recent publications on the history of the Dongjiang Column in time for inclusion in this study. (For instance Wang Zuoyao, *Dongzong yiye* (Guangdong renmin chubanshe, 1983). Useful information is also contained in *Huanan renmin wuzhuang*, esp pp 36 ff and 41 and *Gongfei zhanli panduanbiao*; for a contemporary reference, see Kusano, *Konichi Shina*, p 307.

The relative weakness of the anti-Japanese resistance was the most likely reason for Japanese advances in Canton province in early 1945 (*Xianghe bao*, 3 February 1945). As we have seen Liao was involved in the shift of forces from Canton to the north as part of the truce arrangement between the KMT and the CCP. The rest of the forces concentrated in the Hong Kong area (*Yinianlai (sanshiwunian) zhi zhonggong*, pp 30-1). The rebuilding of the forces went ahead only slowly (*Nanxian xunhui*, p 150). In March a meeting is reported of the 'Armed Operations Work Committee' held in Hong Kong on 21-22 March 1947 (*Gongfei yu minmeng zhi jian*, pp 6 f, 10). Its leaders were, among others Zeng Sheng, Wang Zuoyao, Lin Ping and Feng Baiju, and it was partly financed by contributions from Overseas Chinese (*ibid*, p 11). The Southern Branch Office of the CCP (Huananju) called for better organisation and integration of existing, largely independently acting groups in May 1947. In August the establishment of a '*Liangguang zongdui*' (Canton and Guangxi Column) was announced, the core of which was apparently the Dongjiang Column (*Yantai ribao*, 8, 11, 13 and 19 August 1947, and *Bonhai ribao*, 6 August 1947). These sources do not provide us with much specific information. On the military situation in general, see *Xinhua ribao (Taihang ban)*, 11 November 1947. It was claimed that the strength of the guerrilla forces in southern Canton province had reached more than 9,000 men towards the end of 1947 (*Xuefeng bao*, 16 November 1947; see also *ibid*, 2 and 13 November). KMT estimates are rather lower with 7,000 men for 1948 operating in Dongjiang, Beijiang and the northern areas of northern Canton province (*Gongfei zhanli panduan biao*). The East River Column was either under the direction of the Southern Branch Bureau of the CCP or the South China Work Committee (*Nanfang gongzuo weiyuanhui*; interview with Kuo Hualun, 1982). Fang Fang was also active in the Dongjiang area in the late forties (Xia Yan, 'Jinian Pan Hannian tongzhi', *Zhengming*, p 71).

See also 'Guangdong diqu', in *Zhonggong suo xuanchuan [neizhan dier zhanchang] zhi yanjiu*, pp 31-9, and Luo Chun, 'Huanan renmin wuzhuang'. Also 'Huanan dihou jiefangqu (Dongjiang he Qiongya) gaikuang', in *Kangri zhanzheng shiqi jiefangqu gaikuang*, (nd), pp 123-32.

I was interested during my stay at Peking University in autumn 1984 to discuss the question of 'Chinese patriotism in Canton province' against the background of these fairly modest resistance forces, with Chinese scholars from various research institutes, but it seems still premature to venture on any conclusions. On the Southern Bureau, see *Huiyi nanfangju*, vol 1, (Chongqing (Chungking), 1983), comp Chongqing xiandai gemingshi ziliao congshu bianweihui.

Notes to Chapter Two

1 *Liao Chengzhi de yisheng*, p 26.
2 *Ibid*. See the reproduction of his letter to his mother of 31 August 1937.
3 *PD*, 17 June 1983 which simply states that he 'was sent to the KMT area'. According to Arai, *Shu Onrai no jissen*, p 176, 'Liao received an order from Mao Zedong in October 1937 and it was decided that he should work in areas under the control of Chiang Kaishek.' According to *[Renzhong] Renwuzhi*, (Taipei), p 308 Liao was appointed Secretary of the South China Office after the outbreak of the war against Japan. When Liao returned to Guangdong he was appointed member of the Committee for South China, the 'Nanfang gongzuo weiyuanhui'. See also *Zhonggong ganbu jiyao*, p 20. Elsewhere it has been mentioned that Liao 'went to Guangdong after the outbreak of the anti-Japanese war and was appointed member of the South China Bureau' ('*Huananju weiyuan*') (in *Feidang zhongyang renshi ziliao*, (Taipei, 1 January 1960), p 83). 'The Communist Party sent Liao Chengzhi down south to engage in activities there. Liao plied forth and back between Canton and Hong Kong, negotiating and discussing the incorporation of Red Army guerrilla units situated in the border area between Fukien and Kiangsi into the New Fourth Army: also he was extremely busy to discuss the strengthening and expansion of the anti-Japanese United Front with the provincial party headquarters of the KMT.' (Kusano Fumio *Konichi Shina sokoku no gensei*, (1942) entry for 24 February 1938).
4 Uemura Shinichi, *Chugoku nashiyonarizumu*, passim; on the background of the students' movement in December 1935, see also Kuo *Analytical History*, vol 3, p 148, and Ilyushechkiĭ, 'Studencheskoe dvizhenie 9 dekabrya 1935 g v Kitae', *Kratkie soobshcheniya Instituta Vostokovedeniya* VII (1952), pp 3-19.
5 See also Shang Mingxuan and Liu Jiaquan, 'Song Qingling yu dierci guogong hezuo de shixian', *PD*, 24 January 1983.
6 Jing Puchun, in *Liaogong zai renjian*, p 2.
7 Xu Dixin, in *Liaogong zai renjian*, p 32.
8 On Pan Hannian's pre-1949 (underground) activities, see Xu Dixin, 'Pan Hannian zai Xianggang', *Zhengming*, (1983.4), pp 69-71 and Xia Yan 'Jinian Pan Hannian tongzhi', *Renmin ribao*, (23 November 1982). He had been purged as early as 1955 ('Pan Hannian nianje'). In 1981 Liao Chengzhi submitted a proposal for Pan Hannian's rehabilitation which was accepted by the Central Committee. The official restoration came with the 'Circular from the Party Central' on 23 August 1982, five years after his death in April 1977. (Lian Guan, in *Kakyoho*, 25 June 1983).
9 Lian Guan, in *Liaogong zai renjian*, p 23 and *Guangming ribao*, 17 June 1983.
10 *Nanfang ribao*, 27 June 1983.
11 Tong Xiaopeng, in *Liaogong zai renjian*, p 19.
12 *Guangming ribao*, 25 June 1983.
13 Ding Cong, in *Liaogong zai renjian*, p 46.
14 Xu Dixin, in *Liaogong zai renjian*, p 32.
15 Donald W Klein and Anne B Clark, *Biographic Dictionary of Chinese Communism, 1921-1965*, (Cambridge, Mass, 1971), pp 509 ff.
16 Tong Xiaopeng, in *Liaogong zai renjian*, p 19.

The War

17 Arai, *Shu Onrai no jissen*, p 176. According to Chu, 'Liao Ch'eng-chih', p 87, he went to Canton in 1938 'and after the city was occupied by the Japanese, he escaped to Hong Kong.' *Liao Chengzhi de yisheng*, p 27 contains a picture of Liao Chengzhi in Hankou, dated December 1937. On that picture he wears a badge of the General Headquarters of the 18th Army Group (Hankou); this was the official name of the '8th Route Army' after the official incorporation of the Communist forces into the forces of the National Government.
18 *Liao Chengzhi de yisheng*, p 28.
19 Kusano, *Konichi Shina*, p 307.
20 Published in February 1938 by Jiuwang chubanshe (quoted by Liu Jiaquan, 'Liao Chengzhi').
21 The CCP sent Liao Chengzhi, Zhang Yunyi, Pan Hannian and Yun Guanging to Hong Kong and Canton in order to set up offices of the Eighth Route Army. Liao Chengzhi was in charge of the Eighth Route Army Office in Hong Kong, and when Zhang Yunyi was transferred to the New Fourth Army, Liao was also in charge of guiding the work of the Office in Canton. Liu Jiaquan, 'Liao Chengzhi'. See also Tong Xiaopeng, in *Liaogong zai renjian*, p 20.
22 Lian Guan, in *Liaogong zai renjian*, p 23. Li Shaoshi was executed by the government in Chongqing on 8 October 1945 (*Biographic Information*). 'Jinian Song Qingling tekan' also contains a picture taken in 1938 which shows Liao Chengzhi, Clark, France, Song Qingling, Liao Mengxing, Deng Wenzhao and Eberstein.
23 Arai, *Shu Onrai no jissen*, p 176 and Liu Jiaquan, 'Liao Chengzhi'. As Situ Huimin puts it: 'At that time he guided our work in South China representing the Party Central' (*daibiao dangzhongyang lingdao le women Huanan de gongzuo*). This should of course not be taken to mean that Liao was in charge of operations in South China in general; most likely he was in charge of 'united front work'. For further information on the CCP organisation in the South, see *Nanfangju dangshi ziliao dashiji*, comp Nanfangju dangshi ziliao zhengji xiaozu, Chongqing, 1986 [Zhongguo gongchandang lishi ziliao congshu]. See also endnote to this chapter on the CCP's party organisation in the south.
24 *Renwuzhi*, p 308, and Kusano, *Konichi Shina*, p 307.
25 Liao Mengxing, *Wode muqin He Xiangning*, p 34. Liu Jiaquan, '"Gonghe" dui kangri zhanzheng de zhongyao gongxian - jinian kangri zhanzheng shengli sishi zhounian', *PD*, 1 September 1985; Liu Jiaquan, '"Gung Ho" and China', *China Reconstructs* (June 1986), pp 56-9 ; Liu Jiaquan, 'Song Qingling yu dageming shiqi de fun yundong', *PD*, 5 May 1985; Liu Jiaquan and Xiao Xing, 'Liao Chengzhi yu Kangri minzu tongyi zhanxian', *Renmin ribao*, (27 May 1984), p 5; Liu Jiaquan and Gan Yongmei, 'Song Qingling yu baowei Zhongguo tongmeng', *PD*, 25 May 1986.
26 Cai Jianguo, in *Liaogong zai renjian*, p 31.
27 Tong Xiaopeng, in *Liaogong zai renjian*, p 20. On Song Qingling's 'Baowei Zhongguo tongmeng', see 'Jinian Song Qingling tekan', p 12. The successor to this alliance after the Japanese defeat in 1945 was the China Welfare Foundation ('Zhongguo fuli jijinhui'), see *ibid*, p 12.
28 Ye Jianying, 'Huiyi Liao Zhongkai xiansheng de pianduan', *Xinhua ribao* (Hankou), 20 August 1938, quoted in Liu Jiaquan, 'Liao Chengzhi'.
29 Situ Huimin, in *Liaogong zai renjian*, p 26.
30 Qian Junrui, in *Liaogong zai renjian*, p 36. See also Xi Siming, in *ibid*, p 118.
31 *Nanfang ribao*, 15 June 1983. Ichikawa Kenjiro, 'Nitchu senso Tonan Ajia kakyo', in 'Nitchu senso to kokusaiteki taio', special issue of *Kokusai seiji*, no 47, (December 1972), pp 75-87. See

also Jean Lacouture, *Ho Chi Minh*, (Paris, 1967), pp 69 ff, quoted by King C Chen, *Vietnam and China 1938-1954*, (Princeton U P, 1969), p 189. Referring to Thailand, Yoji Akashi mentions that 'the list of organisations which the Chinese Communist Party controlled through its Hong Kong bureau, headed by Liao Ch'eng-chih, is long' (*The Nanyang Chinese National Salvation Movement, 1937-41*, (University of Kansas, 1970), pp 97 and 179).

32 Yi Meihou, in *Liaogong zai renjian*, p 85.
33 Yoji Akashi, *The Nanyang Chinese National Salvation Movement*, pp 73-4. On further involvement, see also Mantetsu Shanhai jimusho chosashitsu, comp *Kakyo chosa iho*, vol 1, (Dairen, 1940), pp 46 and 49.
34 The financial support of Overseas Chinese has traditionally played an important role in Chinese revolutionary movements. On the role of overseas support for the (communist) effort in the anti-Japanese war, see for example *Xinhua ribao* of 27 February 1938. On Liao's involvement in attracting and organising such support, Lin-Liu, in *Liaogong zai renjian*, p 82. The mobilisation of Overseas Chinese by the Communists during the anti-Japanese war included for instance the establishment of a 'Federation for National Salvation of Overseas Chinese in Yanan', (*Xin Zhonghua bao*, 12 September 1940), and the holding of a 'Congress of Anti-Fascist Representatives of the Peoples of the East' (*Dongfang ge minzu fan faxisi daibiao dahui*) in Yenan on 27 November 1941 (Nakayasu, *Saikin Shina kyosantoshi*, p 351). See also *Riben touxiang hou de gongchandang*, (December 1947), pp 121-2. It goes without saying that the Chinese government in Chungking had its own links with Overseas Chinese in Southeast Asia. It is not quite clear whether Liao was formally in charge of the Office for Overseas Chinese Affairs within the South China Party Branch (Nakayasu, *Saikin Shina kyosantoshi*, p 432). Elsewhere he has been called 'one of the founders of work in the area of Overseas Chinese Affairs within the CCP (Lin-Liu, in *Liaogong zai renjian*, p 82).
35 Liao also had an influential position in the Hong Kong newspaper *Shishi wanbao* (Nakayasu, *Saikin Shina kyosantoshi*, p 202). On his role in the Hong Kong paper *Huashang bao* and other publications directed towards Overseas Chinese, see Xia Yan in *Liaogong zai renjian*, p 12. According to Liu Jiaquan ('Liao Chengzhi') Liao gave direct guidance to several newspapers for Overseas Chinese, like *Huashang bao* and he also lent support to the *Jiuwang ribao* published in Canton.
36 Liu Jiaquan, 'Liao Chengzhi'.
37 Situ Huimin, in *Liaogong zai renjian*, p 26.
38 *Ibid.*
39 He was of course vulnerable to attacks. The following passage may be intended to clear Liao from any suspicion of having been 'too soft' on the government under Chiang Kaishek, a point on which Wang Ming has been severely attacked: 'In 1940 he took part in a conference organised by the Yangtze Bureau of the CCP in Wuhan. At this conference Wang Ming insisted that the funds and material support gathered by Liao Chengzhi and others should first be handed over to the KMT for which he was severely criticised.' (Arai, *Shu Onrai no jissen*, p 176).
40 Yu Feng, in *Liaogong zai renjian*, p 43. It may be remarked that at least in his student days Liao seems to have paid only scant attention to his own dress and appearance (Tan Juezhen, 'Ryo Shoshi o kataru', *Ekonomisuto*, p 29).
41 Si Mu in *Liaogong zai renjian*, p 18.

42 While Liao's character has usually been described as easygoing, affable, easily approachable, there has also been some criticism concerning his overbearing attitude towards his subordinates (Chang Chuan, 'Liao gong de zuihou shike', p 27).
43 Liao Chengzhi, 'Zenyang shishi yiwu bingyizhi', *Jiefang*, vol 1, no 18 (2 October 1937).
44 'Wang ni chuzou yihou', *Kangzhan daxue*, di 2juan, di 4qi (10 February 1939, fukanhao), pp 4-8.
45 Yin Linping, in *Nanfang ribao*, 23 June 1983.
46 See for instance Li Fanfu and He Ganzhi, *Zhongri guoli de duili*, 1936, and also Song Feiru, *Riben zhanshi waijiao neimu*, (Chungking, 1940), p 138.
47 *Nanfang ribao*, 23 June 1983. The first 'Worker-peasant-soldier Soviet' in China's history was set up in November 1927 in the districts Haifeng and Lufeng in the Dongjiang area.
48 This was confirmed by Kuo Hualun. The military activities of the guerrilla forces were under the direction of the South China Bureau or the South China Work Committee of the CCP (interview, 1982). Recently several accounts of guerrilla activities in Canton province during the war have been published in the PRC but not in time to be included in the present study. See for example, Wang Zuoye, *Dongzong yiye*, Guangdong renmin, 1983, and Guangdongsheng danganguan comp *Dongjiang zongdui shiliao*, Guangdong renmin chubanshe, 1984. According to Liu Jiaquan ('Liao Chengzhi') Liao carried out orders from both the Guangdong Provincial Party Committee and the Central Committee in directing guerrilla activities. Liao was also involved in the coordination of guerrilla activities in Guangdong province when the Japanese had landed in Daya Bay, collaborating with Wu Youheng and Zeng Sheng, and he also assisted Ye Ting who directed military activities in 1939. See also *Guangdong renmin kangri youji zhanzheng huiyi*, Huanan renmin chubanshe, 1951, and 'Guangdong dongjiang yu qiongyai de youjizhan', *Kangri zhanzheng shiqi de Zhongguo renmin jiefangjun*, Peking, 1953 [Zhongguo xiandaishi ziliao congkan].
49 Yang Kanghe, in *Nanfang ribao*, 27 June 1983, and Yin Linping, in *ibid*. See also Xia Yan in *PD*, 15 June 1983.
50 Yu Feng, in *Liaogong zai renjian*, p 44.
51 According to Liu Jiaquan Liao planned the evacuation from Hong Kong together with Zhang Wenbin. See Liao's preface to *Dongjiang zongdui shigao*, (Guangdong Renmin chubanshe, 1983) (quoted by Liu Jiaquan, 'Liao Chengzhi').
52 *Ibid.*
53 Jing Puchun, in *Liaogong zai renjian*, p 3. See also Yang Kanghe, in *Nanfang ribao*, 27 June 1983.
54 *Zhonggong ganbu jiyao*, p 20, and *Renwuzhi*, p 308.
55 *Liao Chengzhi de yisheng*, p 29. There he wrote a poem in which he expressed his anger and hatred towards the enemy.
56 Liu Jiaquan, 'Liao Chengzhi'.
57 *Liao Chengzhi de yisheng*, p 30.
58 This was confirmed by Kuo Hualun, according to whom the arrest took place in May 1942 simultaneously with Ye Ting's arrest (interview 1982).
59 Secondary sources disagree on several details concerning Liao's imprisonment. According to *Feiyou zhongyao jianghua huibian*, p 372, Liao is reported to have said that he had been locked up for four years. It seems unlikely that *Zhonggong ganbu jiyao*, p 20 is correct when placing his arrest in 1943. See also *Fei dangzheng ganbu. Renshi ziliao huibian*, (Taipei, August 1966), p

897, and *Biographic Information*: 'Arrested by Kuomintang in May 1943 and held in prisons in Kiangsi and Szechuan until 22 January 1946.' A further detail was provided by Zhang Wen who recalled how Liao sold his Swiss-made wristwatch for $8 in order to buy food (in *Liaogong zai renjian*, p 35; see also Liu Tianfu, *Nanfang ribao*, 16 June 1983).

60 'Xiangqi le Liao Chengzhi de yifu hua', p 33.
61 Kuo, *Analytical History of the Chinese Communist Party*, Book 4, pp 448-50.
62 *Liao Chengzhi de yisheng*, p 30.
63 Jing Puchun, in *Liaogong zai renjian*, pp 3-4.
64 *Liao Chengzhi de yisheng*, p 31.
65 *Ibid*, p 4.
66 *Ibid*, p 30.
67 Li Xianyao, in *PD*, 6 March 1983.
68 *Ibid*. The account is also found in Gong Ping [Jiangxisheng zhengfu wenshiguan] 'Xiangqi le Liao Chengzhi de yifu hua', *Liaowang*, November 1982, p 33.
69 *Ibid*. See also Xia Yan's reference to paintings made by Liao and shown to him (in *PD*, 15 June 1983).
70 Tong Xiaopeng, in *Liaogong zai renjian*, p 20.
71 Lu Dingyi, *PD*, 19 June 1983. See also Yu Feng, in *Liaogong zai renjian*, p 44.
72 Yu Feng, *Liaogong zai renjian*, p 44.
73 Zhang Wen, in *Liaogong zai renjian*, p 35 and Xu Dixin, *ibid*, p 33.
74 'Although Zhou Enlai protested many times and demanded his release Chiang continued to refuse.' (Arai, *Shu Onrai no jissen*, p 177). See also Tong Xiaopeng, in *Liaogong zai renjian*, p 20. For other references to calls for Liao's release, see Ookubo, *Chugoku kyosantoshi*, p 667. *Chugoku kyosantoshi shiryoshu*, vol 2 (Keiso shobo, 1975) pp 70 ff (on 5 June 1944); *ibid*, p 131 (Lin Zuhan's statement of 1 September 1944), and p 427 for a further statement of July 1945. See also Joseph W Esherick, ed, *Lost Chance in China, the World War II Despatches of John S Service*, (New York, 1974), pp 110-11: 'Later she [Madame Sun Yat-sen] remarked that the brother of a woman who acts as her secretary was in a concentration camp in Kiangsi. (The man's name is Liao [Ch'eng-chih]. He is the son of Liao Chung-kai, one of the original Kuomintang leaders. The case is well known because of the family's prominence.) ...' See also Lin Tsu-han's Report to the People's Political Council of 15 September 1944: '... For instance, those involved in the New Fourth Army Incident were arrested without a trial. Yeh Ting is not a Communist and at that time he came out at the request of the Chinese Communist authorities. Then there are Liao Cheng-chih, Chang Wen-ping and others who were detained in Kwangtung. We hope that these men as well as many other political offenders will be released simultaneously.' (*China Handbook 1937-1945*, (New York, 1947), pp 90-1).
75 Liu Tianfu, *Nanfang ribao*, 16 June 1983.
76 See the editorial in *Jiefang ribao*, 14 June 1945, quoted in *Chugoku kyosantoshi shiryoshu*, pp 412 ff.
77 Tong Xiaopeng, in *Liaogong zai renjian*, p 20.
78 Liao Mengxing, *Wode muqin He Xiangning*, pp 38-40. When Guilin came under threat of occupation the CCP assisted He Xiangning to move to a different place close to where Ye Ting was staying.

The War

79   *Ibid*, p 36. According to Li Renren, however, it was Chiang Kaishek who tried in vain to lure He Xiangning to Chongqing (Li Renren, 'Xiangning laoren zai gui liangsan shi', *Huiyi yu huainian - jinian geming laoren He Xiangning shishi shi zhounia*, pp 168-71), (reprinted from *Guangxi ribao*, 8 November 1962).

80   *Ibid*, p 38. Among those in opposition were Li Jishen, Liu Yazi, Li Zhangda, Cai Tingkai and Chen Cisheng.

81   Liao Mengxing, in *Wode muqin He Xiangning*, p 39, and Li Renren, 'Xiangning laoren zai gui liangsan shi', pp 168-9. On Ye Ting, see also a Soviet eulogy by M Yuriev, 'Ye Ting, Organiser of a Revolutionary Army', *Far Eastern Affairs* (Moscow), no 4, (1979), pp 176-84.

82   Liao Mengxing, *ibid*, p 39.

83   *Ibid*, p 39 where Li Minxin and Li Langru are also mentioned.

84   *Ibid*, p 40.

85   *Ibid*.

86   Jing Puchun, in *Liaogong zai renjian*, p 4.

87   *Ibid*.

88   Lu Dingyi, in *PD*, 19 June 1983. According to Chu, 'Liao Ch'eng-chih', p 87 'He was bailed out by Wu Ching-heng because of his father's contributions to the National Government'.

89   Arai, *Shu Onrai no jissen*, pp 177-8. See also Lu Dingyi, *PD*, 19 June 1983.

90   Xu Dixin, in *Liaogong zai renjian*, p 32.

91   Tong Xiaopeng, in *Liaogong zai renjian*, p 21 and *PD*, 21 June 1983. On this occasion he also met Zhu Xuefan for the first time (*Huashengbao*, 19 June 1983). See also Xu Dixin, *Liaogong zai renjian*, pp 32 f.

92   Huang Dingchen, in *PD*, 16 June 1983.

93   Arai, *Shu Onrai no jissen*, pp 178-9. See also Luo Guangbin and Yang Yiyan *Hongyan*, (Peking, 1977), a novel which is not wholly fictitious.

94   *Nanfang ribao*, 23 June 1983.

95   According to Tong Xiaopeng on 31 March (*Liaogong zai renjian*, p 21). If that is correct it is most unlikely that Liao had in fact been scheduled to fly from Chungking to Yanan on 8 April. I cannot explain this apparent contradiction.

96   *Nanfang ribao*, 23 June 1983. Liao is said to have become involved in the work of the communist delegation to the tripartite talks shortly after his release (Jing Puchun, in *Liaogong zai renjian*, p 5).

97   Huang Dingchen, in *PD*, 16 June 1983. There is also a report on the incident in *Qiqibao*, April 1946, for instance.

98   Jing Puchun, in *Liaogong zai renjian*, p 5. Also Ogawa Heishiro, *Pekin no yonen*, (1977), p 203.

99   Tong Xiaopeng, in *Liaogong zai renjian*, p 21.

100 Lian Guan, in *Liaogong zai renjian*, p 24.

101 Li Mei, in *Liaogong zai renjian*, p 167.

102 Liao at times acted as a spokesman for Zhou Enlai, head of the CCP delegation to the Tripartite Talks: 'The Head of the Chinese Communist Party Delegation (Chou) to the Special Representative of the President (Marshall), Shanghai, September 16, 1946 ... In case there is any matter you want to communicate to me, please contact my associates Messrs Liao Chengchi and Wang Bingnan here.' *Foreign Relations of the United States 1946, Vol X: The Far East: China*, (Washington, 1972), p 194.

'Minutes of Meeting Between General Marshall and General Yu Ta-wei at no 5 Ninghai Road, Nanking, September 1946, 10 am. General Yu Ta-wei said that Mr Liao (member of the Chinese Communist Party delegation office at Nanking), Communist spokesman, had stated that General Chou would not come back to Nanking until the Committee of Three met. General Marshall stated that he had been informed of this same thing by General Chou in a personal letter from General Chou.', *ibid*, p 206.

103 Tong Xiaopeng, in *Liaogong zai renjian*, p 21.

104 *PD*, 19 June 1983. According to Lu, he and Liao were frequently in touch with each other between 1946 and the end of the civil war. He also met again with Lian Guan and Qiao Guanhua who were all close collaborators, *Liaogong zai renjian*, p 24.

105 *Nanfang ribao*, 23 June 1983.

106 'Shortly after He Xiangning had moved to Hong Kong she was looking after two grandchildren - a girl, called Yajian (Liao Jian), then seven and a half years old and a boy of not yet four years, Kaisun (presently Head of the Overseas Chinese Affairs Commission, and better known under his name Liao Hui).' See Zhao Yuanbao, 'Gemingzhe, gemingzhe de muqin', *Huiyi yu huainian - jinian geming laoren He Xiangning shishi shi zhounian*, (reprinted from *Guomin* (Guangzhou), 5 March 1946), p 234. In 1947 Liao had three children, a girl nine years old, a boy six years old and a baby girl of two months, *Biographic Information*.

107 Liao Jian, in *Liaogong zai renjian*, p 154.

108 Jing Puchun, in *Liaogong zai renjian*, p 5. According to *Liao Chengzhi de yisheng*, p 36 he returned in September.

109 On the importance of the study of CCP media for an understanding of the CCP's - and the PRC's - foreign affairs apparatus, see for example remarks on Li Chuli and Xu Bing in *Renwuzhi*, p 1145 and a remark by Gao Yangwen, in *Liaogong zai renjian*, p 39. The recent release of numerous new documents and memoirs in the PRC seems to make previous studies on the origin of the foreign affairs apparatus appear dated. For references to Xinhua's broadcast station, see *Renwu zhuanji*, (periodical), p 393 and *Nitchu yuko undoshi*, p 40 on the reception of these broadcasts in Japan. See Nihon Chugoku yuko kyokai (seio) chuo honbu, comp, *Nitchu uuko undoshi*, (1975).

110 Arai, *Shu Onrai no jissen*, pp 179-82. The lack of precise data on appointments during this period of civil war and confusion is not very surprising. It has also been claimed that he acted as party spokesman for some time (*Five Hundred Leading Communists*, p 22). *Yinianlai (sanshiwunian) zhi zhonggong dangpai gongzuo*, (March 1947), vol 7, p 31 does not list Liao among higher officials in the party structure in South China and Hong Kong.

111 Qian Junrui, in *Liaogong zai renjian*, p 37.

112 Gao Yangwen, in *Liaogong zai renjian*, p 39.

113 See also *Liao Chengzhi de yisheng*, p 36.

114 Jing Puchun, in *Liaogong zai renjian*, p 5. On the evacuation under Liao's guidance, see also Qian Junrui, in *ibid*, p 37.

115 Arai, *Shu Onrai no jissen*, p 180.

116 Tanaka Kyoko, 'Mao and Liu in the 1947 Land Reform: Allies or Disputants?', *China Quarterly*, no 75, (1978), pp 566-93, passim; see also Frederick Teiwes, 'The Origins of Rectification: Inner-Party Purges and Education Before Liberation', *China Quarterly*, no 65, (March 1976), pp 15-53.

117 For comparison, see Luo Chun, 'Huanan renmin wuzhuang. baohu gongshangjie liyi de shishi banfa', (xerox copy from an unidentified book), pp 46-8, on criticism of leftist attitudes in the reform movement in Guangdong in the late forties.
118 Lu Dingyi, in *PD*, 19 June 1983.
119 On President Truman's opposition to Britain's aspirations in Hong Kong, see Harry S Truman, *The Memoirs of Harry S Truman, Year of Decisions, 1945*, (1955), pp 62 and 378 ff.
120 Liao Mengxing, *Wode muqin He Xiangning*, p 41. See also Xu Dixin, 'Pan Hannian zai Xianggang' and Xia Yan 'Jinian Pan Hannian tongzhi'.
121 *Renwuzhi*, p 535. Fang Fang belonged to a group of cadres involved in guerrilla struggle and intelligence work in southern China who later maintained close links with Liao Chengzhi. See for example Xu Dixin, 'Pan Hannian zai Xianggang', p 70. Fang Fang was also active in the Dongjiang area in the late forties (Xia Yan, 'Jinian Pan Hannian tongzhi', *Zhengming*, p 71). Liao's relationship with Fang Fang is not always altogether clear. According to Cai Xiaoqian Fang Fang's political importance during the early fifties was greater than Liao Chengzhi's. Liao was then merely involved in United Front Work, whereas Zhao Anbo and Zhang Xiangshan were responsible for relations with the Japan Communist Party (interview 1982). According to one source Liao supported Wu Jishen against Fang Fang during the Cultural Revolution (Ding Chuyuan, 'Mao fei fadong wenge yu feiwei qiaowu gongzuo', *Qiaowu weiyuanhui diqing yanjiushi*, (5 April 1969), p 88).
122 Liao Mengxing, *Wode muqin He Xiangning*, p 41.
123 *Ibid*.
124 Co-operation between the CCP and other dissenting groups was, however, not always smooth, despite rather successful Communist attempts to penetrate non-Communist political organisations such as the Democratic Alliance *(Minmeng)*. *Wei Guomindang geming weiyuanhui chengli yilia zhi huodong gaikuang*, (1 December 1948), p 74, and *Gongfei yu minmeng zhi jian*, (Zhonglian, 1947). The *Minmeng* also established an American branch, see *Yantai ribao*, 2 February 1947.
125 *Gongfei yu minmeng zhi jian*, p 17.
126 On the early history of international front organisations see for example Witold S Sworakowski, ed, *World Communism. A Handbook, 1918-1965*, (1973), pp 495, 492 ff. Liu Ningyi overtook Liao Chengzhi for a period during the Cultural Revolution.
127 See for example *Yantai ribao*, 13 August 1947 containing a call to Overseas Chinese to contribute funds.
128 See for example *Renwuzhi*, p 5199. Liao Xiao had been appointed secretary of the Shanghai Central Committee and when the office moved to Hong Kong in 1948 he called a meeting of Communist cadres in Taiwan to be held in Hong Kong.
129 *Mu Xin. Nanxian xunhui*, p 150.
130 *Gongfei yu minmeng zhi jian*, pp 6 ff.
131 *Yantai ribao*, 13 August 1947.
132 Xia Yan, in *Liaogong zai renjian*, p 12.
133 Chen, *Vietnam and China*, pp 188-9.
134 *Liao Chengzhi de yisheng*, p 36.

CHAPTER THREE

The Foundations of the PRC's Japan Policy

It seems that the Liao family arrived in Peking in spring 1949.[1] He Xiangning continued united front work and was finally also appointed formal head of the new Overseas Chinese Affairs Commission (OCAC). At about the same time Liao Chengzhi began to be appointed to a host of positions, also mainly in the area of united front work. With victory for the Communist side approaching rapidly, the CCP began to set up Communist-controlled mass organisations. Some of these, such as the New Democratic Youth League (NDYL), were established as sub-organisations of the CCP from which future party members would be drawn.[2] Others, however were intended to function as communist dominated mass organisations charged with mobilising non-party members from all walks of life.[3] From their inception Liao played an important role in a number of these organisations. In 1949, for instance,[4] he was appointed to the World Federation of Democratic Youth,[5] the NDYL, and the All-China Federation of Democratic Youth. Towards the end of the year he was appointed Vice-Chairman of the Overseas Chinese Affairs Commission of the provisional government, the General Administrative Council and was a leading member of the Chinese Peace Committee. He also held leading positions in other organisations but it may be claimed that these appointments outline the areas of activity for which Liao would later become best known in addition to his role in relations with Japan. To many Chinese overseas Liao is perhaps best known as the PRC's most prominent spokesman on Overseas Chinese affairs. The OCAC was formally headed by his mother, but there is no doubt that Liao outranked her. From a human point of view it was a situation which could easily have led to friction, since as a Chinese son he would still owe his mother filial obedience:

> In the beginning of the PRC He Xiangning was a delegate in the Central People's Government and Head of the OCAC. Liao was its first deputy-head, presiding over daily work. ... He Xiangning had her own opinions concerning Liao. When Prime Minister Zhou Enlai learned of this he told He Xiangning with a smile: 'Liao is already a very mature cadre with responsibilities within our party. You, Mrs He, must not always treat him like a little child. From now on I will have him report to you more often, and, if there is a problem you can come and see me.' As a result, He Xiangning also began to smile.[6]

Liao Chengzhi's organisational seniority certainly derived from his high position within the party, as a member of the Central Committee and other party organs, while He Xiangning is not known to have occupied any position of importance within the CCP. At the Second Session of the 7th Central Committee in March 1949 Liao had been appointed a full member of the Central Committee.[7] Although party rules obliged him to obey his party superiors rather than his mother it can be imagined that there may have been situations where loyalty to the party conflicted with the Chinese tradition of filial obedience. The passage just quoted is perhaps the only published indication of occasional friction with his mother, while most (eulogistic) accounts praise Liao's filial attitude towards his mother.8

During the fifties Liao often appeared in his capacity as a member of youth organisations such as the NDYL and the ACDFY. He attended numerous functions and gave countless speeches and was active in executive organs of these organisations.9 His position as highest ranking party member in the OCAC was unrivalled over a long period, but the same cannot be said of his role in the youth movement. He occupied high positions on the executive bodies of the NDYL and the ACDFY, but his role diminished sharply with their reorganisation in 1958.10 When appointed to the NDYL executive in April 1949 he was concurrently made head of the Liaison Office of its Central Committee. On balance it would seem that the main focus of his activity in the youth organisations was not so much united front work within China but was specifically directed towards international front organisations where he became an important PRC representative. To some extent the same is true for his role in the field of Overseas Chinese affairs.11

Liao's ultimate importance and ranking as a politician were to hinge on his appointments within the higher organs of the CCP, such as the Central Committee of which he became an alternate member *in absentia* in 1945 and a full member in November 1949.12 Unfortunately information is scarce about the composition of party offices and committees under the Politburo and the Central Committee, and there are few published sources indicating his membership of other high party organs. He was mentioned repeatedly, however, as Deputy Director of the Central Committee's United Front Work Department, and also occupied an important position in the Foreign Liaison Office of the Central Committee.13 Liao's position in the United Front Work Department after its reorganisation in 1956 is not clear, but it seems safe to assume that he continued to play an important role on two other committees: the Foreign Liaison Office and the External Affairs Committee, both of which appear to have played a major role in co-ordinating the activities of various front organisations. The Foreign Liaison office was responsible for the SCRF, the China-Japan Friendship Society (CJFA), CPDS, AASC, the Journalists' Association ACJWA, the Buddhist Society, the PCA, CPFT and the Memorandum Trade Office among others. It appears that the External Affairs Committee had a sub-committee on Japan which assumed co-ordinating functions in the following organisations concerned with Japan-related activities: CPDS, ACFTU, CPFT, SCRF, ACFDY, AASC and other similar bodies. Liao held positions in almost all organisations under the Foreign Liaison Office and in organisations under the sub-committee on Japan except for the ACFTY, where the leading role was played by Liu Ningyi and, of course, organisations such as the Women's Federation.

Liao's functions within these organisations may be divided into two groups: firstly, activities that focussed on a particular *geographical area*, such as Japan, Hong Kong and other areas with a considerable proportion of Overseas Chinese; Southeast Asia and, for certain periods, also Africa and Latin America. From a *functional* point of view Liao was also heavily engaged in activities carried out within the framework of international Communist front organisations such as the World Federation of Democratic Youth (WFDY), the World Peace Council (WPC) and the Afro-Asian Solidarity Council to which Liao was delegated on the basis of his positions in the ACFDY, the China Peace Committee and such organisations.[14] Liao's role in Japan policy will be more fully described later. It should be emphasised that all his other activities were mainly confined to the first two decades following its foundation when to a large extent the PRC was isolated diplomatically from countries of particular significance such as the USA, Japan and the non-Communist countries of Southeast Asia. One of the important aims of the United States in those years was the political, diplomatic and economic isolation of the PRC following the outbreak of the Korean war. Already in the early stages of the Cold War (after 1947) the CPSU had made use of international Communist front organisations as one way of reducing its international isolation, and organisations under the control of the CCP took an active part in these activities.[15] Some of the goals pursued by these front organisations were frequently regarded as subversive by governments towards whom these activities were directed. In the absence of diplomatic relations the PRC often made use of such organisations as a means of conducting 'unofficial' diplomacy, and attempted to make use of unofficial contacts thus established in order to break out of its isolation.

Although most international front organisations were ostensibly under the control of the Soviet Communist Party there are indications that the CCP attempted to operate more independently even during the early fifties.[16] In addition to formal diplomacy and 'people's diplomacy' carried out through mass organisations, the CCP also entertained formal links at a party to party level with foreign Communist parties, an area even less accessible to academic research than other areas of foreign relations. It seems likely that Liao had some advisory role in particular concerning links with Communist parties in his area specialisation. He may also have been involved in some advisory role on relations with the CPSU regarding questions such as the Afro-Asian movement.[17] Liao's activities repeatedly touched on areas of great importance for intelligence gathering, but for obvious reasons it seems futile to speculate on his links with PRC intelligence organisations.[18]

As previously mentioned Liao's formal position in the government structure of the PRC did not reflect his importance in areas such as foreign policy, in particular relations with Japan. As far as is known, before the establishment of the PRC, he was not involved in the formation of the CCP's views on Japan in any major way.[19] It is difficult to pinpoint a date for the beginning of Liao's career as the PRC's foremost Japan specialist. The most likely date would be either 1952 or shortly thereafter when 'Liao set up a Japan [policy] group under the guidance of Prime Minister Zhou and developed private exchanges between China and Japan'.[20] Two factors in particular contributed to his career in the field of Japan policy. The outbreak of the Korean War, followed by the interruption of links between Japan and the PRC, had made the establishment of formal diplomatic and trade relations with Japan very unlikely for the foreseeable future. This forced PRC leaders to

The Foundations of the PRC's Japan Policy

look for ways to undermine the wall of isolation surrounding the PRC. They decided to employ the concept of 'people's diplomacy' to achieve informal contacts first of all with formal relations remaining the long-term goal. Within the existing network of mass and other organisations set up to conduct 'people's diplomacy' - most notably, mass organisations and international front organisations - Liao already occupied a leading position making him the most likely candidate for the position of Japan specialist, not least due to his personal knowledge of the country, its language and culture, and his links with both Japanese and Overseas Chinese in Japan. Also, his pre-1949 background of leading positions in CCP media is in some respects similar to that of many leading professional PRC diplomats. Nevertheless, there is some doubt as to whether he would have evolved as the leading Japan specialist had there been formal diplomatic contacts between the PRC and Japan right from the establishment of the PRC in 1949.

One last remark has to be added on Liao's appointments to leading positions in the youth movement. Apparently he had no role of national importance in the youth movement before 1949, but he could already look back on many years of experience in the organisation of non-party members in support of the CCP. To mention but a little of this, he himself had been active in student politics in the twenties, in the organisation of Chinese seamen in China and overseas, and had shown himself capable in the field of united front work during his years in Hong Kong. Last but not least, as a son of Liao Zhongkai and He Xiangning, he definitely enjoyed a considerable advantage over possible rivals due to the standing of his parents in the eyes of numerous non-Communist (Overseas) Chinese.

The many new appointments and duties must have meant a considerable change in Liao's personal life. In contrast to available sources for the pre-49 period there are only relatively few sources that convey to us something about Liao Chengzhi as an individual. Consequently, the style of the following pages dealing mainly with Liao's involvement in PRC relations with Japan will also have to change. Nevertheless it indicates, through an analysis of his political activities, the extent to which Liao, as an 'individual politician,' left his mark on the PRC's relations with Japan. This picture will of necessity be on a much more abstract level.

Despite his extremely busy schedule Liao also found time to devote his attention to the theatre, film and the media.[21] Reference has already been made to his love of painting and drawing, and his involvement in an amateur theatre group during his stay in Yanan in 1937. It is easy to imagine that for somebody as lively, witty and humorous as Liao Chengzhi these sideline activities may have brought him more immediate personal satisfaction than his life as a Communist official:

> In early spring of 1949 preparations were under way for the establishment of the China Youth Art Theatre Academy under the guidance of the Youth Federation. At the beginning of April Liao Chengzhi, who was secretary of the Youth Federation at the time, was also appointed head of the Academy. On the day we (first) met him the staff of the Theatre were all awaiting his instructions, and his first words were: 'My name is Liao Chengzhi, my weight two hundred

pounds...' A burst of cheerful laughter immediately narrowed the distance between him and us ... On the eve of the establishment of the PRC he was already a leading person combining many important positions ... but every day he could still be seen going to the theatre, talking and laughing, involving himself deeply in all the affairs of the Academy and showing concern for every member. Sometimes he was really tired out, would lie down on a sofa in the office ... for a rest, and even then would have frequent talks with comrades in the office.22

Liao was involved closely in the theatre for four years,23 during which time he also promoted the setting up of a children's art group.24 The Academy was close to where journalists from the *People's Daily* worked before the office in Wangfujing Road was built, and Liao could sometimes be seen eating a late night snack with some actors at a street vendor's place nearby.25 His activities at the Academy included discussion of the political and ideological content of the plays to be performed, and he also wrote an introduction to 'Fang Zhenzhu', Lao She's first play after 1949.26 He was also very much interested in the growth of the film industry, especially in Hong Kong in the seventies and eighties. Only pressure of work prevented his appearance on the stage in a play (*Pavel Korchagin*).27 At the same time he was an enthusiastic photographer, and in fact presided over the work of the editorial committee of the large picture volume *China* published on the occasion of the 10th anniversary of the establishment of the People's Republic.28 Later he also took his own 8mm films, a luxury few Chinese could afford.29

To understand his role in PRC relations with Japan it is necessary to deal in detail with the history of negotiations between the PRC and Japan on the return of Japanese civilians and the repatriation of prisoners-of-war which contributed essentially to the build-up of relations during the fifties in the face of heavy American pressure, and which laid the groundwork for contact between the PRC and members of the governing conservative Liberal Democratic Party (LDP).

Post-War Negotiations

After the Second World War the allies faced the tremendous task of demobilising and repatriating several million Japanese soldiers. From China alone about three million Japanese were returned to Japan with American assistance. Large numbers of Japanese soldiers had also been captured by the Soviet Red Army during its campaign in northeastern China following the entry of the Soviet Union into the war against Japan. The campaign had been prepared for a considerable period in consultation with the USA, and was one of the biggest operations by the Soviet Red Army in the Second World War.30 Negotiations for the return of Japanese held in the USSR encountered many obstacles. Only a few surveys of these negotiations exist in Western languages. It is certain, however, that reports about the treatment of Japanese in Soviet camps contributed substantially to the negative image of the Soviet Union in Japan. In addition, the way negotiations were conducted, and attempts at indoctrination, did nothing to reduce tension.[31] On 21 April 1950 a TASS communiqué announced the completion of the repatriation programme, adding however that 2,458 war criminals were still being held. Among these were 971 who were transferred to the PRC government. These formed the largest group of 'war criminals' held in the PRC.[32] The remainder consisted mainly of Japanese military personnel who had participated in Yan Xishan's army in North China and had continued to fight the People's Liberation Army (PLA) until 1949. It may be added that some Japanese military personnel had also interfered directly or indirectly in the civil war between the PLA and the national (KMT) administration in many places, refusing to surrender to PLA units and offering resistance until government forces arrived.[33] On the other hand, some Japanese also fought on the side of the Communist forces, later gratefully acknowledged by Zhou Enlai.[34]

In addition to those 'war criminals' there was a much larger group of Japanese civilian residents. While later Communist estimates put the number of civilians at approximately 30,000, Japanese estimates were usually higher and a huge number of Japanese were still missing in China. One should also include here a number of Japanese fishermen detained off the Chinese coast after December 1950.[35] In fact, one of the main features of subsequent negotiations between the PRC and Japan consisted of Japanese government efforts to obtain complete (as far as possible) information about the number of Japanese still in China, as well as efforts to secure the prompt release of all Japanese wishing to leave the PRC. The Chinese side preferred to negotiate through semi-official organisations which could promise full co-operation, while the final implementation would depend on government action not formally bound by any 'private' agreement. One of the difficulties in tracing the negotiations concerning the repatriation of Japanese (and Chinese) to their respective countries lies in the fact that apparently not all understandings reached in formal and informal talks are to be found in written statements issued by the delegations mainly concerned with the issue of return and repatriation.

It became obvious that any improvement in relations between the PRC and Japan would depend to some extent on the successful solution of these questions. Viewed from the eighties the difficulties standing in the way of a prompt solution are easily overlooked. Even before the outbreak of the Korean War Chinese attitudes were still influenced heavily by a deep-seated distrust of a possible revival of Japanese military strength backed by US support. From the PRC viewpoint, one of the major - if not the most important - functions of the Sino-Soviet alliance of 1950 was to deter the potential threat of combined US-Japanese military power. PRC charges concerning possible Japanese re-armament, which, at the time, seemed groundless in the light of Prime Minster Yoshida's public refusal to rearm Japan, may appear to have some justification in the light of several Japanese government documents concerning this topic which were recently declassified and made public.[36] As a result of the Korean War there was severe pressure on all non-Communist countries not to engage in trade and other contacts with Communist countries beyond what was considered acceptable by the USA and her allies.[37] It should not be forgotten moreover that both the Soviet Union and the PRC had been advocates of 'revolution' in Japan.38 The basic direction of Japanese foreign policy towards the PRC and the administration in Taiwan province had been shaped prior to Japan's independence in April 1952. Prime Minister Yoshida Shigeru seems to have contemplated a limited peace with Taiwan, and all-out political and commercial relations with the PRC as the ultimate goal of the Japanese government.39 US policy aimed at isolating the PRC was particularly important during the Korean War, but continued well into the late sixties and remained an important, if not the most important, factor in many Japanese policy decisions concerning the PRC, a point well understood by PRC leaders.

It is not surprising, then, that one of the basic aims of PRC foreign policy was to break out of this isolation, to work towards a lessening of co-operation between Japan and the USA, and to isolate the ROC administration. At this point it is worthwhile recalling that as early as 1948 the CCP had initiated a movement called 'Oppose America, Support Japan' to foster Japanese independence from the United States.40 It is hardly possible to review any foreign policy move by the PRC during this period without keeping these basic aims in mind, a point well illustrated by Robert B Ekvall in his description of the approach adopted by the PRC in the Sino-American negotiations on the return of US civilians after the Korean War:

> The Chinese, by the calculated piecemeal release of the Americans at a rate designed to bring the most benefit in support of their objectives, wished to gain the maximum advantage from an accumulation of quasi-diplomatic contacts and exchanges, such as well-publicized official contact in regular meetings and the issuance of statements of mutual agreement. The sum total of all this would be an impressive picture of the United States and the People's Republic of China, in increasing harmony, moving towards settlement of such matters as embargo and cultural exchange and finally arriving at a meeting at the foreign ministers level which, inferentially, could only result in *de jure* as well as *de facto* recognition. Such a sequence would enhance the international status of the People's Republic of China and, as a useful by-product, would arouse aggravation, frustration, and mounting suspicion of United States motives and policy in the very heart of the Republic of China in Taiwan.41

The approach adopted by the PRC was, however, not new. These tactics had been developed first and most fully in PRC relations with Japan. The PRC was aware, however, that formal relations could only be realised in the distant future. The San Francisco Peace Treaty of September 1951, followed by Japanese independence and the conclusion of a peace treaty between the ROC and Japan, implied that in the face of US opposition Japan would not be able to sever links with the ROC in order to establish formal links with the PRC. Also, the structure of Japan's foreign trade with the US made Japan very vulnerable to US pressure in the event of major Japanese foreign policy changes.42 These circumstances severely limited the choices available to PRC policy, since PRC claims to sovereignty over Taiwan required that Japan break off relations with the ROC before establishing relations with the PRC. The importance of the Taiwan factor in impeding the establishment of formal relations between the PRC and Japan is also illustrated by the fact that the USSR was able to resume diplomatic relations with Japan as early as 1956, while PRC relations with Japan were normalised only in 1972.[43] Although Soviet and PRC foreign policy had remained co-ordinated until the autumn of 1954, the Soviet Union by that time could 'seek a bilateral resumption of diplomatic relations by offering to divorce its problems from China's and accept the basic provisions of the San Francisco Treaty'.[44] It is perhaps ironic that, in many ways, the PRC was more successful in the long run in building durable and stable relations with Japan than was the Soviet Union.

One of the earliest attempts by the PRC to widen its relations with Japan by re-establishing trade ties while fostering the growth and strength of the Japan-China Friendship Association (JCFA) and the Peace Association (PA) had its origins in the preparation and holding of the Moscow Economic Conference in April 1952. This conference had been designed specifically for the purpose of frustrating the American containment policy by trying to increase trade between Communist and non-Communist countries.[45] In February Nan Hanchen had appealed to Hirano Yoshitaro to attend the conference and he, in turn, discussed the matter with Murata Shozo[46] and Ishibashi Tanzan among others.[47] Due to the opposition of the Japanese government the Conference was attended only by Mrs Kora Tomi, joined by two other Socialist Diet members, Hoashi Kei and Miyagoshi Kisuke, who only arrived after the conference had ended.[48] Almost simultaneously invitations had been issued for a Preparatory Conference for a Preparatory Meeting for the planned Peace Conference of the Asian and Pacific Region (*Ajia taiheiyo chiiki heiwa kaigi junbikai*) which was to be opened on 28 May.[49]

The first non-official trade agreement between a PRC and a Japanese delegation was signed on 1 June 1952,[50] and Liao was said to be one of the leading figures behind it.[51] Two weeks later the Japanese foreign ministry published a white book critical of trade with the PRC.[52] For various reasons, including government opposition, the private trade agreement resulted in no significant upturn of bilateral trade. At about the same time there was a First Preparatory Meeting in Peking of the Peace Conference of the Asian and Pacific Region, followed in October by the conference itself, also in Peking.[53] Liao was much praised for his organisational efforts which contributed to the success of the conference,[54] but similar praise was also given to Song Qingling and Guo Moruo as its initiators.[55] In the resolutions of the conference concerning the Japanese question an appeal was made for a peace delegation to be sent to visit the Japanese people 'who are fighting for peace'.[56] Reflecting the moves in Peking, a Japanese Peace Association had also been established.[57] This organisation, as well as the JCFA (formed between October 1949 and October 1950), was ready to join the Japanese Red Cross delegation visiting Peking in January 1953 to start negotiations for the return of Japanese civilians. Previously the Japanese government had tried to approach the problem through the International Red Cross, but without success.[58] On 1 December 1952 an invitation was issued for negotiations on a non-official, non-governmental level.59 In choosing to conduct these negotiations with a Japanese delegation consisting of members not only of the Japanese Red Cross which was allied closely to government thinking, but also of the PA and the JCFA, the Chinese side established a clear link between the objectives of the Peace Conference and the negotiations for the return of Japanese nationals. Thus the ground was prepared for contacts not easily interrupted without endangering the repatriation process. This approach entailed obvious advantages for the PRC over an agreement between both Red Cross organisations, in which the political content would be minimised. When the Japanese joint delegation issued an invitation for a Chinese Red Cross delegation to visit Japan later as a sign of its gratitude for the agreement reached in spring 1953, it was natural that the Japanese government should regard such a delegation as part of the 'grand design' published during the 1952 Peace Conference to broaden contacts and increase PRC influence in Japan by working towards the exchange of numerous delegations.60

As it turned out, participation in the negotiations on repatriation by the JCFA and the PA as well as the substantial co-operation by both organisations in the repatriation programme was a vital factor in enabling them to reach a much larger segment of the Japanese population than had been possible hitherto. The Japan Communist Party (JCP) became involved, issuing an order on 19 January 1953 to expand the repatriation movement in order to 'foster Sino-Japanese friendship on a nationwide scale'. New organisations were created, joined by Japanese returnees from China as well as members of the JCFA, PA and other organisations. A very important factor was also that through these organisations Japanese of all political convictions were reached, including members of the staunchly anti-communist Liberal Party.61 During the negotiations in Peking Liao led the Chinese Red Cross delegation. He was formally acting on behalf of the President of the Chinese Red Cross Society, who was said to be ill.62 At first glance it may have seemed strange that Liao had been chosen leader of the Chinese delegation. His background had little to do with the Red Cross. This was however not the first time that he had been engaged in 'international' negotiations. In 1946 he had taken part in the trilateral truce committee. Also, by this time he could already look back on several years of active engagement in meetings of international front organisations, where Chinese delegates came into regular contact with members of Japanese delegations. During his publicised trips abroad Liao had been a member of the Chinese delegation to a Congress of International Students in Prague (August 1950) and to the First International Conference of the WFDY in Warsaw (November 1950). He had been in Korea between March and May 1951, was a delegate to the Executive Committee meeting of the WFDY in Budapest (May 1951) and visited Korea again for several weeks from 15 March 1952. This dry list understates the drama sometimes involved: during his visit to Korea he got caught in fighting and barely escaped at one stage.63 One account mentions his having been involved in efforts to reach a truce agreement in Korea.64 During the Cultural Revolution he was accused of having obstructed the 'Support Korea, Resist America' Campaign for fear of antagonising other governments. Such an accusation might easily be taken as proof of Liao's 'moderate' leanings but there is no concrete evidence to support this specific point.65 He had been a leader of the first nonmilitary delegation from Peking to North Vietnam (August/September 1952).66 He was subsequently a delegate to the PCAPR, and attended the Congress of the Peoples for Peace organised by the WPC in Vienna in December 1952, returning to Peking towards the end of the month.67 Little is known about his activities during these meetings, but it seems safe to assume that he took the opportunity to discuss with Japanese delegates questions relevant to PRC policy towards Japan. One of the best known Japanese delegates to many of these international conferences was Saionji Kinkazu:

> I met Liao for the first time in 1952. In December of that year the World Peace Conference was held in Vienna. New China, which had just been established three years previously, also sent a large delegation with Song Qingling as honorary chairman and Guo Moruo as its chairman, while Liao Chengzhi and Liu Ningyi were vice-chairmen. Liao's grasp of foreign languages surpassed all others, and he was ... fluent ... in Japanese and English, as well as French and German.68

At that time Liao was the only Central Committee member among the leaders of the delegation (Liu Ningyi became a member in 1956) and thus was held to be *de facto* the highest-ranking leader of the delegation. Since he had also been one of the leading figures behind the Peace Conference of the Asian and Pacific Region Liao's leadership during the repatriation talks was perhaps less unusual than might at first appear. His heavy involvement in the international peace movement and international united front work underlined even more the eminently political character of the repatriation talks. During their stay in Peking, the members of the Chinese and the joint Japanese delegations had a number of formal and informal meetings. Under the communiqué signed on 7 March 1953, more than 26,000 Japanese were able to return to Japan. The published communiqué did not refer to the return of Overseas Chinese in Japan, yet under the same programme more than 2,600 Chinese residents in Japan were able to return to the PRC between June and October 1953.69 In contrast to the Soviet approach to repatriation, the Chinese negotiating techniques had been beneficial to the image of the PRC in Japan:

> A public opinion poll ... taken in late April 1953 after the first boatloads of repatriates had arrived, shows clearly that respondents who had changed their opinion about Communist China reported the repatriation programme as the most important reason (59.3%). For most of them the change of opinion had been to a favourable one.70

In July, shortly before the Korean armistice agreement was reached, a Japanese delegation visited Peking to escort home the remains of Chinese killed in Japan during the war. The visit was made within the framework of the 1953 agreement. During the same visit one delegation member, from the important trade union federation SOHYO, Yanagimoto, was the first 'legally' to visit the Chinese General Trade Union office in Peking, demonstrating the new possibilities for contacts that would not have existed without the 1953 programme for the return of Japanese nationals.71 In this delegation were Lin Suiyong and his daughter Lin

Liyun, both Overseas Chinese from Taiwan province living in Japan. Lin Liyun met Liao Chengzhi for the first time during this visit. Later she moved to the PRC and became a leading official dealing with Japan.[72] In June 1953, shortly before the visit, a Japanese-language periodical entitled *Jinmin Chugoku (People's China)* had been started. It was one of the first publications in the Japanese language, and Liao Chengzhi was the leading figure behind its publication.[73]

Although the repatriation programme had not yet been completed, and was to encounter new difficulties later, a general change of mood in Japan towards relations with the PRC became apparent in June when both houses of the Japanese parliament passed resolutions calling for the promotion of Sino-Japanese trade.[74] In September a commercial mission led by Ikeda Masanosuke of the LDP left for Peking and concluded the second Private Trade Agreement on 29 October 1953.[75] On 30 October 1953 Mrs Li Dequan, Head of the Chinese Red Cross, informed visiting Japanese Diet members that collective repatriation had now been completed.[76] However, an unknown number of Japanese had still not been able to return, and there was uncertainty about the fate of many Japanese missing after the war. Furthermore there was the question of the return of Japanese 'war criminals', a point on which the PRC refused to negotiate for a long time. A new repatriation agreement could not be reached before November 1954, although the next phase of collective repatriation started even before this agreement had been concluded. Between September 1954 and March 1955 an additional 3,000 Japanese returned to Japan. Shortly afterwards, in the summer of 1955, the programme encountered new snags which also contributed to a considerable deterioration in the climate between the PRC and Japan. The desired breakthrough, especially in the field of economic relations, however had been made in 1953 with the signing of the Second Trade Agreement, followed by the Third Trade Agreement in May 1955.

Informal and 'Official' Contacts

Following the First Trade Agreement a number of moves had been made in Japan to organise for the coming upswing in trade with the PRC. In the summer of 1953 the Japanese were given to understand that the PRC was prepared to consider a request for the sending of a trade mission. Subsequently members of the Diet Members' League for the Promotion of Sino-Japanese Relations sent a delegation to the PRC under Ikeda Masanosuke. This was unusual in so far as Ikeda did not belong to the majority party of Yoshida, but was a member of the Jiyuto under Hatoyama which had recently left Yoshida's party. In his welcome speech Nan Hanchen unexpectedly offered to conclude a Second Trade Agreement, adding that they would like to make steady progress in developing Sino-Japanese relations, irrespective of differences in the political system of the two countries. In his recollections Ikeda stressed that it was the Chinese who brought up the concept of 'separation of politics from economics', and it was also the Chinese who suggested the form of barter trade that turned out to be one of the reasons for the relatively slow growth of bilateral trade. Although PRC economic specialists like Nan Hanchen finally signed the communiqué, the Japanese delegation also held talks with Zhou Enlai, Chen Yun (Vice-Premier) and Peng Zhen (Mayor of Peking). During the visit Liao is said to have made great efforts towards its success, but his precise involvement is not clear.[77] He did serve as interpreter during a private talk of more than two hours between Zhou Enlai and Ikeda. By choosing Central Committee member Liao rather than an 'ordinary' interpreter Zhou may have tried to emphasise the importance and the confidential character of their discussions. Also, Zhou may have wished to be accompanied by somebody who would be able to make a thorough analysis of Ikeda's behaviour during this confidential session, a function that Liao apparently also exercised during numerous later negotiations.[78] Similarly, Liao was also frequently the only other Chinese present in private talks between Mao Zedong or Zhou Enlai and highly placed Japanese visitors.

On 30 October 1953 Li Dequan told Japanese parliamentarians that collective repatriation had been completed,[79] implying, in effect, that for the solution of outstanding problems new negotiations would have to be undertaken, thus putting pressure on the Japanese. This relatively tough stance should be seen in the context of a two-pronged PRC approach, combining pressure tactics with other moves meant to make a more favourable impression on Japanese dealing with the PRC.

Until about 1952 the PRC had given open support to JCP moves to initiate a revolution to overthrow the government. When this approach not only failed, but was counterproductive, greater emphasis was laid on 'peaceful' moves to increase links with various groups in Japan who might influence public opinion in the PRC's favour, and increase pressure on the government by causing a split between 'hardliners' in the governing party and groups prepared actively to oppose them.[80]

The slogan 'peaceful co-existence' had been in currency for some time in the international Communist movement.[81] Following the truce in the Korean War two months after Stalin's death the term gained increasing prominence in Communist propaganda, and at meetings of international front organisations. In the meantime Liao had attended a number of such meetings. He participated in the WPC conference held in Vienna from 23-28 November 1953; attended an extraordinary session of the WPC in Berlin in May 1954; and, perhaps most important of all, was also a member of a Chinese delegation to the International Conference on Relaxing World Tension in Stockholm in June 1954. Of great interest is his departure for Moscow as a member of the Chinese delegation on the occasion of Stalin's funeral, but I have been unable to discover substantial information about his role. Following the 'settlement' of problems concerning Indo-China at the Geneva Conference in April, international tension appeared to lessen.

A similar trend could also be observed in the PRC's attitude to Japan. The new tone perhaps was illustrated best by a change in attitude towards Overseas Chinese living in Japan, as reported by a prominent Overseas Chinese from Japan:

> In the summer of 1953 when I met Liao ... in Tianjin he moved and encouraged the members of the Tokyo Association of Overseas Chinese (*Tokyokakyokai*) by saying: 'You're doing your work well',

and gave specific explanations concerning the government's decision to give special treatment to Overseas Chinese returning to China ... Referring to the topic of Sino-Japanese friendship he stressed that they should obey Japanese laws, respect the customs of the Japanese people, strive to promote friendly relations with the Japanese people, but should not enter Japanese political organisations (in Japan), and should also not form special political organisations for Overseas Chinese, nor should they meddle in Japan's internal policies. This is our government's foreign policy ... .[82]

For a considerable period the PRC had been trying to gain Japanese approval for the sending of a Red Cross delegation to Japan, invited by the three Japanese organisations who had negotiated the repatriation agreement as a sign of Japanese gratitude for PRC co-operation in this matter.[83] In July 1954 a peace delegation visiting Peking had addressed a cable to Japan to the effect that the Chinese Red Cross was ready to assist in the return of Japanese 'war criminals', followed by an announcement of the pardon and release of 417 such 'war criminals' in August.[84] One of the Japanese negotiators, Yanagida, had stressed in a cable from Peking that negotiations would have to be carried out through the joint office of the three associations that had previously taken part in talks on repatriation, thus once more making use of the absence of formal relations to carry out 'people's diplomacy'.[85]

While Japan was being drawn increasingly into exchanges of various kinds with the PRC, the PRC had taken the initiative in putting first political, then military, pressure on the ROC by attacking offshore islands under the control of the ROC. These attacks were followed by the development of stronger links between the USA and the ROC as expressed in the Mutual Defence Treaty concluded in December 1954, thus leading to renewed polarisation between the USA and the PRC. However, this did not result in a hardening of the PRC's attitude towards Japan, on the contrary in fact, and coincided with a 'peace offensive' following the end of the Geneva Conference. Part of this 'offensive' was the Sino-Soviet Common Declaration Concerning Relations with Japan of 12 October 1954.[86]

In October 1954 very important talks were held between a Japanese Diet delegation and Chinese officials, including Zhou Enlai. This visit became the starting point for the rapid development of economic, cultural and other 'friendly' (non-official) exchanges between Japan and the PRC.[87] At the same time the Soviet Union and the PRC on 12 October 1954 published a joint declaration concerning the resumption of official ties with Japan. The Japanese Foreign Ministry dismissed the declaration as part of a Communist peace offensive, designed to alienate Japan from the USA. Throughout the year efforts had been made to win the approval of the Foreign Ministry for a visit by an 'official' PRC 'Red Cross' delegation to Japan. Finally towards the end of October 1954 approval was given on condition that the delegation did not use the decision to its own political advantage - apparently a nominal condition to placate opposition to the visit.[88] The Chinese side however had left no doubt about its political intentions, as expressed in a statement by Zhou Enlai on 11 October.[89]

The Foundations of the PRC's Japan Policy

When Mrs Li Dequan set foot on Japanese soil as leader of a Chinese Red Cross delegation this constituted an important step in post-war relations between the PRC and Japan. The mission's presence in Japan signified that the PRC had been able to increase tensions within the Japanese government and the ruling party by making the issue a focus of intra-party dissent. The composition of the delegation, as well as the range of its activities during the visit, proved beyond doubt that its importance exceeded a 'Red Cross delegation visit'. In a talk on 30 October Liao Chengzhi admitted that China's reconstruction would be impossible without the co-operation of other countries, a virtual invitation to discuss the issue of trade with the delegation.[90] The official leader of the delegation, Mrs Li Dequan, a non-party member, was clearly outranked by the deputy leader, Liao Chengzhi, and also by Zhao Anbo.[91] As mentioned before, Liao had already replaced Mrs Li during the 1953 negotiations in Peking, due to her reported illness.[92] Yet, even now, it was Liao rather than Mrs Li who signed the second agreement on the return of Japanese, including a number of Japanese 'war criminals'. Li's name does not even appear as one of the signatories.[93] It was also Liao who announced during the visit that detained Japanese fishermen and their boats would be released.[94] Although it had been anticipated that Japanese government officials would keep away from contacts with the delegation, some important officials, among them Ogawa Heishiro from the Foreign Ministry, later Japan's first Ambassador to Peking, had a number of talks with members of the Chinese delegation.[95] One may assume that the main points discussed concerned the number of Japanese residents still remaining in the PRC and wishing to return, the question of the further release of 'war criminals' and their repatriation, as well as information about Japanese still missing on the mainland.[96] It seems the Chinese delegation made no concessions on these points, although the Japanese had high hopes in that direction.[97] Since the talks were kept confidential PRC inflexibility would not exert a strong negative influence on the overall success of the mission in the eyes of the public.[98]

The very fact of talks between PRC and Japanese government officials having taken place illustrates that it would be wrong to see the negotiations exclusively from the point of view of 'people's diplomacy'. It may be added here that, even before the delegation's visit to Tokyo, Liao had met important LDP members like Sakurauchi Yoshio, Nakasone Yasuhiro and Sonoda in 1954.[99] The significance of the delegation's visit also extended to the important realm of trade. Even before the arrival of the delegation there were strong hopes among the business community that the visit would contribute significantly to the development of trade with the PRC.[100] On returning home Mrs Li presented a report on the mission which included a list of Japanese who had met members of the delegation. This provides a vivid illustration of the appeal the mission had for the Japanese business community.[101] During the visit there were meetings with trade leaders like Murata Shozo, the first president of *Kokubosoku*, a leading Japanese organisation involved in trade with the PRC.[102] It is probably not far-fetched to assume that the visit of this delegation hastened the establishment of the Sino-Japanese Export-Import Association on 15 December 1954. The latter was in fact a 'front-organisation' of the Ministry of Trade designed to retain some sort of control over trade with the PRC in the face of the PRC's 'friendship policy'.103 This move was followed by an internal decision by the Japanese Foreign Ministry on 24 December to approve the visit of a PRC trade mission to Japan.104 Subsequent Japanese governments - whether under Hatoyama, Ishibashi or Kishi - differed in their attitude to trade with the PRC, but all were caught in the same dilemma: they were under pressure to support an expansion of trade with the PRC and at the same time, realised that the PRC's ultimate aim, implementation of formal diplomatic relations accompanied by severance of relations with the ROC, was impossible for the time being.

Concerning the return of Japanese and the repatriation of Japanese 'war criminals' the Chinese side had succeeded in conducting negotiations in such a way that all actions - such as the pardon of 417 'war criminals' (granted before the repatriation agreement) - were to be perceived as 'favours' given by the Chinese side to show its goodwill and friendship.105 At the same time the Chinese did not have to enter into specific future obligations. Formally speaking the delegation was not able to commit the PRC government, and it was pointed out repeatedly that this was due to the lack of normal relations between Japan and the PRC.106

The ROC had protested about the visit and one may also assume that the USA was none too pleased.107 Taking into account the wide links established by the delegation, the publicity effect, and the fact that the mission had been able to enter Japan against opposition both from within Japan and from abroad, one is justified in claiming that, from the PRC point of view, the mission had been very successful indeed.108 There can also be no doubt that it was Liao Chengzhi himself whose activities during the visit were the most important contribution to its success.

The Bandung Conference

For the next two or three months Liao's involvement in Japanese affairs seemingly was reduced while links between Japan and the PRC continued to grow, but Liao was apparently fully occupied with preparatory moves for the coming Bandung Conference of mainly 'third world' countries.109

In June 1954, the Communist bloc and Communist sympathisers in the free countries held a so-called international peace conference (*huanhe jushi guoji huiyi*) at Stockholm. At the suggestion of the Asian delegations, a resolution was passed to call a 'conference of Asian states' in India. Its aim, it was said, was 'to exchange views on questions concerning the Asian states in common, to promote general contacts and understanding in all directions among the peoples in Asia to help ease existing world tensions and produce a peaceful atmosphere.' Assuming the leadership of Asian Communists, the Chinese clandestinely manoeuvred at the preparatory meeting in February 1955, to have this conference held from 6-10 April, before convocation of the Asian-African Conference, and to bring up Zhou Enlai's 'five principles' as the main item for discussion. The Chinese Communists intended the Communist Conference of Asian States to control the Afro-Asian

Conference of the neutralist bloc. So the delegation to New Delhi led by Guo Moruo comprised 38 persons including prominent international front personages like Ding Xilin, Chen Hanshen, Liu Ningyi, Liu Guanyi and Liao Chengzhi.[110]

Among the Japanese participants to the New Delhi Conference were Hoashi Kei and Kora Tomi who had previously been involved in establishing trade links in 1952.[111] Throughout the period Hatanaka was involved in talks in New Delhi and subsequently in Peking.[112] It is highly significant that Liao Chengzhi was involved deeply in these preparatory steps towards the Bandung conference, and it is not surprising then that he was appointed one of the advisers to the PRC delegation.[113] Liao's approach was clearly *not from a bilateral* Sino-Japanese angle, but through the organisational network of international front organisations.

In December 1954 the conservative Yoshida cabinet had been replaced by a cabinet under Prime Minister Hatoyama who was to lead the government for the next two years. As early as the middle of December both Hatoyama and his Foreign Minister, Shigemitsu expressed their intention of normalising diplomatic relations with Communist countries as soon as possible. The theme was taken up again in a major policy speech by Hatoyama in January 1955. In the same month, however, the US Secretary of State, Dulles, argued that measures should be taken to strengthen the isolation of China in diplomatic and economic areas.[114] Subsequently it appeared that the Bandung Conference had contributed to the ambassadorial talks on the 'Repatriation of Citizens and other Substantial Questions' at Geneva which were announced on 25 July 1955,[115] and which in turn seem to have negatively influenced Japanese negotiations on the repatriation issue. During his visit to China in January Murata was clearly involved in significant talks with Chinese politicians like Zhang Xiruo, Qiao Guanhua and Zhou Enlai on strengthening relations between Japan and the PRC; if Liao took part, his presence was not prominent.[116] On returning to Japan, Murata met Prime Minister Hatoyama to whom he reported on the results of his visit, and also on the possible exchange of trade missions.[117] About ten days later it was agreed to send a Japanese delegation to take part in the Bandung Conference, followed by talks between Murata and Suzuki and officials of MITI on ways to 'unify' the channels of trade with the PRC.[118] In March, the first PRC trade delegation led by Lei Renmin arrived in Tokyo, and the Third Private Trade Agreement was signed in Tokyo on 4 May, preceded in April by the conclusion of a Fisheries Agreement.

The Japanese Prime Minister Hatoyama had agreed to send a delegation to the Asian-African Conference in Bandung apparently encouraged by the whole momentum of these developments, but it was a move that also initially met with Washington's disapproval.[119] Hatoyama had sent Takasaki, the Director of the Economic Planning Agency, to Bandung where he held talks with Zhou Enlai among others.[120] During the same period, on 16 April 1955 Ishibashi, then Minister for Trade and Industry declared that the exchange of trade missions could be considered if they were established on a private basis.[121]

Zhou's meeting with Takasaki had come about thanks to Liao Chengzhi's personal efforts.[122] Little has so far been published about the contents of these talks, but, as later events showed, the contact established between Liao and Takasaki Tatsunosuke at Bandung apparently played an important role in re-establishing PRC links with Japan after the disruption of all links in spring 1958.123 For the moment, however, nothing came of Zhou's invitation to Takasaki to visit China.124 In addition, Zhou and Liao later also met Foreign Minister Fujiyama Aiichiro for the first time.125 During the Bandung conference Liao also met Indonesian leaders and accompanied Zhou Enlai to Djakarta to meet government leaders.126 Since Liao was the leading representative of the PRC's OCAC it was a foregone conclusion that the topic of ethnic Chinese in Indonesia would be brought up during the talks.127 Several years later Liao would again be involved in this matter when the question became a major issue between the PRC and Indonesia. He was also present at several functions when the Indonesian Prime Minister Sastroamidjojo visited Peking in the following month (May 1955). During the Conference Liao also won some private sympathy from delegations wholly unrelated to the political success achieved by the PRC delegation:

> Ventilation was ... deficient in the conference rooms. ... in Western suits, and crowded into one room ... the heat ... [was] stifling, causing the delegates to perspire. Liao was also dressed in a Western suit and was suffering likewise. When the chairman requested him to speak he ... said: 'Before starting my speech proper I should like to make a proposal. Should we not take off our jackets? ...' With these words he ... remov[ed] his tie. Needless to say, his proposal provoked laughter from everybody, and gained an enthusiastic response.128

There were other problems unrelated to politics. Qian Ren recalls a confession Liao made after the conference:

> Liao said that after the Bandung conference he returned to China with some members of the Chinese delegation, and while shaking hands at the quay to say farewell an Overseas Chinese gave him some *liulian* fruit as a farewell present. The strange, pungent smell seemed to pervade the whole cabin. His colleagues left to avoid the smell, and ... he finally could not summon up the courage to try them. In the end he threw them secretly into the sea. Not long after he went to South-East Asia again and was once more presented with *liulian*. This time he recalled that in making revolution death was not to be feared. How much less eating *liulian*? Right! And then he opened them and tried first one, swallowing it reluctantly, then a second one ... finally a third and a fourth one ... the more he ate the better they tasted ...129

Several weeks later Liao exchanged tropical Indonesia for the far north: he was a member of the PRC delegation to the Helsinki Peace Conference in June 1955. Both the trip to Indonesia and that to Finland had implications for PRC relations with Japan, since the Helsinki Conference became an additional important impetus for the development of 'visiting' the PRC by Japanese, a development that followed Guo Moruo's initiative in December 1954.130

Notes to Chapter Three

1. Ding Cong, *Liaogong zai renjian*, p 47; Li Mei, *ibid*, p 167, and Wu Maosun, *Jingji ribao*, 24 June 1983.
2. For a list of congresses and meetings of the NDYI since its inception on 1 January 1949 see 'Fei xin minzhuzhuyi qingniantuan disanjie dahui zhi fenxi yanjiu', *Renshi diren*, VI, 5, pp 11 ff.
3. On the role of mass organisations, J R Townsend, *Politics in China*, (Boston, 1980), pp 95-8.
4. For a list of Liao's appointments between 1949 and the end of 1959, see the list of appointments in the appendix covering the first decade of the PRC.
5. This was a united front organisation different from the NDYL; leadership of the Federation entailed co-ordination and overall leadership of its various constituent associations. See A Doak Barnett, *Communist China: the Early Years*, (New York, 1964), pp 38 ff, and *Communist China 1958*, (URI, Hong Kong, 1959), p 162. See *Fuxiaobao*, 26 December 1940 for a report on the unification of the youth movement during the anti-Japanese war.
6. Wu Maosun, in *Jingji ribao*, 24 June 1983.
7. *Liao Chengzhi de yisheng*, p 39.
8. 'During the Cultural Revolution Premier Zhou had him live in a different place in Peking (in hiding) ... to protect him from the "Gang of Four". I visited him once a week and Chengzhi always enquired after ... his mother ... Mother also kept thinking of her child, and when she found out that [he] ... was not coming to wish her good morning, she asked us for the reason, and we had to tell her that he was so busy he could not return ...' Jing Puchun, in *Liaogong zai renjian*, p 7.
9. A survey of Liao's appearances in publications like *People's Daily* or *Zhongguo qingnian* would give an incomplete list of his activities in that area. The history of communist youth organisations has been neglected, despite Hu Yaobang's ascent to the chairmanship of the CCP. It is difficult to obtain a comprehensive list of their major activities. See *Fei xinmin minzhu zhuyi*, pp 11 ff.
10. *Communist China 1958* (URI), esp pp 162 f.
11. Corroborated by a survey of Liao's published activities (not included here). The most complete survey of Overseas Chinese affairs until the Cultural Revolution is Stephen Fitzgerald, *China and the Overseas Chinese. A Study of Peking's Changing Policy 1949-1970*, (London, 1972), recently criticised in C Y Chang, 'Overseas Chinese in China's Policy', *China Quarterly*, 82, (1980).
12. According to Kenneth Lieberthal, *A Research Guide to Central Party and Government Meetings in China, 1949-1975*, (New York, 1976), p 49 this plenum took place from 5 to 13 March 1949.
13. In early 1951 he was Vice-head of the United Front Work Department of the CCP CC (*URS Biographical Service*), also with security and intelligence functions; L P Van Slyke, *Enemies and Friends. The United Front in Chinese Communist History*, (Stanford, 1967), pp 217 and 238.
14. A survey of Liao's involvement in the youth movement based on reports published by NCNA confirms that his activities were limited, covering mainly the period until 1957. He was once listed as a Vice-President of the WFDY. Contacts made during meetings of international front organisations may have proved useful later on. Jacques Vergès for example attended an executive committee meeting of the International Union of Students in Peking in 1951 and later played an important role disseminating Chinese views in Africa. He also met Walter Sisulu, Secretary of the African National Congress who visited China after the World Youth Festival in 1953; Bruce D Larkin, *China and Africa 1949-1970*, (1971), pp 16 f. Liao and Liu Ningyi met with African delegates in Soviet financed international front organisations sometimes even before the 1949.

China's Relations with Japan

Liao's activities within the realm of the Peace Movement were most frequent during the years 1955-1963. On the history of the World Peace Council, see for example *Edi caozong xia de guojixing qunzhong zuzhi gaikuang diaocha*, (Taipei, September 1958), pp 2 ff.

15 The best treatment of front organisations is Van Slyke, *Enemies and Friends*. On Japanese front organisations and their links with Soviet and PRC organisations, see *Sayoku dantai jiten*, (comp, Shakai undo chosakai, Kyokuto shuppansha, 1968), passim. For a short survey of groups sympathetic to the Chinese communists before 1949 see *Nitchu yuko undoshi*, p 2.

16 Qian Junrui, in *Liaogong zai renjian*, p 38.

17 On CCP relations with Asian communist parties in the early fifties, Johnson, *The Threat of Soviet Imperialism*, p 360. Even in 1952 the JCP was still regarded as the PRC's main policy instrument towards Japan (Barnett, *Communist China*, p 261). On CCP relations with the JCP, also Paul F Langer, *The JCP Between Moscow and Peking*, and *Zai Zhu Mao fei shiyuan zhidao xia de Riben gongchandang*, (nd), p 15.

18 United Front work (and Overseas Chinese policy) is traditionally closely linked with intelligence work as is Communist media. Liao was prominent in all three. In that context, a number of Liao's closest collaborators in united front work had been involved in intelligence work at least until 1949. See for example Xu Dixin, 'Pan Hannian zai Xianggang', pp 69-70, Xia Yan, 'Jinian Pan Hannian tongzhi', *Zhengming*, p 71 and 'Pan Hannian jianjie', *Zhengming*, (1983,4), p 72.

19 Liao started receiving visitors to the PRC in 1949 (*Mainichi shinbun*, 11 June 1983 and *Guangming ribao*, 20 June 1983). On the formation of CCP views on post-war Japan, see Yamaguchi Ichiro, *Chugoku to Nippon*, (1976), pp 30 ff. Yamaguchi mentions Li Chunqing whose study *Riben wenti gailun* was published in Peking (*op cit*, p 177).

20 Sun Pinghua (*Kakyoho*, 25 June and 5 July 1983) says Liao Chengzhi set up a Japan policy group guided by Prime Minister Zhou. Evidence so far shows the committee would have been set up during the first years of the PRC. For previous references to such a group, see C Martin Wilbur, 'Japan and the Rise of Communist China', in H Borton et al, eds, *Japan Between East and West*, (1957), p 205; A Doak Barnett, *China and the Major Powers in East Asia*, (Washington, DC, 1977), p 126; and Chai-jin Lee, *Japan Faces China. Political and Economic Relations in the Postwar Era*, (Baltimore and London, 1976), p 216. 20 years later Liao is said to have had a similar policy committee on Taiwan, the 'Taiwan unit' (*Zhongyang ribao*, 22 February 1980 'Zhonggong tu liyong qiaobao jinxing tongzhan', and Chen, 'Taiwan in Peking's Strategy', in Hungdah Chiu, ed *China and the Taiwan Issue*, (New York, 1979), p 130.

According to Cai Xiaoqian Liao's activities were limited to united front work in the early fifties, and Fang Fang had a more important position; in the field of CCP/JCP liaison Zhao Anbo and Zhang Xiangshan played major roles (interview with Cai, 1982). This is partly corroborated by a reference in *Liao Chengzhi de yisheng*, p 46: 'From the spring of 1952 Liao presided over "private friendship work towards Japan" (ie people's diplomacy)'.

21 *Liaogong zai renjian*, pp 104 ff.
22 'Liaogong he huaju yishu', in *Liaogong zai renjian*, p 53.
23 *Ibid*, p 56.
24 *Ibid*, p 55.
25 Bo Sheng, in *PD*, 24 June 1983.
26 'Liaogong he huaju yishu', in *Liaogong zai renjian*, p 53.
27 *Liao Chengzhi de yisheng*, p 42.

28 *Ibid*, p 44.
29 *Ibid*, p 72.
30 Lilita I Dzirkals, *'Lightning War' in Manchuria: Soviet Military Analysis of the 1945 Far East Campaign*, (Rand Corporation, 1976), passim; also John Despres et al, *Timely Lessons of History: The Manchurian Model for Soviet Strategy*, (Rand Corporation, July 1976) [R-1825-NA] passim.
31 J J Morris, 'Japan and the Moscow Negotiations with the Soviet Union', *The World Today*, XII (November 1956), pp 438-47; R Swearingen, *The Soviet Union and Postwar Japan*, (Stanford, 1978), pp 41 ff, 102; Borton, *Japan Between East and West*, pp 214, 225. For a recent Japanese account, M Nakata, *Soren gaiko no kosho gijutsu*, (1980), [Soren gaiko, kosho gijutsu chosa kenkyu iinkai hokokusho].
32 See Zhou's statement of 11 October 1954 to a delegation of Japanese Diet members, *Sengo shiryo nitchu kankei*, comp, Ishikawa, p 32.
33 D G Gillin, *Warlord: Yen Hsi-shan in Shansi Province, 1911-1949*, (1967), pp 285 ff; J H Boyle, *China and Japan at War, 1937-1945; The Politics of Collaboration*, (Stanford UP, 1972), p 323.
34 Zhou Enlai's speech of 11 October 1954 (*Sengo shiryo nitchu kankei*, pp 27 f). See also 'Tairiku ni mada Nihonjin nokotte iru!', *Bungei shunju*, 35:3 (March 1957), pp 194, 196.
35 *Nitchu yuko undoshi*, p 71.
36 Yoshida's attitude to Communist China was less one-sided than is sometimes assumed: in 1950 he is said to have been willing to develop trade 'despite ideological differences and artificial trade barriers' (Barnett, *Communist China*, p 259). See also Takano Yuichi, 'The Japan-China Joint Communiqué and the Termination of War', *The Japanese Annual of International Law*, 17, (1973), pp 76-9, who says Yoshida seems to have contemplated a 'limited peace with Taiwan, with the establishment of all-out political peace and commercial relations with the PRC as the ultimate goal of the Japanese Government, as may be seen from his letter of 23 January 1951, to US Special Envoy John Foster Dulles'.
37 *Kihon shiryoshu. Nitchu kankei kihon shiryoshu*, Kazankai publ, (1970), p 125.
38 Harold C Hinton, *Communist China in World Politics*, (1966), p 372. See also *Renshi diren*, pp 3-5, and *Zai Zhu Mao fei*, p 17. *Fei dui Riben de shentou huodong*, (October 1964) [Feiqing yanjiu zhuanbao], pp 26-7 lists Japanese trade unions with close contacts with the CCP. For references to the alleged running of a Communist spy ring in Japan, see *Mainichi shinbun*, 17 July 1950, Ozawa Masamoto, *Uchiyama Kanzo den*, (1972), p 200; also *Nitchu yuko undoshi*, p 33.
39 Uchida Hisashi, 'Legal Aspects of Japan-China Trade Between 1949 and 1975', p 54, and Barnett, *Communist China*, p 259.
40 Jiang Ping, in 'Jinian Song Qingling tekan', p 57.
41 Robert B Ekvall, *Faithful Echo*, (New York, 1960), pp 87-8. The PRC approach was, however, not new; these tactics had been developed first and most fully in PRC relations with Japan.
42 On US influence on Japanese policy esp T J Pempel, 'Japanese Foreign Economic Policy: The Domestic Bases for International Behaviour', *International Organization*, XXXI.4 (Autumn 1977), p 729.
43 On 25 January 1951 a conference on 'the Japan Peace Treaty Question' was held by the Chinese People's Society for the Study of Foreign Affairs (*Zhongguo renmin waijiao xuehui*); Zhang Xiruo was chairman, Qiao Guanhua vice-chairman and Liao Chengzhi a Director (*Nitchu yuko undoshi*, p 43) supporting the view that Liao's position in this policy area was still limited.

44 J W Morley, *Soviet and Chinese Communist Policies Toward Japan, 1950-1957*, (New York, 1958), pp 1 ff; Swearingen, *The Soviet Union and Postwar Japan*, p 84; Hinton, *Communist China*, pp 159, 374. Also John Gittings, *The Sino-Soviet Dispute*, (Oxford, 1964), pp 56 f, and Uchida, 'Legal Aspects of Japan-China Trade', p 40.

45 Murata Shozo, Ishibashi Tanzan, Kitamura Tokutaro, Hirano Yoshitaro, Hoashi Kei and others took part in a Round Table Talk on the International Economic Conference and agreed to strive for participation in the Moscow Economic Conference in April. In a cabinet meeting on 30 January 1952 the government decided to oppose this participation (*NS*, 17 January 1952). This stance is seemingly contradicted by Yoshida's alleged support for moves to restart trade with the PRC: 'Yoshida ... requested the co-operation of Murata Shozo former president of Osaka Shosen ... in helping to improve relations with China. In 1952 Murata visited Peking ...', Ogata Sadako, 'The Business Community and Japanese Foreign Policy: Normalization of Relations with the People's Republic of China', *The Foreign Policy of Modern Japan*, R A Scalapino, ed, (1977), p 179. Note that the Chinese separately appealed to the Japanese to go to Moscow. According to *NS*, on 14 February 1952 Nan Hanchen appealed to Hirano Yoshitaro and others to participate in the Conference. In Japan Hirano was the driving force and the 'Japan-China Trade Promotion Conference (*Nitchu Boeki Sokushin Kaigi*) was formed in May 1952 in response to the World Economic Conference in Moscow that year, but in October 1954, dissolved into the Japan Council for the Promotion of International Trade (*Nihon kokusai boeki sokushin kyokai*) (Uchida, 'Legal Aspects of Japan-China Trade', p 39).

46 Again see Ogata, 'The Business Community', p 179.

47 Ishibashi was one of the initiators of a 'Round-table Conference on the International Economy' (*Kokusai keizai kondankai*). See *Nippon to Chugoku* of 1 February 1952, cited in *Nitchu yuko undoshi*, pp 54-5.

48 *Nitchu yuko undoshi*, p 54.

49 *NS*, 14 May 1952, citing *PD*. The announcement had been made on 12 March. The conference opened on 3 June with Kora Tomi and others attending (*NS*, 3 June 1952).

50 *Sengo shiryo nitchu kankei*, p 24.

51 *Kokusai boeki*, 16 June 1983. See however *Nitchu yuko undoshi*, p 210 which mentions only Xiao Xianqian and Sun Pinghua.

52 *NS*, 13 June 1952. The Japanese Foreign Ministry charged amongst others that Communist Chinese moves were aimed at driving a wedge between Japan and its friends.

53 *Nitchu yuko undoshi*, pp 56 ff; *Sayoku dantai jiten*, pp 1076-7. *Naigai shakai undoshi nenpu*, (Naigai chosakai comp 1965), pp 37 ff lists important events regarding the Peace Conference.

54 Zhu Ziqi, in *Liaogong zai renjian*, p 61.

55 'Jinian Song Qingling tekan', p 12. See also Ma Haide in *Liaogong zai renjian*, p 27.

56 *PD*, 13 October 1952, 'Guanyu Riben wenti de jueyi'.

57 *Nitchu yuko undoshi*, pp 28 f; on 'visiting' as a means to influence Japanese opinion, *op cit*, pp 29 ff. See also Borton, *Japan Between East and West*, pp 218 f.

58 *Nitchu yuko undoshi*, p 60. See also Kasama Shigetoshi, *Nitchu koryushi. Dainiji sekai taisen go*, (1961), p 50.

59 See the report by Xinhua Newsagency, 1 December 1952, repeated by Radio Peking, 3 December 1952 (1952.12.1 Radio Peking appeal *Nitchu yuko undoshi*, pp 59-60); Shimazu, 'Kikoku kosho no omoide' in *Nitchu yuko undoshi*, p 214. On 1 October 1952 the PRC government had issued a

The Foundations of the PRC's Japan Policy

declaration calling for a humanitarian approach to the question of repatriation (Kasama, *Nitchu koryushi*, p 50). Shortly before the 1 December announcement the government promulgated a set of emigration/immigration regulations for non-Chinese citizens, R K Jain, *China and Japan, 1949-1976*, (London, 1977), pp 10 ff; M Y Cho, *Die Volks-Diplomatie in Ostasien, Entstehung, Theorie und Praxis*, (Wiesbaden, 1971), pp 157 ff; Leng, *Japan and Communist China*, pp 72 ff).

60   Leng Shao Chuan, *Japan and Communist China*, (1958), p 74, fn 2. The hesitation of the Japanese government is not surprising if one recalls that the Peace Association had been specifically set up in preparation for the Peace Conference of the Asian and Pacific Region (*Nitchu yuko undoshi*, p 61). The use of the friendship movement as a political weapon against the US and the Japanese Yoshida government is described in 'Nitchu yuko undo o shido suru nikkyo no hoshin', *Koan joho*, no 10, pp 60 ff.

61   This is emphasised in *Nitchu yuko undoshi*, pp 2-3. The application of such united front tactics did not meet with unqualified success (*Koan joho*, no 10, p 65). A further example is provided by incidents during visits to the PRC by former Japanese soldiers led by Endo Saburo in 1956 and 1957, the reason being that some members of the group apparently did not wish to conform to behaviour expected by the Chinese side, Endo Saburo, 'Nitchu jugonen senso to watakushi - kokuzoku. aka no shogun to hito wa iu', *Nitchu shorin*, (November 1974), p 474.

62   Shimazu, 'Kikoku kosho no omoide', in *Nitchu yuko undoshi*, p 217.

63   Jing Puchun, in *Liaogong zai renjian*, p 5.

64   *Nippon Times*, 12 January 1956. Liao had also been involved in a committee to investigate 'US germ warfare' (*NCNA*, 12 March and 31 August 1952). He went to Korea accompanied by Li Dequan who would also accompany him to Japan in 1954 (*Gongfei ganbu jiyao*, p 285).

65   'Jinnianlai gongfei pohai qiaobao', pp 11-12. The campaign also involved the mobilisation of the support of Overseas Chinese, *Gongfei de qiaowu huodong*, (Taipei, April 1952), pp 92-3).

66   *NCNA*, 2 and 3 September 1952; *Shijie zhishi*, 34, 30 August 1952, in Chen, *Vietnam and China*, p 255.

67   *PD*, 13 December 1952. *Gongfei ganbu jiyao*, p 285: *Biographic Information*.

68   Saionji, in *Liaogong zai renjian*, p 146. On the meeting see also *PD*, 13 December 1952.

69   Radtke, 'Negotiations', p 198.

70   Wilbur, *Communist China*, pp 213-4. On the publicity effect, see also *Nitchu yuko undoshi*, p 62.

71   *Nitchu yuko undoshi*, p 81.

72   Lin Liyun, *Liaogong zai renjian*, p 76, and *Kakyoho*, 25 June 1983.

73   *Nihon to Chugoku*, 6-25 (1983); see also *Asahi shinbun*, 11 June 1983.

74   *Sengo shiryo nitchu kankei*, p 68.

75   Ikeda Masanosuke, *Nazo no kuni. Chukyo tairiku no jittai*, (1969), pp 295 ff, 333 ff; Okamoto Saburo, *Nitchu boekiron*, (1971), p 35; Hirai Hiroji, *Nitchu boeki no kiso chishiki*, (1971), pp 63 ff. The first trade agreement had been extended for another six months on 31 December 1952 and Nan Hanchen had stated on 23 June 1953 that the extension would be the last one, and blamed the insufficient results on interference by Yoshida (*NS*).

76   *Nitchu kankei shiryoshu*, p 344.

77   *Kokusai boeki*, 16 June 1983.

78   Ikeda, *Nazo no kuni*, pp 333 ff.

79   *Nitchu kankei shiryoshu*, p 344.

80 In various speeches by PRC government leaders a distinction is made between Yoshida as an 'enemy of China' and the Japanese people (see *Chukyo tai nichi juyo genronshu* end of 1953, but also 1955); there seems to be a change of attitude since Zhou Enlai's talks to Japanese delegations in October 1954 (*Chukyo tai nichi juyo genronshu*, 1955, p 44).

81 See Zhou on normalisation with Japan in a speech on 21 December 1954 in *Riben wenti wenjian huibian*, vol 1, (Peking, 1955), pp 143-4.

82 Chen Kunwang, in *Liaogong zai renjian*, p 131. Also *Nitchu yuko undoshi*, p 34. *Shijie heping yundong wenjian*, 1954-1956 lists Liao as a delegate to conferences of the Movement in Stockholm and Vienna.

83 The Japan Peace Association had issued an invitation to a Chinese Red Cross delegation on 17 October 1953 (*NS*). The Japanese government gave its approval on 3 August 1954 (*NS*).

84 *Nitchu kankei kihon shiryoshu*, p 345, and *Nitchu yuko undoshi*, p 67.

85 *NS*, 31 July 1954.

86 *Riben wenti wenjian huibian*, pp 25-26, and *Nitchu kankei shiryoshu* (1961), pp 6-7.

87 *Nitchu kankei shiryoshu*, (1945-1966 nen), pp 83-4, and *Nitchu yuko undoshi*, pp 67-8.

88 *Mainichi shinbun*, 28 October 1954; see also *Koan joho*, no 7, p 77 and Hatanaka Masaharu, 'Chugoku kojujikai daihyo no rainichi o megutte', *Sekai*, (November 1954) p 92.

89 *Nitchu kankei kihon shiryoshu*, pp 345-6.

90 *Mainichi shinbun*, 31 October 1954.

91 Klein and Clark, *Biographic dictionary*, p 79; *Mainichi shinbun (yukan)*, 30 October 1954, and Matsumoto Shigeharu, *Shanhai jidai*, (1977) p 24.

92 Shimazu, 'Kikoku kosho no omoide', *Nitchu kankei shiryoshu*, p 278.

93 *Sengo shiryo nitchu kankei*, pp 33-4, and *Nitchu kankei shiryoshu*, p 278. The memorandum has apparently not been included in *Riben wenti wenjian huibian*.

94 *Mainichi shinbun*, 2 November 1954, and *Nitchu yuko undoshi*, p 73. The day before Liao had announced preparations for the repatriation of Japanese from Vietnam, thus indicating that talks with Vietnam had been held on the issue (*NS*).

95 Ogawa, 'Chugoku zaikin o oete', in *Keizai to gaiko*, no 665 (October 1977), pp 10-11, and Ogawa, *Pekin no yonen*, p 10. On contacts with other officials see *Mainichi shinbun*, 11 N November 1954.

96 On the Japanese government's disappointment, *Mainichi shinbun*, 3 November 1954, also 1 September and 1 November, *Nitchu yuko undoshi*, p 68 and Hatanaka, 'Chugoku kojujikai', p 92.

97 *Mainichi shinbun*, 28 October 1954.

98 On 31 October, Liao said that the overall number of Japanese in China was 8,000, among them 4,700 women married to Chinese, and that about 940 men wished to remain in China, but he did not give this information as a 'government representative', *Mainichi shinbun*, 1 November 1954.

99 *Kokusai boeki*, 16 June 1983, and *Asahi shinbun*, 11 August 1978. During his visit to Japan, he also met again personal friends like Kusano Shinpei (Kusano, *Liaogong zai renjian*, p 148.

100 *Mainichi shinbun*, 27 October 1954.

101 *Riben wenti wenjian huibian*, vol I, pp 135 ff, and *PD*, 5 December 1954; see also a different report by Li Dequan in *Chuo koron*, 70-3 (March 1955), esp pp 208-10. For an intermediate report on the delegation, see *Guangming ribao* of 15 November 1954.

102 *Kokusai boeki*, 16 June 1983. In January 1955 Murata undertook fisheries talks with Lei Renmin.

103 Hisashi Uchida, 'Legal Aspects of Japan-China Trade Between 1949 and 1975', pp 39 f, and *NS*, December 1954.
104 *NS*, 24 December 1954.
105 *Nitchu kankei kihon shiryoshu*, p 345.
106 *Sengo shiryo nitchu kankei*, p 33 (memorandum of 3 November 1954, item 4). See also *Mainichi shinbun*, 1 September 1954.
107 Editorial in *Mainichi shinbun*, 28 October 1954.
108 The visit was extensively covered by Japanese newspapers. On the publicity effect, see also *Nitchu yuko undoshi*, p 39.
109 On the background to the Conference see Neuhauser, *China and the Afro-Asian People's Solidarity Organisation, 1957-1967*, (Harvard University Press, 1968).
110 *Communist China 1955*, 1956 (URI), pp 27-8. On Liao's appointments to the delegations, see *NCNA*, 11 and 13 March 1955, and *Nippon Times*, 12 January 1956. On the link between these conferences, *Edi caozono xia de*, p 51.
111 *Naigai shakai undoshi nenpu*, Chugai chosakai, comp, 1965, p 98.
112 *NS*, 5 February 1955.
113 *NCNA*, 14 April 1955. The other advisers were Huang Hua, later Foreign Minister, and Chen Jiakang (a prominent Overseas Chinese).
114 Alexander Ching-an Yang, *The Policy-Making Process in Japan's Policy toward the People's Republic of China: the Making of the Liao-Takasaki Trade Agreement of November 1962*, PhD dissertation, Columbia University, 1969, (University Microfilms International, 1978), pp 22 f and Lee, *Japan Faces China*, pp 30-1.
115 Asahi shinbunsha, comp, *Tenkai suru kakumei gaiko*, 1971, p 168.
116 See *NS*, 19 and 22 January 1955.
117 *NS*, 3 February 1955.
118 *NS*, 14 and 19 February 1955.
119 Lee, *Japan Faces China*, p 31.
120 *Nitchu oboegaki no 11nen*, Nitchu keizai kyokai, ed, 1975, p 33 and Dennis T Yasutomo, 'Sato's China Policy, 1964-1966', *Asian Survey* XVII.6 (June 1977), pp 530-44.
121 *NS*, 16 April 1955.
122 *Asahi shinbun*, 12 June 1983.
123 According to Fujiyama Aiichiro Takasaki's talks were not negotiations (interview, 1979).
124 *Nitchu oboegaki no 11nen*, p 33.
125 *Liaogong zai renjian*, p 140.
126 Larkin, *China and Africa*, pp 16-17 and *Tenkai*, pp 9, 115-16. Liao presented a supplementary report on the Bandung Conference to the Standing Committee of the NPC at an enlarged meeting of the 15th session of the NPC on 13 May 1955 (*NCNA>*, 16 May 1955). Interviews held in Japan resulted in contradictory evidence on the significance of Takasaki's meeting with Liao.
127 On Liao meeting Overseas Chinese, see Qian Ren in *Liaogong zai renjian*, p 122.
128 *Ibid*.
129 *Ibid*.
130 *Nitchu yuko undoshi*, p 78. In an interview with Guo Moruo in *Shijie zhishi* Guo had argued for cultural exchange with Japan in order to break out of the present impasse and since that time 'invitation diplomacy' was strongly emphasised (*NS*, 20 November 1954).

CHAPTER FOUR
Economic and Political Relations 1955-1963

On the surface PRC policy towards Japan had been very successful. Only two and a half years after Zhou Enlai had stressed that the PRC was prepared to expand its links with Japan gradually, despite the absence of formal relations, developments seemed to be moving fast. In the second half of 1955, however, the PRC apparently 'altered its objective and raised its price for the solution of outstanding problems between China and Japan'.

Again it was held that establishing full *de jure* relations was fundamental:
Unless and until diplomatic relations were restored the solution of concrete problems relating to trade, fisheries and repatriation would have to be deferred.[1]

The specific issue that was taken up by the PRC as the reason for its hardening attitude was the attempt in July by the Japanese government to re-open the discussion on the return of the remaining Japanese from the PRC to Japan. This took the form of a letter from the Japanese Consul-General in Geneva, Tatsuke Keiichi to the Chinese Consul-General, Shen Ping. The letter used rather trenchant language to make the following points: in the first place it was mentioned that the programme for collective repatriation had come to a halt; secondly, according to Mrs Li's report, 1,069 Japanese were still being held in the PRC as war criminals; thirdly, although the figures for Japanese residents in the PRC coincided with Japanese government figures, there was still the unsolved question of 40,000 Japanese who had been on the mainland, but about whom information was not available. The letter concluded by emphasising that these matters should be settled from a humanitarian point of view, without letting the question of diplomatic relations intrude. The same questions were referred to in a statement by the Japanese Foreign Ministry the following day.[2] The Chinese reply a month later in the form of a letter from Shen Ping, to his Japanese counterpart, Tatsuke Keiichi, - which included a copy of a declaration of a spokesman of the PRC Ministry of Foreign Affairs - was remarkable for its curtness. The whole question of relations between the PRC and Japan, including trade, repatriation and travel was linked to the question of normalisation. While completely rejecting any discussion of the 40,000 Japanese said to be missing on the Chinese mainland the release of Japanese 'war criminals' was said to fall under the sovereignty of the PRC. Refuting any claims of a lack of co-operation in the return of Japanese the question was raised of Chinese residents in Japan who, according to this reply did not enjoy full rights there.[3] This discussion in the form of notes exchanged at consular level in Geneva continued until the end of the year without resulting in any breakthrough.[4]

One naturally wonders why the Japanese government decided to raise the matter in this way at this time and why the Chinese suddenly insisted on full relations before outstanding problems, including trade, could be discussed, reversing its former stance. When Zhou Enlai, in a speech on 17 August, indicated that the San Francisco Peace Treaty alone would not be an obstacle, he added that the aim was to have the treaty with Taiwan abolished.[5] Later PRC statements blamed US interference in Japanese affairs for the lack of a positive response from Japan. Mao Zedong was even more forthright, demanding *de facto* recognition (government contact at ambassadorial level, and moves to end the technical state of war) as a precondition for the release of Japanese prisoners of war.[6]

At about this time negotiations on the repatriation of their nationals after the Korean War took place between the PRC and the US and it may be that the PRC adopted a tough position with Japan in order not to undermine its negotiating position vis-à-vis the USA; just as the latter may have requested Japan not to appear too conciliatory to the PRC on this issue, since Japanese concessions might have weakened the US position. They might create friction between Japan and the USA and also weaken the position of the ROC. It is tempting indeed to suspect a link between the Japanese diplomatic initiative of mid-July and the start of PRC talks with the USA on 1 August 1955, concerning the release of Americans held in the PRC. Without further evidence this interpretation remains speculative. Some time between autumn of 1955 and spring of 1956 the PRC reverted to its former course of gradually strengthening links with Japan without preconditions, but it is difficult to pinpoint the exact date of this change. At times, signals coming from Peking seemed contradictory. For instance in November, Zhou Enlai declared that it would be possible to effect *de facto* re-establishment of relations following the conclusion of private agreements.[7] Possibly following the review of United Front Work in October, and the decision to expand organisational support for this approach the basis had already been laid for a reversion to a softer line.[8]

During this period of tensions between Peking and Tokyo Liao continued to meet Japanese visitors in Peking, the high point being a visit of a delegation of Japanese Diet members in 1955, in the same month that Liu Ningyi led a delegation to the World Conference Against Nuclear Weapons which opened on 6 August in Hiroshima. Although appointed Deputy Head of the PRC delegation to the 44th Conference of the Inter-Parliamentary Union scheduled for 25 August in Helsinki, Liao remained in Peking, attending numerous meetings with members of the Japanese National Council for the Restoration of Diplomatic Relations with China and the USSR. Neither this visit nor other events, such as the first PRC trade exhibition in Tokyo, led to a significant reduction in tension over the repatriation issue. In the meantime, Liao was also active in contacts with leaders and members of foreign Communist parties such as Shiga Yoshio (member of the CC of the JCP)[9] and Paul de Groot, Secretary-General of the Dutch Communist Party, whom Liao had met more than twenty years before in Rotterdam.[10] Towards the end of the year Liao Chengzhi accompanied Mrs Song Qingling on a visit to Burma and India from which he returned in early February 1956.[11] For the remainder of 1956 he did not travel abroad and, although continuing to be engaged in the field of relations with Japan as well as international front organisations, domestic matters seem to have occupied him to a greater degree than in 1955.

Shortly after his return from South Asia Liao was elected one of the five Vice-Chairmen of the Asian Solidarity Committee at its inaugural meeting. As far as relations with Japan were concerned the PRC:

> apparently abandoned all early expectations of achieving *de jure* relations with Japan and reverted to its earlier policy of seeking some basis for *de facto* dealings with the Japanese government on specific problems in the spring of 1956.[12]

Although economic and other exchanges continued to grow and reached a postwar peak in 1956, Prime Minister Hatoyama was in an even more difficult position domestically than in the previous period, and the PRC made little headway in the area of political links.[13] Under these circumstances the PRC once more increased pressure on Japan using the established channels such as trade and the negotiations on the return of Japanese nationals.[14] Prime Minister Hatoyama was willing to respond positively and enter into new talks with Peking.[15] In April it was agreed to extend the Third Private Trade Agreement for another year.[16] This was in fact a compromise since the Chinese had wished to conclude a new agreement providing for the establishment of permanent trade missions as another step towards normalisation. By agreeing to this compromise the Chinese gave notice that the question of a permanent trade office would be brought up again before a new agreement would have to be negotiated. This demand was one of the key problems besetting the long drawn out negotiations on the Fourth Trade Agreement, begun in October 1956 and concluded only on 5 March 1958. The provisions of this private agreement - which included the establishment of trade missions - however, proved not to be feasible, and the Chinese were probably aware that the agreement could not be implemented even before they signed.

The important point to note here is that the original decision to raise the political price for trade links taken in the second half of 1955 was not abandoned during 1956 and 1957, despite a temporary flourishing of trade and other relations between Japan and the PRC.[17] Against this background Japan held a trade exhibition in Peking in autumn 1956, an event which was much publicised and which found Liao Chengzhi in the limelight again.[18] Moreover a number of important Japanese delegations were visiting Peking, including a JSP mission and other parliamentarians. Trade and visitor statistics reached a peak during this period, but in judging the state of affairs one cannot ignore the obstacles which continued to prevent a genuine breakthrough. In talks between Ikeda Masanosuke and Lei Renmin, with Liao Chengzhi attending, it appeared impossible to reach a new, fourth trade agreement, due to disputes over the legal status of Communist Chinese trade negotiators in Japan, and a compromise solution was adopted by extending the existing arrangement until April 1957.[19] For the moment, however, Peking decided not to push too far, as indicated by Zhou Enlai in a speech on 6 November 1956, stressing a 'gradual approach' (*kasaneshiki*), the possibility of a 'peaceful solution to the Taiwan problem' (without excluding the military option), and prospects for the successful conclusion of Sino-American talks after the American presidential election.[20]

Like the talks on a new trade agreement, talks on the question of repatriation did not go smoothly. As early as February 1956 Ni Feijun had hinted at a possible release of 'war criminals', and 335 people were finally handed over on 24 June 1956. In the same month a third agreement on the return and repatriation of Japanese was reached during talks in Tianjin between a Chinese Red Cross delegation and a joint Japanese delegation including Red Cross representatives, the JCFA and the PA. This was the last agreement reached between the Chinese Red Cross and such a joint Japanese delegation. It included provisions aimed at increasing the possibility of Japanese visiting the PRC and PRC citizens visiting Japan. Significantly the Japanese Red Cross - much closer to the government position than the JCFA or the PA - reserved its opinion on that part of the communiqué, implying that the communiqué itself was a compromise insofar as the Chinese had insisted on including clauses it knew the Japanese government would find hard to accept. As with the extension of the Third Trade Agreement the political price had been raised, and the Japanese side was not willing to pay it.

It is striking that Liao, although prominent in the negotiations, did not sign the Tianjin Agreement, despite having previously been first among Chinese signatories. Instead, Zhao Anbo was listed as the first signatory.[21] Although Zhao could by no means be regarded a junior official one may assume that the PRC wished to show its displeasure by having the agreement signed by somebody below Liao's rank. The day the agreement was signed, Zhou Enlai in a speech to the National People's Congress declared that the 'war criminals' had been released for the sake of promoting 'normal' (ie formal) relations, but he criticised Japan for not responding favourably.[22] In this same period the PRC started to strengthen links with the opposition Socialist Party (JSP) which subsequently became an important channel for talks on remaining repatriation problems. In June 1956 the JSP had still been in favour of maintaining relations with the ROC, but had moved gradually closer to the PRC position,[23] most dramatically during the visit of JSP leader Asanuma Inejiro in April 1957. Liao took an active part in rather complex PRC moves to woo certain liberal (LDP) politicians and win over the JSP while attacking politicians supporting links with the ROC and the USA. On the whole he did not appear in the limelight as before. Domestically it was a very busy year. Liao attended meetings of the ACDFY, and took part in domestic united front activities, presiding over and giving a speech at the closing session of the National Conference of Young Industrialists and Businessmen, and also giving a report on behalf of the ACDFY and the NDYL. He was involved in activities of the China Peace Committee, and addressed the 4th National Conference of Overseas Chinese Affairs in June 1956. Most importantly he took part in the 8th Congress of the CCP in September 1956 where he was re-elected to the Central Committee.

The Rupture of Relations with Japan

In late summer 1956 Liao Chengzhi received a mission of former Japanese military men led by Endo Saburo. The mission produced something of a scandal since some members of the delegation did not follow 'normal procedure' and voiced quite outspoken criticism during the visit.24 Who would have thought at that time that little more than twenty years later the PRC would invite Japanese (retired) military officers because they did in fact represent the Japanese defence establishment? Back in 1956 the mood was completely different. The Endo mission was also received by Mao who made statements stressing the common character of nations in Asia, Africa and Latin America, and referring to a united front to be formed by Asia, Africa and Latin America against domination by the USA, Great Britain and France, themes that became prominent during the time of the Sino-Soviet ideological split in the sixties.25

There are various reasons for assuming that certain important developments that took place in 1956 contributed to the Sino-Soviet split. Among events most often mentioned in this context are Khrushchev's de-Stalinisation speech, changing policies towards Yugoslavia and the problem of disarmament and peaceful co-existence. It is not unlikely that questions relating to Japan and the Asian Solidarity movement also played a role. On 19 October the Soviet Union and Japan signed a declaration concerning the resumption of diplomatic relations.26 This should of course not be regarded as an attempt by the Soviet Union to strengthen links between Japan and the whole of the 'Socialist camp', including the PRC. At the same time the fact could not be overlooked that, whereas the Soviet Union's normalisation of relations might result in improved economic links with Japan, the PRC was not in the same position. The Soviet Union could ignore Japan's relations with the ROC but the PRC could not. As mentioned before co-ordination of the policies towards Japan of the Soviet Union and the PRC weakened after 1954, and there may also have been disappointment in the PRC that the resumption of diplomatic relations between the Soviet Union and Japan did nothing to promote the resumption of the PRC's relations with Japan.

Another problem of policy co-ordination concerned relations with 'third world' countries. It seems likely that PRC politicians involved in relations with third world countries - at that time often carried out in the context of international front organisations - would have participated in the co-ordination of policies with the Soviet Union. Liao Chengzhi had visited Eastern bloc countries on numerous occasions and he had first hand experience of the Soviet Union. By the time the Sino-Soviet split came into the open it was also Liao Chengzhi who stood in the forefront of disputes between the communist giants within the Afro-Asian movement. There is however no hard evidence that Liao actually took part in the co-ordination of policies with the Soviet Union during the fifties.

PRC politicians like Liao had frequent meetings with politicians and other figures from Asian and African (including Arab) countries. After the 20th Party Congress of the Soviet Union in February 1956, the Soviet Union had increasingly stressed the possibility of transition towards Socialism by parliamentary means, including such third world countries as Egypt.27 The PRC attitude remained far more critical of countries governed by what it called 'bourgeois' governments, including those which professed some brand of home-made 'socialism'. An early, not so critical, comment is to be found in an article co-authored by Liao, Hu Yaobang and Hu Qili in *Zhongguo qingnianbao* of August 1956.

At the time of the Suez crisis Liao was one of the PRC politicians particularly involved in condemning the invasion of Egypt. He became a Vice-Chairman of the Chinese People's Committee in Support of Egypt's Resistance to Aggression and a member of the Sino-Egyptian Friendship Association which had just been established. Throughout the next year (1957) the PRC endeavoured to strengthen its links with Asian, African and Latin American countries. Moves were undertaken to have a World Peace Conference held in Asia, but according to Saionji Kinkazu: 'The European faction headed by the Soviet Union offered sticky resistance, but the WPC was held in Asia for the first time'.28

This was the so-called Colombo meeting. According to Saionji the decision had been taken at a meeting in Vienna. It is possible that he was actually referring to a meeting that opened on 30 March in Prague, attended by Liao Chengzhi. Following this meeting Saionji visited Peking for consultations about the coming Colombo meeting to which Liao was also appointed a member of the PRC delegation.29 Towards the end of the year Liao was one of the two secretaries-general of the PRC delegation to attend the Conference of Delegates from Asian and African Nations in Cairo in December, and Liao did not miss the chance to have his picture taken in front of a pyramid.30

When Hatoyama's resignation had become inevitable due to internal party opposition he was succeeded in 1956 by Prime Minister Ishibashi. Ishibashi immediately charted a new course for Japan's foreign policy that might best be described as 'independently-orientated'.31 He initiated discussions with US Ambassador Allison on the question of US bases and Japan's defence. On 4 January 1957 he stated his desire to review the question of trade missions in Japan's trade relations with the PRC, raising hopes in the PRC for concessions on a point that had acquired so much importance. Ishibashi fell ill only two months after taking office and was replaced in February by Prime Minister Kishi.32 Even while acting as caretaker Kishi had already attracted the wrath of the PRC media over the proposed entry of guided missiles into Japan.33 His choice as prime minister made it even less likely that Japan would now be prepared to make the concessions that Hatoyama had been unable to make.34

The PRC let political considerations prevail over purely economic ones and decided not to reduce political demands for the sake of increased trade. As it happened, it was the period when heated discussions took place in Peking along ideological lines, leading to the crushing of the 'Hundred Flowers' movement by Mao Zedong and Deng Xiaoping. This was not the time to appear too conciliatory. The argument in Peking may have been that a tough position would eventually help to increase internal dissent against the Kishi government. In an interesting analysis, *People's Daily* of 28 February 1957 argued that Japan's basic policy would not change, but that it would not be able to go against the tide. Such an analysis was a clear rationalisation of and plea for a gradual, realistic approach. On the other hand, Liao Chengzhi had made it clear in talks only a couple of days earlier that restrictions on the number of personnel in trade missions under a Fourth Trade Agreement would be completely unacceptable.[35] The frequent parallel occurrence of seemingly conflicting signals should however not make us jump to simple conclusions concerning factional divisions among Chinese policy-makers. At the same time, it is obviously extremely difficult to assign individual politicians to a particular 'hard' or 'soft' line on the basis of a few randomly selected sources.

Links were strengthened with the Japanese opposition, particularly the JSP which sent a mission headed by Asanuma Inejiro to Peking in April 1957, after its decision to abandon the 'two Chinas' point of view in favour of the PRC at its 13th Congress in January. The mission has been dealt with in detail elsewhere[36] but a few points require emphasis. Having abandoned the traditional 'Red Cross' channel for further negotiations on the pending repatriation issue, talks now continued with JSP representatives.[37] Perhaps this choice was partly determined by the expectation that this move would prove beneficial to the JSP in a way similar to that which had supported the PA and the JCFA in the period of repatriation talks in 1953-54. Altogether two communiqués were published between PRC semi-official organisations and visiting JSP delegations concerning the repatriation issue,[38] while attempts by a Special Diet Committee, led by its member Hirose, to make progress on this issue failed.[39]

The status of Liao Chengzhi during the talks with the JSP mission in April 1957 is not clear. Probably during the same period Liao was mainly occupied by work such as thoroughly reorganising and restructuring the Youth Movement and related United Front Work activities.[40] Although he took part in numerous sessions in talks with the JSP delegation his name appeared as the last but one on the list of participants, and he was listed as a member of the government (NPC) rather than of organisations specifically engaged in welcoming foreign delegations of this kind. Economic issues were also discussed during the visit, but the communiqué did not provide further details. It was much more explicit concerning points of agreement on political issues. Mentioned first were the establishment of diplomatic relations, Asian-African solidarity and 'international peace'.[41] These talks between PRC officials and the JSP delegation contributed to a further collective repatriation programme larger than the one following the 1954 Li Dequan mission but the publicity effect that had been so prominent then, remained rather limited.

During the remainder of the year relations between the PRC and Japan were dominated by scattered attempts to raise the issue of the exchange of trade missions, alternating with increasingly hostile attacks on Ishibashi's successor, Kishi.[42] At the same time it should not be overlooked that Zhou Enlai hinted at the possibility of Japan acting as a 'bridge' in the Pacific, implying the possibility of *rapprochement* with the United States, but the time was not ripe.[43] Talks between Liao and Saionji Kinkazu at the Colombo Conference in May had likewise failed to add new momentum to the question of trade missions. More specific moves in July to have a joint Japanese delegation, including MITI's front organisation, the *Nitchu yushutsunyu kumiai*, engage in further negotiations remained without specific result.[44] Ikeda's talks with Lei Renmin stalled on 3 November.[45] Even the release of Japanese prisoners of war in September following talks by JSP member Arita Hachiro in Peking did not significantly contribute to an improvement.[46]

These developments cast a heavy shadow over the visit in December 1957, of a delegation formally headed by Mrs Li Dequan to Tokyo, and again accompanied by Liao Chengzhi. Attempts by the delegation - and in particular Liao - to achieve an increase in the flow of visitors between Japan and the PRC, and meaningful progress on the repatriation issue, failed and the talks ended in an impasse.[47] It was all the more interesting to note that Liao very consciously tried to establish further links with members of the conservative LDP:

> As far as meeting Matsumura is concerned, Liao Chengzhi - on the occasion of his 1957 visit to Japan - told Miyazaki Ryosuke and Horiike Tomoharu: 'I should like to speak with confirmed LDP politicians.' They recommended as politicians with an understanding of the China problem Ishibashi and Matsumura, which he met for the first time at Ishibashi's residence in Tokyo...[48]

Thus began an acquaintance that turned out to be very significant in re-starting PRC links in 1959 after the rupture only a few months earlier in 1958. Little noticed at the time were his meetings with Ikeda Masanosuke.

In tracing the outlines of bilateral relations between the PRC and Japan during this period one has to keep in mind the constantly changing atmosphere in China, where the Great Leap Forward was about to start with its emphasis on China's ability to jump ahead *independently* of either the Soviet Union, or any outside help. No longer did Zhou Enlai or Liao Chengzhi emphasise the importance of economic co-operation for the reconstruction of the Chinese economy:

> Mori who in February 1958 attended a Japanese trade exhibition, reported that when he was on his return in Wuhan he was asked by a Chinese responsible person 'It seems that people in Japan say that China's construction cannot be realised without Japan's assistance, and his voice showed that it was filled with violent anger'.[49]

In an interview Foreign Minister Chen Yi declared in May that: 'Prime Minister Kishi was thinking that China was forced to trade with Japan, but now great and strong China had no need to be dependent on whatever imperialism'.[50]

Nevertheless, Inayama Yoshihiro was able to conclude a long term trade agreement on steel deliveries towards the end of February which apparently created the conditions for the initialling of the fourth trade agreement a few days later during a visit by Katsumata Seiichi (JSP) to Peking in March 1958 in connection with talks on a Fourth Trade Agreement. PRC insistence on several demands - particularly trade missions - had resulted in the long delay of a new (Fourth) Trade Agreement. During Liao Chengzhi's visit to Tokyo in December the Chinese had expressed a wish to continue talks on a trade agreement, and requested Katsumata Seiichi to pass this message on to Ikeda Masanosuke, leader of a Japanese delegation to negotiate the trade agreement. Liao and Ikeda had met in Tokyo several times, sometimes accompanied by Katsumata himself, and a communiqué had been issued.[51] Despite the harsh political demands - amounting to a quasi-recognition of the PRC - it appeared to Ikeda that Liao, representing the PRC point of view, was nevertheless rather keen on concluding a trade agreement.

As a result of their talks, Ikeda responded to Liao's request and visited Peking again in February 1958. There the talks continued to focus on the question of trade missions and the raising of the PRC flag. Confidential talks between Ikeda and Lei Renmin did not solve the existing differences, although Lei hinted that the tough stance taken by the PRC was due to 'domestic pressure'. In this initial stage of the 'Great Leap Forward', ideological pressure had indeed increased greatly. Whether Lei's remarks were a negotiating ploy is difficult to decide but it is extremely probable that the PRC's Japan specialist may indeed have differed from the tough line taken by the party leadership under Mao Zedong. In his record of the talks Ikeda gives a very lively description of PRC tactics designed to put pressure on the Japanese delegation, including delaying tactics and the tiring out of negotiators.

Liao again had an authoritative role during the talks. At a critical stage when the Japanese delegation threatened withdrawal they considered Liao the only PRC negotiator of sufficient standing to give guarantees acceptable to delegation leader Ikeda. Despite difficulties a Fourth Trade Agreement was finally signed, including a clause making its execution conditional upon the subsequent agreement of both governments.[52] The Japanese government gave qualified approval, attaching conditions to avoid any semblance of quasi-recognition of the PRC by Japan.

The PRC protested against the Japanese government's conditions and the protest was generally considered unreasonable by the Japanese media.[53] The PRC protest clearly foreshadowed 2 May when the so-called Nagasaki Flag Incident was seized by the PRC as an excuse for severing all links with Japan, including the unilateral cancellation of all trade contracts. It is very important to remember, however, that due to the PRC's refusal to accept the Japanese government's conditions, the Fourth Trade Agreement had not come into force. It is therefore technically incorrect to accept the PRC argument that the hauling down of a PRC flag in Nagasaki on 2 May - an act for which the culprit was punished under regulations concerning the damaging of property rather than the national emblem of another government as demanded by the PRC - constituted a breaking off of the Fourth Trade Agreement and therefore justified the PRC's rupture of all relations with Japan.[54] Lei Renmin had pointed out at the beginning of March that it would be 'difficult' to accept a revision of the paragraph concerning the hoisting of the PRC flag mentioned in the agreement. In reaction to the talks in Peking, Taiwan had interrupted its trade talks with Japan, thus putting pressure on Tokyo, and on 28 March the Japanese government announced that it was 'established policy' not to recognise the hoisting of the PRC flag.[55] The following weeks saw increasingly bitter PRC attacks on the Japanese government.[56]

The ultimate reason for the break must be sought in the fact that the PRC at this stage was prepared to put at risk all links with Japan, links that had taken years to build, and gamble for quasi-recognition of the PRC by Japan. It remains tantalising to assume that Liao's obvious desire to conclude an agreement and Lei's reference to 'domestic pressure' indicate a cleavage of opinion among PRC politicians against those who preferred to play for higher stakes. One is reminded of Mao's rejection of a communiqué worked out in 1966 between PRC negotiators and a JCP delegation under Miyamoto Kenji, when high ranking party officials and Japan specialists were overruled by Mao Zedong who wanted to gamble for higher stakes.

After the reorganisation of the PRC Youth Movement further changes had taken place both in government and united front organisations.[57] In the course of a thorough-going restructuring of the PRC's government apparatus in March Liao was appointed deputy director of the Office in Charge of Foreign Affairs headed by Chen Yi. According to one source he was also appointed Secretary of the CCP Work Committee on Overseas Affairs, indicating his influential position in foreign policy making.[58] Liao was also elected to the Second National People's Congress in May as a delegate representing Overseas Chinese, and appointed a chairman of the PRC's Asian and African Solidarity Committee in July. If there were divergences of opinion among policy makers they seemingly did not affect Liao's career, and there was apparently no simple correlation between the dominating 'radical' line of Chinese policy and the career of a 'softliner' like Liao Chengzhi.

The Ishibashi and Matsumura Missions

The interruption of all links with Japan by the PRC in May 1958 has to be seen in the wider context of PRC domestic and foreign policies. Although conclusive evidence is lacking it seems unlikely that the PRC's harsh line towards Japan was caused merely by an attempt to exercise pressure on the Kishi government before the election in May, which Kishi won. In the field of foreign trade links the PRC dramatically increased its efforts to improve its trade relations with Western Europe and Southeast Asia. The PRC went so far as to call for a boycott of Japanese goods by Overseas Chinese and also accused Japan of planning economic expansion in the Afro-Asian region, including Southeast Asia, but predicted that Japan would fail. At the same time the PRC angrily denied that China's reconstruction could only be realised with Japanese assistance.[59] The stage was set for a full-scale attack including moves to isolate Japan from areas traditionally and potentially important for its supply of raw materials. From this perspective the PRC's increasing interest in the politics of third world countries in Asia, Africa and Latin America should not be seen only as ideologically motivated moves to incite world revolution, oppose US influence world-wide and gain influence at the expense of other Soviet bloc countries. It also reflected the PRC's very specific concern with limiting Japan's links with the 'third world'.[60]

One might have expected Liao Chengzhi to be in the forefront of such moves, as one of the PRC's top officials involved in Southeast Asian affairs through his vice-chairmanship of the OCAC, his position in international front organisations and as the PRC's leading Japan specialist. It is, however, all the more striking that he played a very low-key role during the weeks following the Nagasaki Incident. It was Liao who, after weeks of minimal contact with the Japanese, revealed for the first time to Miyazaki Seimin and visiting JSP Diet member Sata in Peking in July 1958 the so-called 'Three Political Principles' with which Japan, in particular the government, must comply before links could be resumed.61 The conditions were fully elaborated and presented to the Japanese public in a report by JSP member Sata on his visit to the PRC in August.62 In his report he quoted the PRC's position as revealed to him by Liao Chengzhi, adding that Liao had presented his statement as representing Premier Zhou Enlai and the Minister of Foreign Affairs, Chen Yi. Although these conditions were tough and 'not negotiable' the Japanese side, including the Minister for Trade, Takasaki (whom Liao had met in Bandung), continued to stress their willingness to reopen trade links.63 This was the beginning of a period of complex manoeuvring for the resumption of trade links against the background of an equally difficult international situation.

August saw the abortive attempt by the PRC to improve its position vis-à-vis Taiwan by undertaking military action in the Taiwan Straits (the so-called Taiwan Straits Crisis).64 This has been called one of Mao's strategic blunders, but it set the stage for the PRC's foreign policy line towards Japan in the coming years, a policy dominated by attempts to reduce the role of the USA in the Far East.

In a meeting with six Japanese delegations in Peking Zhou Enlai called for joint struggle by the 'Chinese and Japanese peoples against the USA', a theme that would become more prominent with the approach of the renegotiation of the security arrangement between Japan and the USA, concluded in 1960. The PRC apparently did not expect any significant policy change by a Japanese government under Kishi. It reverted to traditional tactics, attempting to woo opposition parties and exploit division within the governing LDP in order to put pressure on the Japanese government. One of the first volleys in the intense propaganda campaign against the security link with the USA was fired as early as November 1958, followed by countless attacks in the following year.65

During the first half of 1959 an additional factor influencing the PRC's policy towards Japan was the election struggle. As so often in modern Japanese politics foreign policy was a divisive issue in the elections, and the reopening of links with the PRC also became an important theme. The JSP attempted to make use of the issue and strengthened its links with the PRC, especially during the well-publicised Asanuma mission there in March 1959. Also, the PRC consented to conduct trade on a very limited scale, so-called consideration-trade, a matter that had been discussed mainly between Zhou Enlai, Liao Chengzhi and Iwai Akira of the leftist trade union SOHYO federation in February. It aimed to grant limited access to trade with the PRC to a select group of companies willing to accept political conditions, and which had been 'suitably introduced'.66 The LDP was specifically excluded from participating in this kind of trade, demonstrating the PRC's intention to give one-sided support to the JSP opposition party. Moves by the LDP to suggest a resumption of trade links were frequently dubbed mere election ploys.67

After his talks with Iwai in February Liao left for Moscow to attend the executive meeting of the WPC. Before his return to Peking a JCP delegation had arrived there and it is not clear to what extent Liao was involved in meetings with this delegation.68 While in Peking both the visiting JCP and JSP delegations held meetings resulting in a joint statement indicating PRC support for some kind of an anti-government 'united front'.69 During the talks with the JSP delegation Liao played a leading role. Asanuma was encouraged to agree to anti-US statements which went much further than some other members of the JSP delegation wished, let alone the less leftist-oriented factions at home.70 In spite of these concessions, Zhou virtually rejected the JSP's concept of 'citizens' diplomacy' when in a speech on 15 March he stressed that a breakthrough in PRC relations with Japan had to be achieved by government contacts, and described it as the JSP's task to make the government change its policy.71 Despite vociferous support for the JSP it cannot be denied that the mission had not been able to achieve some of its basic aims.

During the following month (April 1959) PRC leaders were engaged mainly in domestic functions. At the beginning of May Liao Chengzhi left with others to attend a special conference of the executive of the WPC in Stockholm, returning on 18 May. Although the PRC propaganda machine continued to comment on Japanese issues, including the election, no particular new moves were undertaken before voting took place on 2 June 1959. Immediately after the election Ishibashi Tanzan - the former Prime Minister who had previously been involved in contacts with the PRC - wrote a letter to Premier Zhou, attempting to find a way out of the impasse.72 The reply sent by Liao Chengzhi on 21 June mentioned that he had passed Ishibashi's letter to Zhou Enlai and added that Zhou would welcome a visit to the PRC by Ishibashi. Liao referred in particular to the good links existing during the Hatoyama and Ishibashi cabinets, but absolved the PRC of all blame for the deterioration of relations in the subsequent period. Without going into further detail Liao expressed his confidence that talks by Ishibashi with PRC leaders would be of benefit for the improvement of relations between the PRC and Japan.73

Before the election there had been no prospect of LDP links with the PRC but immediately afterwards the PRC changed its position and reverted to its former tactics, strengthening links with dissenters inside the governing LDP. Although a new trade agreement would not be reached before 1962, the first contact between Liao Chengzhi and Ishibashi after the election (Ishibashi had met Liao in December 1957 in Tokyo) proved to be the first stepping-stone to improved relations. On the Japanese side Ishibashi Tanzan, Matsumura Kenzo, Takasaki Tatsunosuke, Okazaki Kaheita and Fujiyama Aiichiro were in the forefront of these moves.74 Liao acted as the leading PRC spokesman during these discussions, next in rank to Prime Minister Zhou and Foreign Minister Chen Yi. During these talks Liao seemed to be directly responsible to Zhou rather than the foreign affairs apparatus.

The new, more conciliatory tactics adopted by the PRC were not only the result of bilateral considerations, but were also brought about by a number of other foreign policy problems for the PRC during this period. Relations with some countries in South and Southeast Asia had started to deteriorate. There was growing trouble on the border with India, a rebellion had broken out in Tibet, and there were clashes with Indonesia over the position of Overseas Chinese there.75

At the same time relations between the Soviet Union and the United States began to improve and there was a marked change of atmosphere, signs of disagreement with the Soviet Union had been growing,[76] and last, but not least, the failure of the Great Leap Forward made it more urgent for the PRC to seek accommodation in some other area such as relations with Japan. Meanwhile Japan had been able to frustrate PRC attempts to prevent it from increasing its influence in Southeast Asia. It is tempting to speculate that the PRC's Japan specialists, or at least some of them, would have supported a change in the previous hardline approach since they must have been particularly aware of the failure of PRC policy towards Japan, but so far evidence to support this hypothesis has been sparse.

The visits to Peking by Ishibashi in August and Matsumura in October 1959 have been dealt with elsewhere.[77] However several points are of particular relevance here. Originally it had been suggested that Ishibashi and Matsumura travel together. Both politicians held a number of talks with LDP leaders before their visit, but Prime Minister Kishi's support must have been very limited although he did not object.[78] Particularly significant was the fact that Ishibashi repeated that he would adhere to his own 'three principles' which had been acknowledged by Prime Minister Kishi and which excluded recognition of the PRC. Before his departure Ishibashi also stated emphatically that he would resist attempts by the Communist leadership to drive a wedge between Japan and the USA. In his meeting with Foreign Minister Fujiyama Ishibashi stressed that he wished to probe the PRC's attitude to the question of 'adjustment of Sino-Japanese relations', and declared he had no intention of broaching trade issues (which were to be left to Matsumura).[79] Liao Chengzhi, on the other hand, in a letter to Kazemi Akira published by Ajia Tsushin on 8 September had stated that the PRC would not retreat from the position expressed in the Zhang-Asanuma communiqué of March 1959.[80] Despite these cautious statements it had been expected that the coming visits would result in a breakthrough.[81] Before meeting Zhou Enlai for the first time on 16 September Ishibashi had three preparatory talks with Liao Chengzhi.[82] Liao reiterated the PRC's tough stance towards Kishi (especially because of Kishi's trip to Taiwan), but during the second talk he also remarked that:

> speaking for myself I can approve of the general content (of your suggestions), but I should like to confer directly with Premier Zhou concerning specific points.

During the third preparatory talk with Ishibashi Liao reacted strongly to the presence of US bases in Japan, and also did not react favourably to Ishibashi's suggestion that Japan might become a 'bridge' between the PRC and the USA. No agreement was reached on these points, and they were moved onto the agenda for Ishibashi's talks with Zhou Enlai.[83] After two talks with Zhou Enlai agreement was reached on the publication of a communiqué.[84] Liao had also been present at these talks, and was entrusted with discussing some final adjustments with Ishibashi before the communiqué was signed on 20 September. Although the communiqué included a strong attack by Zhou on 'outside interference in Japan' (a reference to the USA) and Japan's policy towards Taiwan, it did not make formal relations between the PRC and Japan a precondition for other exchanges.

Following the signing of the communiqué Zhou gave an address in which he praised the talks between Khrushchev and Eisenhower as beneficial towards the relaxation of international tensions, and added that: 'China is not participating in the summit conference since both countries (ie the PRC and the USA) do not recognise the other diplomatically'.

It does not seem far-fetched to assume that this comment was meant to imply criticism of the Soviet Union. Of similar interest was Ishibashi's comment during a press conference on 26 September to the effect that Zhou had greatly approved of Ishibashi's suggestions concerning disarmament:

> Japan's Self Defence Force and the PRC's forces are both armed at the urging of the United States and the Soviet Union, and is it not the case that this is not to our mutual advantage?

Even more interesting was Zhou's statement to Matsumura that 'East is East, West is West, and China and Japan have to build ever-lasting friendship,' a comment that Furui noticed to be quite unusual. With the benefit of hindsight, Furui later interpreted this to refer to the impending shift in Sino-Soviet relations.[85]

After the publication of the communiqué Kawashima, Chief-Secretary of the LDP, and the Chief-Secretary of the Cabinet, Shiina, voiced their opposition, for which they were attacked by the *People's Daily*.[86] This attack could not conceal the fact that Ishibashi's visit marked a significant change in the PRC's attitude to relations with Japan, since it had now become clear that the PRC had dropped its precondition of diplomatic links before other exchanges could take place, thus preparing the ground for Matsumura's visit. Although Liao's name did not appear in the communiqué his preparatory talks with Ishibashi and his presence during Ishibashi's talks with Zhou Enlai again revealed him as the PRC's chief negotiator in questions relating specifically to Japan, ranking only below the prime minister.

Matsumura's visit soon afterwards took place on a much grander scale than Ishibashi's. He was accompanied by a number of other LDP politicians, including Furui Yoshimi and Tagawa Seiichi, at that time Matsumura's private secretary.[87] Journalists of Japan's major news services travelled with them.[88] Matsumura had several talks with Zhou Enlai and Chen Yi with Liao present, as well as preparatory and unofficial discussions with Liao Chengzhi himself.[89] As had always been the intention the talks were kept confidential and no joint communiqué was issued.[90] Some of the topics and results can be surmised from published reports and speech texts. One of the main aims of this trip was the question of economic exchanges.

> Concerning trade Matsumura [wanted] ... to abandon the 'friendship trade' completely, and to conclude a unified general trade agreement. Zhou did not go along with this proposal, and a two-pronged approach was adopted, including both 'general' and 'friendship' trade.'[91]

According to Furui, Okazaki Kaheita suggested to Matsumura the particular arrangement for an agreement on 'general trade', later to develop into the so-called L-T trade.[92] After his talk with Zhou Enlai, Matsumura concluded that cultural and economic exchanges could be conducted on the basis of non-interference, but he was not explicit on the point of diplomatic relations as a precondition for such exchanges. According to one journalist's report Zhou insisted on the PRC's 'three conditions' put forward in June.[93] In his address at a farewell party Zhou referred to the link between 'politics and economics'.[94] By terming both economic and cultural links 'political' Zhou indicated that the PRC was prepared to reduce its previous demands for full political relations before such exchanges could take place. It may be added that Matsumura had been handed a letter from Zhou Enlai to Takasaki, the Minister for Trade and Industry, containing a formal invitation to visit the PRC next spring. While this was not immediately realised, it prepared the ground for Takasaki's later visit during which the L-T agreement was concluded.

The conciliatory stance during talks with Matsumura and Ishibashi contrasted with the joint communiqué issued at the end of the visit of the JCP delegation under Nosaka Sanzo.[95] During that visit the PRC was represented by Liu Shaoqi, Zhou Enlai, Peng Zhen, Wang Jiaxiang and Liao Chengzhi. This would indicate that Liao was also involved in liaison between the CCP and the Japan Communist Party at party level, but his precise function in contacts at party level is unclear.

In the heat of polemics over the approaching revision of the security treaty between the USA and Japan it was not to be expected that the Ishibashi and Matsumura missions would produce immediate results in the area of trade. The immediate effect on the LDP, which led to a split between a 'pro-Peking' group and the 'mainstream' factions was highly significant during the crisis over the revision of the Security Treaty.[96] While Matsumura was still in Peking, however, the visit by a Japanese delegation under Katayama Tetsu on the occasion of the 10th anniversary of the foundation of the PRC was concluded with a communiqué providing for a small, but significant concession. The PRC agreed to revive regulations concerning emergencies at sea involving Japanese fishing boats, thus *de facto* restoring a part of the Fisheries Agreement at a time when the PRC had broken off *all* agreements. It should be noted that the communiqué was signed one day before the departure of the JCP delegation and shortly after the arrival of the Matsumura mission.[97] It is a fairly good example of a favourite PRC tactic of having visits of various missions coincide in order to put pressure on delegations not to initiate moves which may prove disadvantageous to the other. Liao took part in meetings with all three delegations and was thus in the best position to discern differences between their viewpoints and obtain first-hand accounts of the domestic political situation in Japan from Japanese of quite different political colours.

Despite the small, if significant, conciliatory gestures the increasing heat of the PRC campaign against the signing of the Revised Security Treaty made further progress in its relations with Japan quite unlikely for the time being. In the following months Ishibashi, Matsumura and Miki formed the core of dissent against some aspects of Kishi's policy, resulting in a 'split' within the LDP that was widely reported in PRC media.[98]

Takasaki and the Resumption of Informal Relations

While the PRC attempted to maximise its pressure on the Kishi government over the security link with the USA, disagreement and tensions between the Soviet Union and the PRC increased. One result of this was greatly increased PRC activity within the Afro-Asian movement.[99] This took place against the background of strained relations with India over the border question and with Indonesia on the question of the status of Overseas Chinese. Also, the CCP began to take an increasingly independent stance within the international Communist movement.[100] Liao Chengzhi's activities in 1960 covered all these areas.

Tensions with Indonesia had risen to fever pitch towards the end of 1959, and Liao became a prominent speaker on the issue, reflecting his position as Head of the OCAC (he had succeeded his mother as chairman in April 1959). He was also involved in the resettlement of refugees from Indonesia in 1960, in particular in February when he travelled to Canton and Hainan to meet refugees.

In the same month he had talks with Yasui Kaoru, Chairman of the Standing Committee of the Japan Council for Prohibiting Atomic and Hydrogen Bombs, which led to the invitation of a PRC delegation headed by Guo Moruo to Japan.[101] Yasui had talks with Ishibashi and Matsumura on Japan's links with the PRC, as did Iwai Akira of the SOHYO trade union federation.[102] In March moves were made to invite a PRC delegation to Japan. PRC media continued to exploit these developments by stressing the split that had developed within the LDP.[103]

During this period Liao was increasingly engaged in the Afro-Asian movement in preparation for his visit to the Afro-Asian Conference at Conakry.[104] He and Liu Ningyi were the leading members of the delegation. Liao was appointed a member of the Executive Committee which included Oginga Odinga (Kenya), Joshua Nkomo (Rhodesia), J Kozonguizi (Southwest Africa), Ahmed Tlili (Tunisia) and Patrice Lumumba (Congo). In a speech on 13 April, he said that:

> The Chinese people entertain specially close and warm feelings for the African people in their struggle against colonial rule and for national independence ... [because] we were also regarded by the imperialist aggressors as a so-called 'inferior race' and our people suffered the same bitterness of slaughter, plundering and enslavement at the hands of foreign colonialists.[105]

In the same speech he attacked the Western imperialist powers, the USA, Great Britain, France, Belgium and Portugal as 'paper tigers',[106] anticipating some of the themes prominent in the famous article 'Long Live Leninism' published in *Red Flag (Hongqi)* on 16 April, indicating that the split between the PRC and the USSR had now become public. Just as 'Long Live Leninism' was to be attacked by Otto Kuusinen only a few days later,[107] the Soviets also subsequently criticised Liao's statements at the conference in Conakry.[108] On his return to Peking in May Liao kept meeting Asian and African delegations, and although he expressed his 'firm support for the 16 May statement by Khrushchev' on 17 May 1960, his subsequent statements on the Algerian question were interpreted by some as indicating the

PRC's reservations about the move by the FLN to win independence from France by negotiation.[109] At the height of the struggle against the Kishi government in June[110] Liao was one of the leading PRC politicians participating in talks with members of a JCP delegation visiting the PRC.[111] Tension within the international communist movement heightened at the Bucharest conference of communist parties in this period.[112] Liao's involvement in the affairs of the International Communist Movement was also evidenced by his presence at the farewell to a delegation to Korea in May, and to a delegation led by Peng Zhen to the 3rd Congress of the Rumanian Workers' Party in June. Having met the JSP leader Takeuchi Takeshi at the beginning of July, Liao was the leading member of a delegation attending the Enlarged Conference of the Executive of the WPC, passing through Moscow on his way to Stockholm. It must be assumed that differences between the CPSU and the CCP over the future of the WPC played an important role in these discussions. The same is most likely true of the visit of a delegation led by Li Fuchun to North Vietnam in September to the 3rd Congress of the Communist Laodong Party and the celebration of the 15th anniversary of North Vietnam in which Liao took part as a delegation member.[113] In September 1960 Liao saw off a delegation of the Sino-Soviet Friendship Association to Moscow. In November, one day before leaving as a member of the PRC government delegation for Moscow to attend the celebration of the 43rd anniversary of the October Revolution, he also attended a welcome reception in Peking for the Soviet Friendship Association delegation led by V N Stoletov. On his return from Moscow Liao was also present at functions in honour of Ho Chi Minh in Peking in December, and met JCP leaders Hakamada Satomi and Nishizawa Tomio on their way home from Moscow. Liao was clearly involved in the argument about the strategy adopted by Communist parties towards imperialism, and it seems natural to assume that he was engaged in persuading members of Asian Communist parties to come round to the CCP point of view, just as he had been in the forefront of CCP attempts to push their point of view in the Afro-Asian movement.[114]

Despite Liao's busy schedule he also remained active in the field of PRC policy towards Japan. His contacts with JCP representatives have been referred to already. Following preliminary attempts in 1959 several organisations were set up in Japan in January-February 1960 in order to co-ordinate efforts for re-establishing links with the PRC. In his talk with Yasui Kaoru in February, however, Liao Chengzhi used uncommonly strong language to condemn the Kishi government making it clear that the PRC would not engage in any talks with Kishi, and he expressed his confidence in the 'victory against the reactionary clique' in Japan. All subsequent visits of Japanese delegations were coloured by attacks on Kishi. Kishi succeeded in having the Revised Security Treaty with the USA ratified but in a talk with Secretary-General of the LDP, Kawashima, on 20 June, was forced to express his intention to resign after the exchange of ratification instruments. Immediately afterwards, and before Ikeda had been formally appointed Kishi's successor on 19 July, moves were started within the LDP to renew the dialogue with the PRC. On 27 July Ikeda had talks concerning foreign policy towards

Economic and Political Relations

Communist countries with Takasaki Tatsunosuke who had been previously engaged in contacts with PRC leaders and who was going to play an important role during the next two years in Japan's relations with the PRC. Takasaki himself would eventually become Liao's opposite number as 'guarantor' for the famous L-T trade agreement (the initials L and T standing for Liao and Takasaki).[115]

Ikeda also reacted positively to Zhou's statement that trade between the PRC and Japan did not necessarily depend on government agreement (30 July). PRC contacts with the JSP continued after the fall of the Kishi cabinet and resulted among other things in a further agreement on 'consideration trade'.[116] The most interesting development in this period however was the visit to Japan of a PRC Trade Union delegation under Liu Ningyi at about the time the JSP delegation was on its way to the PRC (July-August 1960). The decision to send a delegation to Japan, consisting of Liu, Chen Yu and Sun Shengxuan was published on 9 July and took the Japanese by surprise. Also, the PRC sent a cable to Yasui Kaoru on 20 July to announce the dispatch of a delegation to attend the 6th World Conference for the Prohibition of Nuclear Weapons.[117] These were the first PRC delegations sent since Chen Yi had announced the breaking off of all contacts in 1958. On 26 July the new Japanese government approved the visit, but decided to avoid any formal contact with the Liu Ningyi mission. Despite this position the government regarded the mission as the opportunity for informal contacts with Japanese leaders and groups and as important for exploring possibilities for an improvement in relations. There may be a number of reasons why Liu rather than Liao was chosen to lead this delegation. The delegation had been sent at very short notice, the occasion for the visit being the 10th anniversary of SOHYO, making it reasonable to choose the trade union leader Liu Ningyi. To have sent Liao at this stage might have caused the Japanese to assume that the PRC was overeager to improve relations. Nevertheless both delegations included some of the PRC's most important Japan specialists like Zhao Anbo, Sun Pinghua, Wu Xuewen, Zhao Puchu, and Lin Liyun and Wang Xiaoxian who accompanied the delegations as interpreters, but were later promoted to leading positions. In addition to contacts with SOHYO and functions on the occasion of the anti-nuclear conference, delegation members had talks with members of the JSP (including Asanuma), the JCP (Nosaka, Miyamoto, Shiga and Hakamada) and staff members of the PRC-Japan Fisheries Association.[118] On 5 August, Zhao Anbo and Sun Pinghua had a met Takasaki for nearly three hours. On 7 August Liu Ningyi and others met Matsumura Kenzo but little is known about the substance of these talks.[119]

Back in Peking Liao Chengzhi had participated in the talks with Nakajima Kenzo which led to the signing of a joint statement on cultural exchanges.[120] Shortly afterwards Zhou Enlai had a meeting with Hozumi Shichiro (JSP) and members of a visiting JCFA delegation. He handed them a complete record of his (Zhou's) talks with Suzuki Kazuo which contained suggestions concerning the re-establishment of exchanges. Agreements on trade, fisheries, postal services and transport were to be concluded between the governments of Japan and the PRC on the basis of the previously announced 'three principles'. Special attention was given to a passage referring to the possibility of 'friendship trade' in addition to the 'consideration trade', which from its inception had never been intended to serve as a vehicle for a substantial expansion of trade links.121

The stage was set for a resumption of links at pre-1958 level. In further talks with Hozumi in which Liao Chengzhi took part, agreement was reached on specific questions concerning private contracts. Despite some optimism in Japan PRC attacks on the new Japanese government under Ikeda continued, and he was accused of pushing a foreign policy of even greater dependence on the USA. Also, Hozumi's report made it clear that, even now, political strings would be firmly attached to any new 'friendship' contract. Hozumi took care to deny rumours that the PRC would be forced to make concessions in the political area due to its economic difficulties (in the aftermath of the Great Leap Forward).122

There seems to be little doubt that such economic considerations did indeed play an important role in moves by the PRC to increase its trade with Japan. Perhaps more important than purely economic considerations may have been the realisation that, as a result of the Sino-Soviet split, the PRC would have to make efforts to reduce its isolation from its other neighbours as far as possible, an opinion voiced by Matsumura Kenzo on 3 September.123 It thus appeared very likely that once more the PRC would attempt to involve conservative LDP politicians in order to extend its links with Japan. Shortly afterwards Takasaki left for a visit to Peking, after discussing the visit with Prime Minister Ikeda on 20 September 1960.124 One day after his departure the LDP declared its willingness to resume trade with the PRC starting with trade on a private basis. Takasaki had stated that he was not going to have 'political' talks during his visit. The very fact that he had been invited by Premier Zhou Enlai and Liao Chengzhi in his capacity as Deputy Head of the Office of Foreign Affairs proved that the significance of this visit went beyond what was called an 'inspection trip of the PRC's economy'. Takasaki was also accompanied by a number of Japanese businessmen. In the evening of 11 October Takasaki replied to an address by Zhou, stating that neither the Chinese 'nor the Japanese citizens' were to blame for the fact that 'normalisation of relations' had not yet been achieved. In a press conference at Haneda on his return Takasaki also mentioned that he had pointed out to Zhou that the present form of (friendship) trade produced obstacles, but Zhou had not agreed. Although Liao's name does not appear in published records of the talks, Takasaki also mentioned that he would like to have 'Chairman Liao Chengzhi' invited, not by the government or political parties, but by private institutions in order to promote visits which would reduce misconceptions and misunderstandings.125

It is difficult to give a precise assessment of the influence Takasaki's talks may have exercised. They may have changed the 'mood', as reflected in Fujii Kenzaburo's expectation that prospects for trade contracts were now bright. It would go beyond the scope of this study to detail subsequent moves by various Japanese individuals and organisations to improve trade relations with the PRC.126 Continuing political attacks on the Ikeda government illustrated however that the PRC was not prepared to drop politics for the sake of rapid growth of trade.127 The

Vice-Chairman of the Japanese trade organisation *Nihon Kokubosoku* was asked about Japanese attitudes to the PRC's 'three principles' but, on explaining Japanese reservations, was unable to elicit further comment on the matter. During Yadotani's visit Liao had been in Moscow. His relatively long absence from the 'Japanese scene' at an important juncture in relations with Japan apparently was not due to any diminution in his standing. One may assume that his activities in October and also his participation in the talks in Moscow requiring his absence from contact with the Japanese, went beyond mere ceremonial functions, but unfortunately there is little information available about this period.

'Friendship Trade'

In January 1961 Liao again stepped into the limelight, in particular during the visit of a JSP delegation led by Kuroda Hisao.[128] In the previous month Prime Minister Ikeda had stated that, since agreements on postal and meteorological exchanges would not entail diplomatic recognition, his government was prepared to conclude such agreements with the PRC. Any hopes for an easy solution to pending problems were dashed however when Liao on 20 January, in an address to the JSP delegation stated flatly that Ikeda's suggestion was 'nothing but a gesture to deceive the people', and insisted on adherence to the 'three principles'.[129] Highpoint of the JSP visit was undoubtedly a meeting with Mao Zedong, when Mao repeated openly that he regarded the 'Chinese people a direct ally of the JSP', and dissenters in the LDP, 'the anti-mainstream politicians Matsumura, Miki, Ishibashi, Takasaki and Kono as indirect allies'.[130] Towards the end of the talk Mao referred to Ikeda as being too scared as a consequence of the protests during the security treaty crisis to prohibit contacts with the PRC. Addressing Liao - the only other PRC politician to add a few words here and there during Mao's talk - Mao said that 'apparently Comrade Liao Chengzhi has received an invitation from Okazaki (Kaheita), Comrade Liao will you go?' Liao answered 'It's not yet been decided'.[131] The visit never took place. Mao pointed out possibilities for trade although in his speech he did not comment further on the way this should be done.

Zhou Enlai had previously met Suzuki Mosaburo and expressed his readiness to exchange trade delegations without discontinuing the existing 'friendship trade'. It was also reported that the PRC was interested in receiving a Japanese business delegation including those with power and influence in 'big business'.[132] Perhaps the best indication of the change in PRC policy towards trade with Japan was provided in the report by Matsumoto Shichiro.[133] According to him the PRC saw no likelihood of Ikeda concluding a governmental trade agreement with the PRC.[134] He expressed the opinion, however, that the PRC would gradually try to increase the volume of trade such that the Japanese government would be forced to become involved due to the necessity for government guarantees. While this sounds a plausible rationale for the PRC policy change towards a 'gradual approach', the fact remains that it was not the Japanese government but the PRC that had to adapt to new circumstances after the successful conclusion of the Revised Security Treaty. Despite these indications of change it was going to take many more delegations and even more talks before a 'private' trade agreement concluded in 1962 provided for trade missions with quasi-diplomatic status. Full diplomatic status remained unattainable for the time being, and the desired break in relations between Japan and the ROC was as distant as ever. Throughout the coming months Liao would be closely involved in these complex negotiations which cannot be treated here, although they clearly deserve a separate study.

One may conclude, then, that Liao's role lay mainly on the political side of these talks, and not so much in technical details of trade exchanges. Unlike Mao's approach, Liao was much more specific on political questions related to PRC-Japan relations, as far as one can judge from published records. This is well illustrated in the summary of Liao's speech addressed to *Nihon Kokubosoku* President, Yamamoto Kumaichi, on 25 February 1961,[135] during a visit that became the foundation of a lasting friendship between Liao and Yamamoto.[136] Perhaps not surprisingly Liao devoted much attention to the interlocking questions of Japan's relations with the PRC and the ROC against the background of relations with the USA. It is striking that Liao largely avoided the slogans and clichés, so well known from PRC media and Mao's pronouncements, in talking about the United States. The key to the 'Taiwan question' as well as to PRC relations with Japan lay in Washington, he said and was as frank about this point as about the PRC's short and long term economic difficulties. To Liao, contacts with LDP members were not only useful for the sake of relations with Japan; they were a channel through which he could try to obtain further information about US intentions, since some LDP politicians with whom he developed close contact were also active in sounding out the possibility of changes in US attitudes to the PRC. At this period, for example, Takasaki Tatsunosuke and Nakasone Yasuhiro visited the US for just that purpose. Liao was not the only prominent Japan specialist whom Takasaki, Matsumura and others met, but there was no doubt that despite his temporary absence, his position as the PRC's most senior spokesman on relations with Japan (after Mao and Zhou) was unchanged.

As the Sino-Soviet split deepened, reflected in increasingly antagonistic media statements, an apparently 'tough' PRC approach to the struggle against 'American imperialism' and the necessity for armed struggle and the recent rather flexible approach towards Japan seemed to exist side by side. Matsumoto Shichiro had noted that in his talks with Mao, Zhou and Liao PRC policy towards Japan appeared extremely flexible. The PRC did not expect much from Japanese Prime Minister Ikeda, and a governmental trade agreement appeared out of the question, but it was now held that a gradual approach would 'inevitably' lead to government involvement. Yamamoto Kumaichi had also obtained this impression. At the same time the Japanese side seemed to take a more relaxed approach to the question of trade with the PRC, and there were frequent discussions within the LDP's 'Foreign Relations Research Group' on relations with the PRC and US attitudes. While some LDP politicians even favoured recognising the PRC diplomatically, the majority did not. Nevertheless Ikeda was in favour of an expansion of trade. He wished to reduce the political aspects of the so-called 'friendship-trade', and both Ikeda and the LDP chief-secretary Ohira called for an increased role for the semi-governmental trade organisation *Nitchu yushutsunyo kumiai*.

Moves on both sides towards a *rapprochement* reflected the true substance of a new situation, but their overall tough stance forced the PRC to continue ideological verbiage that harmonised with the aggressive language it used in the debate with the Soviet Union. In his speech on 20 January 1961 Liao had strongly attacked some of Japan's ruling conservative politicians for obediently following the policies of 'US imperialism', and scathingly refuted previous suggestions by the Japanese government of 'so-called governmental postal and meteorological agreements' as a fraud. While news of the disaster of the Great Leap Forward continued to spread abroad, Liao also refuted:

> the small handful of imperialists and reactionaries who perceive with glee the serious natural disasters from which China is suffering and who are of the opinion that China will have to beg from them ... We warn these imperialist elements and their running dogs, your joy is premature, and let's see who will persist in the end: 'he who laughs last laughs best'.

This should be compared to Mao's emphasis on the split within the LDP in his speech on 24 January. Elaborating on the usefulness of such splits he compared them to similar splits that existed between the USA and its Western European allies. Public attacks on Ikeda became much stronger in June in connection with his visit to the United States and talks with Kennedy. PRC leaders made it clear that they did not expect any substantial policy change under Ikeda, just as they did not expect any substantial change from Kennedy.[137] At this juncture how did the PRC leaders perceive their chances of exploiting disagreement within the ruling LDP by exerting pressure on the Ikeda government by supporting what Mao had called the PRC's 'indirect allies' within the LDP? Zhou Enlai gave some surprisingly pessimistic (or should we say 'realistic'?) comments on this point:

> When Takasaki visited China last year he repeatedly offered to devote the remainder of his life to (the promotion of) Sino-Japanese relations. But at present, Takasaki does not hold actual power, being a member of the anti-mainstream faction in the LDP, ... Also, one cannot exclude (the possibility) that he will be influenced by his surroundings. As soon as Fujiyama became foreign minister he lost his courage to act in accordance with the Bandung spirit.

Despite these reservations Zhou was still in favour of promoting trade with Japan:

> With regard to Sino-Japanese trade, we do not expect a governmental trade agreement. Why? Because it's impossible. Without an improvement in Sino-Japanese relations, without formal state relations, how would it be possible to conclude a governmental agreement? What we hope for are private trade relations.[138]

China's Relations with Japan

These pronouncements appear to indicate that PRC leaders entertained rather realistic ideas about the limits of their possibilities for influencing Japanese politics through the bait of trade. Although they attacked Ikeda they seemed prepared to find a way to improve trade relations in the near future. Despite denials that the PRC was under strong pressure to increase its trade with non-Communist countries as a result of economic and political difficulties there was a genuine wish to increase trade beyond the constraints of the existing 'friendship trade' structure, which was clearly not sufficient for the PRC's needs. Lack of diplomatic relations was one obstacle. Perhaps more serious was the strong pressure on Japan from the United States not to support PRC economic development through increased trade. In his talk with Yamamoto referred to above Liao was quite open about this point:

> what is the (main) problem in Sino-Japanese relations? That is the problem of America ... Seen from its military strategic importance in modern times Taiwan has no significance at present. Well, if that is so, why does America not abandon Taiwan? America tries to put obstacles between China and Japan by using Taiwan ... Because America is involved ... the Japanese government cannot normalise relations with China unless it breaks relations with Taiwan. Just like us Ikeda has a headache because of this problem. What can we do about this? We will wait. There is nothing else to do but to wait ...

Subsequently Liao referred to the fact that Egypt had established relations with the PRC:

> (Nasser) did not break relations with Taiwan. There was (still) a Taiwan embassy in Cairo, but Nasser had a Chinese (ie PRC) governmental trade mission established in Cairo. Subsequently he concluded a governmental trade agreement. Soon afterwards he established relations with China. As a result the Taiwan embassy withdrew.

He added that it would be impossible to maintain relations with Taiwan while establishing relations with the PRC. It does not seem far-fetched to assume that the PRC would have liked to pursue a similar strategy towards Japan, and the establishment of the semi-governmental L-T trade and the subsequent stationing of trade missions in Peking and Japan may have been designed to frustrate Japan's links with the ROC in Taiwan. Liao added some seemingly conciliatory remarks on the PRC's attitude towards Taiwan. He agreed that an (important) means to change the minds of the Taiwanese (towards the PRC) was to compete in the area of living standards, although he admitted that this was by no means an easy task:

> I would like to make it clear that we do not wish to overthrow Chiang Kaishek. It would be fine if we could conclude a united front with them, if only America would withdraw from Taiwan. ... if Chiang Kaishek were to come to Peking we would all go to welcome him. The solution to the Taiwan problem lies in driving America out. We do not insist that Japan would have to break relations with Taiwan and establish relations with the PRC (instead).

Economic and Political Relations

Over twenty years later Liao's remark seems to have some relevance to the present situation. It is difficult to judge whether this reflects his own, fairly flexible viewpoint which certainly contrasts with the PRC's tough position in the period 1966-71. Despite signs of PRC flexibility little progress was made in 1961 although contacts with members of the LDP's anti-mainstream faction continued.

The PRC might not have wished to make any concessions *before* Ikeda's trip to the United States, the debate on the police-demonstration law and, in particular, the pending discussion of the PRC's membership in the UN in autumn 1961. Also the need to take the interests of the PRC's 'direct' and 'indirect' allies into account always remained. One of the most important allies, the JSP, was not of one mind concerning their attitude towards the PRC. Disunity on this point was the main reason for the delay in sending a third mission to the PRC.[139] Despite visits by Kuroda, Tanaka and Okada the visit of the delegation planned for the spring was delayed until January 1962.[140] During this period relations with the JCP were strengthened, first during a visit of JCP parliamentarians to Peking in June,[141] and during a visit of a delegation of the party organ *Akahata (Red Flag)* in November, when a contract was signed concerning a Japanese translation of Mao Zedong's Selected Works.[142] While attacks on Ikeda intensified another LDP member, Utsunomiya Tokuma, who also spoke to Liao Chengzhi during his visit, reported on 28 June that, despite Ikeda's talks with Kennedy, the PRC line towards relations with Japan was relatively soft, confirming earlier signs of a tempering of the PRC position. Superficially, however, the PRC's fierce ideological attacks continued:

> Under the influence of the vicious, double-faced policy of Kennedy, the Japanese government adopted what on the surface is seemingly a so-called low profile, unlike that of the Kishi government, with the intention of cheating the people. At the same time there is the plan to strengthen the reactionary rule of Japanese monopoly capital in Japan itself which is following American imperialism by means of the Fascist bill that suppresses the Japanese people - 'the bill to prevent political violence' - as well as a series of [other] reactionary bills.[143]

Liao Chengzhi may well have appeared a 'moderate' to some Japanese visitors. Acting as a PRC spokesman in the field of Afro-Asian politics and in the growing Sino-Soviet dispute, he seemed to emerge as a radical. In his speeches he followed the general sharp line attacking 'US imperialism', and at a rally in Peking charged the USA and Belgium with the murder of Lumumba. In March Liao left for New Delhi to attend a World Peace Conference where the PRC delegation attracted little publicity.[144] Towards the end of the year Liao attended a meeting in Gaza of the Executive Committee of the AAPSO, and also participated in a World Peace Conference in Stockholm where he gave a speech that 'was a renewed and intensified challenge to the general line of Soviet foreign policy.'[145] His published speeches were irreconcilably hostile to 'US imperialism'[146] and also contained open attacks on the 'Soviet line', putting great emphasis on PRC 'solidarity' with 'oppressed' peoples in Asia, Africa and Latin America with which the PRC, but not the Soviet Union, shared a history of colonial oppression.[147] Throughout the year he also attended numerous functions for visitors from third world countries, in particular from South-East Asia and Africa, meeting Burmese, Nepalese and Laotian leaders as well as Indonesian President Sukarno and Kwame Nkrumah.

Despite Liao's attacks on the Soviet line[148] he also repeatedly met members of Soviet friendship delegations to the PRC. Little is known about the contents of such meetings which could hardly have ignored the growing gap between the Communist giants. Looking ahead to 1962 Liao continued to speak at functions within the Afro-Asian movement and Communist front organisations, speeches the content of which could easily lead us to misjudge the international situation relating to the PRC as well as the PRC's internal situation.[149] In addition, the PRC continued attempts to construct a united anti-US front in Japan in order to put pressure on the government. In January 1962 the JSP sent its long-delayed third mission to Peking led by Suzuki Mosaburo which signed a communiqué including many points pressed for by the Chinese Communists.[150] Relations continued to be characterised by friction over a number of points, intensified by splits within the JSP and differences with the JCP, also courted by Peking.[151] During meetings with opposition parties Liao continued to charge the 'reactionary cliques of the United States and Japan' with the murder of Asanuma Inejiro (at a meeting with Yasui Kaoru),[152] and claimed that 'there is no way to change and conceal the iron-hard reality that American imperialism is the factual ruler of Japan'.

Liao also called the Ikeda government a 'running dog of American imperialism'. His speech culminated in a call to 'strengthen the struggle until American imperialism has been driven from Chinese territory (ie Taiwan) and from Japanese territory'.[153]

Despite a temporary lull in Sino-Soviet tensions around this period key phrases denoting the PRC point of view such as 'The East wind prevails over the West wind' did not disappear from PRC propaganda. Also, the PRC wished to create the impression that its main opponent, the USA, was in an increasingly difficult position, and it did not fail to point to Japan's 'economic crisis'.[154]

Under these circumstances would the PRC be willing to enter into serious negotiations with Japanese conservatives? While the PRC attempted to portray an image of its own strength and the power of the 'international revolutionary forces' PRC leaders were well aware of the true situation. The PRC was in the middle of an unprecedented economic and political crisis. In the aftermath of the Great Leap Forward, industry and agriculture in particular had received devastating blows, resulting in starvation and a large exodus of refugees. Tensions with India and the Soviet Union erupted in military clashes. In May and June military activities on both sides of the Taiwan Straits heightened the crisis. In October the PRC reacted to border clashes with India by escalating the conflict into a limited war.

Against this background PRC moves to increase links with the Japanese conservatives may appear somewhat surprising at first. Even within the same year (1962), on 9 November a new trade agreement was concluded, which clearly reduced the importance of the existing 'friendship trade', despite the fact that this trade had been designed to gain maximum political leverage on companies trading with the PRC. The JSP had been heavily involved in the 'friendship trade' and it is doubtful whether the new agreement was welcomed by all JSP members.[155] The JSP continued efforts to retain an important function in PRC trade with Japan, but efforts by Suzuki Kazuo who, for example, left the PRC in March after a stay of more than two months seems to have had only limited success.[156] In April 1962 Liao Chengzhi issued statements that provided a rationale for the change of policy. While continuing attacks on 'imperialists' and the Japanese government he pointed out that, in Japan, medium and small enterprises, not to mention some 'capitalists' were increasingly opposed to American policy towards Japan. He thus included them as potential members of an anti-US united front, and in doing so justified future links with sections of Japan's 'big business'.[157] A few days later Ookubo Masaharu, Matsumura's secretary, left for a 'goodwill visit' to Peking, and he prepared the ground for renewed intensive contacts between conservative politicians like Matsumura, Takasaki and Okazaki who had previously expressed strong interest in the promotion of trade links with the PRC.[158] These moves were not only supported by politicians 'friendly' towards the PRC. Virtually simultaneously with Ookubo's visit Minister Sato (MITI) issued a statement that created considerable excitement in Japan,[159] and even American opposition was apparently unable to stem the tide.[160] Subsequently there was complex manoeuvring in Japan between various individual politicians and sections of the administration (especially those concerned with trade and foreign affairs) which have been described elsewhere in great detail.[161] The PRC also employed 'confidential diplomacy' when Vice-premier Chen Yi sent Sun Pinghua to Japan in the summer as member of a PRC *go* (a Chinese board game much played in Japan) delegation to Japan thus creating opportunities to get in touch with Matsumura Kenzo and Takasaki Tatsunosuke.[162] Another occasion for contact with Matsumura, Takasaki, Utsunomiya and Okazaki Kaheita were visits in early August by Sun and Zhao to attend the annual anti-nuclear conference.[163]

The most detailed published record of the talks leading up to the L-T trade agreement is provided by Tagawa Seiichi who was one of the members of the delegation that visited the PRC between 12 and 25 September.[164] In their recollections both Tagawa and Furui Yoshimi (also a member of that delegation) emphasise that, right from the start of the talks, there was a conspicuous lack of emphasis on 'politics', especially when compared to the previous visit in 1959,[165] although the PRC of course was well aware of the intensive links of the delegation with LDP leaders Ikeda, Fujiyama, Miki and Kono.[166] As Ambassador Ogawa Heishiro pointed out later, an article in the pro-Communist Hong Kong newspaper *Xunhuan ribao* on 9 September raised the expectation that the PRC would not let the delegation return empty-handed.[167] This Matsumura mission paved the way for a second mission led by Takasaki who signed the trade agreement in November.[168] As in previous important negotiations, Liao Chengzhi played a leading role, second only to that of Zhou Enlai and perhaps Chen Yi.[169]

Despite the initial de-emphasising of politics the Matsumura delegation was surprised to find that political questions were, in fact, a major issue during the first discussion between Zhou Enlai and Matsumura, also attended by Chen Yi and Liao Chengzhi.[170] Zhou criticised Japanese press reports stating that both sides had agreed to separate political and economic issues. The refusal to separate politics and economics was of course one of the basic points of the 'three principles', with which the PRC had persevered since 1958, and Zhou could hardly let these press reports go unchallenged. He also attacked some Japanese politicians who, he said, had become involved in US attempts to create an 'independent' Taiwan.

Matsumura refuted these reports and suggested an exchange of journalists in order to improve communication and understanding between the two sides.[171] An additional political point raised was Japan's position on the question of the PRC's membership of the United Nations.[172] On 19 September Sun Pinghua handed over a draft memo in preparation for a joint communiqué.[173] Matsumura's main objection was that it might create the impression that the Japanese side had accepted the PRC demand concerning the 'inseparability of politics and economics'.[174] When Liao Chengzhi met Matsumura later on the same day he attempted to persuade Matsumura, and when Matsumura refused Liao answered:

> this draft was completed by working throughout last night, and has the approval of Prime Minister Zhou ... in order to redraft it I will have to get Prime Minister Zhou's approval once more.[175]

After a discussion lasting for more than an hour Liao left with the remark 'since I am going to reconsider the draft I request the Japanese side to do the same'.[176]

According to Tagawa Seiichi the new draft produced by Liao answered Matsumura's objections. There was one passage the Japanese delegation could not accept, which again might create misunderstanding concerning the difficult point of 'inseparability of politics and economics'.[177] A meeting with Zhou had already been arranged for the afternoon, and Matsumura asked Tagawa to discuss the suggested change with Liao who declared that he personally found the passage acceptable, but that he was not sure about Premier Zhou Enlai's opinion.[178] When the delegation met Zhou it became clear that the new draft had been accepted. In his reply to Matsumura's address, for the first time Zhou Enlai referred to Liao and Matsumura as 'liaison officers for Sino-Japanese relations.[179] Perhaps the most vital passage in the short memo was the following sentence:

> Both sides agree to strive for the normalisation of relations between both countries, including political and economic relations, by (a series of) gradual and cumulative measures.[180]

Political relations were thus no longer a pre-condition for economic contacts. Zhou subsequently touched on a number of issues concerning both countries and, despite his continuing emphasis on the so-called three political and three trade principles, it was fairly clear that the function of the speech was to a large degree a face-saving device.[181] Liao Chengzhi's position once again had been very prominent, and was underlined by Zhou Enlai's suggestion made during his second talk with Matsumura that Liao and Matsumura should act as guarantors under an agreement to be finalised by the Takasaki mission. Matsumura suggested Okazaki instead of himself. Finally it was agreed that the guarantor should be decided during the visit of the Takasaki mission.[182]

Zhou Enlai also expressed some expectations concerning future specific political concessions by the Japanese. He declared that he did not expect Ikeda to recognise the PRC and break off relations with the ROC, but he expressed his hope that as a realistic and minimal political concession Japan might abstain in the vote on the China question in the coming session of the United Nations. He acknowledged that the Ikeda government was different from the Kishi administration in several respects, but he did not think that this amounted to a substantial change, and thus basically confirmed the PRC evaluation of 1960.[183]

Even more interesting in the light of Sino-Soviet relations at the time were Zhou's remarks refuting the idea of a (Chinese) 'Yellow Peril' that still existed in the minds of some Japanese, and stressing that this was a European term designed to 'pour cold water' on Asian solidarity. He pointed out that American trade policy served aggression and contrasted it with that of the PRC: 'East is East, and for the sake of the development of the East the countries of the East have to join in mutual co-operation'.[184] In his farewell address Matsumura also mentioned that Zhou and Chen Yi had referred to this topic:

> East is East, and Asians have to change (the course of) world history ...
> We belong to one body, and we should strengthen our relations between countries of the same race and culture.[185]

These were clear references to 'Asianism', and suggested a fundamentally different outlook from the 'European' Soviet state, but in his speech Chen Yi took care to deny that there were differences between China and other Socialist countries.[186]

Asian co-operation was also taken up again during the Takasaki delegation. During the second meeting with the delegation Zhou referred to the tragic past:

> since the Sino-Japanese War (of 1894-95) Japan has committed aggression against China for eight decades, and caused great damage to human life and property ... We have a deep grudge ..., but compared to the two thousand years of friendly relations between China and Japan this is only an insignificant period. We are making efforts (now) to try and forget this grudge ... Forgetting our grudge let us strengthen Asia by joining hands. An Asia strengthened in such a way would not challenge others militarily, but should there ever again be pressure from outside Asia we might (be able to) defend ourselves.[187]

Liao Chengzhi also played a key role in the negotiations with the Takasaki delegation which have been described in English in detail elsewhere.[188] He again acted as Zhou's representative when Zhou did not participate in the talks himself.[189] The problem of the inseparability of politics and economics was brought up again, but Zhou agreed to have this principle listed as the PRC's point of view without forcing its acceptance by the Japanese delegation.

Rapprochement

The agreement constituted a significant breakthrough in PRC trade relations with Japan, enabling the PRC to obtain badly needed goods for the development of its sadly lagging economy during a critical period, and also laying the basis for a more stable, long-term economic relationship than had been possible under the so-called private trade agreements of the fifties. Due to its semi-governmental character it also carried political weight, as stated by Chen Yi:[190]

> This agreement may be called a private agreement as well as a governmental agreement. Why? Because the Chinese negotiators are members of the government, and the Japanese negotiators, too, are influential LDP politicians who, just like the business representatives have close links with the Japanese government. To carry this argument further, there, is no problem concerning a governmental trade (agreement) as far as the Chinese side is concerned. This is the fault of America which is scheming to create two Chinas, and of Japan which maintains relations with Chiang Kaishek.[191]

Chen Yi's comment on the semi-governmental character of the agreement was hardly exaggerated since it was the foundation on the basis of which trade missions were exchanged in 1964-65, in all but name assuming consular functions.[192]

The agreement had been achieved against a background of tough rhetoric in the Sino-Soviet dispute. At times the PRC's rhetoric had also dampened Japanese expectations of a thaw, as for example, during Guo Moruo's meeting with Hirano of the Japanese Peace Association.[193] In April Liao had provided a rationale for the broadening of links with Japan as a means of driving a wedge between Japan and the United States. The argument seemed partly justified by US opposition to an expansion of Japanese trade links with the PRC.[194] It goes without saying that it also encountered opposition from the ROC. The L-T agreement however did not lead to a break in relations between the ROC and Japan, as in the case of Egypt, and it is very doubtful whether PRC leaders had ever entertained real hopes in that direction. The ultimate reason for the PRC's change of policy should be sought in an attempt to prevent increasing isolation after the Sino-Soviet split and other such crises besetting PRC foreign policy in 1962. In addition to a general desire to strengthen foreign trade links there were more specific problems such as the need to obtain products such as ammonium sulphate, vital for economic recovery, from countries more or less independent of the Soviet Union and the United States.[195]

It is perhaps amazing that the *rapprochement* with Japan took place during a period of heightened 'revolutionary' rhetoric. The CCP was also able to improve its party-level links with the Japan Communist Party, already referred to. Towards the end of 1962 a delegation under Hakamada Satomi went to Peking and had important discussions with Communist leaders including Mao Zedong and Liu Shaoqi.[196] Little has been revealed about the contents of these talks but it appears that they were very important in achieving agreement on major issues in the Sino-Soviet dispute. If Liao took part in these talks published records do not reflect his role. The *rapprochement* was demonstrated during the meeting of the 5th Central Committee on 15 February 1963, also reported in PRC media[197] and followed by increased co-operation between the parties in the coming months.[198]

Liao's visibility in the area of relations with Japan and the Afro-Asian movement seemed to be reduced during the first part of 1963, although he continued to attend numerous functions. No overseas trips were reported until the end of the year but he remained active behind the scenes. Towards the end of April he sent Sun Pinghua and Wang Xiaoyun to Japan as members of an 'Orchid Growers' delegation. Of course, as revealed by Sun himself the reason for their presence in Japan was not to discuss orchid cultivation but to hold talks with Matsumura and Takasaki on the possibility of establishing private trade missions which were eventually established in the summer of 1964.[199] One might have expected Liao himself to lead a delegation to Japan after previous suggestions for such a trip. One simple factor preventing this at that time could have been his numerous engagements in connection with receiving and resettling Overseas Chinese returning from India in the aftermath of the war.[200] A political reason might have been the deterioration of relations with the Soviet Union. Talks between the PRC and the Soviet Union ended in stalemate on 25 July. At a time when PRC foreign policy preached 'revolution' it would have been rather difficult for Liao to lead a mission which would have to express strong support for 'revolutionary' aims and support for the JCP without alienating the JSP and provoking strong reaction from members of the ruling conservative party.

The Moscow talks ended on the same day the Partial Test Ban Treaty was signed by the USA and the Soviet Union, a symbol for Soviet-American collusion in the eyes of the PRC. One of the first meetings of an international front organisation after this event was to be the 9th Anti-Nuclear Conference in Japan to be held in Hiroshima in August. As early as 1 August a meeting was held in Peking at which Liao Chengzhi delivered a speech which set the keynote for the PRC delegation to the conference, and which maintained an uncompromising attitude.[201] The PRC knew itself supported by the JCP.[202] Liao sharply attacked the Test Ban Treaty as a fraud and accused the Soviet Union of collaborating in this fraud instead of concentrating on the fight against American 'imperialism', and of surrender to the United States. He also included East Germany, Czechoslovakia, Bulgaria and the French and Italian Communist parties, in his attack. Referring to the impending Hiroshima Conference Liao warned that it would face:

> a complex international situation. Within Japan, American imperialism, Japanese reactionary circles and their accomplices are busy deploying their schemes, planning to split the alliance of patriotic democratic forces, wrecking the struggle of the Japanese people for the prohibition of nuclear weapons and nuclear war and against American imperialism, to destroy the Ninth World Conference ...[203]

He thus indicated that the PRC was not prepared to surrender its position for the sake of maintaining a facade of unity. The conference became the scene of clashes not only between the Soviet and Chinese Communist delegations but also between the JSP and SOHYO who supported the Test Ban Treaty, and the JCP which espoused the PRC position.[204]

After the conference another JCP delegation visited the PRC from 3-22 September but, apart from reports of meetings with Deng Xiaoping, Peng Zhen, Mao Zedong and Liao Chengzhi, little was publicly announced.[205]

Despite the strong support for the JCP and 'revolution', trade links with Japan seemed to be scarcely affected. Following the L-T agreement the First Trade Protocol was signed at the end of negotiations between Suzuki Kazuo and PRC representatives on 27 December 1963.[206] In his welcome address on 17 December Liao referred to the significance of these links in time of international tension which, as he put it:

> was created by the United States, ever more hysterically hostile towards China. These days, however, Sino-Japanese trade is not only uninterrupted, but is gaining new ground. This is due to the fact that the forces demanding peace and independence for Japan, the forces of the Chinese people, the forces of peace in the world have been strengthened compared to the past.[207]

A more sober appreciation was given by Jain:

> by this agreement, Shinkichi Eto remarks, Japan became the only country in the world to trade with substantial freedom both with Taiwan and with the Chinese mainland. An important feature of the L-T memorandum was that trade contracts concluded in accordance with its terms could not be annulled arbitrarily by any one side. Unlike the so-called 'friendship trade', the L-T trade arrangement was direct and more reliable and had the official backing of the Japanese Ministry of International Trade ... On 16 November 1962 the 'Japan-China Over-All Trade Liaison Council' was established in Tokyo, with Tatsunosuke Takasaki as its first Chairman, to facilitate implementation of the L-T Agreement.[208]

As a result of the L-T agreement trade increased significantly in 1963.[209] This was followed by an even more dramatic increase in 1964, but it has to be noted that, after the great impact of the agreement on the stabilisation of trade in 1963, the share of trade conducted on the basis of protocols and contracts within the framework of the L-T agreement, dropped dramatically in 1964. Between 1965 and 1969 under the L-T agreement Japanese exports dropped to approximately 10% of total exports, to remain at that level until 1973 when this form of trade was finally abolished. As far as imports were concerned the share of L-T trade remained more constant. Except for 1963, 'friendship trade' continued to account for most of Japanese trade with the PRC in subsequent years. After several years of stagnation at a slightly lower level trade picked up again significantly in 1970, to be followed by another dramatic increase between 1972 and 1973 as a result of the normalisation of relations between the PRC and Japan.[210]

Despite the fact that the L-T agreement provided for the exchange of goods which could be obtained only with difficulty under the existing friendship trade pattern, it would be easy to overrate the economic effect of the agreement. It did exercise an important function in giving trade a significant boost in 1963, but it failed to provide a 'politically neutral' framework for trade as desired by a large section of the Japanese business community, since its introduction did not lead to a phasing out of the 'friendship trade' pattern. Also, the Japanese government had actively sought to involve the government-backed Export-Import Association in the yearly negotiations, but the agreements reached in December 1962, as well as later ones, were negotiated by other groups and organisations.

The significance of the L-T agreement should not only be judged by its immediate economic results. It provided a starting point for the dramatic increase in the flow of visitors and cultural and other exchanges, and allowed the PRC to achieve a much higher exposure in Japan. Also, it enabled the PRC to expand its contacts with Japanese individuals and organisations to a much larger degree, especially after the stationing of L-T trade missions.[211] Most important of all was the fact, already referred to, that through the L-T the PRC had been able to elevate the level of contacts with Japan to a semi-governmental one.[212] Increased trade with Japan had apparently not been affected by the PRC's public crusade for revolution.

On 23 August the Japanese government had agreed on deferred payments for the Vinylon plant to be exported to the PRC, an important step in the expansion of trade involving the sale of whole plants. The Second L-T Protocol was signed on 2 September 1963. PRC willingness to continue its wide links with Japan was symbolised by the establishment on 4 October of the Sino-Japanese Friendship Association, of which Liao Chengzhi became president.[213] It was the first PRC friendship association directed towards a country with which the PRC did not maintain diplomatic relations, and thus underlined the importance attached to the links with Japan.[214] In marked contrast to PRC statements supporting revolution only a few days before, speeches delivered on the occasion of the establishment of the SJFA emphasised the desirability of expanded links with Japan. It was a classic example of the application of united front tactics which sought at the same time to win allies among leftists (including 'revolutionaries') and 'neutral' conservatives from within the establishment and not to shy away from presenting a quite different, often contradictory, image to members of both groups. In his speech as head of the newly-founded SJFA Liao stressed the development of economic and cultural links as future tasks of the SJFA, and he referred again to the 'Bandung principles' as the basis on which to strive for the establishment of diplomatic relations as well as for peaceful coexistence. Which image presented by the PRC was the correct one? The revolutionary one, or the one that stressed peaceful coexistence? One may, of course, explain this contradictory stance by referring to Marxist-Leninist dialectics which, stated in an oversimplified way, justify all tactics that bring about revolutionary success. Perhaps it was merely a repetition of the ancient political art of making people hear only what they want to hear.

Notes on Chapter Four

1. Barnett, *Communist China*, p 268. This episode was interpreted differently by Lee: 'Apparently encouraged by Chou's friendly conversation with Takasaki and his opening of the ambassadorial talks with the United States, the Chinese government initiated a direct diplomatic contact with Japan. Chou was apparently confident that the combination of Japan's domestic political conditions - particularly Hatoyama's favourable disposition - and of an expected new thaw in Sino-American relations would be conducive to the process of this decisive diplomatic step. The channel used for this purpose was an exchange of diplomatic notes between Japanese and Chinese consuls-general at Geneva - Tatsuke Keiichi and Shen Ping, respectively. Even though a spokesman of the Chinese Foreign Ministry publicly refuted Tatsuke's first note to Shen, dated 15 July 1955, in which Japan asked for an investigation of 40,000 Japanese nationals still missing in China, Shen, in his secret reply dated 17 August, proposed that in order to promote normalisation of Sino-Japanese relations and contribute to further relaxation of international situations, the Japanese government send a delegation to Peking to discuss trade, exchange of persons, status of overseas residents, and "other important problems" of mutual interest...' (*Japan Faces China*), pp 31-2). *Tenkai suru kakumei gaiko*, p 120 follows a similar line of thought. Firstly, it should be noted that it was the Japanese who again raised the topic of repatriation through the Geneva channel; secondly, prior developments had pointed to the acceptance of a steady and slow increase in the scale of trade and other relations before raising the issue of formal diplomatic recognition. Thirdly, Communist Chinese reactions were characterised by irritation as a result of a perceived insult and loss of face, since the Japanese implicitly accused them of ill faith, or worse, by asking 'for an investigation of 40,000 Japanese nationals still missing in China'.
2. *Sengo shiryo nitchu kankei*, pp 34 f.
3. See complaints concerning the treatment of Overseas Chinese in Japan in a *PD* editorial, 14 September 1955. *PD* of 4 November 1955 charged the Japanese government with forcibly repatriating Overseas Chinese to Taiwan province. Compare Endo, *Nitchu jugonen senso*, p 483.
4. *Senso shiryo nitchu kankei*, pp 34 f.
5. *NS*, 17 August 1955. Zhou's speech gave rise to much speculation; see 'Shu Onrai wa do kotaeta ka?'. Lee mentions that Zhou did not demand 'the immediate abrogation of the Japan-Taiwan peace treaty' which 'was not a necessary precondition for the normalisation of Sino-Japanese diplomatic relations (*Japan Faces China*, p 32). By publicly stating his aim - to isolate Taiwan diplomatically - Zhou must have known that he asked Japan to embark on a course which was totally unacceptable at that time not only to numerous Japanese, but also to the USA.
6. *NS*, 2 and 14 October 1955.
7. *NS*, 14 November 1955. The tone of a *PD* article of 15 December on Japanese foreign policy, and a similar broadcast by Radio Peking the following day, was quite unconciliatory (*NS*). See also the attack on Foreign Minister Shigemitsu in *Dagongbao* (Tianjin) of 19 February 1956 (*NS*).
8. *Feiwei qiaowu gongzuo zhi yanjiu*, (periodical), pp 8-9. Factional cleavages may have been at the root of such policy oscillation although one cannot exclude the possibility of conscious alternation of policies to 'soften up' the Japanese. It might be added here that these changes in policy towards Japan do not always coincide with the cyclical change between 'hard' and 'soft' lines in the PRC's general policies, with all its implications for our assumptions on changes in PRC foreign policies. There is an obvious need to subject traditional periodisations based on general

Economic and Political Relations

foreign policy statements to detailed comparisons of regional policies and bilateral relations. In my view, a promising approach would be to compare policies towards Western Europe and Japan since 1952, or say policies towards Iran, Chile and Angola during the seventies and eighties.

9   *NCNA*, 31 August and 3 September 1955.
10 *NCNA*, 15 September 1953.
11 See also *Nippon Times*, 12 January 1956. A picture in *Liao Chengzhi de yisheng* p 50, shows him together with other members of the delegation in front of the Taj Mahal.
12 Barnett, *Communist China*, p 270.
13 Furui Yoshimi, *Nitchu juhachinen*, (1978) p 68; Wilbur, *Communist China*, pp 215-6.
14 'Saikin ni okeru Nitchu kankei dakai undo ni tsuite', *Kuan joho*, no 63, pp 53 ff, no 67, p 71. In February hints were given on the impending release of war criminals (*NS*, 28 February 1956).
15 According to Furui, Hatoyama had declared on 29 March 1956 in a session of the Foreign Relations Committee of the Diet that 'if the other side seeks talks there is no reason to refuse them' (*Nitchu juhachinen*, p 68). See also Yasutomo, 'Sato's China Policy', p 534.
16 *Kokusai boeki*, 16 June 1983.
17 Saburo Okamoto, *Nitchu boeki ron*, 1971, pp 47-80. Zhou called for visits by Shigemitsu or Hatoyama in May, aware that such a visit would imply *de facto* recognition of the PRC by Japan (*NS*, 9 and 16 May 1956). In the same vein, Liao repeated in August that the Chinese government would do everything possible to realise contacts with Hatoyama and Shigemitsu (*NS* 20 August 1956, quoting Kyodo).
18 *Kokusai boeki*, 16 June 1983.
19 *Nitchu kankei kihon shiryoshu*, pp 353 and 112-3. See also *NS*, 11 and 12 October.
20 *NS*, 6 November 1956, and *PD*, 25 December 1956. The gradual approach was maintained into 1957; see for instance, *NS*, 4 and 21 January and 6 March 1957.
21 Nitchu boeki sokushin giin renmei, comp *Nitchu kankei shiryoshu 1945-66nen*, (1967) p 290 (28 June 1956). See also *Nitchu kokko kaifuku, kankei shiryoshu*, Nitchu kokko kaifuku sokushin giin renmei, comp, 1972, p 359.
22 *Nitchu kankei kihon shiryoshu*, p 352.
23 Oomagari Tadashi, *Asanuma Inejiro. Sono hito, sono shogai*, (1961) p 153. On the change of policy adopted at the 13th Congress of the JSP, see *NS*, 17-19 January 1957 (comment [2]).
24 See Endo, *Nitchu*, pp 256-7, 474, 491. See also *Feiqu guancha baogao*, (periodical), pp 42-3.
25 Doi Akio, 'Mo Takuto shuseki to no kaidanki', *Tairiku mondai* (December 1956) pp 26-30. This conflicts with Armstrong's general description of Peking's foreign policy during that period: 'However, until the end of 1957 the main thrust of Peking's policy was still "unit", with even Western European allies of the US praised in 1956 for "demanding peaceful co-existence", and Thailand and the Philippines earning favourable mention for asserting their independence.' J D Armstrong, *Revolutionary Diplomacy, Chinese Foreign Policy and the United Front Doctrine*, (1977) p 74.
26 Hellmann, 'Japanese Domestic Politics', passim; also Fukui Harukiro, 'Foreign Policy Making by Improvisation - The Japanese Experience', *International Journal*, XXXII.4 (Autumn 1977) pp 791-812 and 'Nisso daketsugo no nitchu kankei', *Ajia keizai junpo*, (November 1956 chu) p 305.
27 Gittings. *Sino-Soviet Dispute*, pp 60-1.
28 Saionji Kinkazu, 'Chunichi yukyo no seiritsu', *Nitchu yuko undoshi*, p 232.
29 *Nitchu yuko undoshi*, p 233.

30 *Liao Chengzhi de yisheng*, p 56. On the Cairo Conference, Hinton, *Communist China*, p 76, fn 89, and *Yijiuwuqinian gongfei paichu yu yaojin gezhong daibiaotuan diaocha*, (Taipei, January 1958), p 18.
31 On the development of Ishibashi's ideas on foreign policy, Masuda Hiroshi (ed), *Sho Nihonshugi: Ishibashi Tanzan gaiko ronshu 1913-1967*, (Soshisha, 1984), passim. See also Tagawa Seiichi, *Matsumura Kenzo to Chugoku*, (1972), p 80 and *Nitchu yuko undoshi*, p 90. See also *PD*, 25 December 1956 and Radio Peking 14 December 1956 (*NS*).
32 Barnett, *Communist China*, p 272 and Hinton, *Communist China*, p 374.
33 *NS*, citing an editorial in *Dagongbao* (Hong Kong), 13 February 1957.
34 Hinton, *Communist China*, p 374.
35 *NS*, 26 February 1957.
36 Wilbur, *Communist China*, p 211. See also the communiqué signed by Zhang Xiruo and JSP leaders, in *Nitchu kankei shiryoshu* (1967), pp 86-7.
37 K W Radtke, 'Negotiations Between the PRC and Japan on the Return of Japanese Civilians and the Repatriation of Prisoners of War', *Leyden Studies in Sinology*, (Leiden, 1981), pp 191-213. *Nitchu kankei kihon shiryoshu*, pp 355 ff, 116 ff.
38 The April communiqué contains a brief passage indicating that 'border crossing of residents' had been a topic. *Nitchu kankei shiryoshu* (1961), p 11 dates the communiqué 22 April 1957, while other sources mention 24 April, for instance, *Nitchu kankei shiryoshu* (1967), p 423. The agreement of 29 August 1957 is reproduced in *Nitchu kankei shiryoshu*, pp 297-8; also in *PD*, 3 September 1957 (see also 'Arita Hachiro shi to Chukyogawa no kaidan oboegaki', in *Chukyo tainichi juyo genron shu (1958)*, p 148.
39 *Nitchu kankei kihon shiryoshu*, pp 355-6.
40 The Third Conference of the NDYL resulted in a downgrading of the role of this organisation and a strengthening of CCP control in order to prevent excessive 'independence'; there was also widespread criticism of NDYL leaders ('Gongfei qingniantuan juxing "disanci quanguo daibiao dahui"', *Renshi diren* VI.8, pp 13 f; *Fei xin minzhuzhuyi*, esp pp 25 ff). Liao was re-elected to the CC of the organisation.
41 *Nitchu kankei kihon shiryoshu*, shiryo 36, pp 113-5, 22 April 1957, and *Chukyo tainichi juyo genron shu*, 1961, pp 156 f.
42 On 2 June 1957 Kishi had supported the ROC's policy of a counterattack against the mainland during his visit to Taipei, and he was also attacked during the following days when he visited Southeast Asia (*NS*, 2 and 5 June 1957), as well as during his subsequent visit to the United States (*NS*, citing *PD* of 24 June 1957).
43 *NS*, 3 July 1957; see also 8 June 1957, and Wilbur, *Communist China*, p 211.
44 This was partly due to the refusal of conservative negotiators to yield to PRC demands. *NS*, 13, 16 and 20 July 1957.
45 *NS*, October 1957. See also *Nitchu kankei kihon shiryoshu*, pp 127-8.
46 *Nitchu kankei kihon shiryoshu*, shiryu 43, pp 125-6, *PD*, 3 September 1957, and *Nitchu yuko undoshi*, pp 84-5.
47 The mission also attempted to discuss the question of an exchange of journalists (*Gongfei duiwai xuanchuan celüe yunyong fangshi ji wo ying cai zhi duice*, Taipei, 1972, p 25).
48 Tagawa, *Matsumura Kenzo*, p 81.
49 *Nitchu yuko undoshi*, p 98, quoting *Nihon to Chugoku*, p 221.

50 *NS*, 9 May 1959, quoting *Xinhua*. It is not unlikely that Chen's criticism may also have implied criticism of the Soviet Union.
51 Furui, *Nitchu juhachinen*, p 69.
52 Ikeda, *Nazo no kuni*, pp 331 ff, esp 354 ff. Hisashi Uchida, 'Legal Aspects of Japan-China Trade Between 1949 and 1975', p 56, and Furui, *Nitchu juhachinen*, p 69.
53 For the government statement issued on 9 April 1958 see *Shiryoshu, Nitchu kankei kihon shiryoshu*, document 47, p 134.
54 Lee, *Japan Faces China*, pp 36 ff.
55 *NS*, 4 March 1958.
56 *NS*, March 1958, and 28 and 30 March 1958.
57 See the joint editorial of *PD, Guangming ribao* and *Dagongbao*, 1 April 1958; *NS*, 1 and 13 April 1958.
58 This included the 'Duiwai wenhua lianluo ju', which was renamed 'Duiwai wenhua lianluo weiyuanhui' on 11 February 1958. In addition to well-known Japan specialists like Zhang Xiruo and Chu Tunan one of its members was an intelligence specialist, Zou Dapeng (*Gongfei jinyinianlai zhongda cuoshi jiqi qingkuang zhi fenxi*, (Taipei), p 868).
59 *Gongfei jinyinianlai zhongda cuoshi*, p 68.
60 *Nitchu yuko undoshi*, p 98.
61 On the political and economic background of this period, Hinton, *Communist China*, p 377. On 12 May Chen Yi gave an open invitation to West German traders to replace the Japanese. On 29 May *Dagongbao* (Peking) referred to Kishi's plans for economic expansion in the Asian-African region (cited according to *NS*). A number of appeals were made to boycott the sale of goods in Southeast Asia, some especially directed toward Overseas Chinese (for example on 5 and 7 July 1958). At the same time, Japan was accused of economic expansionism in the Asian-African - region, in particular in Southeast Asia (*Dagongbao* (Peking), 28 June and 29 July, Peking Radio on 28 June and *PD*, 6 September 1958). On 16 August 1958 Zhou referred to the combination of US capital and Japanese technology 'for economic aggression' in Southeast Asia (*NS*); see also *Dagongbao* of 29 July 1959 on 'Japanese weapons exports to Southeast Asia' (cited according to *NS*). This was later followed up by attacks on Japan's expansionism in Africa and Latin America (*NS*, quoting *PD* of 4 January 1960) and attacks on Japan's 'March to the Tropics' (*nanshin*), an allusion to Japan's occupation of Southeast Asia during World War II (*NS*, citing *PD*, 11 February 1960). It may be added that the PRC's attempt to expand into the Southeast Asian market was not invariably welcomed; in April 1959 the Malay government prohibited the import of fibre goods on the grounds of PRC dumping practices (*NS*, 2 April 1959). See also the Japanese government report on PRC trade with Southeast Asia (*NS*, 20 February 1959).
62 On 7 July 1958 (*NS*), and *Nitchu kankei kihon shiryoshu*, p 435). See also Uchida, 'Legal Aspects of Japan-China Trade', p 42, and *Kokusai nenpo*, 1958.
63 *Nitchu kankei kihon shiryoshu*, pp 144-51.
64 According to *Asahi shinbun, (yukan)*, 23 June 1958, Kishi even expressed regret over the flag incident.
65 It seems not unlikely that the 'crisis' was planned and prepared for as far back as 1957 when Peking decided to extend fishing exclusion zones, *Nitchu kankei kihon shiryoshu*, pp 40-124.
66 Eto Shinkichi and Tatsumi Okabe, 'Content Analysis of Statements in Regard to Japan Made by the People's Republic of China - Source Materials: The People's Daily in Two Periods in 1958',

67 'Hairyo torihiki ni kansuru Iwai Akira hokoku', in *Nitchu kankei shiryoshu* (1967), p 196: it also contains the gist of Liao Chengzhi's talk to the delegation on 13 February. Uchida, 'Legal Aspects of Japan-China Trade', p 42. *Developing Economies*, 3.1 (March 1965), pp 48-72. For examples of such attacks, see the 'Comment' in *PD* of 7 November 1958 and Chen Yi's statement on 19 November followed by a comment of Japan's Foreign Ministry (*Nitchu kankei kihon shiryoshu*, pp 153-6).

68 *NS*, 3 February 1959. Foreign Minister Fujiyama in a speech in a session of the Foreign Relations Committee of the Diet appeared prepared to discuss the conclusion of 'technical' agreements with the PRC such as a postal agreement, but according to *Asahi shinbun* admitted that 70% of his proposal was due to election campaign tactics. It might be added that the ROC moved on 28 February 1959 to prevent any talks at ambassadorial level.

69 Langer, *The JCP Between Moscow and Peking*, p 95, which also contains a list of important meetings between the JCP and JSP during this period.

70 'Shakaito hochu to kokumin gaiko (Nihon no ushio 1)', *Sekai*, 161, (May 1959), pp 44-7. According to *Asahi shinbun* of 12 September 1958 the first joint JSP-JCP action in regard to China had occurred in the same month.

71 *NS*, 18 March 1959.

72 *NS*, March 1959.

73 *Nitchu kankei kihon shiryoshu*, p 435.

74 *NS*, 1959, pp 191-203, document 16. *Nitchu yuko undoshi*, p 105. 'Ishibashi hochu to Jiminto (Nihon no ushio.2)', *Sekai* 167 (November 1959), pp 259-62; Furui, *Nitchu juhachinen*, p 70.

75 Furui's account does not always tally with Matsumura's and Tanawa Seiichi's, but there is no room here to deal with these divergences.

76 Gittings, *Sino-Soviet Dispute*, p 120.

77 *Ibid*, p 117.

78 See documents 16-18 for October 1959, in *NS*, pp 191-216. *Kokusai nenpo*, 1959, p 129; Tagawa's recollections (he accompanied Matsumura as his secretary) in Tagawa Seiichi, *Nitchu kosho hiroku. Tagawa nikki - 14nen no shogen*, (1973), pp 10-31, and Furui, *Nitchu juhachinen*, pp 71 ff.

79 *NS*, document 16, 31 August 1959. LDP Secretary-General Kawashima had approved of Ishibashi's visit on condition that it be undertaken as a private visit (*NS*, 27 August 1959).

80 *NS*, 3 September, 1959.

81 *NS*, 8 September, citing an Ajia Tsushin report.

82 The ROC ambassador to Tokyo, Zhang Lisheng expected a 'considerable present' for Ishibashi from the Communist side in an attempt to split the LDP (*NS*, 7 September 1959).

83 *NS*.

84 'Ishibashi hochu to Jiminto (Nihon no ushio 2)', *Sekai*, 167, (November 1959). *Nitchu yuko undoshi*, p 105. *Kokusai nenpo*, (1959), p 129.

85 Uchida, 'Legal Aspects of Japan-China Trade', p 43.

86 Furui, *Nitchu juhachinen*, p 37.

87 *NS*, 11 and 20 September.

88 Tagawa, *Matsumura Kenzo*, pp 102 ff; Furui, *Nitchu juhachinen*, pp 20, 37, 71 f, 77, 89 f; Matsumura Kenzo and Kazemi Akira, 'Chugoku wa ikaga deshita ka?', *Chuo koron*, 75-2 (February 1960), pp 178-88.

89 Tagawa, *Matsumura*, pp 20, 98.
90 *NS*, loco cit; *Nitchu kankei kihon shiryoshu*, p 172.
91 *NS*, 25 October 1959.
92 Furui, *Nitchu juhachinen*, p 77.
93 *Ibid*, p 7. The initials stand for Liao Chengzhi and Takasaki Tatsunosuke.
94 *Ibid*, p 77.
95 *Nitchu kankei kihon shiryoshu*, p 172, 'Matsumura Kenzo jiminto komon sobetsuen ni okeru Shu Onrai sori no enzetsu'.
96 *NS*, 26 September 1959.
97 For an evaluation, see also *NS* for October 1959.
98 *Nitchu kankei kihon shiryoshu*, pp 170-2.
99 *NS*, 5 November quoting *PD* which refers to an article in *Yomiuri shinbun* of 4 November 1959. On 9 March 1960 Radio Peking calls Ishibashi, Ishii and Kono 'rising anti-Kishi forces'. See also *PD*, 22 March containing praise for these politicians, quoted according to *NS*, same dates.
100 Robert Boardman, 'Ideology, Organisation and Environment: Sources of Chinese Foreign Policy Making', Adomeit et al (eds), *Foreign Policy Making in Communist Countries*, pp 112-49.
101 Gittings, *Sino-Soviet Dispute*, p 120. Hinton, *Communist China*, p 169 and Zagoria, *The Sino-Soviet Conflict, 1956-1961*, (Princeton University Press, 1962), pp 320-3.
102 *PD*, 22 February 1960 and *Chukyo tai Nichi juyo genronshu*, (1961), p 21. The tone of Liao's welcome speech was already indicated by its title: 'The struggle against the Japanese and American reactionaries will inescapably lead to victory'. See also *NS*, February 1960, p 40, comment 11, and 21 February 1960, p 3. The question of a visit by Guo was raised by Yasui on his return to Japan in a meeting with Ishibashi and Matsumura (*NS*, 3 March 1960).
103 *NS*, 9 March 1960, comment, p 57. 'Iwai ra ... Ishibashi to iken kokan'.
104 *NS*, citing Radio Peking (9 March) and *PD* of 4, 6, 10 and 22 March. See in particular *NS*, comment no 13 for April 1960, and 26 May 1960.
105 *Sannianlai gongfei paichu yu yaojin gezhong daibiatuan diaocha*, (1961), pp 378-80.
106 V P Dutt, *China and the World. An Analysis of Communist China's Foreign Policy*, (Praeger, 1967), p 273.
107 *Ibid*, pp 272-3, quoting *NCNA*, of 14 April 1960.
108 Gittings, *Sino-Soviet Dispute*, p 121.
109 *Vneshnaia politika i mezhdunarodnye otnosheniia KNR, 1949-1963*, vol 1, (Moscow, 1974), p 302.
110 Neuhauser, *Third World Politics*, p 34. Larkin, *China and Africa*, quoting *Peking Review*, 13 July 1962, p 8.
111 For an overview, see *Nitchu kankei kihon shiryoshu*, pp 422 ff.
112 *NS*.
113 Gittings, *Sino-Soviet Dispute*, p 123; E G Furin, '1960nen kyosanto kaigi no kaisoroku', *Shakaishugi seiji keizai kenkyu.kenkyu shiryo*, VII-3, (March 1964), pp 24-41.
114 *Liao Chengzhi de yisheng*, p 62. See also *Renwuzhi*, (48 nian), p 126, and *Sannianlai gongfei paichu* (1961), pp 369-70.
115 I have so far been unable to obtain detailed information about Liao's role as a member of the delegation led by the President of the PRC Liu Shaoqi. Other members included Deng Xiaoping, Peng Zhen, Li Jingquan, Lu Dingyi, Yang Shangkun, Hu Qiaomu, Liu Ningyi, Kang Sheng and

Liu Xiao (Li Tienmin, *Liu Shao-ch'i. Mao's First Heir-Apparent*, Taipei, 1975, p 109). Judging by the simultaneous presence of Liu Ningyi and Liao Chengzhi it seems likely that both attended by virtue of their *party* position with regard to united front work.

116 This description is mainly based on *NS* for that period.

117 *Nitchu kankei kihon shiryoshu*, pp 437 and 178-80.

118 It is difficult to prove whether Liao was responsible for these moves. Compare also Zhu Ziqi's account of the delegation sent to Tokyo in the following year: 'On Liao's recommendation Ba Jin led a delegation to attend the World Conference against Nuclear Bombs in Tokyo in 1961 which reaped great success, and won the praise of Chairman Mao and Prime Minister Zhou. (Zhu Ziqi, in *Liaogong zai renjian*, p 62). Zhu Ziqi's article is clearly eulogistic, and cannot be taken as conclusive evidence that Liao both initiated and directed similar activities.

119 Oomagari, *Asanuma*, p 215.

120 This description is mainly based on *NS*, 29 July 1960, which contains a detailed report on the Liu Ningyi mission on pp 288-94; see also *Nitchu yuko undoshi*, p 113.

121 *NS*, 25 July and comment no 13 on p 133.

122 *NS*, August 1960, and Uchida, 'Legal Aspects of Japan-China Trade', pp 42-3.

123 *NS*, August 1960; for Hozumi's report, see comment no 21, 20 September 1960, and 'Shu Onrai danwa', in *Nitchu kankei shiryoshu*, (1961), pp 66-72.

124 *NS*, 'Chukyo no tainichi sekkin wa Chuso sokaku ga gen'in'.

125 *NS*.

126 *NS*, comment no 5, 8 October 1960, pp 183-6, and *Nitchu kankei kihon shiryoshu*, p 185.

127 The best treatment is Yang, *The Policy-Making Process in Japan's Policy Toward the People's Republic of China: The Making of the Liao-Takasaki Trade Agreement*, passim.

128 It is perhaps surprising that *PD* opened a series of attacks on Ikeda virtually coinciding with the visit of the Takasaki delegation (*NS*, 11 and 12 October). On 11 December *PD* reported criticism by Ishibashi Tanzan to the effect that the new Ikeda cabinet made Japan follow the United States even more than the previous Yoshida foreign policy had done (quoted according to *NS*). See also Lee, *Japan Faces China*, pp 42 f.

129 *Nitchu kankei shiryoshu*, 1961, p 130 ff. See also NCNA, 7, 8, 20 and 24 January 1961, and *Nitchu kankei shiryoshu (1961)*, pp 130-4, (Liao's welcome address on 20 January 1961), and pp 134-40 (for Mao Zedong's speech, present Kuroda Hisao, Liao Chengzhi and others). See also the detailed summary in comment no 9, *NS*, for 20 January 1961, and the summary of events in February, pp 8-9 for Kuroda's assessment of PRC policy towards Japan.

130 Quoted according to Uchida, 'Legal Aspects of Japan-China Trade', p 55. *PD*, 21 January 1961, as quoted in *Chukyo tainichi juyo genron shu*, 1961, p 197, 'Yubin kisho kyotei musubenu - Ryo Shoshi no Kuroda shakaito komon kangeikai de enzetsu (yoshi)'. For Liao's welcome address, *Nitchu kankei shiryoshu (1961)*, pp 130-4. Zhou commented on 26 January 1961 as follows: 'How can we conclude inter-governmental agreements prior to the establishment of diplomatic relations? What we expect now are relations between private concerns.' Uchida, 'Legal Aspects of Japan-China Trade', p 55. See also Ikeda's press conference on 28 January 1961.

131 *Nitchu kankei shiryoshu*, 1961, pp 135 ff; *Nitchu kankei kihon shiryoshu*, p 187, and 'Mo Takuto. Shu Onrai kaikenki', *Sekai* 184, (April 1961), pp 140-51, (24 January 1961). See also Lee, *Japan Faces China*, p 45.

132 *Nitchu kankei shiryoshu*, 1961, p 140.

Economic and Political Relations

133 *NS*, 14 January 1961.
134 *Nitchu kankei shiryoshu (1961)*, pp 134 f, and *NS*, 20 January 1961, comment 9, p 30.
135 See Ikeda's statement in the House of Representatives on 1 February 1961.
136 *Nitchu kankei shiryoshu*, 1961, p 154, and comment no 8, 31 January 1961, *NS*, on p 29.
137 *Kokusai boeki*, 16 June 1983.
138 Yang, *The Policy-Making Process*, pp 67 ff.
139 *Nitchu kankei shiryoshu (1961)*, p 148.
140 In January an agreement had been reached on the sending of a third delegation to leave in March (*NS*, 28 January 1961).
141 *NS*, January 1961, including detailed comment no 7 for December, and *NS*, 20, 21 and 28 January; see also entry for May 1961. For a brief survey, *Fei dui riben de zuzhi shentou*, pp 24-5.
142 Full details in *NS*, comment no 9, 13 June 1961. On Yoshio Shiga, see *Communist China 1961*, vol 2, URI, 1962, quoting *PD*, 1961.6.24. For Liao's welcome address on 19 June 1961 see *Riben wenti wenjian huibian*, pp 27-32. For an abridged version of Liao's speech based on *PD* of 20 June 1961 see *Chukyo tainichi juyo genron*, p 137.
143 *NS*, 2 November 1961; Liao is not mentioned.
144 *PD*, 20 June 1961.
145 *Gongfei renshi ziliao huibian*, (Taipei), p 166; *NCNA*, 16 March, 9 April 1961.
146 W E Griffith, *Albania and the Sino-Soviet Rift*, (Cambridge, Mass, 1963), pp 126 and 144. For the text of Liao's speech, see *NCNA*, 11 December 1961, *PD*, 12 December 1961, and *Peking Review*, 51, (22 December 1961), pp 12-14. See also *Shin Chugoku nenkan*, 1962, p 252-5. It was this meeting in Stockholm which brought differences on the peace movement into full public view (*Ajia keizai junpo*, 560 (1963 nen 12 gatsu/chu), p 9.
147 See for instance Liao's September speech 'American imperialism is the root of the threat of nuclear war', *Chukyo tainichi juyo genron shu*, 1962, p 97.
148 Griffith, *Albania and the Sino-Soviet Rift*, pp 125-6 amd 144.
149 These were also inherent in his praise for the armed struggle in Algeria (*Peking Review*, 13 July 1962, pp 8-9).
150 See *Qiaowubao*, March 1962, Larkin, *China and Africa*, p 162.
151 *NS*, comment no 7 30 December 1961, and 1 January 1962, p 10.
152 See entries in *NS* for January 1962, July 1962, p 101, 7 and 8 July and August 1962.
153 *PD*, 5 January 1962.
154 *NS*, January 1962, pp 13 f.
155 *PD*, 20 April 1962 reports on the 'Isolated position' of the United States, while *PD* of 4 June 1962 commented on Japan's export problems. See also *NS*, comment no 3, p 85 4 June, and comment no 3; *NS*, 17 July citing a *Xinhua* report.
156 *NS*, September 1962.
157 *NS*, January 1962, p 26.
158 *NS*, 7 April 1962, comment no 1, p 52; *PD*, 20 April 1962, and *NS*, April 1962, pp 52-3.
159 *NS*, January 1962, pp 13 f, and *PD*, 5 January 1962.
160 Yang, *The Policy-Making Process*, pp 78 f.
161 *Nitchu yuko undoshi*, p 122.
162 *Ibid*.
163 *Jingji ribao*, 24 June 1983.

164 Okazaki Kaheita, *Chugoku mondai e no michi*, p 41, and *NS*, July 1962, p 101.
165 *Nitchu kosho hiroku*, pp 32 ff, and *NS*, 12 September 1962, and the comment on pp 126-9.
166 *Nitchu kosho hiroku*, p 35. For Matsumura's record of Liao's statement, *Ibid*, p 36. See also Furui, *Nitchu juhachinen*, pp 75 ff.
167 *Nitchu kosho hiroku*, pp 32 ff. See also Okazaki, *Chugoku mondai e no michi*, p 118. Another important member was Ogawa Heiji, a member of the Ikeda faction and one of Ikeda's 'brains'.
168 *Nitchu kosho hiroku*, p 34.
169 See *Feiri maoyi jingwei*, (Taipei, July 1964), p 13.
170 This is apparent from *Nitchu kosho hiroku*, pp 35 ff. Referring to Matsumura's visit of September 1962 Sun Pinghua stressed that Matsumura discussed the development of long-term general trade with Zhou Enlai; this remark should however not be interpreted as slighting Liao's role. See also Okazaki Kaheita, *Watakushi no kiroku*, (1979), p 141.
171 *Nitchu kosho hiroku*, pp 39-40.
172 *Ibid*, p 40.
173 *Ibid*, p 41.
174 *Ibid*.
175 *Ibid*, p 42.
176 *Ibid*, p 43.
177 *Ibid*.
178 *Ibid*.
179 *Ibid*, p 44.
180 Tagawa, *Nitchu kosho hiroku*, p 44; Okazaki, *Chugoku mondai e no michi*, p 53. See also *NS*, 20 September 1962.
181 Tagawa, *Nitchu kosho hiroku*, pp 43-4.
182 *Nitchu kosho hiroku*, pp 46 f, and *NS*, September 1962, p 128.
183 According to Furui, *Nitchu juhachinen*, pp 75 ff it was Okazaki who had suggested this form of trade to Matsumura (confirmed by Okazaki, *Watakushi no kiroku*, p 136). Zhou suggested Liao and Matsumura as guarantors (Tagawa, *Nitchu kosho hiroku*, p 46). For further details on questions relating to the L-T trade, see also *Nitchu oboegaki no 11nen*, Nitchu keizai kyokai, 1975, in particular pp 40 ff 'Okazaki koso'.
184 *Nitchu kosho hiroku*, p 47, and *NS*, September 1962, p 128. Furui also refers to the hope expressed by PRC politicians that Ikeda may not simply duplicate Kishi's policies, in *Nitchu juhachinen*, pp 75 ff.
185 *Nitchu kosho hiroku*, p 48; for similar statements, see *ibid*, p 37, and Furui, *Nitchu juhachinen*, p 174.
186 *Nitchu kosho hiroku*, p 149. *NS*, September 1962, pp 127-8. Okazaki, *Chugoku mondai e no michi*, p 323. D Petrov collected several such statements under the heading 'Policy Based on Racialism' to attack the *rapprochement* between Peking and Tokyo in his article 'Japan and the Mao Group's Foreign Policy' in *International Affairs*, (Moscow, December 1968), pp 30-7. In summing up his observations in China, Matsumura stressed that Peking's policy is motivated 'not only by Communism, but ... apparently (by) the nationalist consciousness of the Han race'.
187 *NS*, September 1962, p 128.
188 Okazaki, *Watakushi no kiroku*, p 141.

Economic and Political Relations

189 Lee, *Japan Faces China*, pp 143 ff. Jain, *China and Japan*, p 70 f. Also Eto Shinkichi, 'Post-War Japanese-Chinese Relations', *Survey*, 18.4 (1972), pp 56-65. *Peking Review*, 11 January 1963, p 20.
190 Okazaki, *Watakushi no kiroku*, pp 43 and 141. Also Okazaki, *Chugoku mondai e no michi*, p 189.
191 See also Furui, *Nitchu juhachinen*, pp 75 ff, and Jerome A Cohen, ed *The Dynamics of China's Foreign Relations*, (Harvard University Press, 1970) Harvard East Asian Monographs, 39, p 50: 'In terms of their functions, these offices were undoubtedly substitutes for consulates.'
192 *Nitchu kankei kihon shiryoshu*, p 216 (Chen Yi's speech on 9 November 1962). See also Petrov, *op cit*, p 32.
193 This was confirmed to me by Japanese officials serving in Peking in an unofficial capacity 'on loan' from the government. See also Cohen, *The Dynamics of China's Foreign Relations*, p 50; Furui, *Nitchu juhachinen*, pp 75 ff.
194 *NS*, June 1962; A S Whiting, *The Chinese Calculus of Deterrence*, (Ann Arbor, 1975), pp 37 f.
195 Dennis T Yasutomo, 'Sato's China Policy, 1964-1966', p 542.
196 See Tagawa's remarks on the slump in agriculture in *Nitchu kosho hiroku*, p 33.
197 *NS*, December 1962, p 179.
198 *NS*, 15 February 1963, and *PD*, 28 February 1963.
199 *NS*, March and April 1963.
200 *Jingji ribao*, 24 June 1983. See also Tagawa, *Matsumura Kenzo*, pp 97-8.
201 *URS Biographical Service*.
202 *Riben wenti wenjian huibian*, vol V, '...Liao Chengzhi zai shoudu gejie renmin zhichi dijiujie jinzhi yuanzidan qingdan shijie dahui dahui shang de jianghua (1 August 1963)', pp 204-14, and *ibid*, '... Liao Chengzhi zai shoudu gejie renmin qingzhu dijiujie jinzhi yuanzidan qingdan shijie dahui shengli dahui shang de kaihuici (24 August 1963)', pp 233-5. See also *NCNA*, 1, 21 and 22 August.
203 *Ibid*, p 205. For Liao's speech concerning the Conference, *PD*, 25 August 1963.
204 *Ibid*, p 213.
205 See also Zhao Puchu's attack on 'right wing' socialists in *PD*, 25 August 1963.
206 *NS*.
207 See also Jain, *China and Japan*, p 68.
208 *NS*, December 1962, p 177.
209 Jain, *China and Japan*, p 67.
210 For remarks on certain problems, see *NS*, November 1962.
211 Okamoto, *Nitchu boeki ron*, pp 137 ff, 'Yuko boeki to LT boeki'. For a brief survey of pre- and post-war trade dynamics, Ikeda, *Nazo no kuni*, pp 273 f; also Langdon, 'Japan's Foreign Policy', p 174.
212 *PD*, 5 October, 1963, and *Riben wenti wenjian huibian*, vol V, pp 75-6.
213 See also Sun Pinghua's comments in *Kakyoho*, 5 July 1983.
214 *PD*, 5 October 1963. For Liao's speech at the foundation meeting, *Riben wenti wenjian huibian*, vol V, pp 75-6, and *Nitchu kankei kihon shiryoshu*, p 221.
215 Lee, *Japan Faces China*, p 73.

CHAPTER FIVE
Friends and Foes: 1963-1971

Liao Chengzhi himself was involved on both fronts. As head of the SJFA he had appeared conciliatory, following a united front approach that was lenient towards 'useful allies' - however 'reactionary' their ideology - while insisting on strict ideological discipline in the case of socialist or communist parties or organisations.

Following the Hiroshima Conference clashes between pro-Soviet and pro-CCP groups continued at an even higher level at the Warsaw meeting of the World Peace Council in November-December.[1] Liao led the PRC delegation and made scathing attacks on the Soviet position. Of special interest was his speech of 28 November referring to previous disagreements within the peace movement.[2] In personal recollections he pointed out that there had been voices opposing national liberation movements at the Stockholm meeting of the WPC in 1961.[3] In another part of his speech he accused proponents of 'disarmament at any price' of racism:

> It is those people above all who regard disarmament as their 'overriding duty' and force (this point of view) on oppressed people striving for their independence, who mentally as well as physically disarm people who are struggling against imperialism and colonialism. These are true divisive activities that wreck anti-imperialist forces, this is nothing more than *an expression of European and North American national chauvinism, ... which aids American imperialism in pushing its own neo-colonialism.*' (my emphasis)[4]

This was not completely new, but what appears to be novel was Liao's accusation of 'European and North American chauvinism', a side swipe at Soviet 'European' attitudes. Liao carefully avoided the term 'racism' when referring to Europe and North America but there can be little doubt that many of his listeners would interpret his remarks in this way; he underlined that the struggle was mainly directed against 'American imperialism'. At that time it had become obvious that the Soviet Union was a 'European' power in Chinese eyes. It would not be long before Mao in an interview with Sasaki Kozo, leader of a JSP delegation to Peking in July, would accuse the Soviet Union of land robbery in Asia and Europe. On the same occasion Mao expressed his support for the return of the Kurile Islands that had been occupied by the Soviet Union in 1945 but are still claimed by Japan.

Such remarks were obviously not made carelessly. They should be seen as part of a carefully orchestrated policy that played up to nationalistic feelings in countries also affected by 'Soviet expansionism' as an important factor in a united front that was directed against both the United States and the Soviet Union. Japan occupied a rather particular position in the front. In PRC parlance, geographically Japan belonged to the 'first intermediate zone'.[5] In other words Japan was said to lie in a region where (virtually) all countries were developing countries. Politically, however, it was claimed to belong to the 'second intermediate zone', sharing many aspects of national interest with developed countries in Europe,

America and Oceania (Australia, New Zealand). It is not surprising then, to find that PRC policies towards Japan are a mixture of the themes we find expressed in PRC policy towards developing countries as well as towards developed countries.

Mikhail Suslov, Secretary of the Soviet Central Committee, saw no need to explain Peking's policies by referring to 'theories':

> ... At the same time the Chinese government makes feverish attempts to improve relations with Britain, France, Japan, West Germany and Italy. It is quite clear that they would not refuse to improve relations with the United States but as yet do not see favourable circumstances for such an endeavour.6

One result of this 'double-pronged' policy was to increase tensions among leftist groups in Japan,7 while efforts continued to win over a section of the Japanese 'bourgeoisie'. These themes were elaborated in a number of speeches directed towards Japan by Mao Zedong and other Chinese Communist leaders in 1964. Despite the split among the leftist groups this policy seemed to pay off. Towards the end of September 1963 relations between the ROC and Japan started to deteriorate visibly over the question of trade between Japan and the PRC, and the so-called Zhou Hongqing case.8 Despite efforts by among others former Japanese Prime Minister Yoshida, who visited Taipei at the beginning of the year and held several talks with Chiang Kaishek, it seemed at first that the PRC was going to make new headway in its relations with Japan during the first half of 1964. Repeating previous reasoning Mao justified dealing with 'big business' in a talk with Japanese visitors in January, also referred to in the organ of the JCP, *Akahata*.9 Tagawa Seiichi, one of the key figures involved in the L-T Agreement, visited Peking in February.10

Tagawa continued talks on the practical implementation of a programme to allow Japanese to visit graves in the PRC. He also discussed the question of trade promotion,11 and preliminary talks were held on the question of an exchange of journalists. More generally, Tagawa wanted to explore the situation after France's recognition of the PRC. He had gone in a private capacity but had been in close touch with government and other LDP members. Tagawa's talk with Liao on 12 February touched on a wide variety of subjects. Commenting on the question of diplomatic relations Liao said that it would take some time before relations could be 'normalised' but, in the meantime, there was room for improvement in other areas. Liao appeared rather optimistic with regard to possibilities for a further expansion of trade.12 Tagawa reacted to previous suggestions and mentioned that the Japanese side was presently considering ways to achieve the reciprocal stationing of trade officers (trade missions) to facilitate trade negotiations.13 The PRC appeared to be particularly interested in reaching some sort of agreement on an air link with Japan. There were references to talks going on at that time between All-Japan Airways (Zennikku) on a Shanghai-Kyushu link.14 The proposed airlink would be rather small-scale, and its importance would mainly lie on the political rather than the economic side. It is easy to imagine that the conclusion of such an agreement would have accelerated the worsening of relations between the ROC and

Japan, but it is doubtful whether the PRC believed that such an agreement would gain the necessary approval of the Japanese government. The fact that such talks were taking place constituted an additional political advantage, albeit a small one.

Tagawa's talks with Liao Chengzhi, Wu Xuewen and others did not bring about immediate specific results but laid the basis for negotiations on a more formal level to be held in April. These talks had also indicated the possibility of an agreement on the exchange of journalists between Japan and the PRC. In his book *Nitchu kosho hiroku (The Secret Record of Sino-Japanese Negotiations)* Tagawa revealed the important place that preliminary talks on such an exchange had occupied.[15] The revelation came one year after Miyoshi Osamu and Eto Shinkichi had bitterly attacked Matsumura Kenzo and others for having conceded undue political control over Japanese journalists in agreements since 1968.[16] After Liao had reacted favourably to Tagawa's proposal for an exchange of journalists, Tagawa had a detailed conversation with Wu Xuewen and Ding Tuo on this subject.[17] Wu did not insist on diplomatic recognition as a precondition for the conclusion of an exchange agreement but demanded guarantees by the Japanese government that PRC journalists would receive the same treatment as those from other countries.

In these talks the PRC showed itself in favour of a 'gradual approach' towards the establishment of formal relations, a point of view repeated by Zhou Enlai in Ceylon (Sri Lanka) during a visit to Southeast Asia when he touched on the PRC's relations with Japan.[18] Shortly before this speech Zhou had been to Dacca where he met Song Qingling who was to join him on his visit to Ceylon.[19] Liao Chengzhi was not an official member of the delegation, but had apparently met Zhou Enlai in Dacca, and informed him of the outcome of his talks with Tagawa.[20]

As Zhou's cautious appearance in Pakistan had demonstrated, the PRC was willing once more to appear 'moderate' and 'flexible' even to the extent of curbing attacks on Pakistan's links with the United States, if this would serve the formation of a useful 'united front'. True to united front tactics however the PRC would not tolerate 'deviations' from a 'true revolutionary' point of view where the groups which were regarded as the 'leftist' core of such a united front were concerned. By 1964 the JCP seemed to represent such a leftist core in Japan. During this period relations with the JCP became particularly close, demonstrated during the visits by several JCP delegations to the PRC. Following common practice few details on the content of any talks were made public.[22] Liao was deeply involved in these talks and, judging by PRC newspaper reports was the highest-ranking among the PRC Japan specialists to participate. Before visiting Peking one of the delegations had gone to Moscow,[23] and subsequent events showed very clearly that the JCP tended towards Peking in the dispute between the CPSU and the CCP; this stance was an important factor in an internal split within the JCP in May. In the meantime, a public row had broken out between the PRC and the JSP which objected to a NCNA report on a party congress which had attacked by name leading JSP politicians who did not belong to the pro-Peking wing.[24] While Peking's 'united front' could include conservatives useful to PRC strategy, it could not afford to tolerate 'ideological deviation' among its closest leftist sympathisers.

Shortly after the JCP delegation had left Peking Matsumura Kenzo arrived there on 12 April to negotiate the stationing of trade officials in Tokyo, as well as an agreement on the exchange of journalists. At about the same time a PRC trade mission led by Nan Hanchen which included Xiao Xiangqian visited Japan from 8 April to 21 May. The mission held many talks with Japanese business leaders as well as with members of the JCP and JSP.[25] The PRC had previously conceded that an agreement on the exchange of journalists did not depend on the conclusion of a governmental agreement. On 25 March Xiao Xiangqian - who together with Ding Tuo had arrived in Japan in advance of the economic mission - declared that, in the absence of diplomatic relations, such an accord should be reached within the framework of the L-T agreement.[26] In doing so he emphasised the political character of such an exchange. The traditional viewpoint of the Japanese Journalists' Association had been to conduct any such exchange quite separately from other matters such as trade in order to reduce as far as feasible the possibility of political restrictions.[27] Back in Peking Matsumura agreed to conclude an agreement on the exchange of journalists within the framework of the L-T 'pipeline'. Unlike post-1968 agreements he was able however to prevent the inclusion of 'political principles' governing the reporting of Japanese journalists from Peking. The ground for an agreement on the establishment of a trade liaison office and the reciprocal stationing of trade officials had already been prepared during Tagawa's talks, and did not present any particular difficulties.[28] The discussions also touched upon the possibility of agreements on postal, meteorological and telecommunications exchanges, but did not achieve any results.[29] Published records indicate that most technical points were discussed with specialists such as Lu Xuzhang and Sun Pinghua from various PRC government departments. Liao Chengzhi did participate in some talks, but his active role may have been limited since major questions concerning the political framework of the agreement had already been solved. Liao was a signatory of the 'Memorandum of the Agreement between Matsumura Kenzo and Liao Chengzhi' on 18 April 1964.[30]

Worsening Relations

Only three weeks later clouds began to overshadow the growing contacts between the PRC and Japan. Problems had arisen over the financing of a sale of a Kurashiki rayon plant and on 30 April Liao declared that the agreement to buy such a plant had therefore lapsed.[31] Formal communication to this effect followed on 7 May.[32] Nan Hanchen, then still in Japan, requested a meeting with Minister Sato on this point; Nan appeared quite conciliatory.[33] For the time being the PRC apparently wished to do nothing to aggravate the situation, and Zhou Enlai confirmed this impression when he met members of an LDP delegation led by Kitamura Tokutaro and Kawasaki Hideji a few days later.[34] In the following month staff of the new trade mission arrived in Tokyo, and trade fairs were held in Tokyo and Osaka.

China's Relations with Japan

At the same time, however, Japanese links with the ROC started improving again, symbolised by the arrival of the ROC's new ambassador Li Daoming to replace Zhang Lisheng who had been recalled in September 1963. The Japanese government - still led by Prime Minister Ikeda - refused approval for a visit to the PRC by Japanese youths. It also refused entry permits to PRC Japan specialists Zhao Anbo and Wang Zhaohua who had wished to participate in the 10th Anti-Nuclear Conference as members of a PRC delegation, a refusal which was met with a sharp protest by the Peking newspaper *Dagongbao*.[35] Permission was given for five PRC trade officers to be stationed in Tokyo, but only after the Japanese government had imposed strict rules on the limitation of their activities.

The PRC reacted to these restrictions in a relatively mild way and the reason should be sought in Peking's anxiety to do nothing that might jeopardise the chances for Ikeda's re-election as Prime Minister. Despite earlier reservations there was a realisation that any other prime minister might change the relatively moderate attitude of the current government. PRC concern was evident from repeated questions to members of visiting Japanese delegations about Ikeda's re-election chances. This concern should be seen not only in the light of bilateral relations between the PRC and Japan but also against the background of growing international tension first and foremost over the escalation of the war in Vietnam.

PRC attitudes towards 'American imperialism' and the Soviet Union continued to harden. Liao Chengzhi told a mass meeting in Peking on 9 August that the PRC might adopt 'practical measures' to support the Vietnamese Communists. His statement was one of the toughest warnings delivered by the PRC so far and hinted at the possibility of PRC involvement along the lines of its participation in the Korean War.[36] Shortly after Mao had referred to Soviet 'land robbery', Khrushchev was removed from power in the Soviet Union, followed by the first PRC nuclear explosion.[37] These events may have led PRC leaders to hope for a reconciliation with the new Soviet leadership, perhaps assuming that the PRC's new status as a nuclear power might persuade the Soviets to be more conciliatory. Any such hope was soon dashed, and the nuclear explosion proved quite damaging with regard to the PRC's Japan policy. It highlighted differences with the JSP over the question of (nuclear) arms. When a JSP delegation under Narita Tomomi and Katsumata Seiichi went to Peking all that could be achieved was a communiqué purposely limited to points of agreement.[38] Contacts with other JCFA delegations, a JCP delegation under Yoshida and talks with JCP leader Miyamato showed Liao present at various functions, but it is difficult to assess to what extent he actually participated in these talks.[39] In the ensuing weeks he failed to attend a number of functions where he would normally have been expected. It is not certain whether this irregular appearance is the result of incomplete records, or whether there were deeper reasons. He may have engaged in confidential travels abroad. Another possible reason may be the power struggle involving the United Front Work Department, with which Liao was closely connected. The tensions came to the surface at the 1st Session of the 3rd NPC when Li Weihan was dismissed. It took nearly fifteen years for Li Weihan to refer in detail to his 'illegal dismissal', which he said had been partly due to his links with Overseas Chinese.40 Moreover, nothing had come of a visit to Japan, although he had been expected to lead a delegation there in May.41 Later in the year Liao led a delegation to Rome to attend a congress of the Italian Peace Committee. There were only a few reports on this visit in PRC media.42 Despite Liao's low exposure there were no obvious indications that he was facing 'political problems', and there is no clear reason for his low profile.

There were some signs though, that PRC relations with Japan were about to deteriorate. Shortly before Liao's departure for Rome the Ikeda cabinet had been replaced by a new one headed by Sato. Liao later denied that the PRC was apprehensive about Sato due to the fact that he was former Prime Minister Kishi's half-brother, but there is no doubt that the PRC was seriously concerned. With Sato's election, relations between Japan and the ROC improved significantly, and attempts by the PRC to strive for the establishment of diplomatic relations with Japan came to a virtual standstill until 1972, when Sato resigned.

In quite a different field of PRC foreign policy an incident occurred that, at that moment, seemed to be an isolated failure of the PRC's 'revolutionary' foreign policy towards Third World countries. Early in 1965 Burundi broke off relations with the PRC.43 For the moment, however, developments elsewhere in the Third World may have led PRC leaders to believe in the success of this strategy. In January 1965 Indonesia left the United Nations, and there was talk about the possibility of the creation of a 'new United Nations', a suggestion also repeated later in the year by Liao Chengzhi.44 However, it is not clear whether the PRC ever regarded such a move as a realistic option.

As far as Liao was concerned the most pressing problem confronting him at the beginning of 1965 was probably Sato's election as prime minister. According to common practice the PRC at first muted its public concern about the new cabinet, but it is striking that for many months to come PRC leaders stressed that they 'were still watching and waiting' which way Sato would go.45 As early as 14 January Liao Chengzhi expressed the view to visiting LDP member Utsunomiya Tokuma that Sato's willingness to co-operate with the USA on Vietnam may have arisen from his hostility to the PRC, thus drawing a clear connection between relations with Japan and developments in South-East Asia.46 For the time being the PRC would continue to watch Sato carefully but Liao added that Sato had already taken a number of measures repugnant to the PRC and continued that he had not changed his intention to visit Japan at some stage, but a definite decision would be taken after consultation with Premier Zhou and other government leaders. The visit Liao referred to had been intended to coincide with the signing of the agreement on the implementation of the third year of the L-T accord, but had had to be delayed as a result of the Japanese refusal to accept a delegation under Peng Zhen.47

Another important problem confronting PRC relations with Japan was the question of credit for plant purchases by the official Export-Import (Exim) Bank of Japan. Since some 'sales were financed by the funds made available by the Export-Import Bank of Japan, one might say that Japanese firms acted under official encouragement'.48 On 26 January the Japanese government refused Hitachi Shipbuilding an Exim credit. In one of his regular talks with Japanese journalists49 Liao made it clear next day that, if as a result of the Yoshida letter no Exim credits were available for the purchase of a plant from Nichibo, this would greatly damage L-T trade. This tough position was repeated in a speech by Liao to Japanese L-T and other trade representatives, adding that if present obstacles could be removed, trade would flourish.50

In January a JCP delegation under Miyamoto Kenji had visited Peking.51 Although information about such exchanges between delegations at (Communist) party level is generally sparse, another reason for not underlining Liao's possible role in these talks may have been the consideration that such overexposure of Liao as a 'revolutionary' could have damaged efforts to win approval for Exim credits. Relations deteriorated quickly, however, followed by the announcement on 15 February that a contract for the purchase of a urea plant would be annulled.52 By now, the question of the pending Liao visit to Japan had acquired symbolic significance. Three weeks later Liao announced that under the present circumstances his planned visit could not take place.

Liao Chengzhi continued to engage in talks with Japanese delegations but hopes for change must have been slim. Sun Pinghua, a leading Japan specialist who had arrived in Tokyo in August 1964 as staff member of the L-T mission, returned to Peking in April, probably for consultation on the problems of plant credits and the 'deferred' (cancelled) Liao mission.53 As late as 24 March Liao had stressed that relations with Japan hinged on the question of the Yoshida letter, in other words on the question of Exim credits. This pronouncement seemed to imply that, despite Japan's increasing involvement in US Vietnam policy, the PRC was still prepared to work for an improvement in trade relations. Prospects dimmed however, when on 31 March the PRC declared that contracts with Hitachi Shipbuilding had lapsed due to the expiry of the deadline before the question of credit could be solved.54 It seems that the PRC had largely given up hope of importing big plants with Exim credits under the L-T arrangement. In April there was an opportunity for high-level contact between PRC and Japanese officials during Zhou Enlai's visit to Bandung on the occasion of the tenth anniversary of the Bandung conference. Zhou in fact did meet a highly-placed LDP official but on 30 April, Liao, who had not joined the PRC delegation this time, denied that the meeting had been a 'formal talk'.

While the international situation became ever more tense the PRC must have found it increasingly difficult to make concessions to the Japanese government under Sato, while continuing to preach 'resolute struggle' against the USA and 'its followers', during visits by Zhou Enlai, Chen Yi and Liu Ningyi to countries in Africa and Asia in March-April 1965. Liao himself was soon in the limelight again as PRC spokesman at the Afro-Asian Solidarity Conference in Winneba, not far from the Ghanaian capital, Accra.55 During the previous few months there had been heated debate among PRC leaders over the escalation of the Vietnam war, in particular concerning the question of co-operation with the Soviet Union in the face of the worsening crisis. The Winneba Conference became another stage for hostile verbal exchanges between the CPSU and the CCP and, if Liao's appearance was any indication of the PRC position, it seemed unlikely that the PRC was ready for co-operation with the Soviet Union.

In an interview on 8 June, shortly before his trip to the Second Afro-Asian Solidarity Conference in Algiers, Liao set out in detail the PRC position on a number of questions concerning relations with Japan. He appeared to avoid giving the impression that L-T trade was dead. At the same time he indicated that there would be no discussions between the Japanese and PRC delegations - a view also expressed by the Japanese government who had attempted to send a delegation comprising delegates from all major parties, including the opposition JSP.[55] Several weeks before the conference the left wing of the JSP led by Sasaki Kozo had been able to gain the upper hand in the JSP to the barely concealed pleasure of the PRC.[57] The JSP now refused to take part in the Japanese delegation, since it did not wish to have to commit itself to a position which would bring it into conflict with the PRC delegation.[58]

As is well known the conference never got off the ground.[59] Even before the failure became irreversible the PRC had manoeuvred itself increasingly into isolation in its attempt to polarise world opinion not only against the USA but also the Soviet Union.[60] Liao took part in a number of the activities of the PRC delegation. He is also reported to have visited Egypt with Luo Qingchang and Ke Hua on 19 June.[61] Among the members of the delegation was yet another Japan specialist, Xiao Xiangqian, and despite previous denials it seemed not unlikely that the PRC was prepared for talks on relations with Japan. On his return from Algiers Liao emphasised that PRC relations with Japan were closely bound up with the Vietnamese question. The connection had been made before, but its repetition now presaged a hardening line. During one of his regular talks with Japanese journalists on 15 June Liao appeared particularly concerned about the effect of the joint communiqué of the US-Japan committee on trade and the economy. He denied that the postponement of the Afro-Asian Solidarity Conference constituted a setback for PRC foreign policy (which it obviously was). Perhaps most surprising of all was the optimism Liao professed concerning the future of PRC relations with Japan. This optimism was based on an assumption previously expressed, to the effect that Japan's national interest would of necessity be in conflict with the national interest of the United States. The implication was that sooner or later Japan would adopt a position more independent of the US, and that such a change would lead to an improvement in PRC-Japan relations. Liao tried to put the blame for the obstacles in current L-T negotiations squarely on Sato's shoulders. At the same time he pointedly referred to the great possibilities for plant import under the 'friendship trade' arrangement. He denied the possibility of peaceful coexistence with the USA. Peaceful coexistence with Japan, on the other hand, was said to be not only possible but necessary. The implication was that the PRC would not deal with a Japanese government that would follow the line of US foreign policy.[62]

At the beginning of July Nan Hanchen had talks with conservative politicians in Japan. His initial attitude seemed flexible. On 3 July, however, he gave a speech which created a great stir in Japan because of its toughness and the threat of allowing trade links with Japan to deteriorate unless conditions were met.63 Nan subsequently even refused to meet the presidents of Nichibo and Hitachi Shipbuilding.64 Speeches by Nan Hanchen and Liao Chengzhi toward the end of July raised some doubt about PRC willingness to maintain links not only with conservative LDP members, but even with members of the JSP.65 In a clarification of Nan's statement of 28 July Liao added that the postponement of a visit by Kosaka Zentaro was not linked directly to the refusal of the Japanese government to issue visas to the youth delegation and to Japanese criticism of Nan's previous speech. Liao expressed PRC dissatisfaction with present 'informal' contacts when he stated that visits by 'former prime ministers' and 'former ministers' had to be followed by the visit of an active leading government member.66 An additional reason for PRC reluctance to undertake new moves towards LDP conservatives may have been developments within the LDP itself. Liao added as his 'private' opinion that the internal situation within the LDP was getting more and more complicated as a result of the death of Kono and Ikeda, and the PRC may have preferred to wait for the outcome of factional alignments within the LDP.

China's Foreign Policy in Crisis

During the second part of 1965 the PRC encountered a number of serious policy failures. In Africa, a number of states broke off relations.67 In South Asia, the PRC had tried to play an active role in the Indo-Pakistan war in September, but these attempts were counter-productive. On 30 September, Lin Biao's comments on 'People's War' were published and ironically, an abortive coup took place in Indonesia followed by a massive rout of all Communists there. This put an end to all dreams that may have existed in Peking concerning a Peking-Jakarta axis as the focal point for an international front directed against the USA.68 PRC policy towards the rest of South-East Asia had also undergone some change. Just as the PRC had increased exports to South-East Asia when it broke off links with Japan in 1958, Japanese government circles noted that PRC exports to that area were on the increase again, accompanied by capital export and technological assistance.69 Okazaki Kaheita led the Japanese team to negotiate the 4th Protocol under the L-T agreement and noted that the PRC line had hardened conspicuously. This was followed by an unusually strongly worded speech by Foreign Minister Chen Yi on 29 September in which he indicated that trade with Japan would be kept at the present level.70 During the following days the Indonesian events must have occupied the minds of PRC policy makers. It must have been clear that the increasingly radical line of PRC foreign policy would not lead to early success and there were reports on intense discussions on foreign policy during this period.

In a speech on 2 October Liao focused his attention on two points, trade and the position of Hong Kong. He nevertheless complained that Japan discriminated against the PRC even more than against the Soviet Union. As far as cash purchases were concerned the PRC would rather deal with Western Europe than Japan, taking up a threat that had been regularly used since the fifties (and is not unknown these days either). Liao also appeared fairly conciliatory on Hong Kong but warned that the use of Hong Kong as a base against Vietnam might result in a change of PRC attitudes.[71] In a press interview the same day Liao made it clear that the question of Exim finance was not just an economic problem: he explicitly stated that 'deferred payments' (ie credits) other than through the Exim Bank were not acceptable.[72] As predicted by PRC leaders L-T trade stagnated in the subsequent period, in contrast to the 'friendship trade' conducted at the autumn fair in Canton.

Following the obvious failures of its foreign policy in a number of areas the PRC took pains to 'explain' and 'justify' its present line, without giving any indication of an impending change, as expressed both in Liu Ningyi's speech of 5 November and the joint editorial of 11 November in *People's Daily* and *Red Flag*. There were calls for a struggle by the Japanese people against 'the expansion of American aggression' in Vietnam and against the Japanese treaty with Korea, reminiscent of similar calls during 1958 and preceding the Security Treaty crisis.[74] In contrast to 1958 relations with Japan were not broken off. The need to maintain links was apparent when toward the end of the year Zhou Enlai declared that even a Sino-American war would not interrupt trade with Japan.[75] There may have been a number of reasons for this. Trade had reached a significantly higher level than during the fifties, and disruption would have greater negative effects on the PRC itself. There may also have been the argument that by politicising existing links more leverage would be obtained than by cutting them completely. The Fisheries Agreement concluded on 17 December 1965 was an example of such politicisation which was also to affect virtually all other agreements until 1971-72.[76]

There is no way of discovering whether Liao Chengzhi personally agreed with these changes in Japan policy. Despite his vociferous attacks on the 'Soviet revisionists' especially at functions of the Afro-Asian Solidarity movement, and explicit attacks on 'imperialism', he may have realised that radical policies as such would not change Japanese attitudes in the foreseeable future. Perhaps more than any other PRC Japan specialist Liao had gained a reputation as someone especially able to get on with LDP conservatives. This factor, together with attacks during the Cultural Revolution that was soon to follow, may create the impression that Liao, as representative of a more 'moderate' line, may have been forced against his convictions to go along with the radical line. At that time, however, nobody knew what the Cultural Revolution was going to be like, and how it would affect PRC leaders themselves. It is easy to argue in retrospect that Liao *must* have been opposed to more radical politics personified by what was later to be called the 'Gang of Four' (or five, if Mao Zedong is included). He is likely to have had inside knowledge of the direction of attacks on Li Weihan a year before. Seen against the background of the times, there is a certain internal logic in PRC attacks on the Soviet Union as well as on the United States, and it is not unlikely that even a 'moderate' like Liao may in fact have been personally convinced that a generally harder line was correct in the face of the growing Vietnam crisis, accepting the worsening of relations with Japan as an inevitable by-product of the deteriorating international situation, while at the same time engaging in damage-limitation.

The recall of PRC ambassadors in January-February 1966 underlined the fierce debate on PRC foreign policy after the failures of 1965 and the ongoing tension with the Soviet Union in the face of the Vietnam crisis.[77] At this point the JCP tried to work for a reduction of tension between the CPSU and the CCP for the sake of a common front on Vietnam. An article in the February issue of the Chinese *Red Flag (Hongqi)* had already charged the Soviet Union explicitly with working towards a 'Soviet-American-Japanese Alliance in order to oppose China, Korea and the peoples of all Asian countries ... ', thus adopting an extremely harsh attitude.[78]

A JCP delegation left for the PRC on 8 February, went to Hanoi on 17 February and returned to the PRC on 27 February.[79] A second JCP delegation under Miyamoto Kenji had left for Shanghai on 9 February. Formal talks with a CCP delegation began on 3 March. The JCP delegation left again for North Korea on 11 March, to arrive back in Peking on 21 March.[80] On 25 March the JCP announced that it would not participate in the 23rd Congress of the CPSU, thus indicating their agreement with the CCP on that point.[81] According to later JCP reports a comprehensive agreement had been reached in talks with CCP leaders, but when the delegation met Mao Zedong on 28-29 March, Mao apparently tore this up, laying the foundation for the subsequent bitter and long-lasting split between the two parties.[82] As usual, there was little reporting in PRC media of activities during the long discussions. Attention should be paid to the fact that Liao Chengzhi was mentioned ahead of Liu Ningyi in virtually all published reports as a member of the CCP delegation.[83] For example, during a reception on 27 March, shortly before Mao's intervention, the list of participants was as follows:

Zhu De, Peng Zhen, Kang Sheng, Liao Chengzhi, Lin Feng, Liu Xiao, Liu Ningyi, Liu Ren, Zhang Zongxun and Zhao Yimin.[84]

Although one should not overrate the importance of such rankings, the list at least indicates that Liao's reduced visibility in the second part of 1965 need not be interpreted as an indication of a lessening of his standing in the hierarchy.

It has been argued that another Japan specialist, Sun Pinghua was partially blamed for errors of judgment concerning the JCP, leading to a weakening of his position, but it is not clear whether this was also true of Liao.[85] Later, Matsumura blamed himself for having misjudged Sato, thus damaging Liao, Sun Pinghua and Wang Xiaoyun during the GPCR, and he worried whether Nan Hanchen, too - who was rumoured to have committed suicide - may have been adversely affected.[86]

Even before the break-up of talks with the JCP, Liao Chengzhi had sent a private letter to Sasaki of the JSP to inform him that he would now be willing to head a delegation to Japan.[87] This message was likely to have increased pressure on the Sato government which had previously refused entry to missions led by Peng Zhen and Liu Ningyi. By refusing Liao the Sato government would be refusing the PRC's most senior Japan specialist, specifically responsible for contacts with Japanese conservatives and business circles.[88] The PRC reaction was surprisingly low key, perhaps because the PRC had decided that it could not afford a break with Japan. Another related reason might have been that Liu Shaoqi undertook a visit to South Asia (Pakistan, Afghanistan, Burma) in March-April which was called a 'victory for peace diplomacy', and this was clearly not the time to mar this image by high-handed attacks on the Japanese government.[89]

Other events during 1966 however showed clearly that no softening of PRC attitudes was to be expected. In January a 'friendship' delegation of the Nichibosoku had visited the PRC. Their report contains summaries of addresses by various PRC politicians. In addition to the 'factual content' of the speeches a comparison between them also provides a revealing picture of the various styles used by PRC politicians to address an important Japanese delegation. Zhao Anbo's speech is characterised by its 'serious' approach to both trade and political questions.[90] Lian Guan's address is highly politicised in language reminiscent of his utterances during the Cultural Revolution, highly abstract and devoid of humour.[91] It appears that Lei Renmin - who was already ill - had originally prepared a more optimistic speech, but had changed the tone in response to the worsening political context.[92] Although Zhou Enlai went into great detail on matters such as the importance of an air agreement, his talk was mainly characterised by the repetition of general statements, and it seems that various passages these addresses were more or less straight copies from other speeches.[93] From a rhetorical point of view Liao's speech was by far the most lively and, although short, full of irony.[94] One of the reasons for this may have been the fact that he spoke in Japanese, which, contrary to normal practice, on that occasion was translated into Chinese for the benefit of other PRC members present.[95]

In April moves to negotiate a second L-T agreement were answered in the form of an invitation by Liao Chengzhi to Matsumura Kenzo.[96] On 19 May a communiqué was signed by Matsumura and Liao expressing the willingness of both sides to negotiate a second agreement.[97] Matsumura was the most senior Japanese involved in L-T trade but he was already ageing. At a reception on 13 May Liao appeared to hint that the PRC would like to see Fujiyama Aiichiro succeed Matsumura.[98] In a speech on the same day Liao seemed to express greater certainty about the new line of PRC foreign policy after the debates of the previous period. He referred to a number of recent policy speeches by PRC government and CCP leaders and emphasised the 'resolute support for the Vietnamese people in their struggle against the USA'.[99] At the same time he repeated the previous rationale for continued contacts with Japanese conservatives by stressing that visits such as Matsumura's were particularly important at a time when the USA wished to 'restrain' the PRC.[100] The reiteration of this rationale was rather significant at this time, only a few days after the 'official' start of the Cultural Revolution. Despite all their limitations the semi-governmental contacts with Japan were, with the exception of the PRC's diplomatic outpost in Cairo, virtually the only regular form of contact with any country at the peak of the Cultural Revolution. Very soon however it would become obvious that despite the importance of the Japanese link Liao's position as the PRC's most senior Japan specialist was under attack.

Liao under Attack

Signs of some impending change could already be seen in the reorganisation of one of the semi-governmental organisations responsible for contacts with the PRC, the Chinese People's Association for Foreign Cultural Relations, now renamed Chinese People's Friendship Association for Foreign Cultural Relations.[101] At about this time Qiao Guanhua began playing a more important role in PRC contacts with Japan (Qiao was later purged for alleged links with the so-called Gang of Four).[102] One of the first signs of an attack on Liao came in the form of an article in *People's Daily* on 5 June openly attacking the OCAC for lack of emphasis on 'politics' and demanding the 'revolutionisation' of the Commission.[103] Under domestic pressure Liao apparently attempted to maintain a good atmosphere during talks on trade with Matsumura in May, despite his attacks on the Sato Cabinet.[104] During a subsequent visit in the summer of 1966 Furui noticed that following a minor incident Liao was forced to read a stern message of warning to the delegation, a rather uncharacteristic move for someone like Liao.[105]

Throughout the Cultural Revolution attacks on policies espoused by Liao were mostly limited to the field of Overseas Chinese affairs. Being a closely guarded area of PRC policy-making, foreign policy was one of the few areas that remained relatively untouched by 'revelations' during the Cultural Revolution. Public revelations such as Lin Biao's purported collusion with the Soviet Union often had an implausible ring. It is therefore not surprising that we find hardly any source attacking Liao for following a 'revisionist' policy line towards *Japan*, in contrast with attacks on Overseas Chinese policy. The accusation of a lack of emphasis on 'politics' in the OCAC perhaps also may be taken as a lack of emphasis on 'ideology' in Liao's dealings with Japan. As we have seen in our comparison of speeches by various politicians addressing a Japanese trade delegation, Liao's speech was indeed largely free from *politspeak*, and for that reason may have sounded more convincing to his non-Communist audience. Also, the refusal to have a delegation under Liao enter Japan was not answered by a propaganda barrage, perhaps due to Liao's personal influence, since he would be aware of the fact that such an overreaction might only be counterproductive. But by this time, Liao's influence was already on the wane. Despite a number of reports of attacks on Liao, and the availability of some Red Guard posters containing such attacks, it is still impossible to trace in any detail the history of his gradual downfall. Attacks on the OCAC and Liao increased in August,[106] but Liao continued to appear at public functions, including the National Day parade.[107] Despite Zhou's attempt to protect the celebration of the birthday centennial of the symbol of United Front Work, Sun Yatsen, there were even reports that the house of Mme Sun (Song Qingling) had been sacked.[108] In her recollections Liao's sister Liao Mengxing mentioned that her mother had 'loyally supported the GPCR at the celebration of the birthday centennial of Sun Yatsen',[109] but there was a new spate of attacks on Liao in November, and he did not appear in public as would have been expected.[110]

When asked by Okazaki Kaheita about the meaning of the Cultural Revolution Liao reportedly avoided a straight answer and said that:
> Because there is somebody studying it professionally I will let him explain, and I was introduced to Zhao Anbo, and for more than an hour Zhao gave me a detailed explanation.[111]

This was followed in December by reports of Zhou criticising Liao Chengzhi in public for errors committed during a meeting with a Japanese Youth Delegation earlier in the year but this limited criticism seems to have been intended to preempt more dangerous Red Guard attacks and thus protect Liao.[112] Throughout this period Japanese newspaper reports of the PRC's policy towards Japan seemed to play down the inherent risk of a dramatic change.[113] With the reorganisation of the PRC's foreign trade organs in autumn and the shunning of trade with firms which had 'links' with the JCP (or the USSR) it was clear that change was on the way.[114]

While Liao's star was falling, Liu Ningyi's was soon to rise, and in contrast to Liao, Liu became the focus of attention when the PRC started propaganda attacks against Japan after a failed attempt by Liu to lead a delegation there to attend the Anti-Nuclear Conference.[115] Originally the delegation was scheduled to be headed by Tang Mingzhao with Wu Xueqian as deputy leader, but the PRC raised the political stakes considerably by replacing them with Liu and Zhang Xiangshan.[116] This was not only directed against Sato but was also an expression of the importance attached by the PRC to a meeting which was expected to become a forum of argument with the JCP since Zhang Xiangshan was reputedly in charge of relations with the JCP.[117] When the delegation was predictably refused entry to Japan, PRC journalists stationed there took over its task with the result that the Anti-Nuclear Conference broke up in confusion.[118] Shortly after the visit Chen Yi indicated to visiting JSP members that the responsibility for Sato's 'reactionary policy' would not be laid on the shoulders of the Japanese people. This meant that he excluded the possibility of breaking off relations as had occurred in 1958.[119]

Within the context of the Cultural Revolution Liu Ningyi's role in the affair had virtually made him into a 'martyr', and his star continued to rise. On 17 August it was announced that he had been promoted to the position of secretary of the 'Party Central'.[120] About this time reports appeared that Liao Chengzhi had been attacked in wall posters. In Japan a move was made to have a delegation led by Liao visit Japan but Okazaki Kaheita recognised that such a visit could take place only after a substantial change of Japanese policy, probably under a different prime minister.[121] It is reasonable to assume that the cautious attempt to invite Liao had been made with an eye on his endangered position, which in turn threatened to affect the whole framework of semi-official links. As the Cultural Revolution progressed 'friendship trade' had also been affected; companies with close links to the JCP were now excluded from access to this form of trade.[122] This was of course a result of the failure of the JCP mission under Miyamoto, but could also be seen within the context of the Sino-Soviet split. It is interesting to note that some PRC politicians justified the Cultural Revolution by referring to tension with the Soviet Union 'in order to be prepared', while others refuted this interpretation.

In August it became evident that Liao's fortunes were definitely declining. As late as 6 August he was still mentioned ahead of Liu Ningyi in an account of a mass meeting welcoming Liu after his abortive attempt to lead a delegation to Japan.[123] On 13 August Liu was given considerably more attention in a report on another mass meeting attended by both politicians. The first function after Liu's appointment as secretary of the Party Central on 18 August showed Liao in a conspicuously low position.[124] This was confirmed by Liao's low ranking in an account of the National Day celebration on 2 October,[125] as well as in subsequent reports. During a visit of LDP Diet members towards the end of August an incident occurred when 'inexperienced members' of the delegation were accused of having misrepresented Chen Yi in an interview with Japanese journalists. In a rather uncharacteristic manner Liao Chengzhi appeared and read a written protest threatening discontinuation of the visit. Liao then failed to meet members of the delegation again before their departure, the reason given being his 'health'.

Japanese delegations returning from the PRC stressed the stability of the PRC's economic situation and professed optimism about the conclusion of a second L-T agreement.[126] Nevertheless there was palpable Japanese concern, all the more justified by reports of attacks on Sun Yatsen and Song Qingling in mid-September, not long before the celebration of Sun's birthday centenary on 11 November.[127] This was not merely an attack on an individual. It should be seen as an attack on essential elements of united front strategy which had hitherto maintained a common revolutionary heritage symbolised by the figure of Sun, and to which both Communists and non-Communists could refer. As one of the architects of the PRC's united front strategy Zhou Enlai lost no time in defending Sun and his widow.[128] Although under attack Liao had been deeply involved in preparations for the celebration of the anniversary and the attacks on Sun and Song naturally also reflected on him, one of the main exponents of CCP united front work.

There are some indications that, in the period between September and October, Liao Chengzhi kept fighting in order to defend his position. Towards the end of September the so-called '32 person appeal' was published in Japan, attacking the Sato government's policy and calling for an improvement in relations with the PRC. The appeal adopted many slogans recently propagated by the PRC and should be seen as a dramatic initiative to keep contacts alive.[129] In response to this action Guo Moruo and Liao Chengzhi in turn on 5 October published a so-called '52-person appeal' in support of the Japanese action. It was a clear demonstration of their willingness to maintain the proven channels of communication between the PRC and Japan which appeared threatened.[130] A few days later Liao travelled south to receive refugees from Indonesia, and in a widely noted speech provided one of the first clues that Lin Biao might soon become the CCP's *only* vice-chairman.[131] Towards the end of October Liao was criticised by Red Guards.[132]

The celebrations of Sun's birthday centenary continued to attract much attention in the media, but it could hardly be overlooked that Liao was treated with less than usual prominence, although the media devoted much space to printed speeches by Song Qingling and He Xiangning.133 Okazaki visited the PRC in November to discuss the continuation of trade

> When I went to Peking ... due to the fact that my counterparts were engaged in taking care of Red Guards the negotiations hardly proceeded.134

Elsewhere it was remarked that during the negotiations the atmosphere was characterised by 'touchiness' hitherto absent from such negotiations.135

According to wall posters that appeared on 14 December in Peking Zhou Enlai had criticised Liao's shortcomings in the area of youth exchanges with Japan, and other Red Guard publications also contained attacks on Liao.136 It seems reasonable to argue that Zhou may indeed have expressed limited criticism of Liao Chengzhi in order to defend him, in a manner reminiscent of his protective tactics at the time of Liao's arrest by Zhang Guotao.

In the meantime PRC policy towards Japan kept changing. In a striking deviation from previous united front tactics strong support appeared for splinter and minority groups within the JCP and other left wing organisations.137 Somewhat surprisingly at this stage it was also decided to strengthen links with the trade union federation SOHYO, with which there had been serious differences on the question of (nuclear) armament.138 During the SOHYO visit to Peking a joint communiqué was published which hardly touched on controversial issues. One may guess that the driving force behind this move was Liu Ningyi, who had been deeply involved in trade union contacts before. Despite all efforts undertaken by Japanese and some PRC politicians the L-T negotiations for 1967 disappointed the hopes of Japanese business, and although detailed figures were not revealed the agreed target showed a drop compared to the previous year.139 The drop was not only an indication of displeasure with the Japanese government's policy, but was partly due also to differences on quantities and categories of goods to be exchanged under the agreement. Also, trade with Western Europe was on the increase, and general domestic instability too will have affected the talks. It is hardly surprising that in the turmoil of the Cultural Revolution a number of contracts that had indeed been concluded were subsequently breached.140

The situation took a more serious turn when unconfirmed reports appeared of the suicide of Nan Hanchen, a leading figure in the PRC's trade with Japan. This was confirmed five weeks later.141 In January, as revealed 16 years later, Liao was deeply enmeshed in the power struggle.142 His public appearances had become rare.143 Liao himself came under renewed attack in mid-April 1967. These attacks were directed mainly at his role as head of the OCAC, and also against Chen Yi and Liao as representing United Front Work Organisations. They have been dealt with extensively by scholars of the PRC's policy towards overseas Chinese and need not be repeated here. However, one of the particular charges raised against Liao was his apparent opposition to Lin Biao, which seems to be confirmed by the fact that Liao was one of the first higher ranking officials to be rehabilitated following the fall of Lin Biao.145 Following these attacks Liao appeared once more in public in his capacity as member of the National People's Congress on the occasion of the May Day celebrations in Tiananmen Square in Peking, and he also took part in talks with a Japanese delegation under Matsumura which led to the signing of an agreement on the extension of L-T trade on 19 May 1967.146 In June 1967 attacks followed which contained among other things the charge that Liao had been guilty of personally protecting a 'spy'. One of his last appearances published by PRC media was on 3 July when he appeared at a function for overseas Chinese expelled from Burma in connection with 'cultural revolutionary' activities.147

On the same day Sato's visit to Taiwan scheduled for September was announced. This announcement contributed to the worsening of trade relations between the PRC and Japan. The first five-year L-T agreement was about to expire in December 1967, and at one stage it seemed as if the PRC would refuse to negotiate a new agreement.148 During these months a number of Japanese businessmen were arrested on spying charges, and a further row developed concerning the visit of a PRC youth delegation to Japan.149 There was little news to encourage LDP politicians such as Matsumura, Okazaki, Furui, Fujiyama, Tagawa and others. There was speculation that the current L-T agreement might lapse, to be followed by a different sort of short-term agreement valid for one year only, thus fundamentally altering the character of the L-T agreement which had been set up to create stability. After a period of uncertainty Zhou Enlai asked a JSP member, Sekino Hisao, to convey to Matsumura Kenzo that the Japanese should send a small delegation to discuss the way trade might be continued. The Japanese were concerned about the way the message had been sent indirectly, thus foreboding difficulties, and their anxiety did not prove groundless. Liao - reportedly ill - did not appear during the talks; instead Liu Xiwen, Wang Xiaoyun, Sun Pinghua, Lu Jun and Chen Kang took part.150

By now it had become clear that Liao Chengzhi had become a victim of the Cultural Revolution, but there were also further reports of his impaired health.151 Other apparent victims were Sun Pinghua and Wang Xiaoyun who were temporarily absent from the public political scene. Some of Liao's subordinates remained in the field of their previous assignments, and others were added. As was to be expected, there were also changes in hierarchical order among the old and new Japan specialists.152 Liao's fall has been linked to attacks on the Overseas Chinese Affairs Commission, which seems to have been abolished some time in 1968,153 but in view of the chaotic state of affairs in the PRC during this period it seems a rather futile exercise to ascribe this to any particular reason, or the outcome of logical decisions on the basis of clear cut policy differences. Viewed superficially it seems reasonable to date his downfall shortly after his dropping from public view. There were reports of attacks on Liao in February 1968, which however do not constitute conclusive evidence that he was still politically active at this time.154 He Wen has argued with some justification that if Liao had still held some kind of official position by the summer of 1968 he should have appeared at the signing ceremony of a new agreement on trade with Japan, now renamed Memorandum Trade - thus omitting Liao's name from the title.155

Experiences in the Cultural Revolution

At that time little news about Liao Chengzhi filtered through to Japan. In October 1968 Saionji mentioned to Tagawa Seiichi that Liao was still suffering from heart disease, and that he was sending medicine to him.[156] At about the same time it was alleged that Liao, among other charges, had offended Mao's wife, Jiang Qing, and that he had been purged.[157] In March 1968 an official source confirmed that Liao had been under political attack. In 1969 during a party congress that elevated Lin Biao to the position of personal successor to Mao Zedong, Liao lost his seat on the Central Committee. Later, on 2 October 1970 Saionji Kinkazu mentioned to Hoashi Kei that Liao had been severely attacked during the early period of the Red Guard movement. He was suspended from his posts and efforts by his friends to restore his reputation had failed.[158] The first subsequent 'official' public reference to Liao came in 1971 during a visit of a Japanese delegation shortly after the fall of Lin Biao, when Zhou Enlai expressed his regret that Liao was unable to be present 'due to a heart condition'.[159] Japanese observers agreed that this reference augured a policy change from the icy relations that had prevailed since the beginning of the Cultural Revolution. However, it would still be several months before Liao himself reappeared in public, and his return to an active schedule took even longer.

It was many years before more detailed sketches of Liao's life during this period were published. The publication of these recollections was a political act in itself. They may paint a biased picture of what happened to Liao during these years of turmoil, but it is worthwhile presenting some episodes in translation.

Marshall He Long was also attacked during the Cultural Revolution and his widow later described how Liao helped the family during these difficult times:

> It happened towards the end of 1966. At that time He Long and I were already isolated from the world ... In order to escape the claws of the 'Gang of Four' our children had assumed different names and had gone into hiding, drifting aimlessly in society without anybody to support them. He Long worried day and night about his children, and frequently dragged his ailing body up and leaning against the window called his children's names in a weak voice. What tortured him most was the fate of his youngest daughter Liming. She was only sixteen at that time. Liao's family was also in dire difficulties then. The gates of his residence were pasted all over with large posters that said 'Burn Liao Chengzhi alive'. Here I have to add that hitherto we had respected each other and got along well without however having had much social intercourse. One evening Pengfei, Xiaoming and Liming found themselves in difficult straits. They ... put a call through to the children of the Liao family to find out how they were faring. They would not go to their house and bother them if they themselves had problems. ... we heard the warm voices of Jing Puchun and the children of the Liao family ...: 'Where are you? Come over to our place right now, we have been thinking of you.' ... they wanted to have

our children stay with them, and when they found out that Liao was not there, asked for his whereabouts. The children replied that he could not remain at home, and was now in Zhongnanhai and could not return home frequently. It was only later that we learned that they had given Liao Chengzhi a ring, telling him about the arrival of the three children of He Long, and that Liao had urged them to let them all stay. Our three families were deeply moved by the sincerity of the Liao family, and received the greatest (possible) comfort and consolation. In the evening Pengfei and Xiaoming held counsel: for the three of them to stay would be asking too much and might bring disaster on the Liao family, all the more so since at present Liao found himself in the same situation. They could not bear [to] cause him even greater abuse, and decided to move on to Tianjin and find ways and means [to survive there], leaving only Liming to stay at Liao's place. When told about these plans Jing Puchun did not want to let them go, but was unable to detain them. Liao urged her by phone not to let the children suffer any difficulties concerning their livelihood. Jing Puchun produced money and food ration coupons and gave them to Pengfei and Xiaoming. Both brother and sister were hard up in those days. Liming stayed on with the Liaos. One day Liao had come to see his mother who was ninety years old ... During his brief visit Liao had Liming come to him and said to her warmly: 'All right, you stay with us'. Jing Puchun loved and spoiled her as if she were her own daughter, and whenever the house was searched by 'rebels' Jing Puchun hid her in He Xiangning's room... personally declared off limits to any intruders by Prime Minister Zhou. In this way our children enjoyed the full protection and care of the Liao family. Living in the Western Hills we were not aware of the situation. Until He Long drifted into unconsciousness and before dying he kept on muttering unceasingly 'my daughter, my daughter'. How great would his consolation have been had he been aware [of the situation] in his grave. I learned about the whole affair only in 1972 when I returned from Guizhou. When I met Liao I expressed my gratitude to him and the family, but he only laughed 'Don't mention it, it was our moral duty.'[160]

Liao's daughter Liao Jian also referred to He Long's daughter staying at their place, and adds that in 1967:

He Long and his wife were both put under arrest by the 'Gang of Four' ... Once father was about to leave. He had already gone into the yard when he returned again to Youming's room and urged her not to go anywhere else and stay where she was ... It was on that occasion that father left home only to meet us again after five years had passed.[161]

Liao was apparently not put into prison. According to Jing Puchun:

During the Cultural Revolution Premier Zhou had him live in a different place in Peking (in hiding) in order to protect him from the

'Gang of Four'. I visited him once a week, and Chengzhi always enquired after the health of his mother... Mother also kept thinking of her child, and when she found out that her child was not coming to wish her good morning, she asked us for the reason, and we had to tell her that he was so busy he could not return.[162]

Although he was not totally isolated he could not see visitors freely. One of his few visitors was his grandchild Yu Yanwen who was brought up in Liao's house:

But the good times did not last long, the 'Cultural Revolution' started and grandpa and us were separated for five years. I remember how one day in winter when I was four or five, grandma took me along to give grandpa some things. At that time there was nobody in our family except for grandma and myself who were able to see grandpa. The reason that I was permitted to see him was probably because I was an ignorant child. When we arrived at grandpa's room he was just lying on his bed reading. His hair was all white, and a thick full beard covered his emaciated face and cheeks. When grandpa saw me he dropped the book, full of joy, called me by my nickname and stretched out his hand to draw me towards him. I anxiously tried to hide in grandma's arms. Grandma tried to get me to say 'grandpa', in Cantonese, but I shut my mouth and stared at grandpa without saying a word. Later grandpa told me that I let him give me a kiss only after he had drawn a picture for me and played blind man's buff. Whenever grandma took me to see grandpa later on I always had him make drawings for me. Grandpa used a pencil to draw portraits, cats, dogs, taught me how to write one, two, three ... on cigarette boxes, in newspaper margins. When I left him there were usually four or five drawings in my hand. I fixed them onto my bed; when looking at them I would start thinking of grandpa ...[163]

Liao's daughter Liao Ming recalls that:

When I graduated in March 1969 I was considered 'a youngster fit for receiving education', and was 'assigned' to a labour camp in Qinghai. Father was already being kept in isolation at that time, and it was only after putting in many requests that I received approval to say goodbye to my father before I left. I had not seen father for several years. He looked frighteningly emaciated, and his hair had become almost completely white. Forcing a smile I said goodbye to him. He urged me whatever happened not to abandon myself to despair, to study and work hard, and write many letters. Father accompanied me to the gate. I kept looking back many times. He waved his hands with a smile on his face while something like sparkling crystals seemed to be floating in his eyes ...[164]

Liao was able to send his daughter a letter dated 27 July 1969, as well as two drawings which he had entrusted to her mother who smuggled them out and sent them to Liao Ming. His letter reads as follows:

> Thank you very much for giving me *The Song of Ouyang Hai*. I read it several times from cover to cover, and I felt that it gave me new spirit, it has some undescribable power ... You sent me a very good book [indeed], but I [kept wondering] what I could give you in return. I could not sleep because of this and drew two pictures for you. They are not good as paintings, but at least they are able to convey my feelings. The first one is a general impression of what I felt during the Long March. Never forget that revolution consists of endless hardships and bitter experiences, and victory is only obtained after innumerable sacrifices ... All of you grew up like plants in a hothouse, but be always on your guard and never forget your roots.165

One of Liao's two drawings depicted a mother who had to leave her baby in the care of an old gentleman during the Long March because both parents had to carry on fighting while the March went on and could not carry their child any further. Liao explained in his letter that the parents were killed during the March, and added that if the baby had survived he would not even know his parents' names:

> When I was imprisoned in Jiangxi I frequently thought of this scene, and some time in the future, when I have time, I should like to paint it in oils ...166

Soon afterwards Liao's mother He Xiangning was taken into hospital after she had injured her leg in an accident. Her daughter-in-law Jing Puchun was:

> very worried at that time. I gave Prime Minister Zhou a ring to tell him what had happened and requested him to let Chengzhi go to the hospital and visit his mother. Prime Minister Zhou agreed immediately and sent a car to pick me up, and we went to fetch Chengzhi and take him to the hospital. He Xiangning had not seen him for a long time and was very happy when she saw him. Some time later Prime Minister Zhou also arrived to see He Xiangning ...167

Some time in 1970 Liao's heart trouble worsened,168 and Zhou apparently intervened again to allow him to have proper treatment. Later Liao met one of his former colleagues, Wang Jiaxiang, as told by Wang's wife Zhu Zha:

> My deep friendship with Liao dates from the period of the 'Cultural Revolution'. In 1970 Wang Jiaxiang was persecuted by Lin Biao and Kang Sheng, and sent to a labour re-education camp in Xinyang, Henan province. He subsequently suffered from infectious TB and was granted permission by Mao Zedong to return to Peking for treatment, lying next door to Liao's sick room. Wang Jiaxiang and Liao had been comrades-in-arms for a long time collaborating in foreign affairs. Now they were staying in the same hospital as neighbors they could not even see and talk to each other freely. All that they could do was to pray in their hearts for each other's speedy recovery.169

Between 1971 and 1972 Liao was gradually rehabilitated politically. The first official indication was, as already mentioned, Zhou's reference to Liao during an unscheduled speech.170 Little is known about the specific steps accompanying the rehabilitation, but one source mentions that he may have had to attend the so-called 7 May Cadre School for some time, a particular form of 'political re-education'[171]:

> It was in 1971. Father had just been given some freedom, and was being treated in the media as someone who 'still exists' [politically]. Just then my younger brother Kaisun discussed the question of marriage with his wife, Mrs Zhao. She comes from an ordinary family, and had been a ballet dancer. She worried ... about many things. One of her fears was that the families were not equal, and that after father's rehabilitation to his original position he would look down on her. Secondly, she had injured her legs. Should she ... not be able to dance again on the stage after her operation, she would have no more prospects of a career, and would be looked down on by people even more. When Kaisun told his father about her anxieties father took up his pen ... and wrote a letter to his future daughter-in-law: 'First I should like to tell you that yours are unnecessary worries ... I've been an actor myself, and have some understanding of the mind of an actor. ... your illness ... is unfortunate, but it is not at all serious, and I am confident that it won't influence your artistic future negatively. ... Secondly, you are also of the opinion that we may become influential again, and once 'liberated' we may become arrogant, to the degree that we won't recognise our friends any more.[172]

It goes without saying that Liao was able to persuade her. It is interesting, to note that this is not the only reference to 'class distinctions' with regard to the Liao family by persons who considered themselves of inferior rank or social standing. Not unusual, of course, in pre-Communist society, but worth noting as a phenomenon also explicitly and without reserve referred to in Communist China.

How did Liao Chengzhi tolerate his dismissal from office and virtual house arrest? According to various reports his spirit does not seem to have been broken. An official involved in Overseas Chinese affairs in Canton province, Yi Meihou, confirms this impression:

> In the middle of the 'Cultural Revolution' we all received blows, but he was full of confidence in the future. When he saw me in Canton he told me with a streak of humour that having survived disaster (in the first place) good fortunes were sure to come later on, and he encouraged me to look forward.[173]

Was Liao's ability due to his confidence in the 'future of the revolution', or was it the result of a basically optimistic character? I must say that I incline towards the latter view, although Liao may indeed have couched his optimism in 'revolutionary' jargon, as reported by Wu Hengxin:

> I am an Overseas Chinese who returned (to the PRC) from Mauritius. In 1952 my father, Wu Yinggui, visited China to attend the Political Consultative Conference as an Overseas Chinese leader from South Africa and he took me along to see He Xiangning and Liao. I remember how my contacts with foreign countries and my medical

research suffered severely during the 'Cultural Revolution'. My scientific material was completely destroyed, my work as a medical doctor came to a halt, and endless 'house searches' and 'interrogations' made it impossible to feel at ease. When I saw that some Overseas Chinese living in the PRC despaired of the situation and left (the country) I also wavered. At this decisive moment I went to ask Liao for advice. He was also in a difficult position ... When I had finished talking he said to me: 'This situation can't go on for long, don't be afraid.' Subsequently he began to mention my participation in the movement 'To Oppose the USA and Aid Korea'. He mentioned one by one what I had achieved since my return to China, as if making up an inventory of family treasures, and urged me not to make a break with my past without full consideration of everything involved. Finally he also personally made arrangements for some measures to protect me, which made my eyes fill with tears of gratitude. It was not long before he himself was in a situation more dangerous and worse than mine, but when I saw him he always talked in an optimistic way as if he was fundamentally unconcerned about what would happen to him...[174]

Liao's attitude is all the more astonishing since he was also afflicted by a heart condition which worsened in about 1970. There were many reasons why he might have despaired. His efforts to build up a viable policy towards Overseas Chinese abroad and in the PRC had been virtually destroyed, with no hope of improvement in the foreseeable future. Relations with Japan had worsened so much in the course of the Cultural Revolution that all hopes of being able to achieve the main goal to which Liao had devoted so many years - the establishment of relations - were gone. Most of Liao's political activities had involved 'contacts with foreign countries' which were now considered 'criminal' during this wave of open xenophobia. The whole idea of united front work had been disgraced.

Of course some projects in which Liao was particularly involved were also affected. During the Cultural Revolution the Overseas Chinese University and Jinan University ceased functioning. The situation was not much better on farms for Overseas Chinese settled in the PRC. Liao's personal involvement in the affairs of Xinglong farm has already been mentioned. According to a later report the:

Gang of Four slandered Xinglong Farm as a 'murky basis of the capitalist class' during those ten years. They smashed the sign that carried characters in He Xiangning's style. They also fabricated four big cases in which more than 200 persons were implicated. After the smashing of the Gang of Four the joy of these Overseas Chinese knew no bounds. They took the initiative and burned firecrackers [to celebrate], and hung up the signboard 'Xinglong Farm' at the gate.[175]

Despite Liao's professed optimism, these experiences must have had traumatic effects on him as on so many others. His rehabilitation in 1971-72 after Lin Biao's eclipse did not mean that the situation would revert to what it had been before the Cultural Revolution. Although Liao was to play a very important role during the seventies, focussing on Japan much more exclusively, he knew he still had to be careful, and he told Gao Yangwen (later Minister for Coal Industry) about it:

> In spring 1972 in order to see a doctor I returned to Peking from the place where I had undergone re-education by forced labour. I had nowhere to stay in Peking, so I had to put up temporarily at the guesthouse in Wang Daren Lane. One day an attendant told me that He Xiangning lived next to the guesthouse, and that Liao was also staying there. This was happy news ... Liao was thus in good health, and had considerable freedom. Could I see him? Would it reflect badly on Liao if I went to see him? I hesitated. One day I was just at the entrance gate of the guesthouse when suddenly a sedan started moving away from the gate next door. One glance and I knew it was Liao. I could not restrain myself and waved ... Liao looked, opened the car window and asked when I had returned, and where I was staying. I told him that I had become his neighbour. He immediately invited me to come over to his place. From then on I frequently visited his place for a chat. He was still as friendly and warm as before, but more cautious in talking about things. He said that luckily Prime Minister Zhou's all-round protection had enabled him to manage through [all these] difficult [times]. ... since the Lin Biao Incident, the Prime Minister had presided over work [in party and government], and things had taken a turn for the better. He also warned me that the struggle was still quite fierce, problems were complicated, and one had to be cautious in everything. But his deep hatred towards the 'Gang of Four' and his firm belief in the future of the country still showed in Liao's behaviour and manner of speaking. He said that the gang had perpetrated too many evil things, and had become estranged from the masses, and they would be overthrown in the end.[176]

Liao was also an artist and despite his many party and government duties during the fifties and sixties he involved himself deeply in the growing film industry including that in Hong Kong. Of course there was political relevance to this area of activity, too, but it is not difficult to imagine that Liao may have conceived of this as an outlet for his artistic talent. The Cultural Revolution put an end to his cultural activities and Liao once mentioned that 'Prime Minister Zhou had told him that he would not let him manage cultural affairs [any longer]'.[177]

This of course was a result of the fact that, until Mao's death, 'leftists' had been able to dominate the media, and therefore perhaps should not be seen as a restriction that was directed against Liao personally. Like so many other people involved in the arts Liao was gagged, despite the fact that he enjoyed many privileges as a member of the élite. His restoration to public life was however not accompanied by an immediate restoration of material privileges.[178]

Liao and China's Japan Policy during the Cultural Revolution

Liao's reinstatement in 1971-72 was limited, enabling him mainly to take part in one of his former areas of activity, PRC relations with Japan. Liao had dropped from the scene in the course of 1967. In March of the following year the L-T agreement (bearing his name) was replaced by a new framework for trade, the so-called 'memorandum trade' based on one-year agreements and thus unable to lead to a stable trade relationship.[179] A distinctive difference also was its explicit political character due to the inclusion of political conditions which had been absent from the L-T arrangement. The same applied to a revised agreement on the exchange of journalists, important details of which were in fact kept secret, leading to later charges in Japan about the willingness of Japanese negotiators to agree to PRC curbs on the freedom of the Japanese press.[180] Zhou Enlai himself passed judgment on the old L-T agreement which according to him 'had not produced good results during the past four years', thus virtually denying the merits of an agreement bearing Liao's name, an agreement that had been intended to prepare the way for formal diplomatic relations through a gradual approach. During the Cultural Revolution 'gradualism' was more or less synonymous with 'capitulation' and 'opportunism', and it is not surprising that until 1972 'gradualism' was replaced by an all-or-nothing approach dominated by political slogans.

What should not be overlooked, however, is that most elements of the new approach had already been in evidence since 1965, shortly after the inception of the Sato cabinet. Naturally, the question arises as to who was mainly responsible for the general formulation of policy towards Japan and its implementation during the period from 1965 until about 1972. There are some who maintain that this change of policy was a result of Liao's personal failure. Matsumura Kenzo was rather worried by the possibility that information he (and others) had given to Liao may have been relied on by Liao, leading him to misjudge future trends, and this may have been the reason (or one of the reasons) for criticism of Liao Chengzhi.

In fact several factors contributed to both Liao's decline and the change of policy, some of these factors operating quite independently. First of all there was the personal factor. Attacks against Liao contain a lot of personal invective, and it is often not clear whether the main underlying reasons for these attacks were of a personal nature or were indeed connected with matters of policy. When meeting Hoashi Kei on 2 October 1970 Saionji Kinkazu remarked that:

> Liao Chengzhi was severely attacked during the early stage of the Red Guard Movement. After having been suspended from his positions Liao's close friends made an attempt to redeem his reputation, but unfortunately they failed.[181]

Despite the enormous number of publications on the Cultural Revolution it is still very difficult to trace the factional infighting that took place then, and at the moment it seems impossible to come to a conclusion as to Liao's position and relations with regard to the constantly changing pattern of factions and cliques.

Secondly, the fact that the foreign policy apparatus at both party and government levels was in considerable disarray for long periods should not be overlooked. One point is clear - scanning the record of appearances and functions of politicians still involved in relations with Japan after Liao's departure virtually no single person could have been said to have taken over Liao's dominant position. A characteristic of policy-making before 1965 seems to have been the direct personal link with the highest party leadership, in daily routine represented not by Mao but by Zhou Enlai and Liao Chengzhi. Since such a direct link was not re-established between Zhou (or someone else of his stature) and a remaining Japan specialist it is quite likely that there was little room for initiative by those Japan specialists, all the more so since political survival during this period demanded a high degree of adaptation to the current line of the party leadership.

PRC policy underwent a dramatic change between 1968 and 1972, most visibly in relations with the United States and other non-communist countries, including Japan. As far as I can see as yet there is no clear indication how policy-making operated during this period, and in particular how the approach towards the United States influenced policy in other areas, such as Japan policy. There is no clear cut relationship. In 1969 the PRC vigorously denied Soviet slanders of China to the effect that 'China may follow Japan and compromise itself with the US'.[182]

Attacks on Japan and 'Japanese militarism' heightened after the Sato-Nixon Joint Communiqué of November 1969.[183] There were even further setbacks to trade with Japan following the announcement of 'Zhou Enlai's Four Principles' at the Canton Trade Fair in April 1970. In May Mao appealed for a united front against the USA. The secrecy surrounding foreign policy-making in particular during this period of rapid changes makes it all the more difficult to grasp how policy towards Japan was formulated during Liao's absence from the public scene.

Under 'normal' circumstances such a study could give us a fairly good idea of Liao's role in foreign policy making *before* his eclipse by analysing the changes *due* to his departure from the scene. Unfortunately, so many other factors were simultaneously affecting foreign policy-making that it is exceedingly hard to isolate precisely which changes were due to Liao's eclipse; likewise to pinpoint the reasons that led to Liao's relatively early, but slow rehabilitation. As mentioned above there is some indication that the fall of Lin Biao may have been directly connected with the rehabilitation not just of Liao, but also of a number of other high cadres just below the very top of the party élite. Liao's rehabilitation took place during the same period that also saw a rather sudden change in the PRC's Japan policy away from the icy winds of 1970 to the establishment of diplomatic relations in September 1972. It is tempting to ascribe this change partly to Liao's rehabilitation. The improvement of relations with Japan however can only be understood against the background of the rapidly changing international situation, in particular the decision by the PRC to strengthen its links with non-Communist countries such as the USA as well as the PRC's entry into the United Nations.

Notes to Chapter Five

1. Griffith, *Sino-Soviet Relations*, p 17.
2. *Peking Review*, vol VI, no 49, (6 December 1963), pp 13-15, and *PD*, 30 November 1963. *Ajia keizai junpo*, 560 (1963.12.*chu*), pp 9-14. Griffith, *Sino-Soviet Relations*, p 17. Also *Pravda*, 29 November-4 December 1963.
3. *Ajia keizai junpo*, 560 (1963.12.*chu*, pp 9-14; *PD*, 30 November 1963.
4. *PD*, 30 November 1963.
5. *NS* annual overview for 1964 has a more sophisticated interpretation than the more common one identifying Japan as a member of what was later called the 'second world'. Also Peter Van Ness, *Revolution and Chinese Foreign Policy*, (Berkeley, Los Angeles, London, 1970), p 58, Hinton, *Communist China*, p 53, and Armstrong, *Revolutionary Diplomacy*, pp 89-90.
6. D Lach and E S Wehrle, *International Politics in East Asia Since World War II*, (New York, 1975), p 212.
7. Including severe criticism of the JSP right wing.
8. The ROC's irritation is described in Furui, *Nitchu juhachinen*, p 82; also Lee, *Japan Faces China*, p 47.
9. *Akahata* editorial, 1 February 1964. See *PD*, 28 January 1964 and *NS*, 27 January for Mao's speech giving a rationale for 'uniting with suppressed big business in Japan' against the common enemy USA.
10. Tagawa, *Nitchu kosho hiroku*, pp 52 ff.
11. For a good summary of the February trade talks, *Feiri maoyi jingwei*, pp 41 ff.
12. Tagawa, *Nitchu kosho hiroku*, p 56.
13. *Ibid*, Furui mentions that Minister for Home Affairs Kaya Okinori - who was opposed to relations with Peking - was in a position to put obstacles in the way of setting up offices due to his power over immigration issues (*Nitchu juhachinen*, pp 81-2).
14. *Ibid*. Also *Asahi shinbun*, 6 November 1983. It may be recalled that establishing an air link was mentioned by Zhou on 6 November 1956 (*NS*) in a talk on 'normalisation' of relations with Japan. The points were raised again by Zhou in Colombo in a widely noted press interview, *PD*, quoted in *Sengo shiryo nitchu kankei*, pp 292-3. Also Okazaki, *Chugoku mondai e no michi*, pp 193-4.
15. Tagawa, *Nitchu kosho hiroku*, pp 52 ff, 56 ff. See also Tagawa, *Matsumura Kenzo*, p 20, and Furui, *Nitchu juhachinen*.
16. Miyoshi Osamu and Eto Shinkichi, *Chugoku hodo no henko o tsuku*, (1972), esp pp 111 ff.
17. Tagawa, *Nitchu kosho hiroku*, p 57.
18. *Asahi shinbun*, 26 February 1964.
19. For Zhou's speech, *NS*, March 1964, pp 49-50: 'The gradual approach serves the improvement of relations between both countries, but in this manner it will be impossible to come to a quick realisation of the restoration of government relations ...' He also mentioned 'marvellous' prospects for revolution in Asia. The *PD* report of 1 March 1964 referred only to 'driving the US out of Asia'. For a more complete record of Zhou's interview, *Asahi shinbun* (*yukan*), 1 March 1964. Also *Asahi shinbun*, 26 and 29 February 1964, and Bin Sun, 'Zhou fei Enlai fu mian-ba-xilian dengguo huodong', in *Feiqing yuebo*, (February 1964), pp 7-21, and *Zhonggong shouyao shilÜe huibian*, (Taipei), p 55. For further comment, Furui, *Nitchu juhachinen*, p 82.
20. *Zhonggong shouyao shilÜe huibian*, p 55. On the visit, also *NS*, comment no 1 for March 1964.

21 *Asahi shinbun*, 29 February 1964 (*yukan*). Such consideration was unnecessary when Zhao Anbo visited Japan (*NS*, overview February 1964) On Zhou's visit and attacks on JSP members who wished to acknowledge 'one China, one China', *NS*, 5 February and comment no 1, 3 February.
22 'Anpo haiki ga saiko mokuhyo', *Sekai shuho*, 14 April 1964; short references are also found in *PD*, 14, 22, 24, 26 March, and 6, 11, 18 April 1964.
23 *Asahi shinbun*, 29 February (*yukan*) 1964.
24 *Ibid*, 3 March and 4 April (*yukan*) 1964.
25 *NS*, April 1964, and Furui, *Nitchu juhachinen*, p 82. 'Nan Kanshin atarashii Nitchu kankei no tame ni', *Ekonomisuto*, 28 April 1964; 'Nan Kanshin no yonjunichi', *ibid*, 2 June 1964. That the mission went to Japan despite entry refusal for Wu says something about PRC eagerness.
26 *NS*, 25 March 1964, p 110.
27 *NS*, 11, 27, 28 and 31 March 1964. Compare also March 1964, p 243.
28 *PD*, 20 April 1964; see the text of the accord in *Nitchu kankei shiryoshu* (1967), p 210; also *Asahi shinbun*, 14 April 1964 (*yukan*). For CCP personnel stationed in Japan in the sixties see *Gongfei waijiao renyuan jiqita haiwai wei guan zhi renshi diaocha*, (Taipei, July 1966), pp 110 ff.
29 *Asahi shinbun*, 14 April 1964 (*yukan*).
30 *Nitchu kankei shiryoshu (1967)*, p 210; *PD*, 20 April 1964.
31 *Feiri maoyi pouxi*, p 43.
32 *Ibid*. The best reference in English is Fukui Haruhiro, *Party in Power. The Japanese Liberal-Democrats and Policy-making*, (ANU Press, Canberra, 1970), esp pp 235-6: 'In protest against these decisions and the attitude of the Japanese government Liao Cheng-chih announced the nullification of the contract with Hitachi on 6 April, and on 30 April the contract with Dainihon Boseki.' Many Japanese standard handbooks do not mention the episode, or only briefly.
33 *NS*, 15 May 1964.
34 *NS*, 21 May 1964. See also Hisamaro Komatsu, 'Chugoku de mita Nitchu mondai - Kitamura shisetsudan ni zuiko shite', *Ekonomisuto*, (1964), pp 26-30.
35 *Asahi shinbun*, 28 July 1964.
36 *Ibid*, 10 August 1964 (*yukan*), and Hinton, *Communist China*, pp 365-6.
37 For Mao's mention of Russian 'land robbery' to members of the Sasaki delegation on 10 July 1964, *Asahi Shinbun*, 2 September 1964 (*yukan*); also 'Gespräch Mao Tse-tungs mit japanischen Sozialisten (Sowjetische Darstellung)', p 202, quoting *Pravda* of 2 September 1964; see Beilage, *Sowjetunion heute*, 1964-18; Hinton, *Communist China*, pp 383, 476. *Nitchu kankei kihon shiryoshu*, p 240. 'Chishima wa Nihon e kaesubeki da', in *Sekai shuho*, 11 August 1964. On the effect of the nuclear explosion on the anti-nuclear JSP, see *NS* comment no 5, 14 October 1964; see also Hinton, *Communist China*, p 487.
38 *Nitchu kankei kihon shiryoshu*, p 241.
39 See 'Anpo haiki ga saiko mokuhyo', p 21. Reports on Miyamoto's visit are included in *PD*, 10, 11, 15 September and 1 October.
40 *PD*, 19 March 1979. See also *Renwuzhi*, 2, p 1332, and Van Slyke, *Enemies and Friends*, p 247. It is tempting to link these changes to the general debate on policy in the Standing Committee of the Politburo (Central Work Conference) held in September-October 1965 (*NS*).
41 'Anpo haiki ga saiko mokuhyo'. According to Japanese journalists in North Korea Liao had decided to accept an invitation by Matsumura Kenzo to visit Japan soon (*NS*, 21 December 1964).
42 *PD*, 24-5, 30 November and 7 December 1964; *NCNA*, 19 November and 6 December 1964.

43 'Chinese officials were expelled from Cameroun in 1961 for allegedly aiding rebel forces, from the Congo in 1964, and from Burundi and Kenya in 1965.' Boardman, 'Chinese Foreign Policy-Making', p 121. It is also possible to point to a series of Chinese setbacks even at this stage by referring to 'Soviet successes with North Vietnam, North Korea, Algeria and Egypt and its mediation of the Indo-Pakistani conflict at Tashkent'. Yasutomo, 'Sato's China Policy', pp 538-9.

44 *PD*, 12 May 1965, and *NS*, January 1965. As a result of tensions with other Communist parties and the rapidly changing international situation there were also changes in the way international front organisations were run. See for example *China News Analysis (CNA)*, 574, (30 July 1965), p 5, and *Asahi shinbun*, 28 January 1965. For a vivid account of the tension pervading some of these meetings, see Zhu Ziqi's account of an international conference in an unnamed country in October 1965, *Wenhuibao* (Shanghai), 21 June 1983.

45 See Lee, *Japan Faces China*, p 49. With continuing verbal attacks on Sato in the period leading to the Cultural Revolution the PRC's moderate attitude to trade with Japan is all the more striking as compared with the break in trade after the Nagasaki flag incident of 1958. Speaking on 14 January Liao said that the anti-China policy had started immediately after the formation of the Sato cabinet but that due to the difficult straits it found itself in as a result of attaching itself to the USA China 'was still watching' the Sato cabinet (*NS*, comment no 3 for 10 January 1965). While Sato's attitude to the Yoshida letter and the refusal to grant Exim-credits was very obvious, in a meeting with Japanese correspondents Liao emphasised that China 'was still watching' (*NS*, 24 March) ; also *NS*, April 1965, overview). More striking still was his remark on 8 June, again to Japanese correspondents, that 'since there was still no clear declaration of Japanese intentions concerning the Yoshida letter China was still "watching"' (*NS*). In July in an even more striking statement Nan declared that prospects for trade were good due to the start of China's new five year plan and that trade with Japan would not be cut off despite some danger due to the widening of the Vietnam War (*NS*, 28 July 1965). When Chen Yi said on 29 September that trade would be limited to its present level the importance lay in the fact that it 'would be continued'.

46 *Asahi shinbun*, (15 January 1965).

47 *CNA* 895 (22 September 1972).

48 Jain, *China and Japan*, p 76.

49 According to Japanese colleagues and journalists, in regular - sometimes weekly - meetings with Japanese journalists he often spoke off the record in a manner reminiscent of Western politicians.

50 *Asahi shinbun*, 1 and 8 February 1965. See also *NS*, 25, 27, 31 January and 7 February 1965; *Kokusai nenpo 1965-6*, p 126. When PRC pressure failed to secure Exim finance Liao stated that Japanese exports of 'large plants' was out of the question, but left open the possibility of exporting 'smaller size plants' (*NS*, 30 April 1965).

51 *PD*, 20 January and 7 March 1965; see also *NS*, comment no 11 for 18 January 1965.

52 Hayashi Shigeru, 'LT boeki dai 3 nendo keiyaku, sono kosho keika to omo na mondaiten', *Ajia keizai junpo* 603 (1965.2.*chu*), pp 12-15, *NS*, 15 February 1965.

53 *Asahi shinbun*, 22 April 1966.

54 *NS* (6 April) says the Chinese told Takasaki's office on 6 April that the agreement expired on 31 March.

55 See, for instance, *PD*, 5, 6, 12, 13, 19, 22 and 27 March 1965; *Peking Review* (21 May 1965), pp 14-17. See also *CNA*, 574 (30 July 1965), p 2. One of the members of the delegation headed by Liao was Wu Xueqian (*PD*, 6 May 1965). See also Neuhauser, *Third World Politics*, pp 52-3.

56 *Asahi shinbun*, 8, 9 and 10 June 1965.
57 *NS*, overview for May 1965. See also *Gongfei dui yafei diqu geguo shentou dianfu huodong gaikuang*, (Taipei, March 1969), pp 9 f.
58 *Asahi shinbun*, 11 and 15 June 1965.
59 *PD*, 13 and 19 May 1965.
60 Even under these difficult circumstances Liao did not always forget his good-humoured conversational tone in talks with Japanese visitors. (*Asahi Januaryaru*, 30 July 1965, p 51).
61 A report on Chen Yi's arrival on 22 June 1965 listed Liao as the main delegation adviser before senior politicians like Fang Yi, Qiao Guanhua, Liu Xiwen and the PRC ambassador to Tanzania, He Ying (*PD*, 23 June 1965). Luo Qingchang has been one of the most important and influential figures in relations with Taiwan and Overseas Chinese.
62 The special issue of *Asahi Janaru* of 20 July 1965 has Japanese analyses of the Asian-African movement and an interview with Nakasone Yasuhiro and Katsumata Seiichi, pp 98 ff. Also Nakasone's comment on China, 'A Liberal-Democratic View', *Japan Quarterly* (1961), pp 266 f.
63 *NS*, 3 July 1965.
64 *Asahi shinbun*, or *NS*, 3 July 1965.
65 *Asahi shinbun*, 31 August 1965.
66 *Ibid*.
67 A Hutchinson, *China's African Revolution*, (London, 1975), p 247.
68 *PD*, 17 October 1966.
69 *Asahi shinbun*, 31 August 1965.
70 *Asahi shinbun*, 30 September 1965.
71 *CNA* 585 (15 October 1965), p 3 quoting *Gongshang ribao* (Hong Kong) of 4 October 1965.
72 *NS*, 2 October 1965.
73 *NS*, monthly overview for November 1965.
74 *PD*, 20 November 1965.
75 *NS*, yearly overview for 1965.
76 *NS*, 17 December 1965.
77 *NS*, January 1966.
78 'Gao yige Su-Mei-Ri lianmeng'.
79 For a brief summary, *NS*, comment no 4, 18 February 1966; *Nitchu kankei kihon shiryoshu*, p 444.
80 *PD*, 1, 4, 12, 22, 27, 28 and 30 March.
81 *PD*, 27 March 1966.
82 *Communist China, 1958*, p 59, fn 3 and K S Karol, *La deuxième révolution chinoise*, (Paris, 1973), p 422. *PD* of 30 March 1966 contains a short report on the delegation's departure. Shibata Minoru and Ito Kikuzo, 'The Dilemma of Mao Tse-tung', *China Quarterly*, 35 (July-September 1968), pp 59-60.
83 *PD*, 1 and 28 March 1966.
84 *PD*, 28 March 1966.
85 *Dalu qingshi fenxi huibian. 1969 nian*, (Taipei, March 1970, p 338.
86 Tagawa, *Matsumura Kenzo*, p 123.
87 *Asahi shinbun*, 25 February 1966, and *CNA*, no 895.
88 *Yomiuri shinbun*, 26 February 1966. *Asahi shinbun*, 26 February 1966, and other sources cited in *CNA* 895 (22 September 1972). See also Ito and Shibata, 'Dilemma', pp 59-60.

89 *NS*, 24 March 1966. *Asahi shinbun*, 2 May 1966.
90 Nitchu boeki sokushinkai, comp, *Nitchu boeki sokushinkai yuko daihyodan hochu hokokusho*, (1966), pp 48 ff.
91 For Lian Guan's report, see *ibid*, pp 55 ff.
92 *Ibid*, pp 65 ff.
93 *Ibid*, pp 89 ff.
94 *Ibid*, pp 99 ff.
95 *Ibid*.
96 *Nitchu oboegaki no 11nen*, pp 92 ff; *Asahi shinbun*, 23, 24, 27, 30 April and 1 May 1966.
97 *Nitchu kankei shiryoshu (1967)*, p 225.
98 *PD*, 14 May 1966, and *Asahi shinbun*, 20 May 1966.
99 Radio Peking (reported by *NS*, comment no 6 for 13 May 1966). I have again been unable to verify such reports so I doubt whether it is justified to claim special significance for Liao's *not* including the USSR in referring to an anti-China military alliance as in *Hongqi*, February 1967.
100 *PD* and *Asahi shinbun*, 14 May 1966.
101 *NS*, 22 April 1966. The strengthening of United Front Work organisations at that stage should not be interpreted as a return to a 'moderate' approach, but rather the organisational preparation for a new approach that would pay more attention to the role of 'ideology' in this area.
102 *PD*, 14 and 20 May 1966.
103 *PD*, 5 June 1966, 'Cujin qiaowu ganbu he guiguo huaqiao sixiang geminghua'.
104 *Nitchu oboegaki no 11nen*, pp 92 f; *NS*, comment no 3, 10 May 1966, and comment no 6, 13 May quoting Radio Peking. See also *Feiri maoyi pouxi*, p 20.
105 Furui, *Nitchu juhachinen*, p 88.
106 It seems that 'In mid-1966, Ch'en Yi, Liao and Fang appointed work teams from the CCP's Foreign Affairs Political Department to carry out the bourgeois reactionary line in the Commission. ... probably in this connection ... an Overseas Chinese Affairs Political Work Conference was held in Peking in April 1966.' Regarding attacks on Liao in August, see Wu Zhenyan 'Gongfei, "wenge" hou de qiaowu bumen gaikuang', *Feiwei qiaowu jianbao*, (1 August 1968), p 2b.
107 Liao attended a number of GPCR functions in August, September and November (*Feiwei renshi ziliao*, 1967, p 346; *PD*, 19 August 1966 and 2 October 1966). *Qiaowubao*, 1966.10.
108 *Asahi shinbun*, 17 and 21 September 1966.
109 Liao, *Wode muqin*, p 44. *PD* of 13 November carried reports of speeches by Liao's mother He Xiangning, Song Qingling and Miyazaki Seimin.
110 Towards the end of October Liao was accused of having obstructed Red Guards (*Feiwei renshi ziliao huibian*, p 346). See also Tagawa, *Nitchu kosho hiroku*, p 65. 'Ryo Shoshi shi ni ihen?' His name was missing from a report of a parade on Tiananmen Square (*PD*, 12 November 1966), but did appear again in a report towards the end of the month (*PD*, 27 November 1966).
111 Okazaki, *Watakushi no kiroku*, p 27. Tagawa, *Nitchu kosho hiroku*, p 68, and Zhang Tianxing, 'Wei wujie renda changweihui fu weiyuanzhang Liao Chengzhi', in *Feiqing yuebao*, 1978.9.
112 *Asahi shinbun*, 16 December 1966. *Zhonggong shouyao shilüe huibian*, p 60; see also *Feiwei renshi ziliao*, 1967, p 346, and Lu Zhenji, *Liaofei Chengzhi beikou zhi mi*, pp 4a-b.
113 For a report on such a possibility, *Asahi shinbun*, 8 November 1966. At times, Japanese optimism appeared not only unwarranted, but unreal - perhaps simply appealing to the Chinese not to

Friends and Foes

     disappoint hopes for continued relations? *Asahi shinbun*, 8 and 10 September 1966. *Asahi shinbun*, 26 January 1967, carried a report headed 'Still safe - Guo Moruo and Liao Chengzhi'.
114 *NS*, 29 September 1966.
115 *PD*, 25 and 31 July 1966. It is noteworthy that Zhao Yimin is listed ahead of Liao in the report on their departure, but the order is reversed on their return. This may be because Zhao as Vice-Chairman of the China Peace Committee was listed right after Guo, head of that organisation, but in Guo's absence Liao as head of the AA organisation would be ranked higher than Zhao.
116 For Sun's protest on 28 July 1966, see *Nitchu kankei shiryoshu (1967)*, p 225.
117 *NS*, 22 July 1966 also refers to the message sent by Zhou Enlai to the Conference on 28 July.
118 *NS*, 28 July 1966, and *PD*, 31 July 1966.
119 See the summary of Chen Yi's speeches on 11 August 1966, *Nitchu kankei shiryoshu (1967)*, p 126, and 6 September 1966, *ibid*, p 127; *NS*, comment no 7 for 21 September 1966. See also *Kokusai nenpo* (1965-6), p 465.
120 *Asahi shinbun*, 18 August 1966.
121 See *Kokusai nenpo (1965-1966)*, pp 127-8, and *Asahi shinbun*, 19, 20, 22 August.
122 *Asahi shinbun*, 1 October 1966.
123 *PD*, 25, 31 July and 7 August 1966.
124 *PD*, 19 August 1966; see also *Feiwei renshi ziliao*, 1976, p 346.
125 *PD*, 2 October 1966, and *Feiwei renshi ziliao*, 1967, p 346.
126 See optimistic articles in *Asahi shinbun*, 8, 10 and 22 September 1966. Furui describes meetings a delegation of LDP Diet members had on a visit to the PRC in late August 1966 and conveys a tense atmosphere, even relating that Liao could not meet the delegation again before their departure, for reasons of illness. It is not unlikely that his absence indicates political problems he already faced during this initial phase of the GPCR (*Nitchu juhachinen*, pp 87-8).
127 *PD* and *Asahi shinbun*, 21 September and *PD*, 13 November 1966.
128 *Asahi shinbun*, 17 September 1966, and *PD*, 13 November 1966.
129 *Nitchu yuko undoshi*, pp 245-6; *Nitchu kankei shiryoshu*, pp 74 f. Lee, *Japan Faces China*, pp 79-80; *Peking Review*, 14 October 1966, pp 33-4.
130 *Nitchu yuko undoshi*, pp 245 ff; *Nitchu kankei shiryoshu*, pp 75-6.
131 See Liao's speech of 28 November 1966, in *Qiaowubao*, no 10 (1966), and *Asahi shinbun*, 18 October (*yukan*), 1966.
132 *Asahi shinbun*, 31 October 1966.
133 For reports on He's and Song's speeches, see *PD*, 13 November 1966.
134 Okazaki, *Chugoku mondai e no michi*, p 234.
135 *Nitchu oboegaki no 11nen*, p 94 ('bimyo ma kuki ga kanjirareta').
136 *Asahi shinbun*, 16 December 1966. It was also reported that Zhou criticised Liao in a speech to Red Guards, 9 December 1966 (*Zhonggong shouyao shilüe huibian*, p 60, and *Feiwei renshi ziliao*, 1967, p 346). Some posters were rather drastic: 'Burn Liao Chengzhi - Fry Liao Chengzhi'. See Gao Yanwen, in *Liaogong zai renjian*, p 41.
137 *Asahi shinbun*, 8 and 15 November 1966.
138 *Asahi shinbun*, 5, 16 and 17 December 1966. This follows a large increase in the number of JSP members visiting the PRC in 1966 (*NS* annual overview 1966).
139 Tagawa, *Nitchu kosho hiroku*, pp 63 ff. Liao attended Mao's review of Red Guards at this time (*PD*, 27 November 1966) but his political role seemed reduced (*Nitchu kosho hiroku*, eg p 68).

140 *Asahi shinbun*, 1 February 1967.
141 Reports of Nan Hanchen's suicide were at first denied by Radio Peking, but confirmed a few weeks later (*Asahi shinbun*, 6, 8 February and 13 March 1967.
142 *PD*, 21 June 1983.
143 In February he was at a reception for a Mission of the Malayan Liberation League in Peking (*CNA*, 18 July 1969), and also the signing of the trade protocol with Japan (*Asahi shinbun*, 28 February 1967).
144 Lu Zhenji, *Liao fei Chengzhi bei kou zhi mi*, p 5b. 'According to the Hong Kong newspaper *Mingbao*, the "Red Flag Forces" of the OCAC continued on 16 April 1967 to put up wall posters attacking Liao for carrying out a revisionist policy in Overseas Chinese work, and pointed out that Liao had not mentioned the name of Lin Biao on purpose in a document, and obviously [tried to] disrupt the relation between Lin Biao and Zhou Enlai.'
145 Chang, 'Overseas Chinese in China's Policy'; Gurtov, 'The Foreign Ministry and Foreign Affairs', in T Robinson (ed), *The Cultural Revolution in China*, (University of California Press, 1971), pp 313 ff; Fitzgerald, *China and the Overseas Chinese*, passim. The attacks were directed mainly at Liao as head of the OCAC (*Jinnianlai gongfei pohai qiaobao*, pp 5 ff. He was also accused of conspiring with Zhang Wentian, Wang Jiaxiang, Li Weihan to plan autonomy of *huaqiao* policies, especially abroad (*ibid*, p 12). Renewed attacks were made in the *Geming qiaobao* on 9 April 1967 (included in *Zhonggong wenhua da geming ziliao huibian*, vol 1, pp 706 ff). See also Lu Zhenji, *Liao fei chengzhi beikou zhi mi*, pp 6a f, and *CNA*, (12 February 1971), p 1; *Feiwei renshi ziliao*, (1967), p 346. Wu Zhenyan, 'Wenge hou de qiaowu gongzuo', p 5a.
146 *Feiri maoyi pouxi*, pp 22 ff.
147 NCNA, 3 July 1967. Regarding attacks on Liao at this time, see M Yahuda, 'Chinese Foreign Policy After 1963', *China Quarterly* 36 (1968), p 105; *Jinnianlai gongfei pohai qiaobao*, pp 7-8; We Zhenyan, 'Wenge hou de qiaowu bumen', p 3a. *SCMP*, pp 5-8 (March 1968) reports Liao as 'one of the counterrevolutionary revisionists who much admired *First Half of My Life*, a book written from the standpoint of feudalism and imperialism to distort history by Pu Yi, and immediately after its publication, they had some copies sent to the responsible comrades of the Party Central Committee and the rest circulated internally as reference material.' From an article, 'Inside Story of Release of *First Half of My Life*' in Canton, *Wen-ko Feng-lei*, no 3, (Cultural Revolution Storm) March 1968.
148 See for instance *Asahi shinbun*, 22 July 1967.
149 *Asahi shinbun*, 11 and 19 August 1967.
150 Akioka Ieshige, *Pekin Tokuhain*, (Asahi shibunsha, 1973), pp 149-50. For further details on the negotiations, Tagawa, *Nitchu kosho hiroku*, pp 70 ff, and *Nitchu oboegaki no 11nen*, passim.
151 *Nitchu kosho hiroku*, pp 75 ff; Lu Zhenji, *Liao fei beikou zhi mi*, p 8a. *Asahi shinbun* carried a report on 2 October 1967 attributing Liao's absence from functions to a possible heart ailment. There were even rumours about his suicide (Ye Yiwen, *Qiaowu gongzuo*, p 3a).
152 Akioka, *Tokuhain*, pp 154-5, mentions 'economic specialists' Liu Xiwen and Wu Shudong (also *ibid*, pp 149-50, 170). Also Furui describes negotiations in early 1967 (*Nitchu juhachinen*, p 200).
153 *Tenkai suru kakumei gaiko*, p 245. See also 'Gongfei zhengsu wei qiaoweihui toumu de fenxi', *Diqing yanjiu congkan*, p 16.
154 Lu Zhenji, *Gongfei zhengsu wei qiaowei toumu de fenxi*, (Taipei, 5 March 1969), [Diqing yanjiu congkan zhi 16], p 5, quoting *Xianggang shibao* of 28 February 1968.

155 *Qiaowu gongzuo*, p 21b. On the name change which had occurred during trade talks in February, Tagawa, *Nitchu kosho hiroku*, p 99.
156 Tagawa, *Nitchu kosho hiroku*, p 115. Arai, *Shu Onrai no jissen*, p 187 writes that Liao became ill in the winter of 1970 ('shinzobyo ni kakatta').
157 *Zhongyang ribao*, 22 February 1969.
158 W L Chu, 'Liao Ch'eng-chih - A Maoist "Liberated" Cadre', p 88, quoting Hoashi Kei: 'Liao ... was severely attacked during the early stage of the "Red Guard Movement". After his being suspended from his posts, his close friends made an attempt to restore his reputation but unfortunately they failed.' See also Zhang Tianxing, 'Wei wujie renda changweihui fuweiyuanzhang Liao Chengzhi', p 78.
159 Chang, 'Liao Chengzhi', p 78. Zhou made the reference to Liao in his speech on 1 March 1971 (Akioka, *Tokuhain*, pp 142-3, 205). also Furui, *Nitchu juhachinen*, p 213, and *Asahi shinbun*, 3 March 1971; *Nihon keizai shinbun*, 10 March 1971. For comment on a link with Lin Biao's fall *Kokusai nenpo*, (1972), p 195; Akioka, *op cit*, pp 145-6; Arai, *Shu Onrai no jissen*, pp 187-8.
160 Xue Ming, in *Liaogong zai renjian*, pp 172 f.
161 Liao Jian, in *ibid*, p 156.
162 Jing Puchun, in *ibid*, p 7. Liao himself referred to his curtailment of freedom as 'ruanjin' (house arrest) for a period of five years (Xia Yan, in *PD*, 15 June 1983).
163 Yu Yanwen, in *Liaogong zai renjian*, p 162.
164 *Ibid*, pp 158 f.
165 *Ibid*.
166 *Ibid*, p 161.
167 Jing Puchun, in *ibid*, p 7.
168 'In 1970 Liao suffered from serious heart trouble, and was saved ... only when he was under the direct care of comrade Zhou.' Lian Guan, in *Guangming ribao*, 17 June 1983.
169 Zhu Zha, in *Liaogong zai renjian*, pp 57-8.
170 *Asahi shinbun*, 3 March 1971; Furui, *Nitchu juhachinen*, pp 213, 216 and Akioka, *op cit*, p 205.
171 Chu, 'Liao Ch'eng-chih', p 88.
172 *Guangming ribao*, 25 June 1983.
173 *Liaogong zai renjian*, p 86.
174 *Ibid*, p 90.
175 *Zhongguo nongminbao*, 28 June 1983.
176 *Liaogong zai renjian*, p 42.
177 Yu Feng, in *ibid*, p 43.
178 After his mother died Liao moved to a smaller house, perhaps partly to avoid any appearance of 'luxury' (Jing Puchun, *ibid*, p 7). It was 1973 before he re-engaged his cook who had been 'demobilised' and sent to his original unit during the Cultural Revolution (Xu Fu, *ibid*, p 101).
179 Akioka, *op cit*, p 151; Okazaki, *Chugoku mondai*, p 187; Furui, *Nitchu juhachinen*, p 95 ff, 199.
180 Eto-Miyoshi, *Chugoku hodo no henko o tsuku*, especially pp 97 ff.
181 W L Chu, 'Liao Ch'eng-chih - A Maoist "Liberated" Cadre', p 88.
182 *PD*, 30 January 1969.
183 On PRC relations with Japan until 1972, see Furui, 'Tanaka goes to Peking', chapter III in T J Pempel, ed *Policy Making in Contemporary Japan*, (Cornell University Press, Ithaca, 1977).

CHAPTER SIX
Enemies Become Friends 1971-78

Lin Biao's rise to power during the Cultural Revolution had been followed by events during 1970-71 foreshadowing his fall in September. During this period the PRC foreign affairs apparatus had been severely damaged. Few details exist but it would appear that as a consequence, PRC strategy was seriously affected, for example, in the field of relations with Japan. It was a time that saw dramatic changes in PRC foreign policy, although slogans tried to create an impression of 'revolutionary' consistency and stability. The most basic change was in relations with the United States. As early as January 1969 the *People's Daily* found it necessary to deny the Soviet 'slander' that the PRC might look for a compromise with the USA.[1] Superficially developments did not point in that direction. In November 1969 the so-called Nixon doctrine implicitly urged Japan to take a more active role in maintaining Asian security.[2] Then there was the Nixon-Sato Communiqué containing Prime Minister Sato's statement that 'the maintenance of peace and security in the Taiwan area is ... a most important factor for the security of Japan'.[3] Against the background of the Vietnam war these changes portended greater integration of Japanese policies into US policy determined to contain Communist expansion. Some observers even saw signs of *rapprochement* between the PRC and the USSR during 1970,[4] but such an image may have been created by the PRC to raise the price of *rapprochement* with the United States and Japan.[5] While secret diplomacy between the PRC and the USA continued, early in 1970 there was a very interesting change in PRC policy towards Overseas Chinese, little noticed at the time, which presaged a cautious and slow return to traditional united front tactics.[6] Policy towards Overseas Chinese had always been a sensitive indicator of PRC foreign policy changes: although difficult to prove, it seems likely that the 1970 change in policy was related to foreign policy changes in other areas.

Available reports show that the OCAC was abolished during the GPCR and its work taken over by the Ministry of Foreign Affairs.[7] This supports the assumption of a close link between both policy areas especially during this period. The main focus of change concerned Overseas Chinese in Hong Kong, Japan and the USA, and to some extent, Southeast Asia. The change also became visible later in 1970 with the restoration of administrative organs dealing with Overseas Chinese affairs in Canton and Guangdong, and included the rehabilitation of purged cadres.[8]

For now there seemed to be no change in the area of relations with Japan. The vehemence of attacks on the Japanese government continued to increase to a degree that surprised Japanese involved in the annual Memorandum Trade (M-T) negotiations. Commenting on talks that took place in March 1970 Furui recalls:

> The Chinese side was much more severe than we had anticipated. Even now when I think of it I wonder why ... They should have been aware that America's policy had started to change.[9]

PRC attacks on the Japanese government, especially Sato, continued until 1972 shortly before the formation of the Tanaka cabinet and the establishment of diplomatic relations.[10] Initially the explanation may be sought in PRC attempts to put maximum pressure on Japan to weaken as much as possible pro-Taiwan groups there;[11] gain concessions on sovereignty over the Diaoyutai (Senkaku) Islands; and forestall moves that might affect PRC claims to sovereignty over Taiwan.[12]

Towards the end of 1970 there were indications that the PRC had started rebuilding its foreign affairs apparatus as far as Japan was concerned. Wang Guoquan and Wang Xiaoyun were involved in talks with the 5th JSP delegation that visited the PRC in October 1970, and continued to play a senior role until 1972 when they were replaced by Liao Chengzhi during a relatively short period which saw both politicians working together in rather similar functions.[13]

Establishment of Diplomatic Relations

The sphere changed completely during the M-T negotiations in February 1971. On this occasion Zhou gave his unscheduled speech on 1 March mentioning Liao in public and delivering him from non-person status. Zhou also referred to the fact that Canada and Italy had already established diplomatic relations and asked rhetorically whether Japan would even trail behind the USA.[14] Soon afterwards Geng Biao became Head of the Committee for Foreign Relations of the Central Committee.[15] In April a US table tennis team was invited to visit the PRC after competing in Nagoya. A close look at the PRC delegation in Nagoya shows that the move was carefully prepared. It included Gao Liang, who later established the PRC United Nations delegation as its first secretary and Jiang Chengzong, a foreign affairs official speaking excellent English.[16] Internally circulating policy documents also indicated a shift.[17] Against this background Zhou's mention of Liao's name does not seem coincidental. It is important evidence for the belief that the beginning of Liao's 'resurrection' was a *consequence* of a general policy change and, moreover, the *timing* of his rehabilitation was well prepared.[18]

As already noted, it is probably going too far to assume that Liao's position was immediately one of great influence, but Hikata mentions that when he visited the PRC in 1971 with a business delegation from West Japan (Kansai), they met Prime Minister Zhou and Li Xiannian, 'I think due to Liao's efforts'.[19] Other recollections also suggest that Liao's role was still limited - confirmed by the public record showing him largely 'out of action' while relations with Japan grew dramatically, except for attacks on Prime Minister Sato and his supporters. The improvement in relations, conducted mostly without Liao's direct participation, has been described in detail elsewhere.[20] It was also expressed in the field of trade, especially in the wake of a much publicised visit to Japan by Wang Xiaoyun in April.[21] It seemed that the PRC wished for a more relaxed interpretation of the harsh political conditions previously attached to trade with Japan,[22] a mood further boosted with the announcement of the Nixon visit to Peking on 15 July 1971.

Matsumura Kenzo, one of the leading LDP politicians advocating closer links with the PRC, died in the following month and Liao Chengzhi and Guo Moruo sent a joint message of condolence to his family. It was Liao's first 'public' duty since the Cultural Revolution, but there was still no indication of his formal position.23 Wang Guoquan led an important delegation to attend the funeral, which, not surprisingly, created enormous publicity in Japan.24 Of course business interests appeared extremely concerned to make use of this opportunity to establish new connections. The Sato cabinet also tried to approach the mission but was rebuffed. Liao must have thoroughly regretted that it was not he who reinitiated contact in Japan. On 17 October he attended a performance in Peking by the Japanese Matsuyama Ballet but apparently his state of health also precluded a full schedule as yet.25 This was confirmed by Akioka who met Liao at Peking airport. Liao had gone there to wish farewell to Saionji Kinkazu, who had just completed his first short stay in Peking since the Cultural Revolution.26 While this was so, Japanese visitors noticed that his health was improving;27 it was learned that two years before Liao had entered hospital after a serious attack of coronary heart disease. Now (towards the end of 1971) he was still undergoing treatment as an outpatient and his weight had dropped from over 90 kilograms to 85 kilograms, but the doctors had told him to reduce to 65 kilograms. In December, Tagawa noticed that Liao still needed a walking stick.28 To make matters worse he injured his leg in 1972 and had to enter hospital.29 His health was often less than satisfactory until he died in 1983, and with no accurate record of this, at times it is difficult to decide whether his absence from certain events and functions was due to ill health or to other reasons. It may be added here that he used a hearing aid for his left ear.30

Wang Xiaoyun remained one of the main Japan specialists but the leading role was played by Wang Guoquan at this time. There seemed to be a clear attempt by 'outsiders' to penetrate this 'establishment' when Yao Wenyuan (later known as a one of the 'Gang of Four') frequently attended meetings of Japanese with Zhou. These and similar efforts seem to have had only limited success. When Foreign Minister Chen Yi died the leftists were not able to push their own candidate. Ji Pengfei succeeded Chen Yi, and there was no marked change of foreign policy.

The next months showed clearly that the PRC would wait until the expected downfall of the Sato cabinet before engaging in major moves to improve relations. There was also some indication when this would happen, most likely after the return of Okinawa to Japanese sovereignty.31 Meanwhile the criticism of the 'gradual approach' towards improving relations had disappeared during the negotiations in December for the 1972 M-T Protocol. As early as July 1971 Guo Moruo had reconfirmed the 'semi-governmental' character of this trade, which had been one of the main characteristics of L-T trade in the first half of the sixties.

Since the fifties one of the great stumbling blocks to the establishment of diplomatic relations had been their existence between Japan and the ROC. With the establishment of diplomatic relations looming larger as a distinct possibility for 1972, the PRC initiated new propaganda moves for the 'peaceful liberation' of Taiwan. This was accompanied by attempts to mobilise Overseas Chinese for the same purpose. Policies were obviously co-ordinated by a higher party committee, but there is no evidence of the extent or degree of Liao's involvement.

Liao's reappearance as an active politician had to wait until April 1972. For about a month he appeared in functions concerning Japan with Wang Guoquan until Wang left the field to Liao completely.[32] During this period however he was consistently ranked ahead of Wang Guoquan.[33] Such ranking does not necessarily imply seniority as far as position within the party hierarchy is concerned, rather it should be seen as a 'signal' of Liao's reappearance as the PRC's most senior Japan specialist. By this time it was clear that establishment of diplomatic relations was only a matter of time, and would probably come soon. This would of course mean that a large part of all future governmental contacts would be rerouted through formal diplomatic channels. Would Liao become a member of the foreign affairs apparatus directly involved in dealing with Japan, or would he remain in the background as a leading figure whose position of power was not well defined? Contemporary Japanese observers were unable to give firm predictions.[34]

During the transitional period, while Liao was acting in tandem with Wang, he met Japanese politicians like Kasuga (DSP) and Miki (LDP) but his role in these talks is unclear. He also took part in meetings with Albanian and US visitors, and received Overseas Chinese businessmen from Hong Kong and Macao among other places. The first decisive and concrete step towards the realisation of a visit by Tanaka Kakuei, the future prime minister, were visits by Furui and by a Komeito delegation in May.[35] As a result there was a:

> straightforward invitation to the would-be Tanaka cabinet to take up the normalisation issue without delay and for Tanaka himself to visit Peking for that purpose.[36]

Although there are studies dealing with these events - in particular Fukui's article 'Tanaka goes to Peking' - it remains difficult to assess Liao's role in these highly confidential talks. Zhou himself devoted considerable time to bringing the negotiations to a speedy and successful conclusion. Liao took part in virtually all important functions. Most of the other high officials involved in the (preliminary) talks and negotiations belonged to the group of Japan specialists who had begun to be rehabilitated in 1971.[37] An important further step in the direction of diplomatic relations was visits by Takeiri (Komeito) and Sasaki (JSP) in July, while Sun Pinghua visited Japan in the same month.[38] Sato had offered to resign on 16 June 1972 and these visits were the first to discuss normalisation after the swearing-in of the Tanaka cabinet on 7 July. These contacts resulted in first informal, then formal invitations, to Tanaka to visit Peking to discuss the matter at the highest level:

> Since the spring of the year there had been a plan among Japanese groups, including the opposition parties, to invite a large non-official delegation from the PRC...[39] An official invitation was carried to Peking by Sasaki ... in July. By late [July] preparations were completed among the twenty-two Japanese groups involved and Tanaka had ... approved the plan. During his conversations with Chou ... however, Takeiri suggested and Chou agreed that the plan should be

cancelled if Tanaka would visit Peking during the fall and ..., if Tanaka should decide to do so before October 1, Takeiri would ... announce the cancellation ... This would be a firm signal to Chou that Tanaka and Ohira had decided to come to Peking in September. On August 5, the day after Tanaka and Ohira had met Takeiri, the cancellation ... was reported in the Japanese press, ... attributed to an anonymous source. On the 7th a 'government source' reported that Tanaka's trip would be in September. The 'anonymous' source was no doubt Takeiri.[40]

Liao should have led that delegation, according to Japanese press reports. Ironically, just as a planned visit in the mid-sixties had fallen through because of worsening relations, it was now cancelled because of an impending breakthrough.[41] Presumably the mission's task would have been to prepare the ground further for diplomatic relations using 'people's diplomacy' as in the fifties and sixties. Obviously this would not only be unnecessary with Tanaka's visit, but would lead to considerable confusion with the more formal channels now being established.

Liao's speech to a Japanese friendship delegation on 7 July 1972 amply illustrates the point. Liao first emphasised again the PRC's firm attitude on the severance of Japanese formal links with Taiwan, and acknowledgement of PRC claims concerning Taiwanese territory and expressed his opinion that normalisation of relations might take place 'perhaps in the spring of 1973'. He then continued:

China has a clear standpoint. There won't be ... wavering concerning the three principles (on Taiwan). How then can state-state relations ... be restored? How about relying solely on the LDP? An old dog has no new tricks. On the road to the restoration of ... relations one cannot but rely on the working people, ... the wide range of the Japanese people.

It seems that America won't allow Japan to restore relations with China before the United States. The LDP, too, won't have the courage to normalise relations before America does.[42] Consequently, we consider that over a long period the united struggle of the Chinese and Japanese peoples will be necessary [to achieve this goal].

Why? The answer is simple. The forces in Japan having money, the gang of militarists still try to exploit Taiwan and to put Taiwan in their pockets.

Of late, the Japanese government has issued a formal statement saying that the area to which the Security Treaty between Japan and the United States applies is unchanged. As before, it covers Taiwan.

Consequently one can say that the Japanese militarists, the wealthy, the leaders of the LDP do not wish to improve relations ...

Part of the wealthy Japanese comes to China and declares their intention 'to give China economic assistance' and refer to ... reparations, but in their hearts think of something different.

In fact Japan has now too many dollars, is stuffed with dollars. Moreover, Japan's [industrial] facilities have reached a period of renewal. All over the place there is pollution. What should be done?

> At this point, they think of the problem of 'reparations'. That is an ingenious method, through 'reparations' they try to sell old machinery and instal new machinery in Japan.
> Consequently we have publicly stated that 'we won't fall into your trap'.
> Therefore, their 'Sino-Japanese friendship' has a certain [ulterior] aim.
> If the talk is genuinely about mutually benefitting relations we will respond [positively]. Selling old stuff and so on - please spare us this sort of thing.

Liao went on to criticise opponents of Japan's relations with the PRC, like the JCP, adding a personal attack on its chairman Miyamoto. He later turned to the subject of Fukuda Takeo as a possible successor to Sato as Prime Minister:

> Before five hours had passed after the four candidates had declared their candidature Washington issued a statement: 'There is hope if it's Fukuda.' Not two hours later Moscow issued a declaration: 'It's convenient if it's Fukuda.' Twelve hours later a statement was issued in Jakarta, and Suharto declared that 'We approve, if it's Fukuda.'
> Things become clear when we see this sort of circumstance.
> I fervently hope to be on friendly terms with the Japanese people for a long time. We have a history of close contact since 2000 years.
> However, to our regret, since the Meiji reforms in 1868, for 103 years the Minseito and the Seiyukai have remained [the same] conservative affair despite changes in the name [of the parties]. It appears that the reactionary conservative government will still continue to be in existence for a certain period.
> Further - to put it differently - an extraordinary fight is necessary in order to change the policies adopted after the Second World War by Yoshida, Kishi and Sato.
> Presently numerous people say that we have entered a new situation - a new era, a new policy -, but we still have to observe [the situation]. ...
> Generally speaking, the prospects for the restoration of state-state relations between China and Japan are bright. It's definitely not an easy road. There are numerous difficulties. But it will be possible to surmount them. Those who stand in the way of Sino-Japanese friendship are unscrupulous. A long fight will be necessary. ...[43]

Does this speech reflect Liao's genuine evaluation of the political situation in Japan? It is perhaps more likely that this talk had been specifically tailored to his audience - a Japanese friendship delegation - without prejudice to secret diplomatic moves involving a wide variety of political leaders in Japan. Liao's reference to the importance of the 'workers' in bringing about the establishment of relations with Japan undoubtedly reflects the political jargon of the Cultural Revolution and should be seen as a concession to the influence of 'radical' politicians in Peking. As for Liao's prediction of the necessity of a 'long fight' he was certainly aware of continuing moves which would very soon lead to the establishment of relations *before* the United States. Liao must have been wondering how the establishment of relations would affect his own role in the PRC's policy making towards Japan.

Various Japanese individuals and groups competed in claiming a particular role during this phase of contact. From the evidence available it seems clear, by this time, Liao had regained his former status as the PRC's number one negotiator in relations with Japan, subordinate only to Zhou Enlai in the first instance, and not the foreign ministry as such. During these confidential negotiations the question of 'reliable channels' was of prime importance. An important role was played by Takeiri of the Komeito, a 'newcomer' in the field of Japanese relations with the PRC. At a more advanced stage the PRC increasingly turned to politicians like Furui, Fujiyama, Tagawa and Matsumoto Shunichi, with whom the PRC, and Liao in particular, had had numerous and extensive contacts over a long period of time.

This caused considerable dissatisfaction within the LDP.[44] One of the main reasons was that, by attaching so much importance to these politicians, the PRC seemed to be reviving its former tactics which sought to drive a wedge between various groups within the LDP divided on policy towards the ROC and the PRC. As a result of this pressure it was decided to send to Peking the first official LDP delegation representing the party *as a whole*. The delegation was led by Kosaka Zentaro and was charged with preparing the ground for Tanaka's visit.

Almost at the same time - a few days before Kosaka's talks - secret talks had been held in Peking by Furui, Tagawa and Matsumoto on the same question, under the camouflage of M-T negotiations.[45] Liao attended these talks which went very smoothly.[46] It is noteworthy that the PRC much preferred dealing with politicians that it could 'trust personally' as a result of contacts gradually built up under Liao's direction during the fifties and sixties. By the same token top party leaders in the CCP must have decided in advance that such talks could best be held with PRC politicians known to the Japanese, Liao foremost among them. It is worth remembering that the first mention of Liao's name came almost at the same time as the PRC's policy change towards the USA became apparent, and it is not too far-fetched to assume that a decision had been taken by then on Liao's rehabilitation. By reinstating Liao the party made use of his political capital built up through frequent and close links with Japanese in all walks of life during the fifties and sixties. Liao needed party approval to devote himself to relations with Japan, but the party also needed him. The main reason for this reciprocal relationship lies in the fact that, throughout the first decades after the establishment of the PRC, Communist leaders were forced to conduct a good deal of 'diplomacy' through informal channels rather than via the network of the foreign affairs apparatus. As will become clear later, PRC leaders had learned to value 'people's diplomacy' so highly that they continued employing this method even after formal diplomatic relations were established. While this is to some extent also true for relations with other countries it is no exaggeration to say that this dichotomy has had more influence in the PRC's relationship with Japan than with any other country.[47]

In contrast to the smooth secret talks between PRC officials, including Liao, and Furui, Tagawa and Matsumoto, problems arose during the visit of the Kosaka delegation. One reason was the inclusion of LDP representatives with reservations about how diplomatic relations with the PRC should be established. Concurrently with the Kosaka delegation, Shiina led a delegation to Taiwan where he was to assure the ROC that links would be maintained. As soon as this news arrived in Peking Liao replied in the form of a stiffly worded speech to the Kosaka delegation. These were the last hitches, however, which did not prevent Tanaka's visit and the planned establishment of relations.[48]

During the Tanaka visit Liao was given a leading role among PRC politicians taking part in the talks. He participated in all sessions between Tanaka and the PRC leaders, being outranked only by Mao, Zhou and the Foreign Minister, Ji Pengfei. His formal position was rather awkward. Officially he was not a member of the Central Committee of the CCP and he was listed as 'adviser to the Foreign Ministry'. According to normal protocol Ji Pengfei would be treated as senior to Liao but despite the lack of conclusive evidence it seems likely that by this time Liao had regained his previous leading position within the decision-making groups of the party and government concerning policy towards Japan. It was perhaps more than merely polite ritual when Liao received high praise for his contribution to the establishment of relations with Japan during Mao's meeting with Tanaka:

> The ceremonial highlight of Tanaka's China journey was his talk with Mao at *Chungnanhai* for an hour in the evening of September 27. ... According to Nikaido, some of their conversation went as follows:
> Mao: 'Did you have a fight with Premier Chou (at their summit meetings)?'
> Tanaka: 'No, I had a smooth discussion with him.'
> Mao: 'Only after a fight can you (Tanaka and Chou) become good friends.'
> Mao: 'He (pointing to Liao Cheng-chih) was born and raised in Japan. Why don't you take him to Japan with you?'
> Tanaka: 'Mr Liao is very popular in Japan, and he may be easily elected to the House of Councillors from a national district.'[49]

On the other hand Mao's praise of Liao need not be regarded as a personal tribute. Liao's good relationship with Zhou has been attested to often but there is little reference to such a relationship with Mao, not surprising perhaps, since up to now in most PRC sources Mao is treated as somehow removed from daily politics.

With the establishment of diplomatic relations a large area of links with Japan would be taken over by PRC government offices including the Ministries of Foreign Affairs and of Trade. Liao had previously held formal positions in relevant government offices. Quite a few former subordinates were absorbed by the foreign affairs apparatus. Similarly there was speculation in Tokyo that Liao might become the PRC's first ambassador to Tokyo[50] but such an appointment would have meant the virtual end of Liao's involvement in the decision-making process in Peking. It would also prevent him from continuing activities in the area of united front work and 'people's diplomacy'. He had started gradually to engage once more in contacts with Overseas Chinese from Hong Kong, Macao and Taiwan.

China's Relations with Japan

There were compelling reasons why the PRC was not prepared to put an end to its 'people's diplomacy'. The establishment of formal relations had not yet solved the problem of the conclusion of some kind of peace treaty. The communiqué published at the end of Tanaka's visit spelled out the need to conclude governmental agreements in all areas hitherto covered by 'private' agreements, in addition to new areas such as agreement on an air link.[53] Japan had broken off its diplomatic links with the ROC, but a number of agreements continued to function. The PRC had to tread carefully if it did not want to create the impression of *de facto* recognition of the ROC. Obstacles related to the Taiwan question delayed the conclusion of an air agreement until 1974. Rather unusual demands (unusual in the history of International Law) like the inclusion of an anti-hegemony principle into the Treaty of Peace and Friendship delayed the conclusion of this treaty until 1978. During these and other negotiations the PRC continued to use existing 'channels' to exert pressure on the Japanese government. Bypassing formal channels, contacts with opposition politicians and individual members of the governing party were used in the same way as they had been during the fifties and sixties.

Of course the Japanese government was not always happy about this situation. On the other hand, it is not far-fetched to assume that in Peking, the co-ordination of formal and 'people's diplomacy' ran into problems at times, and that there may have been rivalry and competition between sections of the bureaucracy. There is, of course, always the assumption that both areas of activity would be controlled by the relevant party organs. Little is known about deficient co-ordination, but there are signs of rivalry on matters of foreign policy within the party itself.

Previously we have seen that Yao Wenyuan attempted to get a direct foothold in the PRC's negotiations with Japan. When Prime Minister Tanaka visited Shanghai after the signing of the communiqué establishing relations he was received by Zhou Enlai and Zhang Chunqiao. The latter assumed a surprisingly high profile, ranking behind Zhou but before the Minister of Foreign Affairs, Ji Pengfei, and Han Nianlong (Liao did not travel to Shanghai), and there was a clear attempt to use this visit to enhance Zhang's standing. However, one should be careful not to portray the period before Mao's death in 1976 as wholly dominated by the 'Gang of Four', of whom Zhang was a leading representative. After Lin Biao's fall contacts were established with non-Communist countries like the USA and Japan, and with Western Europe.[52] There was a clear revival of elements of united front tactics in numerous areas, such as Overseas Chinese policy, the PRC's approach to Taiwan, the resumption of 'people's diplomacy' towards Japan as well as other countries. There seems no doubt that foreign policy arose out of debates and competition between various groups.[53] It is however extremely difficult to ascribe particular moves to the influence of any one group. This applies for example to negotiations between the PRC and Japan on a number of governmental, trade and other agreements and the Treaty of Peace and Friendship, the conclusion of which was delayed by many obstacles. It is questionable whether the information published to date makes it possible to relate specific objectives pursued and negotiation tactics employed by PRC negotiators to the domestic power struggle. However, one good example of the varied approaches taken by different PRC officials may be found in Liao Chengzhi's visit to Japan in 1973.

Liao's 1973 visit to Japan

Diplomatic relations with Japan led to a huge increase in political and economic contacts, and offered new possibilities for PRC pressure on the ROC. Despite much publicised developments relations in some areas proceeded less smoothly than might have been hoped. On the establishment of relations both sides had agreed to the speedy conclusion of formal government agreements on economic and trade exchanges.

The first significant step towards achieving these agreements was a joint visit to Peking by a mixed government-private delegation led by Minister for Transport Nakasone, and Kimura.[55] Both sides again were willing to conclude agreements at an early stage but political obstacles prevented speedy progress. The most important was undoubtedly Japan's relations with Taiwan which continued albeit below formal diplomatic level. For the moment neither side was prepared to grant concessions. Against this political stalemate the PRC used previously applied tactics, engaging in 'people's diplomacy' to exert further pressure on the Japanese government.[56] The Taiwan question was important in Overseas Chinese policy. The first conference on these affairs after the Cultural Revolution was held in Canton from 28 November to 7 December.[57] The next was the widely publicised anniversary celebration of the 'February 28' uprising in Taiwan; prominent participants were Liao, Zhou Jianren, Luo Qingchang and others active in United Front Work and Overseas Chinese policy including that directed to the ROC.[58]

When the Nakasone-Kimura visit did not lead to a breakthrough on the Taiwan question, Liao admitted on 10 March that unless this was solved, air agreement negotiations would not progress. Since this agreement was to be tackled first the statement implied delay for other agreements also. It appeared in an interview with *Yomiuri shinbun* before his visit as head of the largest PRC delegation to Japan.[59]

The delegation was expected to concern itself in three main areas: PRC-Japan relations; discussion of Overseas Chinese problems; and the containment of Soviet influence. It was intended to establish contact with Japanese from all walks of life but especially officials and politicians, including government ministers and the prime minister. The impressive farewell at Peking airport underlined the importance of the mission. Li Xiannian, the vice-prime minister who carried most weight had been present, and Deng Xiaoping, reinstated only a few days earlier, thus emphasising the 'thaw' in PRC foreign policy.[60] One of the most important aims of the mission was to work for the reduction of Japan's links with the ROC.

Delegation members were to seek frequent contact with Overseas Chinese in Japan, including businessmen and it was so successful that it achieved a significant shift in loyalty among many Overseas Chinese from the ROC to the PRC. Also, they would be encouraged to work for the 'reunification' of the fatherland.[61]

China's Relations with Japan

The PRC was concerned at the possibility of increased Japanese links with the Soviet Union, including intensified co-operation in the economic exploitation of Siberian resources.62 This was a development seen as potentially dangerous. Not only might the exploitation of such resources lead to a strengthening of the USSR's economic and military might, especially in the Far East, but increased links would reduce PRC leverage vis-à-vis Japan on a number of issues. The concern was heightened by a feeling of Soviet 'encirclement', perhaps including apprehension at the remote possibility of some sort of link between the Soviet Union and Taiwan.63

During the visit Liao and others spared no efforts to meet cabinet members and leading politicians, including Prime Minister Tanaka. Even a summary of the schedule shows the importance attached to such contacts, especially early in the mission, followed by meetings with opposition politicians and business leaders.64

April 16 Met at the airport by Nikaido Susumu representing the government. Liao meets Vice-Premier Miki.

April 17 Meets Tanaka at the Prime Minister's residence.

Meets Nakasone, Minister of Transport.

Meets Fujiyama Aiichiro who invites Liao to the foundation meeting of the *Nitchu yuko giin renmei* (Japan-China Friendship Diet Members Federation).

April 18 Meets Miki.

Meets Ohira, Minister of Foreign Affairs.

Meets Narita Tomomi, JSP chairman.

Meets Miki and Ohira at a reception.

April 19 Meets Prime Minister Tanaka. No political discussions were held, but a second meeting is agreed.

Meets Kuno, Minister of Postal Communications.

Meets Ezaki, Minister of Self-Government.

Meets Sakurauchi, Minister of Agriculture and Forestry.

April 20 Meets Kono Kenzo.

Meets Takeiri Yoshikazu, Komeito chairman.

April 21 Meets Furui Yoshimi.

Meets Kosaka Zentaro (Economic Planning Agency).

Meets Miki.

April 22 With his wife Liao visits former PM Ishibashi Tanzan, who was ill.

April 23 Meets with representatives of Mitsubishi.

April 24 Talks with Ohira who sets out the Japanese viewpoint on the operational agreements under discussion.

Meets representatives of Koga.

May 1 Meets representatives of the Sanwa Bank, Hitachi Shipbuilding, etc.

May 9 Meets Inayama Yoshihiro, chairman of Keidanren.

May 10 Meets Fuyo representatives.

Meets Furui Yoshimi.

May 14 Meets Prime Minister Tanaka.

Altogether Liao met Tanaka twice and Ohira five times during this visit - rather surprising if one recalls the non-official, 'private' status of the mission. Not all

Japanese politicians and bureaucrats were happy about the intensity of these contacts, not least because they feared that such talks might interfere with attempts to conduct talks through the newly established diplomatic channels.65

After the establishment of formal relations PRC leaders had clearly expected to continue high-level contact with Japanese leaders, but were disappointed.66 One reason was, of course, that the failure to reduce disagreement on links with Taiwan would render high-level visits inopportune since failure to agree at a higher level would conceivably be counterproductive. By April, more than six months after relations were established, there was still little progress in negotiations towards agreements on trade, shipping, aviation and fisheries, all explicitly mentioned in the joint communiqué.67 Towards the end of November and up to early December a Japanese delegation under Togo held intensive talks with a PRC delegation under Han Nianlong, one of the PRC's most experienced negotiators. The Japanese side presented its position on the operational agreements, and at a press conference about prospects for concluding an aviation agreement at an (unspecified) early date, Togo seemed quite optimistic. He was likewise optimistic concerning the other agreements although he added that trade and economic questions would take time.

According to informed sources the question of the existing airlink between Japan and Taiwan had posed a problem.68 At the talks in 1972 Tanaka and Zhou had agreed to give priority to the aviation talks, because of both their symbolic and practical significance.69 An aviation agreement would of course facilitate the conclusion of a postal agreement. Following the Togo mission, the Nakasone-Kimura mission visiting Peking in January 1973 was not able to narrow the gap on the Taiwan question, and further talks on the aviation agreement between February and April achieved no significant progress,70 although Liao stated again in March that the PRC did not object to the existence of an air link with Japan as such.71

The delay also affected talks on fisheries.72 There were also reports that the Chinese remained cool towards Nakasone compared to Kimura, who is said to have carried a personal letter from Tanaka and thus might have been treated by the Chinese as his personal emissary. Another reason may have been that Nakasone already had a reputation as a proponent of strengthening Japanese defences - which may not have gone down well with the PRC at that time.73 It should be noted, however, that it was during this visit that the PRC's changing stance concerning the question of Japanese defence was indicated, 'conceding the right to maintain its own defence forces within certain limits'.74 In March during a subsequent round of talks on an aviation agreement, Japan's air link with Taiwan remained the main stumbling block, delegation leader Wang Xiaoyun openly expressing the serious differences separating the two sides.75 Throughout the whole period the PRC continued to increase public pressure on Japan to gain concessions on the question of the air link. It was hardly a coincidence that it was Wang who, during the March mission, announced the definite arrival date of the Liao mission in Japan, thus underlining the link between the aviation talks and the Liao visit.76

It was Liao's first visit to Japan since 1957. Although he was invited in 1966 by Matsumura Kenzo, the visit did not take place due to the general worsening of relations at that time.77 In April 1972 Liao had again been invited by a group representing the JCFA, trade organisations, the JSP, Komeito, and the Minshato. The visit had been tentatively scheduled for the autumn of the same year, but was postponed in favour of Tanaka's visit to Peking. There is little doubt that, in April 1972, the mission had been seen as contributing to the establishment of diplomatic relations. Now, however, after the establishment of formal diplomatic channels the function of the Liao mission proved somewhat unusual and ambiguous.

The newly-appointed ambassador to Tokyo, Chen Chu had arrived there with other embassy staff only shortly before the Liao mission arrived in mid-April. He succeeded Mi Guojun who had been appointed chargé d'affaires in January. Chen Chu was not a Japan specialist, and was appointed against the expectation of many who thought that Liao or Wang Guoquan would be the first ambassador to Tokyo. He was a high-ranking career diplomat whose previous background made him eminently suitable for keeping an eye on Japan's changing relations with the USSR and the USA.78 As far as bilateral relations between the PRC and Japan were concerned the PRC had made it very clear that the establishment of diplomatic relations would not necessarily mean abandoning contacts established at the 'people to people' level. In a speech delivered in February 1973 Liao also stressed the need for 'joint struggle' by the Japanese and the Chinese people without which it would be unlikely that the aims set forth in the Tanaka-Zhou communiqué could be realised.79 Li Xiannian was even more explicit in March when he mentioned the need to maintain a number of channels in addition to formal diplomatic ones.80

Some Japanese explained this continuing attachment to 'people's diplomacy' by the PRC as due to habit or inertia. Liao's and Li Xiannian's statements make it clear that the tasks of 'people's diplomacy' had been redefined and from now on it would complement formal diplomacy. When in Japan Liao repeatedly emphasised the informal character of the mission and said he was not an official representative of the PRC government.81 He would be formally restored to full membership of the 10th Central Committee in the autumn of 1973, but his party status at the time of his visit was unclear. There was, nevertheless, no doubt that he continued to be regarded as the PRC's leading Japan specialist. As the *Mainichi shinbun* put it:

> This will be the most highly-formed, large-scale mission to be dispatched to a foreign country since the establishment of the People's Republic of China.82

The mission had been thoroughly prepared. Before going to Japan the fifty or so members had been 'interned' in Peking for nearly a month, studying the political and social situation in Japan as well as the economic and historical background.83 The same care also went into selecting travel destinations within Japan and the schedule as a whole. Besides mission leader Liao Chengzhi, members included prominent politicians like Sun Pinghua, Zhang Xiangshan and other veterans, with a number of delegates reflecting Cultural Revolution preferences for 'ordinary' workers. It is notable that the mission included Li Suwen, Vice-chairman of the Liaoning Provincial Committee and known as an expert on Soviet-PRC relations, Ma Chungu, a trade union leader, who became conspicuous as one of the more vociferous spokesmen against the USSR, and quite a number of delegates with links with Overseas Chinese, especially those of Taiwanese origin. It was assumed by some that Zhang was responsible for CCP liaison with the JCP, causing speculation that the mission might try to contact JCP leaders during the visit.[84]

As mentioned earlier the mission was seen off at Peking Airport by Li Xiannian and Deng Xiaoping (who had just been reinstated) and was given an equally public welcome on its return. Overall news coverage of the visit went beyond common practice for PRC accounts of the activities of delegations abroad. Judging by most press accounts in the PRC and Japan the mission was very successful. Some of the more specific points mentioned were that the mission had caused a significant shift of loyalties among Overseas Chinese in Japan, damaging the ROC's position there, and it had given clear warnings to Japanese and Chinese business leaders about links with the USSR. Not all Japanese papers agreed with this assessment. In a biting commentary the *Yamato Shinbun* speculated that the delegation's lack of success, coupled with the unpopularity of the Tanaka cabinet, would lead to a deferment of any high level visit until the formation of a new cabinet.

> Frankly speaking, Liao, who is conscious of the rating to be given him by the Party Centre, upon his return home, deliberately made ... [a] statement, singing his own praises and evaluating the results, which he had achieved, extremely highly.[85]

According to the *Yamato Shinbun* this was a traditional expedient of Chinese politicians in order to strengthen their own position. The JCP party organ *Akahata* however admitted that government officials who had been apprehensive about the mission before its arrival were full of praise on its departure.

The mission addressed itself mainly to Japan and Overseas Chinese living there, but it was obvious that it would try to frustrate Soviet policy aims in the region. PRC media comments on Japanese links with the USSR were fairly low key to avoid any appearance of interference in Japan's internal affairs.[86] However the PRC point of view was well known and it can be safely assumed that its attitude on Japanese-Soviet co-operation in projects like the exploitation of the Tyumeni oil field was expressed during Nakasone's visit to Peking in January 1973.[87] In an interview with the *Yomiuri Shinbun* on 10 March, published two days later, Liao specifically referred to the USSR as China's greatest and most treacherous enemy adding that the proposed oil pipeline from Tyumeni would provide the Soviet Union with additional supplies for its aircraft and tanks during an invasion of China and appropriate countermeasures would be necessary. He reminded the Japanese that co-operation would leave China with 'bitter feelings' towards Japan. On another occasion Liao warned that should Japan materially assist the Soviet Union, it would evoke feelings stronger than those of a 'divorce quarrel'.[88]

One Japanese correspondent reported Japanese foreign ministry officials as saying that the mission was 'more embarrassing than welcome' in its impact on Tokyo's dealings with the USSR[89] and there was concern that during a visit by mission members to the northern island of Hokkaido, Japanese nationalist feelings about the Soviet occupied islands to the north of Japan would be exploited.[90]

Sun Pinghua, secretary of the delegation, stressed his reluctance to comment on these issues early in the visit.[91] Likewise, when visiting JSP headquarters on 18 April Liao emphasised this cautious approach, telling his hosts that the delegation would say nothing that might be 'unbeneficial' to Sino-Japanese relations.[92] Since the JSP and the closely affiliated trade union federation SOHYO both had strong links with the Soviet Union this remark was taken to mean that the delegation would show restraint in statements about the USSR.[93] A few days later, however, the Communist paper *Dagongbao* gave ample room to Japanese critics of Japan's Soviet links.[94] While the mission remained generally cautious in public, it was less restrained during 'private' meetings, particularly with Overseas Chinese in Japan. On 27 April, during a Welcome Rally in Kyoto, Liao called for joint opposition to a 'super-big power' a clear reference to the USSR.[95] Two days later in Osaka he repeated his warning against 'socialist imperialism' which was 'cunning and deceptive by nature'.[96] He also issued a clear warning to Taiwan not to get involved with the Soviet Union by 'playing the Soviet card'.[97] On 2 May in Kobe he referred to the Soviet military threat and added that 'any Soviet aggression by air or ground attack would be repulsed'.[98] Other delegation members made similar statements, Ma Chungu being most conspicuous for strong, ideological language.[99] During his visit to Hokkaido Xu Guang as expected criticised the Soviet Union for its 'annexation' of the four islands to the north of Hokkaido. He referred to China as 'being threatened by Soviet aggression' and strongly implied that the Soviet Union should be regarded as the common enemy of China and Japan.[100]

The USSR finally commented on the Liao mission on 8 May, with articles in *Pravda* on 11 and 16 May also.[101] Some observers noted that on 12 May three Soviet warships had appeared in the Taiwan Straits, possibly as a warning.[102] Rather than putting pressure on the Japanese government the Liao delegation seems to have aimed to impress the public at large with statements on the Soviet Union, thus avoiding charges of interference in Japan's internal affairs, which clearly would have been counterproductive.[103] In fact PRC policymakers at home may have been less apprehensive about the possibility of Soviet-Japanese co-operation. In an intra-party speech in early March Zhou Enlai gave Soviet attempts to gain Japanese and US co-operation little chance.[104] The attacks on the USSR made during the Liao visit should, in the first instance, be seen as warnings to private business and perhaps also as 'statements for the record' designed to antagonise the Soviet Union. It is difficult to judge to what extent PRC pressure contributed to the failure of the Tyumen and Yakutsk projects.[105] US refusal to participate was probably decisive. Against this background it seems likely that Japanese relations with the Soviet Union formed only a minor, if widely noted, task of the mission.

The Taiwan Issue

Far more important was the question of Overseas Chinese in Japan. Together with the *rapprochement* towards the United States there had been a revival of united front tactics including attempts to 'win over' Overseas Chinese as well as American, Japanese, Hong Kong and European intellectuals and political leaders of various colours.[106] Partly these attempts were directed towards building an anti-Soviet alliance, but an important underlying aim was the isolation of the ROC. By winning Overseas Chinese living in Japan and South-East Asia the PRC hoped to damage the Taiwanese economy as well as undermine its political position. Half of the roughly 58,000 Overseas Chinese living in Japan had close links with Taiwan and were thus a potentially powerful weapon to exert pressure on Taiwan 'from within'. With the establishment of diplomatic relations with Japan, the PRC gained new opportunities to increase its influence among Overseas Chinese living in Japan. Also, the nature of existing links between the overseas community and the mainland in the area of trade started to change.[107] It is therefore not surprising that Liao's delegation included numerous delegates with a 'Taiwan' or 'overseas' background, and it sought to take advantage of any possibility of contact with those Overseas Chinese whose loyalty had hitherto lain with Taiwan. There was a clear de-emphasis of previous confrontational tactics, a renewed stress on 'unity', and the mission provided a good example for the revival of united front tactics.[108]

The mission contained members such as Lin Liyun (who acted as an interpreter for Zhou Enlai at the time of the Tanaka visit to Peking) whose relatives still live in the Kansai area of West Japan. Lin's father was in Lin Suiyong, Vice-President of the Association of Chinese Merchants in Kobe.[109] Direct contacts between mission members like Lin and their relatives, including distant relatives, and their friends have had greater power of persuasion among the Chinese merchant circles in Japan than is realised by most Japanese.[110] The mission also included Rong Yiren, a so-called 'national capitalist'. His task was to convince Overseas Chinese that his property had not been confiscated during the GPCR and that his physical well-being had also not been affected - a difficult undertaking in view of the great apprehension which followed reports during the Cultural Revolution.[111]

Despite the impression of a low-key approach it should be noted that, in a speech to Overseas Chinese in Osaka on 29 April, Liao called on his listeners to assist in 'liberating' Taiwan, probably the first time that a PRC leader during a trip to a foreign, non-Communist country, had openly appealed to Overseas Chinese to work together to this end. Japanese derecognition of the ROC meant that such an appeal did not constitute outright interference in Japan's internal affairs.[112]

It was subsequently claimed that 'more than 90%' of Overseas Chinese in Japan had been 'united' behind Peking's banners. More realistic estimates show a swing from 40% who declared their loyalty to Peking rather than to Taiwan before Liao's visit, to about 60% after his departure - still a striking result, obtained despite Taiwanese countermeasures.[113] While such a swing was clearly damaging to ROC interests trade figures for 1973 indicated that the damage was political rather than economic. While PRC trade with Japan rose sharply so did Japanese trade with Taiwan, despite PRC hopes for a decline in Taiwan's links with Japan.[114]

In more than one sense the so-called 'Taiwan question' lay at the heart of the mission. The inability of the PRC and Japan to come to terms on the operational agreements was caused by the refusal of the Japanese government to give in to PRC demands that would have resulted in a severe reduction of trade with Taiwan. The Tanaka-Zhou agreement saw Japan acknowledging PRC sovereignty over Taiwan. Simultaneously, the legal basis of existing agreements and treaties with the ROC had become invalid but the practical effects of this change were limited. Although the aviation agreement between Japan and the ROC had also lost its previous legal foundation, operations continued on the basis of 'administrative permits' from the Ministry of Transport and flights continued *as if nothing had happened*.115 This was difficult for the PRC to swallow, but the Japanese were more determined to maintain such highly profitable links than had perhaps been expected by those who viewed Japanese foreign policy as rather 'weak-kneed'. To some extent Japanese resilience in the face of PRC demands was due to the continuing influence of the 'Taiwan lobby' in Japan. There was also a more general realisation that Japan should not have to pay a higher price for its links with the PRC than did other countries, in particular the United States. It was argued, for instance, that the PRC had agreed to establish a liaison office in Washington at a time when the flag was still fluttering over the embassy of the ROC. In the *Yomiuri* interview of 10 March Liao Chengzhi had tried to anticipate this argument:

> As a result of Kissinger's visit to China a liaison office was established. This does not signify (acceptance of the existence of) two Chinas.

Referring to the semi-governmental trade offices established during the sixties Liao added that:

> The L-T offices started as simple trade offices and were gradually given powers which in fact did resemble diplomatic privileges. (The new PRC-USA liaison offices) are on a somewhat larger scale ..., but are simple liaison offices. The difference is ... that the assistant to the present American president has been visiting China repeatedly ...116

Liao's argument is political rather than legalistic; he holds that such comparisons should be seen in proper historical perspective. In the context of previous relations with the USA the existence of a liaison office in Washington was a significant advance for the PRC, whereas a continuing Taiwanese presence in Japan would be a step backwards, since 'normalisation' should have put a definite brake on such links. Legal specialists in the Japanese Foreign Ministry may not have been impressed by the argument. Moreover, the Japanese defended their position, despite strong PRC pressure, that agreements with the ROC predated recognition of the PRC. The PRC position strongly resembled its demands that the Soviet Union accept the invalidity of former 'unequal treaties' between Tsarist Russia and China. PRC insistence that Japan acknowledge the invalidity of the peace treaty with the ROC concluded within the framework of the San Francisco Agreement was also a considerable obstacle during the protracted negotiations for the conclusion of the Treaty of Peace and Friendship. Contrary to widespread opinion Japanese negotiators did not give in easily to PRC demands during negotiations and were willing to accept long delays to defend their position.117

Addressing Overseas Chinese living in Japan Liao and other members of the mission had frequently tried to convince their listeners that following the *rapprochement* between the PRC and the USA Taiwan would no longer be able to rely on a powerful ally and, in its own interest, should negotiate a peaceful 'settlement' with the PRC while it was still able to gain relatively favourable conditions.[118] References to US 'unreliability' had also figured prominently in speeches during the anniversary celebrations of the 'February 28' incident, when Liao Chengzhi and Fu Zuoyi (a veteran of united front tactics) had been the most celebrated speakers. During the visit to Japan there had also been repeated warnings to Taiwan not to 'play the Soviet card'.[119]

At one stage the controversy over Japanese links with Taiwan even seemed to threaten the continuation of the mission. One day before a planned visit to the site of the 1970 World-Expo in Osaka the delegation became aware of a ROC flag on the premises. It was said that Liao considered filing a protest with the Japanese government through the PRC embassy in Tokyo. The dispute was defused following an apology by the President of the Osaka Chamber of Commerce and Industry, Saeki Isamu. Business leaders made a 'secret' visit to Liao's hotel; Liao appeared conciliatory and agreed to attend a welcome party on the night of the 3rd which had been threatened by the 'flag incident'.[120]

The Liao mission however was not able to gain substantial concessions from the Japanese government concerning the treatment of the 'Taiwan question' in the negotiations on operational agreements, particularly on aviation. Liao had even issued rather over-optimistic statements about the possibility of compromise which turned out to be counterproductive. Despite the indisputable success of the Liao mission it was not an unqualified success. One must assume that one of its tasks had been to make a direct contribution to progress in the stalemated talks on an aviation agreement. There had been considerable reluctance among numerous LDP politicians and government officials to bypass formal diplomatic channels and accept the mission's 'people's diplomacy' as an important complement to more regular negotiations.[121] One immediate result of the mission was an announcement that Foreign Minister Ohira would visit Peking later in the year.[122] This visit, however, was expected to take place only after Prime Minister Tanaka's return from a visit to the USA, the Soviet Union and Europe. Ohira also announced that he would not negotiate on specific matters such as an aviation agreement.[123] As it turned out Ohira's visit eight months later became the turning point in the aviation talks, laying the basis for an agreement. Liao's attempt to advance the talks on an aviation agreement during his April-May visit resulted however in a minor crisis.

In November 1972 the Japanese side had indicated that it would be willing to start negotiations on a fisheries agreement either in April or at the beginning of May 1973, apparently assuming that an aviation agreement could be reached before that date.[124] The existing private agreement was due to expire in 1973, thus putting additional pressure on the negotiating teams.[125] When Liao and Ohira met on 23 April their talks covered problems concerning all four operational agreements.[126] Ohira conveyed his intention to dispatch a negotiating team to

Peking shortly, a suggestion agreed to by Liao.[127] Ohira, apparently encouraged by Liao's optimistic statements may have argued that sending a delegation then would mean that the PRC was under pressure to come up with concessions and would be held responsible if these were not forthcoming. Liao may also have concluded - wrongly, as it turned out - that the Japanese themselves were ready to change their position on existing air links with Taiwan. Indications are, however, that it was the PRC rather than Japan that was pressed for time, and that Liao's optimism was part of a risky strategy to coax Japan into an early agreement.

Nearly a decade before, the PRC had suggested an air link between Shanghai and Kyushu, a move clearly aimed at achieving informal recognition of the PRC. Such a link would have been a rather isolated step at a time when the PRC had not yet begun to build up its own global air network. The situation had changed by the early seventies when such efforts had begun on a large scale.[128] An air link with Tokyo, eventually to be extended to the American continent would have been a very important step in that direction. The question of prolongation rights following the establishment of the Peking-Tokyo route was therefore a substantial issue for the PRC during the aviation talks. By the same token, the PRC also attempted to have similar prolongation rights granted to the ROC airline cancelled. It is sometimes assumed that the 'Taiwan question' was confined to the problem of avoiding aircraft from Taiwan and Peking being next to each other on a Japanese airfield, thus symbolising a 'two China approach' abhorred by both the ROC and the PRC. The talks would also affect PRC plans to build up a global air network, and an agreement detrimental to the ROC might affect its own global network.

The Japanese had submitted a draft proposal concerning an aviation agreement as early as November 1972. It failed to mention the future status of Japan's air link with Taiwan, and met with strong PRC dissatisfaction.[129] A less realistic proposal floated towards the end of the year would have meant the replacement of all existing links between Taiwan and Japan by a single connection between Okinawa and Taipei.[130] The Chinese made a counterproposal in mid-February.[131] Liao Chengzhi confirmed in public on 27 February that the PRC would not object to the an air link between Taiwan and Japan as such, and clearly wished to appear conciliatory.[132] When Nakae Yosuke led a Japanese delegation to Peking in March Wang Xiaoyun pressed for comment concerning the Taiwan air link. The Japanese however explained that such comment would involve a political decision falling outside the competence of the delegation.[133] Uncharacteristically, the PRC agreed to deal with technical questions concerning an aviation agreement before the most pressing political problems had been solved, thus giving an indication of the urgency with which the PRC viewed the negotiations.[134] Wang elaborated that the main stumbling block was not so much the air link as such but the fact that the existing arrangement was so closely linked to the (expired) treaty between Japan and the ROC on which it had been based.[135] This argument was repeated by Liao in his interview on 10 March. He was careful not to criticise Tanaka or Ohira by name in order not to damage relations with Japan but his implicit criticism of the Japanese position showed how strongly the PRC felt.[136] As mentioned above, the

March round of talks was inconclusive, and no new date for the continuation of negotiations was set, although the Japanese government announced its intention of sending a second delegation to Peking at a later stage.137

Speaking on 18 April, shortly after his arrival, Liao did not refer specifically to the aviation talks,138 but in talks with government leaders he seemed optimistic about the chance of an early agreement, as in his talks with Postal Minister Kuno or with Fujii Katsushi, Chairman of the Lower House Foreign Affairs Committee:139

> According to Fujii's explanations, Liao exemplified an extremely optimistic outlook on a[n] ... aviation agreement, saying 'I firmly believe that the negotiations will be concluded in the near future'.140

Some in the Japanese government were saying that there was no need to hurry the talks and that there was no prospect of an early conclusion even if talks at ambassadorial or bureau chief level were set in motion.141 Liao's talk with Ohira on 23 April has been referred to already and it was apparently as a result of this meeting that the Japanese government decided to reopen the talks at short notice.142 On 25 April the Chinese government through the Japanese Embassy in Peking conveyed its intention to receive the Japanese request.143 Acting with unusual speed the Japanese government decided on the same day to dispatch Foreign Affairs Councillor Togo and Aviation Bureau Councillor Goto to Peking,144 where talks started on the 28th.145 Only a few days later a Japanese government source commented on the talks saying that they had:

> merely disclosed more clearly than before that differences in the position of China and Japan had been too great, and that absolutely no progress had been made.146

The talks had ended in failure and Japan had been unable to gain any idea of the concessions the PRC was prepared to make.147 Some members of the Foreign Ministry and the Ministry of Transport thought that early conclusion of an aviation agreement could only be reached through large-scale concessions, including the abolition of the Japan-Taiwan air route. Clearly the LDP would not agree.148

The failure of the talks reflected squarely on Liao since his talks with Japanese officials had set the latest round of talks in motion. There is no conclusive evidence that Liao had been to blame for errors of judgment or inappropriate negotiating tactics, since he may have acted on fairly specific orders from Peking. Immediately after the débâcle he attempted to limit the damage by minimising the significance of the talks:

> The delay of the aviation agreement is not a serious matter, and this is not a great obstacle for the development of Sino-Japanese friendship.

Liao also continued to appear optimistic, as in his statement on 10 May:

> I will meet Foreign Minister Ohira tomorrow and discuss the question of the aviation agreement. Since there are no man-made obstacles I am optimistic that the negotiations will be concluded speedily.149

He thus reconfirmed his impression that both sides had the political will to come to an agreement, virtually implying that Ohira might still make some kind of concession. The Japanese made it clear, however, that they regarded the question of an air link with Taiwan as a matter for Japan alone to solve.[150]

For the time being, attempts at compromise had failed. It is difficult to say whether responsibility for the failure lay with Liao personally, but it appeared that 'people's diplomacy' as practised by the mission had been no more able to prod the Japanese government into making concessions than formal PRC diplomacy. In an interesting comment made to officials of the Komeito Liao declared that:

> Through my visit to Japan I came to understand well that the 'pro-Taiwan faction' is only small in numbers.[151]

In vivid contrast to the past Liao did not blame the Taiwan lobby for Japan's unwillingness to make concessions, a public standpoint designed to downplay existing differences. This is supported by reports that Zhou Enlai did express strong dissatisfaction regarding the Taiwan air link to Postal Minister Kuno.[152]

With the Japanese government's firm stance, both sides now agreed to negotiate on other matters before a solution to the aviation problem was found. Since the PRC had placed so much political value on the aviation talks this should be seen as an important concession. Of course, PRC relations with Japan were not dominated exclusively by political differences. From the early fifties trade had been an important factor. 1973 brought a dramatic increase in PRC trade with Japan but moves to formalise the exchanges proceeded less smoothly than had been hoped. When Nakasone and Inayama had led a joint mission to Peking, followed by PRC missions led by Liu Xiwen, Bai Xiangguo and Li Qiang, there had been considerable optimism about early conclusion of a trade agreement.[153] Failure to conclude an aviation agreement also affected the proposed trade agreement. There were purely economic factors inhibiting a more stable trade relationship. The most important problem was the PRC's inability to deliver all the oil promised to Japan only a short time before.[154] The PRC also had to allay fears among Japanese producers about cheap PRC imports that would create problems for local producers. In comments during the first days of his visit Liao virtually apologised for problems that had arisen due to cheap imports of Chinese raw silk.[155]

It seems most likely that Liao's other talks with business leaders were of a rather general nature. They were frequently followed by invitations for visits during which more specific questions would be discussed.[156] Liao was also able to announce the sending of a large economic delegation to Japan scheduled for the autumn of 1973. In contrast to previous missions this one would include representatives from all major areas.[157] Although Liao also discussed the question of the PRC supply of crude oil and natural gas to Japan, most talks involving economic problems were not intended to produce firm agreements. Both sides apparently regarded them as a good way of confirming their interest in future contacts, also expressed by announcements of visits by various delegations.[158]

After visiting Japan in the spring of 1973 Liao continued to meet members of economic delegations visiting Peking but, judging from published information, his role was limited to more general or political aspects of such talks, as is apparent from his well-documented opening speech during a visit in September 1973 by a delegation under Uemura Kogoro.159 That year also saw agreement on extending the Most-Favored Nations Clause to the PRC. A trade agreement was reached towards the end of the year and signed in January 1974, followed by the signing of other operational agreements. There seems little doubt that during his visit to Japan and during meetings with businessmen on his return Liao was able to create much goodwill. It should be added in fairness, though, that without Japanese eagerness to 'conquer' the PRC market Liao's success would have been more limited.

Among political observers there was considerable interest concerning JCP reaction to the visit of the Liao delegation. There had been rumours that the delegation might seek to contact the JCP. According to one source, Mi Guojun (PRC chargé d'affaires who had arrived in Tokyo on 31 January), the delegation had almost immediately sought this contact and a meeting had taken place with Hakamada Satomi, JCP vice-chairman.160 If such a meeting took place, it did not result in a noticeable improvement in relations between the parties, also confirmed by Liao's interview on 10 March.161 The presence of Zhang Xiangshan in the Liao mission gave rise to some speculation since he was said to be 'in charge of [links with] the Japan Communist Party'.162 Shortly before the mission's arrival JCP Chairman Miyamoto made clear that his party did not intend to make contact on its own initiative.163 Various statements by members of the Liao mission also implied that they would not seek contact. According to Kawasaki Hideji, who met Liao on 25 April, Liao denied the possibility of relations between the JCP and the CCP 'under Miyamoto', adding that Miyamoto was 'not a true Communist'.164

On the whole Liao appears to have been relatively reticent concerning the JCP. Another member of the delegation, Han Xiya commented on the dispute with the JCP in the following terms:

> This is entirely a principled confrontation between Marxism-Leninism and Revisionism. The Miyamoto revisionist group have tried to force a revisionist policy line on China in the past. When Miyamoto came to Peking in 1966 he openly slandered the policy line of China. However, a majority of the JCP members desire revolution and only a handful of persons, including the Miyamoto faction, is challenging the policy line taken by China.165

It is highly doubtful whether Liao was happy about Han Xiya's statement which Han directed towards an audience of citizens from Nagasaki. In the context of the united front strategy adopted by the mission as a whole Han's reference to a majority of JCP members desiring revolution seemed inopportune. His remarks also brought charges of interference in Japan's internal affairs.166 Minister of Justice Tanaka denied that Han's remarks constituted interference since they 'had been made in reply to a question from a Japanese participant at the rally'.167

A few days later Utsunomiya Tokuma (LDP) reported on Liao's position which seemed to differ from Han's statement. According to Utsunomiya Liao said that:

> (1) The JCP is carrying out a propaganda campaign concerning the confrontation between the Chinese Communist Party and the Japan Communist Party saying that the confrontation has been caused

because the Chinese side pressed the JCP to 'encircle cities from rural villages and carry out guerrilla activities' and because the JCP rejected this. This is false propaganda. The cause of the confrontation is differences in the evaluation of the Soviet Union; and
(2) China is taking a guarded position towards the policies of the Soviet Union towards Eastern Europe.[168]

It was the first time since his arrival in Japan that Liao had been reported as referring to the cause of the CCP's confrontation with the JCP. Although both Han and Liao refer to 'revolution' in quite a different context it is fairly clear that, in contrast to Han, Liao tried to *de-emphasise* this controversial topic. His approach was more in tune with united front tactics while Han's pronouncement might frighten off a number of Japanese who would otherwise regard the PRC with some sympathy. Similar differences could also be observed between statements by Ma Chungu and Liao. In contrast to Liao, Ma made use of much more aggressive-sounding ideological language, as when he referred to the 'historical truth of people's liberation which cannot be obstructed by any force'.[169] In a speech to Japanese workers in Kitakyushu Ma told them that 'the struggle of the workers will progress by fighting revisionists and right wing opportunists'.[170] This was addressed to the JCP but he also openly criticised Japan's links with the USA when he told schoolchildren in Okinawa that the PRC 'supports your struggle for the removal of military bases'.[171] On 16 May he mentioned nuclear intimidation by the USSR and the USA and again referred to the possibility of a 'solution' for American bases in Okinawa.[172] Even should Liao have subscribed to Ma's statements his own remarks seem to have been carefully calculated to avoid sounding obtrusive to the average Japanese. In any event, CCP relations with the JCP did not change as a result of the Liao visit.

The JSP was not averse to strengthening its links with the CCP, despite strong links with the Soviet Union. It had been expected that the CCP would try to improve relations with the JSP. JSP Chairman Narita met with Ambassador Chen Chu and Liao Chengzhi, but relations did not improve rapidly, and it was March 1975 before the JSP was invited to send an official delegation to the PRC.[173]

Judging by the publicity given to the Liao mission by the PRC media it would appear to have been treated as an unqualified success and most Japanese media reports convey a similar impression. Most spectacular of all perhaps was the mission's ability to cause a significant shift of loyalty in favour of Peking among Overseas Chinese in Japan. The mission, and Liao in particular, had also held extensive discussions with Japanese business representatives. While Liao was still in Japan announcements were made concerning Foreign Minister Ohira's plans to visit the PRC later in the year, the mission announced the sending of a large scale economic delegation to Japan and also prepared the ground for more intensive contact with Japanese business in general. Nevertheless, the mission had been unable to contribute to a breakthrough in the stalemated aviation talks. There is little doubt that a major aim of the mission was to put pressure on the Japanese government at a time when negotiations through formal diplomatic channels had been unsuccessful. Information provided by Liao must have been the prime reason for the Japanese government's sudden decision to send another delegation to Peking while Liao was still in Japan. When this move failed to bridge the gap concerning the treatment of the 'Taiwan question' in a future aviation agreement, the PRC made an important concession. Peking agreed to 'shelve' the talks for the time being and start talks on the other operational agreements. There is no conclusive evidence as to whether the inability of the Liao mission to persuade the Japanese government was due to an error of judgment by Liao, or whether Liao merely acted on orders from 'higher up'. It is impossible to say whether Liao and other PRC Japan specialists may have raised expectations among PRC leaders that the 'people's diplomacy' conducted by the mission in fact would be more successful than regular diplomacy. The political results of Liao's mission seem to have taught leaders that 'people's diplomacy' continued to be a useful instrument at least in areas such as business contacts or links with Overseas Chinese. On the other hand, it was also to be the last large, high-powered PRC delegation engaging in 'people's diplomacy' that attempted to supplement formal diplomacy during the numerous contacts with high-ranking Japanese government members.

On the whole Liao made a good personal impression on the Japanese public. He was extremely busy during his stay in Japan, and there was some concern about his health, particularly since he had a heart condition. Towards the end of the visit he had to limit the range of his activities and number of his engagements, probably on the advice of the doctor accompanying the mission. It was said that the doctor was to file daily health reports to Peking concerning Liao.[174]

The visit had confirmed to the Japanese that Peking treated Liao as its major Japan specialist. His unqualified return to the political scene and active engagement were seen as symbols for future stable relations. It must not be forgotten that, at that time, the power struggle in Peking was intense and the debate between 'rightist' and 'leftist' - those who wanted to increase trade and other links greatly and those who wanted to keep them at a modest minimum - would continue for some years. Later accounts confirmed that the internal position of politicians like Liao was probably less stable than may have been assumed at the time:

> In May 1973 I reported to Liao ... There were not a few Overseas Chinese who had applied for exit visas because they had been persecuted. I asked Liao how this situation could be rectified and redressed. When I had finished Liao became grave but replied to me categorically:
> 'I am also to some extent aware of the situation but the Central Committee's Overseas Chinese policy has been designed by Chairman Mao and Prime Minster Zhou ... and if it is not carried out the way it should be, then that is due to the legacy of that bandit Lin (Biao). They can't represent the party, and the day will come when Overseas Chinese will see this clearly.'
> He seemed to be deeply moved, and expressed his confidence in the future.[175]

'They' obviously refers to the Gang of Four; Chen may not have remembered Liao's words verbatim but he gives us an indication of the lack of actual authority concerning united front work and how careful even prominent politicians had to be in expressing themselves. However, it would be wrong to underestimate the influence of these anti-radical politicians. Due to events during the Cultural Revolution Liao was a good friend of He Long, in turn a close ally of Wang Zhen, with whom Liao was also on friendly terms. Friends of Liao were able to push He Long's rehabilitation in 1974, all the more remarkable since there may have been rumours even then linking He Long to an assassination attempt on Mao.176

A reduction of Liao's status or visibility at that time, however, would have damaged Japanese confidence in PRC trade policies, which would have contributed significantly to his political survival during the difficult last years of Mao's life. As long as there was minimal agreement among top PRC decision-makers on the need to maintain and perhaps expand links with Japan Liao could be sure of his political survival. To what extent he may have been able to influence policy-making towards Japan at a given moment throughout these years is quite a different question. It would be patently wrong, however, to describe politics between 1971 and 1976 in terms of a quasi-total dictatorship of the so-called Gang of Four.

The Ohira Visit

In August 1973 Liao Chengzhi was formally restored as a full member of the Tenth Central Committee which saw a significant increase in foreign affairs specialists generally, over the Ninth Committee (1969) dominated by Lin Biao.177 For the rest of the year Liao continued to be almost exclusively involved in PRC relations with Japan. He also met Overseas Chinese from other areas as well as residents of Hong Kong.178 Despite the revival - albeit a modest one - of Overseas Chinese policy Liao's share was limited compared to the pre-eminent role he and his mother played in this area during the fifties and sixties. Likewise, he was not restored to the many other positions he had held before the Cultural Revolution. Following the disgrace of Lin Biao the CCP to some extent resumed united front tactics, but none of those who had played important roles in high-level party organisations like the United Front Work Department regained their former status. Liao's revival as a Japan specialist had not been accompanied by his restoration to important positions in other areas of united front policy although he took part in related activities such as the commemoration of Sun Yatsen's birthday on 12 November 1973. Therefore it seems justified to assume that his influence in general during the years until Mao's death and Deng Xiaoping's revival would have been significantly less than before the Cultural Revolution, and it is debatable how far he was able to influence Japan policy during these years. His appearance as 'Adviser to the Foreign Ministry' in 1972, his restoration to the Central Committee and his appointment as Head of the Beijing Institute of Foreign Languages indicated that he may have regained a party position within the Foreign Ministry during this period.

In Japan in April-May Liao had shown considerable optimism about the future of PRC relations with Japan but in a speech delivered at about the time of the Tenth Party Congress his comments were much more subdued. The delay in concluding operational agreements may have been one reason for this, but the tone of the speech seemed to reflect a policy change by top CCP leaders, foreshadowing the xenophobic anti-Confucian campaign of 1974. In his speech Liao repeated many shibboleths of PRC foreign policy of the day, such as the emphasis on 'self-reliance'. His statements on PRC economic foreign policy dampened the overly high expectations of the Japanese business world regarding trade with the PRC, an uncharacteristic move when one recalls the importance of trade during the fifties and sixties as a means of strengthening links with Japan. Having stressed that foreign trade would not expand rapidly, Liao emphasised that the PRC would be willing to conduct technological and economic exchanges on two conditions - loans would be totally unacceptable as would joint development projects. He pointed out that, although comparatively slow, trade growth would be 'extremely' stable, if, perhaps, not 'in a straight line'. He later indulged in personal attacks on 'pro-Taiwan' politicians like Kishi. One reason for returning to such verbal attacks was clearly PRC irritation with the delay in concluding operational agreements.

Throughout the latter part of 1973 talks on the agreements had continued between Ogawa, Ambassador to Peking and Han Nianlong, then Deputy Minister of Foreign Affairs, among others. These negotiations mostly centred on 'political principles' (mainly the Taiwan question) and made little progress.[179] Liao's role in here is unclear. PRC attitudes seemed to have hardened, as observed by Japanese businessmen trading with the PRC. Ambassador Ogawa left the PRC for a visit to Japan in September 1973. Before leaving he had confidential talks with Prime Minister Zhou and Ji Pengfei but no progress was made.[180] Although after his return to Peking in May Liao had been busily engaged in meeting Japanese visitors there is little indication that he took direct part in the formal diplomatic talks on the operational agreements. One can only speculate on this point, but Liao's failure to achieve a breakthrough during his visit and Japanese insistence on continuing talks through formal diplomatic channels may have been important reasons. Whatever Liao's authority in matters of relations with Japan, his formal position in PRC government and foreign affairs remained rather vague to the outside observer.

While Japanese political relations with the PRC continued to be marred by disputes over operational agreements the announcement came of Ohira's visit to Peking on 28 December.[181] This visit was to become the turning point leading to the signing of operational agreements in 1974, perhaps politically most significant, the Aviation Agreement in April.[182] During the visit itself Ohira was able to sign a trade agreement removing several important obstacles. Negotiations were not easy:

> The Chinese proved more demanding and less cordial than at least some quarters in Japan had expected them to be.[183]

Ogawa, the Japanese ambassador, recalls that Ohira was already about to return to Japan without an agreement when the PRC team suddenly shifted its position.[184] Ohira's visit also laid the foundation for talks in March and April 1974, resulting in the long delayed Aviation Agreement. The question of why the PRC was prepared to make concessions at this stage naturally arises. It was most likely the domestic political situation both in Japan and the PRC that brought about this change.

The Tanaka Cabinet's popularity had been waning and with elections due in 1974 there was justified concern in Peking that any alternative would be even less likely to grant concessions. After the Tenth Party Congress, PRC policymakers were faced with an increasingly bitter feud between the 'Isolationists' and their 'Internationalist' opponents, represented by supporters of the 'Anti-Confucius Movement' on one hand, and Zhou Enlai on the other. Any longer delay in coming to an agreement with Japan might further jeopardise the position of the 'Internationalists' and seriously threaten the PRC's foreign policy line.

Zhou was already ailing at that time and by 1975 Deng Xiaoping seems to have assumed quite a few of his tasks.[185] Zhou and Ji Pengfei took an active part in the negotiations, but little information has been published on Liao's involvement. Of course there were also international factors making further delay in concluding these agreements inadvisable. It was no coincidence that, during the negotiations, Zhou announced for the first time in public, PRC production figures for crude oil. Following the oil shock this seemed a good moment to lure Japan with the prospect of PRC oil in exchange for increased imports of Japanese technology and plant.

Ohira himself, as a member of the politically threatened Tanaka cabinet, had an important interest in achieving a foreign policy success at that time. Even after his return to Japan negotiations on the remaining operational agreements were not always easy, complicated greatly by domestic Japanese politics. Differences within the ruling LDP led Ohira to stake his political life on the signing of an aviation agreement before the elections. These developments clearly deserve further study.

As mentioned earlier Liao attended several functions during Ohira's visit but there is little evidence that he took an active part in the negotiations. The same is true of the talks on an aviation agreement in March-April which received wide coverage in the Japanese press. Liao was hardly mentioned although he did take part in the signing ceremony.[186] In early 1974 he was at the departure and welcoming ceremonies for Deng Xiaoping who went to New York in April. On that occasion Deng set out in detail the 'Theory of the Three Worlds' during a meeting of the General Assembly of the United Nations.[187] Liao also attended a meeting between Deng and the delegation of Japanese National Governors and was present at the reception on the occasion of Army Day on 31 July. No particular signs pointed to a diminution in his formal status. Perhaps it was not just accidental that, during major functions attended by Liao in this period, Deng Xiaoping in particular was among the top leaders at the same meetings.

In addition Liao remained actively involved in numerous 'united front' activities, meeting Japanese delegations such as 'LDP Young Diet Members', SOHYO, a JSP delegation as well as a delegation of Chinese of Taiwanese origin residing in Japan and the USA who had attended the Seventh Asian Games.

The Treaty of Peace and Friendship

Since the beginning of 1974 'radical' influence had increased considerably, as evinced by the anti-foreign campaign criticising Confucius and Lin Biao. Radical influence continued right up to the death of Mao Zedong in September 1976. The arrest of the so-called Gang of Four ushered in a transitional period presided over by Hua Guofeng as Mao Zedong's successor in his role as chairman of the CCP. It was not until 1978 that a new group of leaders would appear who set the People's Republic on a course of radical economic reforms.

Domestic politics during this period of about four and a half years were characterised by constant manoeuvring between various groups. It would, of course, be wrong to describe the struggle merely in terms of a clash between the 'radicals' and their 'rightist' opponents. Chinese foreign policy was also in a transitional period; internal divergences of opinion were compounded by dramatic changes in South-East Asia following the occupation of South Vietnam by the North. On the surface Chinese foreign policy remained consistently bent on fighting 'hegemonism'. The practical content of this foreign policy line initially was mainly containment of Soviet influence, including an attempt to prevent a *rapprochement* between Japan and the Soviet Union, particularly economic cooperation in the exploitation of Siberian resources.

After 1975, it becomes increasingly clear that the PRC attempted to gain as much support as possible for its South-East Asian policy. As far as Japan was concerned, the PRC tried to prevent Japan from assuming the role of mediator between Vietnam and the United States. When the PRC felt forced to take action against Vietnam in the winter of 1978/79 it obviously needed to obtain as much co-operation as possible, or at least some kind of 'benevolent neutrality', from countries such as Japan and the United States. Such was the background of negotiations concerning the conclusion of a 'Treaty of Peace and Friendship' (TPF) between the PRC and Japan, the political and strategic functions of which clearly outweighed its effect on Japanese trade with the PRC.

Viewing the period between 1974 and 1978 as a whole it is fairly clear that Liao was less influential in 1974, during the time of increasing 'radical' influence, than in 1978.[188] Yet even Liao's political opponents were aware of the fact that, despite the establishment of diplomatic relations with Japan, the PRC still needed to continue its 'people's diplomacy' in support of its attempt to prod Japan into a TPF, and that Liao's standing in Japan, and his connections there made him virtually indispensable.

As already noted, the negotiations on the operational agreements had been encumbered by the 'Taiwan' factor, and it was widely expected that this would also pose a major problem for the coming talks on the conclusion of the TPF[189] but this was not the case. A new issue arose: the PRC wished to include opposition to 'hegemony' in the main text of the TPF. This had been mentioned in the 1972 Tanaka-Zhou communiqué, but it was a concept hard to define and had never been included in an international treaty before. It is therefore hardly surprising that

Japanese politicians were not prepared to include the concept in the main text of the treaty in such a way as to oblige Japan to take specific action should a third country 'practise hegemony'.190 It was widely assumed, and often confirmed, by PRC politicians that the clause was specifically directed against the Soviet Union.191 However, when the TPF was signed in 1978 the PRC had to accede to Japanese demands for a clause formulated in such a way that 'opposition to hegemony' could not be used to oblige Japan to take specific action, and also designed to than prevent the impression that the TPF was the basis for an anti-Soviet alliance.192 The vagueness of the treaty text as a whole was in stark contrast to the tenacity with which the PRC had pursued the negotiations for more than four years.193

The history of the TPF negotiations has puzzled a number of scholars. If there are no secret clauses, one must conclude that the main effect of the treaty was to be psychological, an expression of an overall willingness to maintain good relations and a common stance towards the Soviet Union and Vietnam. As it was, the treaty was largely a reiteration of the Sino-Japanese joint declaration of September 1972.194 The principle of 'opposition to hegemony' had been included in the Tanaka-Zhou communiqué, but the issue had remained largely dormant during the talks on operational agreements, overshadowed by differences with Japan on relations with the ROC. 'Opposition to hegemony' was raised forcefully in 1974, especially later in the year. As far as the PRC was concerned it became the central issue of the whole TPF, since without the its inclusion, PRC politicians claimed, the treaty would become meaningless.195 It seems hardly accidental that the issue was raised shortly before the conquest of South Vietnam by the North, when politicians in Peking must have been wondering how to counter the increasing influence of North Vietnam in the Southeast Asian peninsula. Again, as already mentioned, in 1978 Peking must have been concerned to hasten the conclusion of the TPF while deliberations were going on concerning military intervention in Vietnam following a Vietnamese invasion of Cambodia.196 Moreover, Peking must have been aware that Japan would find it difficult to sign the TPF, including an 'anti-hegemony' clause *after* a PRC invasion of Vietnam, since this would have virtually amounted to specific endorsement of PRC intervention. This factor may have been the main reason for PRC willingness to accept Japanese insistence on including Article 4 in the Treaty in order to have the TPF come into effect *before* any such intervention. The conclusion of the TPF was followed by the announcement of the establishment of diplomatic relations with the United States. Although these events were not linked there may have been an attempt to create the impression of a budding military relationship among the three countries.197

Besides considerations of strategy and multilateral diplomacy, negotiations towards a TPF were also clearly designed to put pressure on Japanese politicians such as Prime Minister Miki and his foreign minister, Miyazawa.198 The talks stalled repeatedly over political issues which did not seem to affect economic exchanges negatively in the way previous controversies had done. Consequently:

the business community was not involved in the treaty controversy to the extent that it was involved in the politics of Japan's decision to recognise China.199

A further factor complicating the talks was the political turmoil in the PRC before and after the death of Mao Zedong, which seems to have been the direct reason for the virtual interruption of talks during the first nine months of 1976.200

At the same time, the conclusion of operational and other economic agreements had led to a relative depoliticisation of subsequent economic talks, reducing the importance of Liao Chengzhi in the area of more practically orientated talks and negotiations. Throughout the period Liao remained the most prominent of the PRC's Japan specialists, attending countless functions and receiving Japanese delegations, but a mere statistical survey of his activities provides insufficient clues to his importance in the decision-making process. His role becomes somewhat clearer through an examination of the history of TPF negotiations. 1978 was the year in which the succession struggle between Hua Guofeng and Deng Xiaoping was decided in Deng's favour, and which also saw the beginning of a fundamental restructuring of the CCP party organisation as well as government institutions.201 It is only after this that a series of appointments to high party and government positions provides a better idea of Liao's relative standing in the political hierarchy.

Ohira's visit to Peking in January 1974 had achieved a major breakthrough in the stalled talks on an aviation agreement, and although various snags developed in the final stages of talks on this and the remaining operational agreements, there were no further major delays. It was first assumed that talks on the proposed TPF would start only after all operational agreements had been concluded. As early as May, however, there were signs that the PRC wanted to speed up the beginning of such talks, leading the then Japanese foreign minister, Kimura, to declare that talks on the operational agreements and on the TPF could run parallel.202 As already indicated, concern about the situation in Southeast Asia may have influenced this change of attitude. During the same period, Prime Minister Tanaka's position continued to weaken, and there may have been some concern that his successor might be less willing to grant concessions than Tanaka who was also in need of a foreign policy success to bolster his domestic position.203

In addition, Zhou Enlai may have been under pressure to improve relations with Japan at a time when he was under attack during the 'Campaign to Criticise Confucius and Lin Biao'. Even before the Aviation Agreement had come into effect there were hints that the PRC would be prepared to shelve issues such as Taiwan and the dispute over the sovereignty of the Senkaku Islands, held by the Japanese, but also claimed by China.204 Deng had given a clear indication to a delegation under Katsumata Seiichi that TPF talks could take place simultaneously with talks on the remaining operational agreements,205 and negotiations on a TPF began in September 1974 during preliminary talks in New York between Foreign Ministers Kimura and Huang Hua where both were attending a session of the UN General Assembly.206 Formal treaty talks began on 13 November 1974, when Han Nianlong visited Japan to sign the Shipping Agreement.207

Liao had not been deeply involved before November 1974, and it still seemed that negotiations would continue through formal diplomatic channels. The situation changed, however when Miki succeeded Tanaka as Prime Minister in December.[208] In January both sides were still professing considerable optimism concerning early conclusion of a TPF.[209] In that month Hori, a conservative LDP politician, led a delegation to Peking. He had recently changed his attitude to the PRC and Tagawa had played an important role in enabling Hori to visit Peking.[210] The visit took place at the invitation of the PRC government although Hori did not go as a Japanese government representative.[211] The importance attached by the PRC to the mission was also symbolised by the fact that he was the first high-ranking foreign politician received by Deng after his appointment as first among the vice-premiers at the recent meeting of the Fourth NPC, and his election to the vice-chairmanship of the CCP at the second plenum of the Tenth Party Congress. Since Hori was a political opponent within the LDP of Prime Minister Miki it could reasonably be expected that he might make use of pending issues in relations with the PRC to exert domestic political pressure on Miki. Hori met Zhou in hospital but Liao was his most important counterpart, followed by Zhang Xiangshan and Wang Xiaoyun. On returning to Japan Hori reported that the Taiwan 'problem' had not been brought up 'in order not to embarrass a guest'. With regard to the anti-hegemony clause Hori pointed out that apparently Kissinger himself had originally suggested the inclusion of this clause in the 'Shanghai-communiqué'.[212] Subsequently Hori became one of the leading LDP politicians urging Miki to speed up the conclusion of the TPF and, although little is known about the content of his talks in January, they must have influenced his attitude to the anti-hegemony clause as well as the future issue of the re-opening of the Japanese air link with Taiwan.

The first formal meeting of Japanese and PRC negotiators after the exchange of drafts ended on 24 April with no agreement in sight on the 'anti-hegemony' clause.[213] Moves followed by Tanaka, Ohira, Hori and Kono Kenzo to weaken Miki's position.[214] Although Miki had expressed willingness to strive for the conclusion of the TPF before the regular session of the Japanese Parliament ended on 25 May,[215] it soon became clear that he had tried to obtain commitments from the opposition parties not to support the inclusion of the 'anti-hegemony' clause in the treaty.[216] It is not surprising that this domestic situation in Japan provoked an intensification of PRC 'people's diplomacy' to exploit internal divisions.

Peking's next move was made during a visit by JSP leader Narita to Peking in May as a result of which the JSP changed its attitude to the 'anti-hegemony' clause. The overall effect, however, proved counterproductive in Japan.[217] If anything, the visit showed that the PRC would continue to exert pressure on the Japanese government by making use of 'people's diplomacy' outside formal diplomatic channels.[218] Liao played the main role in talks with the JSP delegation. The JSP was still split between pro-Soviet and pro-PRC wings,[219] but in his welcome speech Liao Chengzhi made it clear that opposition to Soviet hegemony would be the focus of the talks. Also rather unusual in a welcome speech was Liao's detailed criticism of the Soviet Union for not being a 'socialist' country.[220]

Enemies Become Friends

The day before Narita arrived Liao met with Japanese parliamentarians, including members of a group within the JSP called 'New Current' (*Atarashii nagare no kai*) who had agreed to 'oppose Soviet hegemonism'.[221] On the same day Ji Dengkui had approved a visit by Foreign Minister Miyazawa to Peking, in a talk with Miyazaki Seimin, but had re-emphasised Peking's inflexibility in its 'anti-hegemony' stance.[222] Right from the start the PRC tried to force a decision on the question of opposition to the Soviet Union even before entering into main talks with the delegations, a somewhat unusual move:[223]

> Sun Pinghua suggested to Kawasaki, secretary of the Narita delegation, that if it was not prepared to accept the Chinese terms, its members might just enjoy a sight-seeing tour in China and return home without a communiqué.[224]

Differences in attitude had been quite clear in the welcome speech delivered by Liao to Narita on 5 May.[225] In talks with Liao on the 8th it seemed as if Narita would not support an anti-Soviet stance, but there were also signs that he might agree to some extent to supporting an anti-hegemony clause.[226] He attempted to avoid the impression of anti-Soviet bias and would not agree to an ideological condemnation of the Soviet Union.[227] Despite some reservations it was clear when Narita and Liao signed the communiqué that there had been an undeniable change in the position of the JSP towards the Soviet Union, certainly as far as opposition to Soviet occupation of Japan's northern islands was concerned.[228] The communiqué did include a reference to the maintenance of relations 'with all countries', but this could hardly be taken to mean that the JSP's basic line was unchanged.[229] The day the communiqué was signed the Japanese government announced the (temporary) recall of Ambassador Ogawa, usually a sign of Japanese government displeasure at Peking's moves.[230] The Japanese government worried that the JSP communiqué would affect negotiations at government level and, as a result of a meeting between Ambassador Ogawa and Miyazawa, it was decided not to pursue negotiations on a TPF for the time being.[231] Despite JSP internal criticism of the communiqué the result was a definite estrangement between the JSP and the Soviet Union.[232]

About a month later Fujiyama Aiichiro visited Peking, where again his major counterpart was Liao Chengzhi.[233] Fujiyama had been in touch with Prime Minister Miki before (and after) the visit. Miki had previously transmitted a compromise suggestion on the anti-hegemony clause (his 'four conditions') through Ambassador Ogawa, but while Foreign Minister Miyazawa acknowledged that an informal PRC reaction had been received it was stressed that the Japanese government was still waiting for an official reply.[234] Miki had made a major concession to include the anti-hegemony clause in the main treaty text provided it was made clear that it was a principle directed against no country in particular.[235] Liao subsequently made it clear that the PRC considered this concession insufficient.[236] Moreover, in a meeting with Fujiyama, Zhou Enlai had emphasised that Miki's previous message had already been answered through Han Nianlong.[236]

The situation was certainly confused, to a considerable extent as a result of conducting talks in parallel, through official and unofficial channels. Liao had been deeply involved in indirect contacts with the Japanese government on the issue of the anti-hegemony clause, but as a Chairman of the CJFA and not a PRC government representative. Since Liao's statements could not be regarded as formal government statements, the PRC could continue to be inflexible towards Miki without having to bear the responsibility for frustrating talks at government level. At that stage, direct contact through official channels did not function smoothly, as shown by the discussion on whether the PRC government had replied officially to Miki's compromise proposal. Miki's next step was to bypass formal channels and ask Kawasaki Hideji to carry a handwritten memo addressed to Zhou Enlai.238 When Kawasaki met Liao on 24 June he promised to transmit Miki's five-point memo to Zhou. The reply to Miki's message was given in the form of a statement by Liao Chengzhi, publicly announced by Kawasaki at an airport press conference after Kawasaki's talks with Liao and other PRC politicians.239 On returning to Tokyo Kawasaki reported Liao's reaction to the effect that Miki's efforts were appreciated but the memo was vague on 'anti-hegemonism', and the clause would have to be inserted in the main text. Kawasaki added that there had been no direct reply from Zhou but that Liao's reaction was, in fact, an official reply.240 Miki's message entrusted to Kawasaki had been transmitted 'formally', but again to what extent Liao's reaction was to be taken as remained somewhat ambiguous. Hardly surprising, then, that the Japanese concluded that 'from now on, professional diplomats would have to work through formal routes'.241

Most likely the PRC was not in a mood for compromise at that juncture. Throughout 1975 talks had been going on between Japan and Taiwan on resuming the air link, broken off after the signinng of the Aviation Agreement with the PRC the previous year. Civil aviation links between Japan and Taiwan were restored on 10 July.242 Shortly before Foreign Minister Miyazawa had issued an ambiguous statement concerning the status of the ROC flag as a 'national flag'.243 Liao criticised this statement in an interview with a reporter of the *Nihon keizai shinbun*:

> Miyazawa has made a statement in which he acknowledged that the (ROC) blue and white flag is a national flag. Does he really assume that this will not affect Sino-Japanese relations? It really is putting a 'two-China' [policy] into practice. There is no one in China who is not indignant. It can't be denied that Miki knew about this . It shows that [they] tried to handle the TPF and relations with Taiwan as one whole. Which country's flag would ... Miyazawa ... have acknowledged? Miyazawa's statement can be summarised in the following three points:
> 1) it tramples on the joint communiqué (of 1972);
> 2) it reflects a 'two-China' policy;
> 3) it begins with an assumption that reflects the opinions of the anti-China group.
> I don't think that people with common sense, ... Japanese citizens, intellectuals and politicians can be expected to let this happen.244

While Liao's reaction was an expression of a cooling-off of relations with Japan, it was a statement which the Japanese side interpreted:

'apparently correctly, as statements for the record, which would not be followed by any retaliatory action.245
Liao's initial comment was later followed by a similar statement from Deng Xiaoping to other Japanese visitors.246

PRC relations with Japan in other areas were hardly affected by these developments but further efforts of the Miki cabinet concerning the TPF remained fruitless. On 24 September Miyazawa met PRC Foreign Minister Qiao Guanhua in New York without reaching agreement. Miyazawa offered to accept the anti-hegemony provision if the PRC would accept four conditions concerning the interpretation of the clause (the 'Miyazawa conditions').247 Miki also sent former Foreign Minister Kosaka Zentaro as his emissary to Peking but, in a meeting with Kosaka on 3 October, Deng criticised the attitude of Miki and Miyazawa.248

The situation became further complicated by the intensification of the power struggle in Peking. Zhou Enlai's death on 8 January 1976, was followed by the fall of Deng Xiaoping, and an anti-rightist campaign during the first months of 1976. This was obviously not an opportune time to undertake new initiatives, all the more since the Japanese political world was rocked in February by the so-called 'Lockheed scandal'. One of the few moves undertaken during this period was a visit to Peking in June 1976 by Fujiyama, where he had confidential talks with Hua Guofeng and Liao Chengzhi concerning the strengthening of economic ties and the TPF.249 It goes without saying that although Liao's direct influence on decision-making may have been greatly reduced during this period, in public at least, he continued to appear in his customary role as the PRC's leading Japan specialist.250

A low point was reached in relations between the PRC and Japan when the PRC took exception to remarks by Miyazawa about the desirability of the security link between the ROC and the USA.251 Several developments in the latter part of 1976 augured the possibility of improvement in relations. In Peking, Mao's death was followed by the arrest of his widow and numerous 'leftists'. Although the struggle for succession continued, mainly between Hua Guofeng and adherents of Deng Xiaoping, himself still in political disgrace, there was a new sense of stability. At the same time Japan's relations with the Soviet Union started to deteriorate considerably, a development obviously welcome to the PRC.252 In Japan, Foreign Minister Miyazawa, who shortly before had visited Peking on a mission for Miki, was replaced by Kosaka Zentaro. In an address to the UN General Assembly Kosaka set out his country's foreign policy position containing a passage which roughly paralleled the PRC's position on the 'anti-hegemony' question.

Throughout 1977 the Japanese government seemed to be vacillating, especially under Miki's successor, Fukuda. At the beginning of January 1977 Kono Kenzo visited Peking, carrying a private letter from Fukuda to Hua Guofeng.253 The immediate response did not seem very encouraging. He was received by Liao Chengzhi, who appeared quite forceful, telling Kono that the PRC 'absolutely would not allow any backsliding' from its previous position. The TPF had also been a topic during talks between Fujiyama and various PRC politicians, including Liao.254 In April Liao received a delegation of young members of the Tanaka faction of the LDP led by former Deputy Chief Cabinet Secretary Yamashita Ganri. The invitation had first been issued in October 1976 during a meeting between Kuno Chuji and Liao, and was a clear attempt to urge the Fukuda cabinet to accept the PRC point of view concerning the TPF.255

For some time in May it seemed that Fukuda himself would tackle the 'anti-hegemony' question in a 'forward-looking' way, only to be seen as backing down somewhat soon afterwards.256 Factional manoeuvres were certainly of importance in Japanese foreign policy decision-making, but it should not be overlooked that other factors, such as Japan's relations with the United States and the Soviet Union also exercised a major influence. Fukuda's vacillation around May indeed was exploited by his political opponents as indecision, but most likely was due to considerations concerning current Japanese negotiations with the USSR on a fisheries agreement. Yet neither Fukuda's moves, nor the attempt by Takeiri Yoshikatsu, who led the fifth delegation of the Komeito to Peking in early spring 1977, led to an early resumption of formal talks on a TPF. Liao was involved in these and other talks, but published sources give little precise information about his role.257 On the surface, the dogged pursuit of the TPF left no room for conciliation with the Soviet Union. In December Liao told a group of Japanese Dietmen that the PRC did not intend to renew the friendship treaty with the Soviet Union.258 With the benefit of hindsight it is interesting to note that only a short time later in 1978, Peking's Sino-Soviet Friendship Association was resuscitated259 but it seems unlikely that Liao's visit to Rumania and Yugoslavia in May 1977 had anything to do with first explorations on a new set of relations with Soviet satellite states.260

Despite the apparent stalemate on the TPF it would be wrong to overlook important developments in relations that took place in other areas. April was the starting point for visits to Peking by Japanese involved in military affairs, who were also received by Liao. If anything, such visits indicated that 'political obstacles' to a rapid conclusion of a TPF would not prevent further improvement in PRC relations with Japan. It is tempting to argue that, in 1977, the continuing succession struggle between the then Party Chairman Hua and his challengers, in particular Deng may have heightened PRC inflexibility in matters of formal foreign policy. There were some indications that domestic tensions before the National People's Congress scheduled for February 1978 also contributed to lack of progress on the road towards a Treaty of Peace and Friendship.261 To all appearances the power struggle was decided only in the second half of 1978. There were some signs, however, that basic decisions on a reorientation of foreign policy towards more active co-operation with non-Communist countries had been adopted earlier.

Changes in Overseas Chinese policy often give valuable indicators for changes in the PRC foreign policy line. As of late 1977 there were numerous signs that the PRC was to restore its complete Overseas Chinese policy bureaucracy which had been virtually out of operation since the beginning of the Cultural Revolution.262 In February 1978 Liao was appointed head of the newly re-established Overseas Chinese Affairs Office and was also involved in the affairs of Jinan University for Overseas Chinese students.263 In the same year he was appointed to several other high offices in the PRC government, most important being as Vice-Chairman of the Fifth NPC Standing Committee, also in February-March 1978.[264]

The change in Overseas Chinese policy was soon followed by indications in mid-February of a softer stand concerning the anti-hegemony clause in discussions with Japan. One may argue that the conclusion of a long-term semi-private trade agreement with Japan at that time may have helped to contribute to a more conciliatory position on the anti-hegemony clause but it is difficult to establish a direct link between the two agreements.[265] As in previous years a 'private' visit by a Japanese politician was used to reinitiate a dialogue at government level on a TPF, when Yano Junya, Secretary-General of the Komeito, led a delegation to the PRC. In a way reminiscent of the involvement of non-government representatives in the negotiations leading up to the establishment of diplomatic relations Yano held extensive talks with PRC politicians on the TPF.[266] It was reported that Liao handed Yano a four-point statement described as being from Deng Xiaoping and addressed to the Japanese Prime Minister.[267] Yano's talks confirmed the PRC negotiating position as set out shortly before to Japanese diplomats in Peking in a series of confidential talks. Further immediate progress towards the conclusion of a TPF were however unexpectedly frustrated by the so-called 'Senkaku Incident'.

Japan and the PRC had previously agreed to shelve the question of sovereignty over the Senkaku (Diaoyutai) Islands. Apparently in response to moves by some LDP politicians, who wished to support Japanese claims by expanding the Japanese presence on the islands, a flotilla of armed Chinese fishing boats approached the islands. The move was no more than a demonstration of counterclaims, but it led to a momentary flare-up of nationalist feeling in Japan and the PRC. It has been suggested that the dispatch of this flotilla had been initiated by opponents of the new line in Peking, to frustrate further *rapprochement* between the PRC and Japan, but available sources do not yet permit an unambiguous interpretation of the incident. Most noteworthy here is the fact that, throughout the crisis, Liao, more than any other PRC politician, tried to play down the seriousness of the incident, virtually promising to 'prevent conflicts caused by Chinese fishing boats'.

Liao's words contrasted somewhat with Deng's whose statements at times show a certain undiplomatic flippancy. Both Vice-Premier Geng Biao and Liao had given assurances to the Japanese but, it should be emphasised, not in the form of official declarations binding on the PRC under International Law.[268] The Senkaku Incident settled, there were further signs of progress, corroborated to the Japanese by US presidential adviser Brzezinski who had visited Peking.[269] When Fukuda proposed a resumption of formal treaty talks it was Liao who in a meeting with members of the New Liberal Club in Peking in June issued the first reaction from a leading PRC politician.[270] Hori's visit to Peking indicated further progress,[271] and five weeks later Foreign Minister Sonoda was able to announce the reopening of formal talks.[272] This was taken as an indication that both sides were by now confident that remaining differences could be solved in the near future.

There were several factors enabling Liao to increase his political weight. In the sixties he had been engaged in the PRC's struggle against 'Soviet revisionism' in meetings of international front organisations, in Overseas Chinese policy, and in PRC relations with Japan. Since his rehabilitation in the early seventies his activities had been mainly limited to Japan. The emergence of tensions with Vietnam meant that it became imperative for the PRC to put relations with the USA and Japan on a firm basis before taking military action against Vietnam.[273]

Throughout 1978, the position of Overseas Chinese in Vietnam (the Hoa) became more difficult. As Head of the Overseas Chinese Affairs Office Liao was closely involved in policy towards Vietnam, while the Vietnamese 'question' also exercised its influence on relations with Japan.[274] It seems reasonable to assume that Liao would have taken part in foreign policy deliberations in high-level party committees beyond the narrow confines of a 'Japan committee' or the OCAC.

According to Tretiak Liao played a major role in the decisive stage of the TPF negotiations,[275] but it is not always easy to detail his precise role. Shortly before the final stage of the negotiations in August 1978 an incident occurred when Zhang Xiangshan purposely leaked details of a meeting between Nikaido Susumu, Deng Xiaoping and Liao Chengzhi in October 1977, with the aim of prodding the Japanese towards a rapid conclusion of the treaty.[276] There is little information about Liao's position during these talks but his presence underlined his status as the PRC's foremost Japan specialist. After the reopening of negotiations had been formally proposed in May, talks were subsequently conducted through formal diplomatic channels.[277] Some Japanese observers continued to appreciate the TPF as a means of fostering bilateral relations, particularly trade.[278] A Foreign Ministry document obtained by the Sankei newspaper confirmed, however, that as far as the PRC was concerned political motives outweighed economic considerations.[279] In addition, Ito, head of the Japanese Defence Agency, stated that 'militarily, it (the TPF) is a plus point for Japan's security'.[280] Japan's largest newspaper, the *Asahi shinbun* also drew a link between the concluding of the TPF in August and Deng's planned visit to Thailand and Pham Van Dong's visit to ASEAN countries, thus emphasising the implications of this treaty for global strategy. Although business leaders welcomed the treaty and its possible stimulating effect on trade there were also some critical voices.[281] When the TPF was initialled in Peking in August it was agreed that it should be signed during a visit to Tokyo of Deng Xiaoping, accompanied by Liao Chengzhi.[282] The visit took place in October 1978 and had a largely ceremonial character, also showing Liao in the limelight again.[283] During the visit Liao copied a poem by Zhou Enlai in his own calligraphic style; during his visit to Japan in April of the next year the unveiling took place of a boulder inscribed according to Liao's calligraphic design and placed in a park in the Arashiyama Hills near Kyoto.[284] On returning to Peking Liao presented a report to the NPC on 4 November 1978 on the visit of the Deng delegation.[285] Several reports appeared indicating an impaired state of health, but his condition still seemed to be satisfactory.[286]

Notes to Chapter Six

1. See also Furui's reaction to the revelation of Peking's confidential contacts with Peking since 1969, in *Nitchu juhachinen*, p 50.
2. R Clough, 'The Taiwan Issue in Sino-American Relations', in Barnds, *China and America*, p 158; Barnett, *China and the Major Powers in East Asia*, p 110.
3. Fukui, 'Tanaka goes to Peking'.
4. J Garver, 'Chinese Foreign Policy in 1970: The Tilt Towards the Soviet Union', *China Quarterly*, (June 1980), passim; Akioka, *Tokuhain*, pp 56 and 182.
5. R G Brown, 'Chinese Politics and American Policy: A New Look at the Triangle', *Foreign Policy*, 23 (Summer 1976), pp 9-10.
6. *Chugoku no kakyo seisaku*, Naikaku kanbo. Naikaku chosashitsu comp (April 1974), pp 63, 70 ff.
7. *Dalu qingshi fenxi huibian*, pp 159, 222, 224, 270 and 638-9. *Zhonggong dui huaqiao*, pp 11, 26 and 31; *Dangzheng zhuanji*, p 381. See also J Taylor, *China and Southeast Asia. Peking's Relations with Revolutionary Movements*, (Praeger, 1974), [Praeger Special Studies in International Politics and Government], p 249.
8. *Ibid*, pp 161, 554 ff; *Chugoku no kakyo seisaku*, pp 63 ff. There was no formal 'rehabilitation' yet of government organisations dealing with Overseas Chinese affairs, but the PRC was paying increasing attention to these. The establishment of formal relations with Japan, and limited formal relations with the US facilitated approaches to Overseas Chinese there and elsewhere (*Asahi shinbun*, 7 May 1973, *Dalu qingshi fenxi huibian*, 1973, pp 208 f); in 1972 Zhou had met Overseas Chinese leaders in Peking, as reported in *Huaqiaobao* (*Dagongbao*, 25 April 1973).
9. Furui, *Nitchu juhachinen*, pp 100 ff.
10. Shibauchi Tadashi, 'Haken mondai to tsunahiki sareru Nihon', *Chuo koron*, (July 1975), p 155; Tagawa Goro, *Chugoku arinomama hokoku*, (1980), pp 182-3. Also *PD*, editorial, 18 September 1971, and previous attacks for example on 11, 16 and 20 June 1970. As during the late fifties, Japan's role in Southeast Asia was also attacked (J Glaubitz, 'Balancing Between Adversaries: Sino-Japanese Relations and Soviet Interference', *Pacific community*, IX.1 (October 1977), p 40).
11. As a protest against Sato's policies the position of head of the LT office in Tokyo had been left vacant for some time, with a relatively young official temporarily in charge but soon after Sato's resignation Xiao Xiangqian arrived in Tokyo to assume leadership (*Nitchu yuko undoshi*, p 166).
12. Yu-hsi Nieh, 'Hintergründe des chinesisch-japanischen Inselstreits', *China Aktuell*, (May 1978), p 280. Zhang Aizhe, *Gongfei dui haiwai huaqiao*, 1971, p 10. H C Hinton, *The China Sea: The American Stake in Its Future*, (New York, 1980), [Agenda Paper No 12], p 14.
13. Akioka, *op cit*, pp 196, 200-1 and 221.
14. Akioka, *op cit*, pp 205 and 142-3; Furui, *Nitchu juhachinen*, pp 216 and 213. See also *Asahi shinbun*, 3 March 1971, and *Nihon keizai shinbun*, 10 March 1971.
15. O Weggel, 'Die Volksbefreiungsarmee: Fraktionsstreitigkeiten, Krise des Selbstverständnisses und Heilungsversuche zu ihrer Überwindung', *China Aktuell*, (March 1981), p 185. An early indication of the problems faced by the foreign service during the early seventies was the need for Zhou and others to exercise 'self-criticism' during a conference with PRC ambassadors abroad who had been temporarily recalled (Arai, *Shu Onrai no jissen*, pp 184-5).
16. Akioka, *op cit*, p 199.

17 'Shu Onrai kokusai josei ni kansuru himitsu enzetsu' *Chuo koron* (November 1976), pp 161-74, containing the text of a confidential intra-party speech on foreign relations by Zhou Enlai. See also 'A Study of "On Policy"', *Peking Review*, (27 August 1978), p 13. R Wich, 'The Tenth Party Congress: The Power Structure and the Succession Question', *China Quarterly* 58 (April-June 1974), pp 246-7. *Dalu qingshi fenxi huibian*, 1971, pp 380 f. Akioka, *op cit*, p 97, *Dalu qingshi fenxi huibian*, pp 430 f.

18 Liao was also one of the first Chinese officials to talk publicly on the Lin Biao affair on 20 August 1972 (*Kokusai nenpo 1972*, p 168.

19 *Asahi shinbun*, 11 June 1983.

20 Fukui, 'Tanaka goes to Peking', and *Zhonggong dui huaqiao*, p 11.

21 Akioka, *op cit*, p 211. Wang Xiaoyun had secretly met Mikasa, the Emperor's younger brother, *Dalu qingshi fenxi huibian*, p 335.

22 *Asahi Evening News*, 25 June 1970, and Akioka, *op cit*, p 219.

23 Zhang, *Liao Chengzhi*, p 76, and *URS Biographical Service*.

24 Tagawa, *Matsumura*, p 154.

25 It seems that Utsunomiya Tokuma was the first Japanese to meet Liao again in his home. Akioka, *op cit*, pp 145-6.

26 Akioka, *op cit*, pp 114-5.

27 Tagawa, *Nitchu kosho hiroku*, p 317.

28 *Ibid*, pp 318-9. 322. Liao was said to be too ill to appear at the signing ceremony for the MT communiqué on 1 March 1971 (Akioka, *Pekin tokuhain*, pp 205, 142-3). Also Furui, *Nitchu juhachinen*, p 213, and *Asahi shinbun*, 3 March 1971; *Nihon keizai shinbun*, 10 March 1971.

29 Liao Yiyuan, in *Liaogong zai renjian*, p 107.

30 See for instance the photo showing Liao in a flight simulator during his visit to Japan in 1973, *Liao Chengzhi de yisheng*, p 93.

31 Shibauchi, p 1769.

32 This is shown by an analysis of reports of meetings with various delegations during this period; an LDP delegation in April; Miki's visit in the same month; delegations by *Yomiuri shinbun* and the Komeito, and Furui's visit in May; visits by Sasaki and Takeiri in July, and Kosaka in September.

33 According to Akioka, *op cit*, p 208, Wang fell ill shortly before the formalisation of relations between Tokyo and Peking.

34 As confirmed by the following account Liao did not yet take part in Central Committee meetings, for instance: 'My deep friendship with Liao dates from the period of the Cultural Revolution. In 1970 Wang Jiaxiang was persecuted by Lin Biao and Kang Sheng ... Wang Jiaxiang and Liao had been for a long time comrades in arms working together in foreign affairs. Now that they stayed in the same hospital ... they could not even see and talk to each other freely. When the situation had somewhat improved, Liao and his wife one day came to the place where we were staying. They had just sat down when a beaming smile appeared on his face and he said to Jiaxiang: "At the third plenum (ie the third plenum of the 9th CC in 1972) yesterday Prime Minister Zhou transmitted Chairman Mao's high estimation of your life's achievement ... when beardy Wang (Wang Zhen's nickname) heard it he asked me to tell you this immediately...' Zhu Zha (Wang Jiaxiang's wife), in *Liaogong zai renjian*, p 57. Liao's absence from the Central Committee makes it likely that at least during the early seventies his involvement in CCP foreign relations committees was limited, although he was Head of the Beijing Institute of Foreign Languages

(Beijing waiguoyu xueyuan) and so linked to the diplomatic apparatus (*Jingji ribao*, 24 June 1983).
35. See also Ohara Shinichiro, 'Junan ni natta ga gensoku wa magezu' in *Sekai shuho*, (13 June 1972), pp 64-8, and Furui, *Nitchu juhachinen*, p 235.
36. Fukui, 'Tanaka goes to Peking', p 16. In dealing with this period I have drawn extensively on this study by Fukui and Lee, *Japan Faces China*, pp 106 ff.
37. D Tretiak, 'Who Makes Chinese Foreign Policy Today (Late 1980)', *The Australian Journal of Chinese Affairs* 5 (1981), p 145.
38. Lee, *op cit*, pp 116-7, 121. Also *Dalu qingshi fenxi huibian*, p 335; *Nitchu juhachinen*, pp 237 f.
39. See also *Nitchu yuko undoshi*, p 185.
40. Fukui, 'Tanaka goes to Peking', p 24.
41. Zhang Tianxing, 'Wei wujie renda changweihui fuweiyuanzhang Liao Chengzhi', *Feiqing yuebao* 3, p 78.
42. The negative forms in 'yurushimasumai' and 'yuki wa nai desho' have both been translated as 'won't'.
43. Ryo Shoshi, 'Chugoku no tainichi seisaku to gaiko seisaku' in *Ajia keizai junpo* 872 (August 1972, chu), pp 12-16.
44. The LDP was not pleased that the PRC turned to Furui, Fujiyama, Tagawa and Matsumoto (see also Fukui, 'Tanaka goes to Peking', p 26). On Liao's participation in the negotiations with Furui in September, see Furui, *Nitchu juhachinen*, pp 124 ff and *Kokusai nenpo 1973*, p 168.
45. Furui, *Nitchu juhachinen*, pp 123 ff, 235. See also Tagawa, *Nitchu kosho hiroku*, pp 356 ff.
46. Furui, *Nitchu juhachinen*, pp 124 ff.
47. Lee states: 'Just as Chou En-lai bypassed his Ministry of Foreign Affairs and used Liao Cheng-chih and other nonofficial experts of Japanese affairs, who often conducted preliminary diplomatic negotiations with their Japanese counterparts in Japanese, Tanaka and Oohira relied more heavily on their personal emissaries than on senior governmental bureaucrats, for they did not have a high opinion of policy innovation albeit technical expertise, among the ranking officials in the Japanese Ministry of Foreign Affairs' (*Japan Faces China*, p 119). This argument ignores the fundamental difference between China's 'people's diplomacy' and Japanese foreign policy making with its interplay of officials, factions, and parties (as well as business), since the PRC Foreign Ministry, so to speak, has always been bypassed by the relevant CCP committees.
48. Tagawa, *Nitchu kosho hiroku*, pp 371 ff.
49. Lee, *Japan Faces China*, pp 122-3.
50. *Ibid*, p 131.
51. *Kokusai nenpo 1974*, p 104.
52. See Zhou Enlai's confidential intra-party speech of March 1973, in 'Shu Onrai kokusai josen ni kansuru nimitsu enzetsu'.
53. Following internal policy deliberations a two day conference of PRC ambassadors abroad was called in August 1972, Arai, *Shu Onrai no jissen*, p 184.
54. Barnett, *China and the Major Powers in East Asia*, p 115, notes 86, 97. C T Hsüeh, *Dimensions of China's Foreign Relations*, (Praeger 1977), p 11; A M Halpern, 'China and Japan since Normalisation', p 11; *Yomiuri shinbun*, 18 January 1973 (*yukan*); *Sankei shinbun* and *Asahi shinbun*, 29 January 1973; *Mainichi shinbun*, 17 December 1973; *Dalu qingshi fenxi huibian*,

1973, pp 66-8; Akioka, *op cit*, p 181; Shu Onrai, 'Kokusai josei ni kansuru himitsu enzetsu', p 175; Uchida, 'Legal Aspects of Japan-China Trade', p 69.

55 'Ryo daihyodan, Nihon taizai no ikkagetsu', p 97.

56 *Zhonggong dui huaqiao*, pp 10 f.

57 For English translations of the speeches by Liao and Fu Tso-yi, see *The Twenty-Sixth Anniversary of the 'February 28' Uprising of the People of Taiwan Province*, Foreign Languages Press, (Peking, 1973); see also *Peking Shuho*, 15 (1973), and *Dalu qingshi fenxi huibian*, pp 138-9.

58 *Yomiuri shinbun*, 12 March 1973. See also J Domes, *China nach der Kulturrevolution*, (München, 1975), p 312, and *Osteuropa*, XXIII no 5, p 335. E Von Gröling and M-L Näth, *Die Aussenpolitik Chinas*, (München-Wien, 1975), p 25. R N Clough, 'Sino-Japanese Relations: A New Era?', *Current History* 65 (no 385) (September 1973), p 110.

59 At the airport to send the delegation off were Li Xiannian, Deng Xiaoping, Guo Moruo, Wu De, Fu Tso-yi and others. Apparently it was Deng's first function after rehabilitation except for a meeting with Sihanouk, underlining the PRC's intention to present a new image. *Asahi shinbun*, 16 April 1973 and *Nihon keizai shinbun*, 16 April 1973. Japanese Ambassador Ogawa describing the farewell said that Li Xiannian was then the vice-premier with real clout. Ogawa was probably the second foreigner to meet Deng after reinstatement, (Ogawa, *Pekin no yonen*, pp 25-6).

60 *Nihon keizai shinbun*, 30 April 1973; *Asahi shinbun*, 15 April 1973; *Yomiuri shinbun*, 17 April 1973.

61 Among others, *Asahi shinbun*, 22 January 1973 (*yukan*). *Far Eastern Economic Review*, 23 April 1973 and R K Jain, *China and Japan, 1949-1976*, pp 117, 122. 'Amongst the objectives were restraining the Soviet Union and efforts towards the "liberation of Taiwan"', *Nihon keizai shinbun*, 30 April 1973; *Asahi shinbun*, 15 April 1973. Zhou summarised these points in an intra-party speech on foreign relations ('Shu Onrai kokusai josei ni kansuru himitsu enzetsu', pp 161 f). The delegation coincided with Soviet moves to strengthen links with Japan. Before the Liao visit exchanges of letters between the highest leaders and other contacts had shown a Soviet wish to increase contacts with the Japanese and it was also expected that Liao would carry private letters from Ji Pengfei and Zhou (*Nihon keizai shinbun*, 20 April 1973, yukan). The day after Tanaka's letter was delivered to Brezhnev (7 March) Zhou announced the dispatch to Tokyo of a Liao mission (Nakamura Koji 'Treading the Siberian tightrope', *Far Eastern Economic Review*, 14 May 1973).

62 See Liao's talk to Overseas Chinese merchants in Osaka on 29 April which contained a warning to Taiwan not to play the Soviet card (*Asahi shinbun*, 30 April 1973).

63 'Ryo kaihyodan, Nihon taizai no ikkagetsu', in *Asahi janaru* (18 May 1973), p 97. For a chronology of Liao's visit see *Ajia keizai junpo* 902 (June 1973, chu), pp 28 ff; *Chugoku geppo*, nos 174-5. See also *Dalu qingshi fenxi huibian*, 1973, pp 237-47, 258-65 and 324-8. For further general reports on the visit see *Asahi janaru*, 18 May 1973, pp 97-9, and 'Yuko o miyage ni Chugoku daihyodan kikoku', in *Sekai shuho*, 5 June 1973, pp 10 ff.

64 After Nakae Yosuke had stated as recently as March that regular negotiations would be continued through diplomatic channels (*Yomiuri shinbun*, 20 March 1973) some observers wondered whether the delegation's contacts with government members were too frequent (*Yomiuri shinbun*, 22 April 1973). While the mission was generally regarded a 'diplomatic event', (*Mainichi shinbun*, 15 April 1973), Liao was at pains to maintain its informal character (*Shinano Mainichi*,

23 April 1973). The need to maintain a number of channels in addition to the normal diplomatic route was also emphasised by vice-premier Li Xiannian (*Asahi shinbun*, 18 March 1973).

65 After normalisation, the expected high level contact did not occur, although it appeared that the Chinese side must have been starving for it, *Sekai shuho*, 22 January 1974, pp 30-1.

66 'Oohira hochu koku kyotei no zenshin o kakunin', p 30 f. At the talks in 1972 Tanaka and Zhou agreed to begin with the Aviation Agreement, due to its symbolic and practical significance. Tadokoro Takehiko, 'Ichinen no kiseki to kongo no mondai (tokushu. Nitchu seijoka no ichinen [1])', *Ajia rebiyu* (March 1973), p 12. See also *Yomiuri shinbun*, 14 May 1973, and *Sankei shinbun*, 21 May 1973.

67 Ji Pengfei stated that it would be impossible to have PRC and Taiwan planes together at Haneda. The Japanese draft aviation agreement did not refer to the air link with Taiwan (*Asahi shinbun*, 12 and 18 March 1973, and Tadokoro, 'Ichinen no kiseki', p 13). A proposal floated towards the end of the year would have entailed the replacement of all other links by a connection between Okinawa and Taipei, *Asahi shinbun*, 6 and 21 December 1972.

68 Tadokoro Takehiko, 'Ichinen no kiseki to kongo no mondai', p 12.

69 Ibid.

70 *Asahi shinbun*, 12 March 1973.

71 *Yomiuri shinbun*, 5 May 1973.

72 *Dalu qingshi fenxi huibian*, 1973, p 66-8. See also Uchida, 'Legal Aspects of Japan-China Trade', p 69; *Asahi shinbun*, 18 (*yukan*), 19, 19 (*yukan*), 20, 20 (*yukan*), 21 and 22 January 1973. There were even doubts whether the sending of the Nakasone-Inayama mission at that stage was premature (*Asahi shinbun*, 22 January 1973 (*yukan*)). Hopes were raised for technological co-operation in oil exploration, one of the means to reduce Japanese interest in co-operation with the USSR (*ibid*). For some time there seemed to be prospects for a Chinese delegation to visit Japan in March or April led by politicians such as Liu Xiwen, Bai Xiangguo or Li Qiang (*Asahi shinbun*, 22 January 1973 (*yukan*)).

73 'In early 1973 Chou En-lai told Takeo Kimura that "Inasmuch as Japan constitutes a nation, weapons of self-defence are essential to it." Not long thereafter, Liao Cheng-chih stated: "I cannot support the US-Japan Security Treaty structure but its functions directed toward China have already lost substance, and we will not take particular issue with it ... Japan will probably have to rely on America's nuclear umbrella for some time to come."' Barnett, *China and the Major Powers in East Asia*, p 115. *Yomiuri shinbun*, 18 January 1973 (*yukan*); *Yomiuri shinbun*, 22 January 1973, 27 January 1973 (Takeo Kimura's account); *Sankei shinbun*, 29 January 1973; *Asahi shinbun*, 16 October; *Mainichi shinbun*, 17 December 1973.

74 *Asahi shinbun*, 10 and 12 March 1973. One of the main objections was not so much the existence of an air link, but the link with the treaty between Japan and the ROC. The Japanese negotiating team was not authorised to deal with the formal-legal aspects of the Taiwan question (*Nihon keizai shinbun*, 16 March 1973).

75 *Yomiuri shinbun*, 17 March 1973.

76 *Nihon keizai shinbun*, 16 April 1973.

77 For further details, see *Dalu qingshi fenxi huibian*, 1973, pp 65 f and 207, and Lee, *Japan Faces China*, p 131. Wang Guoquan would have been a serious candidate for the position of ambassador had he not fallen ill (Akioka, *Pekin tokuhain*, p 208).

78 'Ryo daihyodan. Nihon taizai ni ikkagetsu', p 97.

79 *Asahi shinbun*, 18 March 1973. Nakae Yosuke, a high-ranking foreign affairs official stated that regular negotiations would continue through diplomatic channels (*Yomiuri shinbun*, 20 March 1973).
80 *Nihon keizai shinbun*, 17 April 1986. 'Ryo daihyodan, Nihon taizai no ikkagetsu', p 96. *Yomiuri shinbun*, 22 April; *Mainichi shinbun*, 15 April 1973; *Shinano Mainichi*, 23 April 1973.
81 *Mainichi shinbun*, 15 April 1973.
82 'Ryo daihyodan. Nihon taizai no ikkagetsu', p 95.
83 On Zhang Xiangshan's role in liaison with the JCP, see Nakamura Koji, 'The Wedge Drivers', in *Far Eastern Economic Review*, 23 April 1973, and *Asahi shinbun*, 21 January 1976.
84 *Yamato shinbun*, 16 May 1973. 'Ryo daihyodan. Nihon taizai no ikkagetsu', p 95.
85 A *Dagongbao* article of 22 April quoted Japanese observers approvingly who wished to keep Japan from too close contacts with the Soviet Union.
86 *Asahi shinbun*, 22 January and 12 March 1973.
87 *Mainichi shinbun* and *Asahi shinbun*, 15 April 1986.
88 Nakamura Koji, 'The Wedge Drivers', in *Far Eastern Economic Review*, 23 April 1973; Nakamura, 'China Wedge', in *Far Eastern Economic Review*, 28 May 1973. See also *Asahi shinbun*, 16 April 1973.
89 *Asahi shinbun*, 16 April 1973.
90 In an interview Sun Pinghua denied that the mission's aim included political functions beyond 'friendship' (*Nihon keizai shinbun*, 17 April 1973).
91 *Mainichi shinbun*, 18 April 1973.
92 'Ryo daihyodan, Nihon taizai no ikkagetsu', p 98.
93 See the attack on the Soviet Union published in *Dagongbao* on 22 April 1973.
94 *Akahata*, 23 May 1973, according to *Daily Summary of the Japanese Press*, and *Asahi shinbun*, 21 May 1973.
95 *Asahi shinbun*, 30 April 1986. 'Ryo daihyodan. Nihon taizai no ikkagetsu', p 98.
96 *Ibid.*
97 Kyodo, 2 May 1973, in *SWB*.
98 *Dagongbao*, 30 April 1973; *Yomiuri shinbun*, 17 May 1973; *Nihon keizai shinbun*, 17 May 1973, and *Yomiuri shinbun*, 10 (*yukan*) and 17 May 1973. 'In Kitakyushu, Ma Chunku said to Japanese workers that workers' struggles will progress by fighting revisionists and Rightwing opportunists.' Observers interpreted Ma's remark as an indirect criticism of the JCP. (*SWB*, Kyodo, 4 May 1973).
99 *Asahi shinbun*, 21 May; *Mainichi shinbun*, 4 May 1973 (*yukan*).
100 *Pravda*, 11 and 16 May ('Provokatsionnye vylaski'), 1973. *Shinano Mainichi*, 17 May and *Asahi shinbun*, 21 May 1973.
101 *Asahi shinbun*, 21 May 1973.
102 *Asahi shinbun*, 19 May and 12 March 1973. See also *Asahi shinbun*, 22 January 1973. Liao had also referred to the Soviet Union in his interview in March (*Yomiuri shinbun*, 12 March 1973), as China's greatest and treacherous enemy. The proposed oil pipeline from Tyumen would help supply Soviet aircraft and tanks invading China, and with this in mind, (China) would have to take considerable countermeasures. He reminded the Japanese, that co-operation would leave China with 'bitter feelings' towards Japan. See also Jain, *China and Japan*, pp 117 and 122.
103 'Shu Onrai kokusai josei ni kansuru himitsu enzetsu'.

Enemies Become Friends

104 *Asahi shinbun*, 19 May 1973.
105 *Ibid*, 7 May 1973.
106 *Dalu qingshi fenxi huibian*, 1973, pp 208 f; K C Chen, 'Peking's Attitude Toward Taiwan', *Asian Survey* XVII.10 (October 1977), p 903-18; *Asahi shinbun*, 21 May 1973; the delegation concentrated on a wide alliance rather than on confronting the Taiwan faction (*Nihon keizai shinbun*, 29 April). 'Direct contacts between these mission members and their immediate relatives and friends have greater persuasion among the Chinese merchants' circles in Japan than the Japanese people can imagine (*Asahi shinbun*, 13 May 1973; see also *Shinano Mainichi*, 14 May, *Yomiuri shinbun*, 13 May 1973). 'One of the factors of pressure on Japan was the fear that the PRC might revive propaganda against 'revival of Japanese militarism' and one could not exclude an anti-Japanese movement in Southeast Asia. (*Yomiuri shinbun*, 21 March 1973).
107 *Nihon keizai shinbun*, 29 April 1973.
108 Lin Liyun, in *Asahi shinbun* and *Yomiuri shinbun*, 13 May 1973, and *Shinano Mainichi*, 4 May 1973. See also *Kakyoho*, 25 June 1983.
109 *Asahi shinbun*, 21 and 27 April 1973.
110 *Ibid*, 27 April 1973.
111 Kondo Tatsuo, 'Kappatsuka suru Chugoku no toitsu sensen kosaku (tokushu. Nitchu seijoka no ichinen [5])', *Ajia rebiyu* (March 1973), p 41. At a meeting on 11 May overseas quite a few Chinese attended who had hitherto not shown up at pro-Peking meetings (*Asahi shinbun*, 13 May 1973). Liao called on them to contribute to the liberation of Taiwan (Kyodo, *SWB*, 12 May 1973). See also *Mainichi shinbun*, 20 April 1973 (*yukan*): 'It is no longer possible for our compatriots who have gone to Taiwan to rely upon the US. Even if they want to rely on other forces, China will not permit this. The Taiwan people also will not permit this. Tung Chi-wu was also clear in his warning against Taiwan-US collaboration.'
112 'Honichi seikai no kawakiri toshite Sohyo taikai ni shusseki suru Chukyo yojin rainichi no igi', p 42, Kyodo, 12 May 1973 (in *SWB*), and *Far Eastern Economic Review*, 28 May 1973, as well as *Asahi shinbun*, 13 and 21 May 1973.
113 Tadokoro Takehiko, 'Ichinen no keseki to kongo no mondai', p 13.
114 Ohara Shinichiro, 'Ashibumi jotai o dasshita Nitchu kankei', p 14. Tadokoro Takehiko, 'Ichinen no kiseki to kongo no mondai', p 11.
115 *Yomiuri shinbun*, 12 March 1973.
116 Tadokoro, 'Ichinen no kiseki', p 11.
117 *Mainichi shinbun*, 20 April 1973 (*yukan*).
118 *Ibid* and 30 April 1973.
119 *Yomiuri shinbun*, 4 (*yukan*) and 5 May 1973.
120 *Ibid*, 17 April 1973; *Asahi shinbun*, 16 April 1973.
121 *Nihon keizai shinbun*, 11 May 1973 (*yukan*); see also *SWB* citing Kyodo of 11 May 1973.
122 *Nihon keizai shinbun*, 11 May 1973 (*yukan*); see also *SWB* citing Kyodo of 11 May 1973. Further attempts to 'resolve the difficulties blocking conclusion of these agreements, including the deadlocked aviation', were undertaken by Fujiyama Aiichiro who had succeeded the late Ishibashi Tanzan as President of Kokubosoku (*JTW*, 23 June 1973).
123 *Yomiuri shinbun*, 5 May 1973, and *Sankei shinbun*, 21 May 1973.
124 *Yomiuri shinbun*, 5 May 1973.
125 *Nihon keizai shinbun*, 23 April 1973 (*yukan*).

China's Relations with Japan

126 *Yomiuri shinbun*, 24 April 1973; *Mainichi shinbun*, 26 April 1973.
127 *Yomiuri shinbun*, 16 March 1973. Tadokoro Takehiko, 'Ichinen no kiseki', p 13; *Dalu qingshi fenxi huibian*, pp 287 and 385; *Dalu qingbao*, p 769.
128 *Asahi shinbun*, 6 December 1974; Tadokoro Takehiko, 'Ichinen no kiseki', p 12.
129 *Asahi shinbun*, 21 December 1972.
130 *Ibid*, 12 March 1973.
131 *Ibid*.
132 *Ibid*, 10 and 12 March 1973; *Nihon keizai shinbun*, 16 March 1973. See also Tadokoro Takehiko, 'Ichinen no kiseki', p 12.
133 *Asahi shinbun*, 18 March 1973.
134 *Kokusai nenpo 1973*, pp 105 f.
135 *Asahi shinbun*, 12 March 1986.
136 *Yomiuri shinbun*, 20 March 1973.
137 *Ibid*, 19 April 1973.
138 *Ibid*, 24 April 1973.
139 *Ibid*; *Asahi shinbun*, 23 April 1974.
140 *Yomiuri shinbun*, 26 April 1973.
141 *Nihon keizai shinbun*, 23 April 1973 (*yukan*); Tadokoro, 'Ichinen no kiseki', p 13.
142 *Yomiuri shinbun*, 24 April 1973; *Mainichi shinbun*, 26 April 1973.
143 *Ibid*.
144 *Ibid* and *Yomiuri shinbun*, 26 April 1973; *Asahi shinbun*, 29 April 1973.
145 *Tokyo shinbun*, 2 May 1973 (quoted according to *Daily Summary of the Japanese Press*).
146 *Nihon keizai shinbun* and *Mainichi shinbun* of 5 May 1973 and *Yomiuri shinbun*, 1 May 1973.
147 *Tokyo shinbun*, 2 May 1973; *Yomiuri shinbun* and *Shinano Mainichi*, 11 May 1973.
148 *Yomiuri shinbun* and *Shinano Mainichi*, 11 May 1973, and *Asahi shinbun*, 18 May 1973.
149 *Ibid*.
150 *Ibid*.
151 *Komei shinbun*, 18 May 1973.
152 *Asahi shinbun*, 22 January 1973 (*yukan*).
153 Liao referred several times to the problem of low Chinese oil supplies Japan, due among other things to limited harbour facilities (*Yomiuri shinbun*, 24 April 1973), and *Asahi shinbun*, 23 April and 10 May 1973. On Chinese oil exports during the early seventies, see R W Hardy, *Chinese Oil*, (1976), especially p 54.
154 *Nihon keizai shinbun*, 20 April 1986.
155 *Ibid*, 9 May 1973 (*yukan*), and *Asahi shinbun*, 19 May 1973.
156 *Mainichi shinbun*, *Asahi shinbun* and *Yomiuri shinbun*, 22 April 1973.
157 *Yomiuri shinbun*, 24 April 1973; *Asahi shinbun*, 10 May 1973, Kyodo, 15 May 1973 (in *SWB*).
158 *Asahi shinbun*, 5 and 7 September 1973. See also *Asahi shinbun*, 2 and 4 September and *Kokusai nenpo 1973*, p 156.
159 *Dalu qingshi fenxi huibian*, 1973, pp 208-9.
160 *Ibid*, pp 20 ff.
161 *Far Eastern Economic Review*, 23 April 1973.
162 *Asahi shinbun*, 14 April 1973.
163 *Nihon keizai shinbun*, 26 April 1973; *Akahata*, 9 May 1973.

164 *Sankei shinbun*, 7 May, and *Akahata*, 6 May 1973; and *Tokyo shinbun*, 7 May 1973.
165 *Asahi shinbun*, 12 March 1973.
166 *SWB*, FE 4291/A3/3 (10 May 1973).
167 *Nihon keizai shinbun*, 9 May 1973.
168 *Dagongbao*, 30 April 1973.
169 *SWB*, 4 May 1973, quoting Kyodo.
170 *Yomiuri shinbun*, 10 May 1973 (*yukan*).
171 *Nihon keizai shinbun* and *Yomiuri shinbun*, 17 May 1973.
172 Lee, *The Japan Socialist Party*, pp 276-7.
173 Bing Xin in *Liaogong zai renjian*, p 52.
174 Chen Zongji, in *ibid*, pp 87-8.
175 On He Long's rehabilitation, see Xue Ming's recollections in *PD*, 29 June 1983. The unconfirmed assassination attempt has been described in detail by Shi Shu, 'Mao (Zedong). He (Long) chuanqixing zhi andou'.
176 *Current Scene*, XI.10 (October 1973), pp 22-6.
177 See also Chen Zongji in *Liaogong zai renjian* p 87.
178 Ogawa, *Pekin no yonen*, pp 38 ff.
179 *Ibid*, p 40.
180 For Ohira's comments in Hong Kong before travelling on to Peking in January 1974, see *Asahi shinbun*, 3 January 1974, as quoted in *Kokusai nenpo*, 1974, p 105.
181 See 'Ohira hochu koku kyotei no zenshin o kakunin'. A detailed account starting in January 1974 of the air agreement negotiations is also found in *Dalu qingbao*, pp 41 ff. See also *Feiwei jiben ziliao huibian, waijiao zhuanji*, (Taipei, June 1975), pp 305 f.
182 Golam W Choudhury, 'Trends in China: Post Mao Policy in Asia', *Problems of Communism* (July-August 1977), p 22.
183 For Liao's comments on the visit, see *Asahi shinbun*, 8 January 1974, as quoted by *Kokusai nenpo*, 1974, p 107. On the final phase of Ohira's negotiations, see *Kokusai nenpo*, 1974, pp 106-7: apparently Zhou offered no concessions on matters of principle (Ogawa, *Pekin no yonen*, p 23). During the decisive phase of the talks Ohira even threatened to leave Peking without reaching an agreement (*Mainichi shinbun*, 18 January 1974, as quoted by *Kokusai nenpo*, 1974, p 106; see also Ogawa, *Pekin no yonen*, pp 40-1. With the conclusion of the first operational agreement on trade, the Memorandum Trade ended (*Kokusai nenpo*, 1974, p 113).
184 According to the Japanese ambassador in Peking, Ogawa, Deng Xiaoping carried out most tasks of Zhou Enlai after Zhou fell ill (Ogawa, *Pekin no yonen*, p 28). This was also confirmed by a PRC source: 'In 1975 ... it was learned that Chairman Mao had asked Comrade Deng Xiaoping to take charge of the Party Central Committee's day-to-day work.' Liu Ying 'Mourning Comrade Zhang Wentian with Profound Grief' *FBIS*, 29 August 1979, L9. The rehabilitation of Zhang Wentian itself is intriguing, since there is also a link with Wang Zhen, who in turn had close links with He Long and Liao Chengzhi. Zhang had been director of the Party Central Committee's Propaganda Department and principal responsible person of *Liberation Weekly* during the thirties (Deng Xiaoping's Eulogy on 25 August, in *FBIS*, 27 August 1979, L2 ff. Arai, however, claims that during that period Zhou had been isolated from his colleagues (Arai, *Shu Onrai no jissen*, pp 248-9). These views are not necessarily contradictory. The important question, obviously, is to what extent the so-called gang of four was able to influence foreign policy making during this

period; it would be wrong to assume that this area was under the complete control of one or other group. Despite the 'radicalism' of the group around Jiang Qing, Zhou's report to the National People's Congress referred to the need for Japanese co-operation in China's modernisation drive. (Shibauchi, 'Haken mondai', p 158).

185 The conclusion of the air agreement with Peking led to a (temporary) cancellation of the agreement with Taipei (*Kokusai nenpo* 1974, pp 112 ff). For further references to the operational agreements, including a fishery agreement, see *Kokusai nenpo*, pp 112 ff, Kim Hong N, '"Anti-hegemonism" and the Politics of the Sino-Japanese Peace Treaty: A Study in the Miki Government's China Policy', *Asia Quarterly* 2 (1977), p 102, Glaubitz, 'Balancing Between Adversaries', p 31, and Ishikawa Tadao, *Watakushi no mita Nihon gaiko*, (1976), pp 71 ff.

186 See also *Dalu qingbao*, pp 346 f.

187 A Taiwanese researcher has argued, however, that the death of Liao's patron Zhou Enlai should have reduced Liao's influence (Zhao Jian, interview in 1982). Generally speaking, a good indication of the relative standing and influence of politicians can be obtained by tracing their ability to restore members of their personal clique to positions of power, or to initiate their posthumous rehabilitation. The rehabilitation of He Long was slow in coming (see for example Xue Ming, in *PD* of 29 June 1983). A close friend of Liao, Xia Yan was released from prison in July 1975 (*Liaogong zai renjian*, p 13). It is, however, premature to attempt conclusions on the basis of such limited data; there is an obvious need for large-scale statistical surveys which may be aided by bibliographical aids listing obituaries in various journals such as the classified bibliography in the journal *Gongdang wenti yanjiu*.

188 Y H Park, 'The "Anti-hegemony" Controversy in Sino-Japanese Relations', *Pacific Affairs* 49 No 3 (Fall 1976), p 476; it was interesting to note that the pro-Communist Hong Kong evening newspaper *Xinwanbao* denied that the PRC had tacitly approved Japanese possession of the Senkaku (Diaoyutai) islands (*Yomiuri shinbun*, 17 August 1978; see also *Nihon keizai shinbun*, 30 May 1979, and *JTW*, 20 May 1978). For further references on the negotiations for a treaty see Park, op cit; Shibauchi, 'Haken mondai', passim; Kim, 'Anti hegemonism', passim; Miki tried to blunt the anti-Soviet thrust of PRC moves by attempting to have his interpretation of 'anti-hegemony' accepted (the so-called 'Four Principles'), *Mainichi shinbun*, 16 June 1975 (*yukan*), and Shibauchi, 'Haken mondai', p 165.

189 Park, 'The "Anti-hegemony" Controversy', pp 478 and 488.

190 Park, ibid, p 479; Kim, 'Anti-hegemonism', pp 107-8; Shibauchi, 'Haken mondai', p 160; *Kokusai nenpo*, 1975, p 98. See also *Pravda*, 25 August 1978.

191 Strategic implications of the treaty were underlined during Deng Xiaoping's press conference at the end of his visit in late 1978 (*JTW*, 4 November 1978).

192 *JTW*, 26 August 1978. See also *International Herald Tribune*, 14 August 1978, 'The Historic Document is Thin in Content'.

193 *JTW*, 26 August 1978.

194 Kim, op cit p 107; Park, op cit, p 477; Shibauchi, op cit, p 154.

195 It was also suggested that Deng Xiaoping's visit to Thailand was related to the Treaty on Peace and Friendship (*Asahi shinbun*, 15 August 1978).

196 Despite the PRC's xenophobic appearance during the political campaigns of 1974-75 the *rapprochement* with the United States continued to grow. Zhou Enlai's report to the Tenth Party Congress, for instance, has been interpreted as an indication of such a *rapprochement* ('Dui Mei

zhengce', p 23). There are further 'hard' indications: a Chinese machine industry mission to Japan in 1975 is said to have presented a list of desired weapons (*JTW*, 15 July 1978). Liao, Zhang Xiangshan and Sun Pinghua met Iwashima Hisao, Head of the National Defense College's First War History Research Department and a top expert on US military strategies, during a visit in April 1977 (*JTW*, 7 May 1977). Widely noted also was Zhang Zaijian's visit to Tokyo in September 1978 (*JTW*, 16 September 1978). On strategic implications, see also Glaubitz, 'Balancing Between Adversaries', p 44. *PD* commented in October 1978 that the ratification of the treaty may have 'far-reaching and positive influence for peace and security in the Asia and Pacific Region' (*PD*, 23 October 1978). Japanese sources reported that Brzezinski's visit to Peking may have contributed to the re-opening of the treaty negotiations (*Sankei shinbun*, 9 August 1978, and *Yomiuri shinbun*, 13 August 1978). For Carter's approval of the treaty, see *Nihon keizai shinbun*, 14 August 1978. From evidence available so far it is not clear whether the parties concerned simply wished to conjure up an *image* of strategic co-operation, or whether co-operation was more substantial. Finally the Treaty also contributed to a change in attitude towards defence among the Japanese opposition, for instance the Komeito (*JTW*, 28 October and 25 November 1978). On the other hand, it is doubtful whether North Korea welcomed these developments which would have seemed to make Peking less interested in any 'adventures' on the Korean peninsula (*Nihon keizai shinbun*, 5 September 1978, and *JTW*, 4 November 1978).

197 Hirano Minoru, *Gaiko kisha nikki* (jo, ge), (1979), pp 125 ff.
198 *Asahi shinbun*, 29 October 1975. Although negotiations on the further implementation of the long term trade agreement concluded in February were held shortly after the conclusion of the Treaty of Peace and Friendship trade does not seem to have been the major factor for the conclusion of the treaty at that moment. See also *International Herald Tribune*, 14 August 1978.
199 Kim, op cit, p 116; Park, op cit, p 489. Zhou Enlai had died on 8 January 1976.
200 On the power struggle between Hua and Deng in summer 1978, *Sekai nippo*, 6 and 9 August 1978, and *Sankei shinbun*, 4 and 8 August 1978. For Li Xiannian's remarks concerning Deng visiting Japan instead of Hua Guofeng, *Nihon keizai shinbun* and *Shinano Mainichi*, 5 August 1978; see also *Yomiuri shinbun*, 10 August 1978.
201 'Glaubitz, Balancing Between Adversaries', p 32.
202 *Dalu qingbao*, p 765.
203 Kim, 'Sino-Japanese Peace Treaty'; Shibauchi, op cit, p 158; Park, op cit, p 476. On Deng's agreement to exclude the Taiwan issue from the agenda of the treaty negotiations, *SWB*, FE/4274/A3/4 (9 October 1974); also Nieh, 'Hintergründe', p 281, and Glaubitz, 'Balancing Between Adversaries', p 33 and *SWB*, FE/4171/A3/11.
204 *Feiwei jiben ziliao huibian, waijiao zhuanji*, p 305.
205 Shibauchi, op cit, p 153; Kim, op cit, p 102.
206 Kim, op cit, pp 101 ff; Shibauchi, op cit, p 154; on Han Nianlong's recently increased importance in Japanese affairs, Ogawa, *Pekin no yonen*, pp 4, 42. The shipping agreement was initialled in November 1974 (*Yomiuri shinbun*, 2 November 1974, as quoted in *Kokusai nenpo*, 1974, p 114).
207 The new composition of the Miki cabinet implied a strengthening of the 'pro-Taiwan' influence (Park, op cit, pp 477 f, 485; Kim, op cit, p 103, and Shibauchi, op cit, pp 154, 163-4).
208 Kim, op cit, p 103; Ishikawa, *Watakushi no mita Nihon gaiko*, p 75.
209 *Asahi shinbun*, 14 January 1975.
210 Shibauchi, op cit, p 154; Kim op cit, p 103.

211 *Asahi shinbun*, 22 January 1975.
212 Shibauchi, op cit, pp 163 ff; Kim, op cit, pp 106 ff and Glaubitz, 'Balancing Between Adversaries', p 34.
213 Shibauchi, op cit, pp 166 ff: Park, op cit, pp 480 f.
214 Kim, op cit, p 103.
215 Park, op cit, pp 479 ff; Shibauchi, op cit, p 164 ff.
216 Shibauchi, op cit, p 166; Park, op cit, p 480.
217 Lee, 'The Japan Socialist Party', p 276; Park, op cit, p 480, and Ishikawa, *Watakushi no mita Nihon gaiko*, p 93.
218 *Asahi shinbun*, 5 May 1975.
219 *Ibid*, 6 May 1975 (*yukan*).
220 *Ibid*, 4 May 1975.
221 *Ibid*, 5 May 1975.
222 *Ibid*, 7 May 1975 (*yukan*).
223 *Ibid* and Lee, 'The Japan Socialist Party', pp 276-7.
224 Ishikawa, *Watakushi no mita Nihon gaiko*, p 94.
225 *Asahi shinbun*, 8 May 1975 (*yukan*).
226 *Ibid*, 10 May 1975.
227 *Ibid*.
228 *Ibid*, 13 May 1975.
229 *Ibid*, 12 May 1975 (*yukan*).
230 *Ibid*, 13 May and 13 May (*yukan*) 1975.
231 *Ibid*, 19 May 1975.
232 Kim, op cit, pp 109-10; Ishikawa, *Watakushi no mita Nihon gaiko*, p 98 f. See also *Yomiuri shinbun*, 12 August 1978 (*yukan*).
233 *Asahi shinbun*, 13 June 1975 (*yukan*).
234 Park, op cit, p 482; Kim, op cit, p 110 and *Kokusai nenpo*, 1975, p 97.
235 *Yomiuri shinbun* as quoted by *Kokusai nenpo*, 1975, p 97.
236 *Asahi shinbun*, 13 June 1975 (*yukan*).
237 Ishikawa, *Watakushi no mita Nihon gaiko*, p 100.
238 *Ibid*.
239 *Asahi shinbun*, 1 July 1975.
240 *Ibid*, 1 July 1975 (*yukan*).
241 Kim, op cit, p 113.
242 *Asahi shinbun*, 10 July 1975; *Kokusai nenpo*, 1975, p 101; Kim, op cit, p 114; see also Clough, *Island China*, p 198.
243 *Asahi shinbun*, 10 July 1975.
244 *Ibid*, 12 July 1975; Hsüeh, *Dimensions of China's Foreign Relations*, p 116.
245 *Asahi shinbun*, 22 July 1975.
246 Choudhury, *Trends in China*, pp 23-4. *Kokusai nenpo*, 1975, p 97; Kim, op cit, pp 112 f.
247 Park, op cit, p 484 and Kim, op cit, p 113.
248 Yu, 'Mao Zedong sihou', p 40.
249 See for instance Liao's attendance at functions following Mao's death, in *PD*, 9, 10, 13 and 19 September 1976.

250 Glaubitz, 'Balancing Between Adversaries', p 35.
251 According to Glaubitz, op cit, p 35, the nadir of Sino-Japanese relations was reached towards the end of 1976; on CCP activities to drive a wedge between Japan and the Soviet Union, Yu Zhi, 'Xianjieduan zhonggong yu Ri Su de sanjiao guanxi', *Zhonggong yanjiu* 126, p 78.
252 On Kono's meeting with Liao Chengzhi, *Peking Review*, 21 January 1977. On Fukuda's revived interest, see Glaubitz, op cit, p 35.
253 Yu, 'Mao Zedong sihou', p 40.
254 *JTW*, 30 April 1977.
255 On Fukuda's vacillating attitude, see *JTW*, 25 June 1977, which also reported the postponement of a visit to Peking by Hori, previously announced (*ibid*, 4 June 1977). At this time, Liao was active during numerous meetings with members of the Keidanren mission (*PD*, 1, 3 and 5 April 1977 and *JTW*, 9 April 1977).
256 *Peking Review*, 29 January 1977; *JTW*, 29 January 1977 and Glaubitz, op cit, p 35. *PD*, 20, 22, 23 and 24 January 1977.
257 1977.12.11 *Sankei shinbun*, 11 December 1977, as quoted by Glaubitz, *Schwerpunkte der Aussenpolitik Japans 1977-78*, May 1978.
258 H Gelman, 'Outlook for Sino-Soviet Relations', *Problems of Communism*, no 28, (September-December 1979), p 259.
259 *PD*, 5, 22 and 25 May 1977. *Liao Chengzhi de yisheng*, p 96.
260 *JTW*, 11, 18, 25 February and 4 March 1978.
261 Although there is no information about the resurrection of a central organ corresponding to the OCAC abolished during the late sixties it would be incorrect to claim that this meant the absence of Overseas Chinese policy. See for instance *Dalu qingshi zhaiyao huibian (1975nian 1yue 8ri - 5yue 29ri)*, (Taipei, May 1978), p 194 for information on 1975; the OCAC had not been mentioned at the Fourth NPC in 1975 (Zhi Xing, 'Zhonggong xin dangquanpai zhi duiwai tongzhan huodong', *Feiqing yuebao*, 21.2, pp 45 ff. For an early report on the revival of central level policy in 1977-78, *Mingpao* (Hong Kong), 2 August 1978. Chang Chuan points out that the change in Overseas Chinese policy was indicated when Xinhuashe's *Dankao xiaoxi* on 28 November 1977 reprinted - possibly at Liao Chengzhi's suggestion - an article from the Hong Kong magazine *Zhengming* which commented on the reasons for Overseas Chinese wishing to leave the PRC (Chang Chuan, 'Liao gong de zuinou shike', p 28).
262 See Chen Wen, in *Liaogong zai renjian*, p 93 and Liu Xizheng, in *Nanfang ribao*, 27 June 1983. On further involvement see also *Guangming ribao* of 27 June 1983.
263 The State Council established the Overseas Chinese Affairs Office in 1977; the date of Liao's formal appointment may in fact coincide with the establishment of this office. See Xu Simin, in *Liaogong zai renjian*, p 119. It has been reported that Liao had been suggested for this office by Li Xiannian, but this could not be confirmed independently (see Luo Bing's column 'Beixing fangyu' in *Zhengming* 70, August 1983, pp 9-10. 'Li Xiannian yu Xianggang shiwu. - Shei jiren Liao Chengzhi zai qiaoban gangao ban de zhiwu?').
264 On the agreement, *JTW*, 25 February 1978; *PD*, 7, 15, 16 and 17 February contains references to Liao Chengzhi's meetings with Inayama during talks on the long term trade agreement.
265 *JTW*, 25 March and 8 April 1978; *PD*, 15 March 1978.
266 *JTW*, 25 March 1978.
267 *Ibid*, 22, 29 April and 6 May 1978; *Japan Times*, 8 September 1979.

268 *JTW*, 3 June 1978.
269 *Ibid*, 8 July 1978.
270 *Ibid*, 27 May 1978.
271 *Ibid*, 8 July 1978.
272 *Ibid*, 15 July 1978.
273 As mentioned before, Liao was involved in meeting Overseas Chinese through the seventies, but we know little about his formal membership of party and/or government bodies in charge of policy until about 1977 when most institutions dealing with such affairs abolished during the GPCR were restored (Chang, 'Overseas Chinese in China's Policy', passim). On Overseas Chinese policy in 1975-6, see *Dangzheng zhuanji*, p 367. During 1978 when the position of Overseas Chinese in Vietnam (*hoa*) was taken up as a point of tension between the PRC and Vietnam Liao had already regained a conspicuous position among those officials dealing publicly with this question (eg, *PD*, 16 June 1978, and Woodside, 'Nationalism and Poverty', p 407). For details on the last phase of negotiations between Vietnam and the PRC on the '*hoa*', see *Nihon keizai shinbun*, 4 and 29 August 1978; *Asahi shinbun*, 8 and 29 August 1978; *Yomiuri shinbun*, 8 August 1978. He was formally appointed Head of the Office on Overseas Chinese Affairs of the State Council and in this capacity took part in conferences (*Guangming ribao*, 27 June 1983), and Zhuang Xiquan, in *Liaogong zai renjian*, pp 80 ff; see also *Nanfang ribao* 27 June 1983.
274 Tretiak, 'The Sino-Japanese Treaty of 1978', passim.
275 *Nihon keizai shinbun* and *Asahi shinbun*, 6 August 1978.
276 For brief chronological accounts of the negotiations, see *Nihon keizai shinbun*, 12 August 1978, and *Yomiuri shinbun* (main edition and *yukan*), 21 July 1978; *PD* reveals very little on progress achieved. Liao acted as one of Peking's authoritative spokesmen on the negotiations (eg *JTW*, 10 June 1978) but reports in *PD* (9-14 August) suggest his presence at talks with Sonoda during the final stage of the negotiations was limited to largely ceremonial encounters.
277 *Nihon keizai shinbun*, 12 August 1978, *Asahi shinbun* (*yukan*), 30 August 1978 and *The Times*, 14 August 1979.
278 *Sankei shinbun*, 13 August 1978.
279 *Sankei shinbun* (*yukan*), 16 August 1978.
280 *Sekai nippo*, 22 August 1978. Quite a few Japanese observers maintained that Japan had made most concessions (*Asahi shinbun*, 10 August 1978).
281 It had been expected that Hua Guofeng would go to Tokyo but he himself announced Deng's visit (*Asahi shinbun*, 13 August 1978) which may be interpreted as a public humiliation of Hua.
282 The delegation was given 'the grandest reception ever given for a foreign visitor' (*JTW*, 21 October 1978). Deng, Liao, Huang Hua and Han Nianlong were accompanied by their wives (*PD*, 23 October 1978). In reporting the formal ceremony protocol demanded that the counterparts of Prime Minister Fukuda and Foreign Minister Sonoda, Deng Xiaoping and Huang Hua be listed ahead of Liao (*PD*, 24 October 1978) but Liao was repeatedly listed ahead of Huang in other reports (*PD*, 23-27 and 30 October 1978). Later he was also listed ahead of Huang in a report on the farewell of Deng Yingchao leaving for Japan in April 1979 (*PD*, 9 April 1979).
283 *Liao Chengzhi de yisheng*, p 110.
284 *PD*, 5 November 1978.
285 Reports ranged from a slight cold (*Sekai nippo*, 5 August 1978) to hospitalisation (*Nihon keizai shinbun*, 12 August 1978).

Eventide

The conclusion of the TPF meant that the tasks set out in the 1972 Tanaka-Zhou communiqué had been accomplished. The establishment of diplomatic relations in 1972 had not immediately ended 'people's diplomacy'. Until 1978 contact at government level had remained limited, both in quantity and level.[1] Yet it took another year before an agreement was reached to hold regular annual high level consultations between Foreign Ministry officials alternately in Peking and Tokyo.[2] Deng Xiaoping's visit, and a second brief stopover on his return from Washington indicated a qualitative change in relations between Peking and Tokyo.[3] Liao himself had predicted this change in a speech in Osaka.[4] 'People's diplomacy' had continued until the conclusion of the TPF; what would its future be like now that regular diplomatic channels had acquired more importance, accompanied by a big increase in trade? Would there be a significant change in Liao's position as a 'leading Japan specialist'? Deng's direct involvement in confidential and public contacts with Japanese leaders automatically reduced Liao's relative importance, at least where public appearances were concerned.[5] The same seems to apply to other Japan specialists.[6] Another factor was concern among Japanese previously involved in people's diplomacy on the Japanese side. On 27 August 1978 the NCNA carried an article by Liao, designed specifically to counter disquiet among Japanese who had been active in 'people's diplomacy', that they would now be forgotten. This article, entitled 'We won't forget the well-digger when we drink water', alluded to a well-known Japanese proverb. Some days later it was suggested in Peking that, during Deng and Liao's visit to Tokyo, new steps would be taken in the area of 'people's diplomacy', such as a large 'friendship mission' to Japan and twinning Japanese and PRC cities.[7] Notwithstanding the role that such exchanges can play, it seemed clear that this new 'people's diplomacy' had a lesser role to play in support of formal diplomacy than had been the case in the past.

This point was proved during Liao's next visit to Japan in May 1979 on the PRC liner *Minghua*.[8] Although he and other high-ranking members of the mission had a number of meetings with Japanese politicians - among them Tanaka Kakuei, Sonoda, and former Prime Minister Fukuda - and influential business leaders, published reports do not suggest that the mission achieved particular goals during the visit.[9] One of the most interesting meetings was perhaps Su Yu's courtesy call on Yamashita Ganri, Director-General of the Defense Agency:

> It was the first meeting between a high official of the Chinese People's Liberation Army and a Japanese defense chief. General Takehiko Takashina, chief of the Joint Staff Council was also present.[10]

The mission became notorious for the large number of family members of prominent Communist leaders present and resulted in charges of nepotism and corruption in Peking. An article in *Yomiuri shinbun* of 7 August 1979, reported a Hong Kong member to the second session of the 5th NPC saying on 6 August that the question had been brought up at the recent session of the NPC and had been the focus of criticism by many representatives. It seems that not only the China-Japan Friendship Association but two other organisations were independently charged with selecting some participants. It was suggested that about 10%, or 60 people taking part in the trip, had been included as a result of backstage manipulation. There were also charges of bringing back goods purchased in Japan which were not declared to PRC customs. In an apparent whitewash attempt one of Liao's eulogies stressed that the 1979 mission had 'definitely not been an amusement trip'.[11]

The mission included Liao's wife, Jing Puchun, Su Yu and his wife, Chu Qing, Deng Xiaoping's daughter and son, Deng Lin and Deng Ken, and Li Xiannian's wife, Lin Guimei. Liao's sister Mengxing was not a member of the delegation, but visited Japan the following year.[12] With them travelled the wives of a number of prominent victims of the Cultural Revolution: of Tao Zhu, He Long and Luo Ruiqing. Also present were He Long's daughter, married to Liao's son, and her son and daughter, the widow of the late Wang Jiaxiang, with whom Liao had developed strong bonds of friendship, the wife of Zhu Zhongli, Geng Biao's daughter, Geng Ying, and the late Luo Ronghuan's widow Ling Yueqin.

It is not surprising then, that there were even rumours that Liao's position was endangered by charges of nepotism[13] although his prestige seems not to have suffered to any great extent. A weakening of his official position would have led to serious questions abroad about Peking's foreign policy towards Japan and also towards Overseas Chinese at a time when Liao was also thought useful in Peking's recently initiated campaign for 'reunification' with Taiwan.[14] On the surface the career of Liao's son in the area of Overseas Chinese affairs may also simply seem the result of Liao using his influence on behalf of a close relative but it is also possible that the CCP decided to use the Liao family name for propaganda purposes even after Liao's death. Even in the case of a nephew of Liao's who reached a senior position at Jinan University for Overseas Chinese caution should be exercised before ascribing his position to nepotism without further evidence.[15]

About the same time that the restructuring of Overseas Chinese affairs was taking place there was also a renewed emphasis on policy towards Taiwan, with repeated calls for 'peaceful reunification' and direct talks with ROC leaders. Even before that Liao had been one of the most prominent figures delivering speeches on the anniversary of the 28 February uprising. Now there was a concerted buildup of appeals for reunification by various Communist politicians who sought to create the impression of an increasingly conciliatory position. Referring to Ye Jianying's offer of 'peaceful reunification' published in 1981 PRC sources claimed later that:

> In fact, the mainland and Taiwan are having contacts unintermittently. The other side was informed of the draft of the 9-point proposal three years before its publication. Therefore, the proposal was not a propaganda offensive.[16]

Political attacks on Liao at this stage would necessarily have created serious doubts abroad about the credibility of the new initiative.[17]

Meanwhile, clashes between the Khmer Rouge, closely allied with the PRC, and the Vietnamese presaged Vietnam's invasion of Cambodia, followed in turn by the PRC invasion of Vietnam in February-March 1979. Although the confrontation caused a minor upsurge in nationalist propaganda, Liao was not significantly engaged in any campaign to increase nationalist feeling among Overseas Chinese, and this theme did not play a role in PRC propaganda towards Taiwan.[18]

In the second half of 1979 there was a considerable reduction in Liao's public engagements and appearances,[19] almost certainly due to deteriorating health. He had begun to lose weight, and it was finally decided to send him to Stanford in the United States for heart surgery. By this time he had already suffered three attacks of myocardiac blockage.[20] Liao was told that, even if the operation was successful, he could not expect to live for more than another three years.[21] He entered hospital in the PRC for a time in 1979, possibly for a different operation.[22] He was not daunted by the dangers of a heart operation: 'There is no way I can go on working without having an operation, and is there any sense in going on like this?'[23]

Two of Liao's heart arteries were blocked completely, and the remaining one was 80% blocked.[24] Two other such operations before and after Liao's operation were unsuccessful.[25] Liao left for the United States after the spring festival 1980 in March, and returned to Peking in May:[26]

> In May 1980 I (Jing Puchun, Liao's wife) accompanied Chengzhi on his way back from America to Peking ... Liao paid attention to his diet as he had been told to by his doctors. As a result, there was a conspicuous reduction of his body weight. One day he happily told me: 'You see, have I not recovered completely?' In fact, I knew very clearly that notwithstanding his [healthy] appearance somebody with a heart ailment like Liao Chengzhi could not possibly recover completely. From May 1980 until the end of May 1983 when he entered hospital (shortly before his death) Liao took on a workload much heavier than that of a healthy person for a full three years, working more than ten hours nearly every day, including Sundays and holidays...[27]
>
> At times he went to meetings in three or four different places on one ... day, sometimes receiving five or six groups of foreign guests. Usually he left early in the morning to return only in the middle of the night. After his operation he worked entirely like a young man ...[28]

Liao's visitors were mainly Japanese, Overseas Chinese from further afield and Chinese from Taiwan, Hong Kong and Macao:

> On returning home he would still study quite a few important documents and answer letters from ordinary people. On top of all this, he would still glance over publications from Japan, Hong Kong and Macao.[29]

Despite work pressure Liao remained concerned about his own family, including his grandchildren, as related by his son Liao Jian:

> When our child entered school ... my wife and I hoped very much that he would be able to study foreign languages. Father was Honorary Chairman of the Academy of Foreign Languages, where many of his

former subordinates were working, and we hoped through father's connections to have our child attend the middle school attached to the Academy. When father heard about this he set two conditions: school results ought to be better than 80 marks, and the exam papers should be shown to him. Then he wanted to examine his grandchild in person and have a talk with him in English, and asked him to sing a song in English. When his grandchild stood in front of him and sang the 'Straw Hat Song' from the Japanese film *Witness* father was beaming happily all over his face. When we moved to have him apply for school entrance father did not react. Later we gave up raising this topic. Did father not like his grandson? No. The bond between grandfather and granchild was very strong ...30

Of course this episode was told with a purpose in mind, to show Liao Chengzhi as an incorruptible politician who refused to support nepotism.

Common sense should tell us that, even after recovering from such an illness, Liao would find his influence seriously curtailed and career prospects diminished, to say the least. Contrary to such expectations there was seemingly no open challenge to his position during the last three years of his life. There are, however, a number of precedents where important Chinese politicians have been able to preserve considerable authority in similar situations. We will return to this interesting problem in the concluding chapter of this study.

During Liao's absence from the active political scene in the first half of 1980 it was Zhang Xiangshan who occupied the most senior position among PRC Japan specialists. Zhang acted as a stand-in for Liao during the visit of a Japanese delegation led by Nakasone, but his range of activities was conspicuously limited compared to Liao's.31 There is also no indication that he might have replaced Liao either in party functions or in other fields of activity, such as Overseas Chinese affairs. High-ranking Japanese delegations were also received by politicians like Deng and Hua. Judging on the basis of evidence collected so far, none of the PRC's Japan specialists took Liao's place during such meetings. It took several months before he had recovered. His first public function dates to the end of June 1980, but his schedule remained severely limited up to September 1980.32

The first important issue to arise between Japan and the PRC after Liao's recovery was the PRC's unilateral cancellation of projects worth more than $1 billion at the beginning of 1981. The crisis was eventually settled through intense negotiations lasting several months. Many such talks were conducted in Japan by visiting PRC politicians. Gu Mu went to Japan in April; Zhao Ziyang arrived towards the end of May, accompanied by Huang Hua and others. Gu led another high-ranking ministerial delegation to Tokyo towards the end of the year. There were also various other channels to discuss political and economic questions, such as the semi-governmental Consultative Council on Long-Term Trade Agreements. The overall impression was of a qualitative change in PRC relations with Japan which were increasingly dominated by the need to maintain and expand a complex economic relationship, which in turn demanded regular contact and consultations very different from those of the heyday of 'people's diplomacy'. This is not to say, of course, that informal, personal ties had suddenly become unimportant. It is quite likely that Liao's presence during numerous meetings in Peking had a more than ceremonial character. Yet even so, his role as a politician active in direct negotiations between the PRC and Japan had conspicuously diminished. In the remaining two years Liao appeared in the limelight only thrice: first in 1981 in connection with the PRC's moves towards reunification with Taiwan, during the trial of the 'Gang of Four' as one of their prominent victims, followed by his involvement in the so-called textbook crisis that soured Japan's relations with the PRC in 1982. Even before Ye Jianying's withdrawal from the forefront of politics, Liao had become the PRC's most prominent spokesman on reunification with Taiwan, second only to Ye himself.[33] PRC propaganda efforts concerning Taiwan reached a high pitch with Ye's nine-point proposal on reunification published towards the end of September 1981. The report gained rather unexpected support from former Prime Minister Fukuda who visited Peking in November and had several talks with Liao and 'Taiwan specialist' Luo Qingchang whose career is closely linked to that of Liao himself. Fukuda also met other PRC politicians previously involved in Japanese affairs like Gu Mu, Han Nianlong and Ji Pengfei. Fukuda's visit gained particular importance since it was later claimed that there had been informal contact(s) with the ROC on Ye's nine-point proposal, and it was suggested that Fukuda was either told of these contacts of might have sounded out Taiwan on this matter. His change of mind created quite a stir in Japan:

> Fukuda's backing for China's reunification plan almost amounts to the Japanese government's official endorsement of the proposal because Fukuda had reportedly co-ordinated views on the Taiwan issue with Chief Cabinet Secretary Kiichi Miyazawa and other government leaders before his visit here. Since he is a senior leader of the Japanese pro-Taiwan politicians, Fukuda's stand in favour of Beijing's peace plan for Taiwan can be also taken to be a position common to pro-Taiwan Japanese leaders, including Prime Minister Nobosuke Kishi and Hirokichi Nadao, former Lower House speaker.

Important as Fukuda's change of heart may have been, it presented a mainly psychological blow without specific consequences. Liao continued to be active in moves on Taiwan, most conspicuously in an open letter to ROC President Jiang Jingguo in July 1982, in which he also referred to his presonal encounter with Jiang in Moscow roughly five decades earlier.[34] Liao's letter did not remain unanswered, but the Taiwanese answer heaped scorn on his offer to negotiate.[35]

At about the same time, in summer 1982, the so-called textbook crisis occurred over charges that the Japanese government had gone along with, if not encouraged, changes in Japanese history textbooks designed to cover up the truth of Japan's naked aggression towards East Asian countries in the thirties.[36] Similar charges soon came from South Korea, the ROC and elsewhere in Asia. There is strong reason to believe that, initially, the textbook crisis had been played up for political reasons just as charges of a 'revival of Japanese militarism' had suddenly surfaced in 1975. It was generally asserted later that Liao had intervened personally to contain a possible worsening of relations over the affair.[37] It is even possible that the matter had been brought up by the Deng faction to defend itself against charges by domestic enemies that it was overly 'pro-Japanese', and might have gone too far in the direction of military co-operation with Japan and the USA. This affair marred preparations for the celebration of the tenth anniversary of the establishment of relations with Japan. Liao was due to lead the delegation, but in August, shortly before his departure he fractured his leg and thus missed his last opportunity to see the country of his birth.[38]

In September 1982 Liao was appointed to the politburo of the CCP.[39] More than two years had passed since his heart operation; with perhaps one more year still left this appointment to the highest office Liao had ever held obviously did not signify a new starting point on the road towards more power. Just as Liao's appointment to the Central Committee in 1945 was largely seen as recognition of past merit, his membership of the politburo was most likely a distinction in honour of his merits in the area of foreign relations and Overseas Chinese policy. Another reason may have been the wish to elevate his status in order to make him an acceptable partner in talks with representatives of the Guomindang (KMT) from Taiwan.[40] Following his elevation to the politburo he was also mentioned as having been nominated for a Vice-Premiership of the PRC at the coming session of the National People's Congress, an honour which fate prevented him from receiving.[41] Song Qingling had likewise been accorded a high position in the PRC government shortly before her death, namely that of chairmanship of the PRC, in order to lend greater weight to calls for 'peaceful reunification'. On formal grounds of seniority there seems to be no doubt that when Ye Jianying had to cease activities Liao became the highest authority on Taiwan.[42] He was similarly involved in Hong Kong affairs, and it had been assumed that he did in fact exercise influence on PRC policy towards the Chinese territory of Hong Kong.[43] I am unable to furnish conclusive evidence but I would argue that the apparent lack of any independent power base - compared to other top leaders in the politburo and the Military Affairs Commission of Party and State - seems to lend weight to the argument of those observers who regard his appointment to the politburo as 'image building' to create the impression abroad of a 'moderate' line towards Hong Kong, Taiwan and Overseas Chinese.[44] Moreover, Liao's health kept deteriorating.

Liao was already 74 when he fractured his leg and had to attend functions and conferences in a wheelchair.[45] After surgery he could move only with difficulty, supported by two nurses.[46] While his spirit seemed unbowed this further experience will have heightened Liao's awareness of his own fragile condition, and it was during this period that he engaged in compiling a book entitled *Huiyi yu huainian* commemorating his parents, one of his last acts as a filial son.[47]

Before this accident Liao had taken part in preparations for the shooting of a film about the life of his father Liao Zhongkai and featuring Liao as a child. The film was completed several months later, and it is easy to imagine that in Liao's condition it should have evoked strong deep sentiments, causing him to look back on his life as a whole. Tang Xiaodan, a well known film director recalls that when he and Yang Gongmin, the principal director:

> went to Liao's residence for a visit to obtain details about different figures ... Liao still remembered many things that had happened in his childhood as if they had happened yesterday. Liao said that:
>
> 'The most important characteristic of my father was a scar above his left eyebrow. He enjoyed flowers and trees. On returning home he would not enter the house straight away but have a look at flowers and trees first. He would prune superfluous leaves. Father had a passionate love for classical poetry and often used quotations from old poems to express his feelings. He had written quite a few classical poems when he was imprisoned by Chen Qiongming. Father's movements were brisk, walking with fast strides, but he talked at a normal speed. He could speak Cantonese, Hakka, English and Japanese. His eyes were full of expression, his dress correct - normally wearing Western style clothes - and he loved to wear a brimmed hat which gave him a lively look. My mother was not particular about the painting materials she used, and applied very ordinary pigments. She had beautiful hair.'
>
> Liao further referred to personal characteristics of some historical figures such as Sun Yatsen who was about five centimetres taller than Liao Zhongkai; Wang Jingwei was about 180 cm tall, well-spoken and accompanied his speech with gesticulations with hand and feet. Hu Hanmin was very short-sighted, and about 170 cm tall, with a longish face that did not show any emotions. Chen Qiongming had the habit of glancing at people sideways. Lin Zhimian frequently wore the traditional long scholar's garment like a gentleman from Shaoxing. Referring to Liao Zhongkai's education of Liao Chengzhi and Liao Mengxing, Liao recalled that, when his father was appointed head of the financial section of the Generalissimo's headquarters, as well as head of Canton province, he often left home early and returned late. Yet, even when work was pressing, he would still want to inspect my homework and that of my sister and would also have us take part in manual labour. At that time I was enrolled in a religious school. When I returned home during term breaks I would shine my father's shoes until his white leather shoes were gleaming.[48]

In October 1982 Liao's Japanese alma mater, Waseda University, conferred an honorary doctorate on him on the occasion of the 100th anniversary of its foundation.[49] In Liao's absence his son Liao Kaisun, attended the ceremony in Japan and received the document. He also presented a collection of paintings by Liao Zhongkai and He Xiangning to Tokyo Central University (Chuo daigaku) and the Girls' Art Academy (Joshi bijutsu daigaku), institutions attended by his parents early in the century.[50] Liao's thoughts must have gone back to the days when he was enrolled at the high school attached to Waseda and to his activities as a leftist student in the twenties. He was still thinking of visiting Japan in 1983:[51] 'If only my health permits I should like to visit Japan again - any date would be satisfactory.'

Liao had been invited to visit Japan in the autumn, but would he ever be able to start on his last visit?52 He does not seem to have lost his deep-seated optimism, but at times he must have wondered whether meetings with friends and acquaintances would be the last occasion to meet them in this life.

> For seventy five years I've seen rivers flow and flowers fall,
> In Berlin and Tokyo, leisurely walks in forests along river banks,
> San Francisco and Egypt, a quick glance at flowers,
> Carved in my mind - Peking, Shanghai and Yanan,
> How can I ever forget the Long March - a prisoner in ropes
> Run out of luck, streams that escape my memory.
>
> My temples like silver, with wobbly teeth, but
> My offspring's grown up, and can look after themselves.
> It's not easy to reach the honour of a grave at Babaoshan,
> In the smiling company of dew-sprinkled flowering plum trees.53

There were also quite a number of nostalgic moments, for instance when Liao's closest collaborator in the area of Overseas Chinese affairs, Zhuang Xiquan, entered the CCP:

> On 30 December 1982 Liao came to me to congratulate me on receiving the glorious honour of becoming a party member of the CCP at the advanced age of 95. When I was sworn in Liao pressed my hands and wished that I would still be able to work for another ten or twenty years.54

Liao was also involved in collecting material on CCP history, in particular its southern branch where he had been active before 1949.55 On 15 April 1983 there was a symposium and meeting of former members of the southern branch office. Here Liao raised the question of rehabilitation of a former collaborator, Zhang Wenbin, just as he had been one of those urging Pan Hannian's rehabilitation.56

His leg had healed by February 1983.57 Liao continued a heavy schedule, attempting to foster youth exchanges between Japan and the PRC, meeting visitors from Japan, Overseas Chinese and other foreigners. Towards the end of April he met Sakurauchi Yoshio, a Japanese politician whom he had met nearly thirty years before.58 He brought greetings from Prime Minister Nakasone and former Prime Minister Suzuki, as well as Kono Kenzo. Liao mentioned that he did not feel quite fit. A few days later Sun Pinghua led a delegation to Japan carrying greetings to Liao's Japanese friends in person. Sun did not meet Liao again, and was unable to bring greetings back to him.59 By this time it was an open secret that Liao was a leading candidate for the post of Vice-President of the PRC.60

In May Liao left Peking for over two weeks, visiting among other places Hangzhou:61

> The weather was hot, which put a great strain on Liao both mentally and physically. When he returned to Peking on 19 May he had been

suffering from a cold for some days and was running a slight temperature. He was short of breath, and coughed all the time. We urged him to see the doctor at the hospital, but he shrugged it off: 'It's nothing.' On 20 May sick as he was, Liao took part in an activity concerning foreign policy. When he really could not carry on any longer he entered hospital. Although he kept coughing and his temperature refused to drop he still kept receiving guests and studying documents without taking even one day's rest. On 31 May he felt a slight turn for the better and left hospital. On 1 June he accepted the invitation for a 'Glow-worm evening party on 1 June' at the primary school of his grandchildren.[62] He did not feel strong enough to attend and had to send his apologies, but dedicated a couplet for the school: 'Study well every day, progress every day'. On the evening of that day he forced himself to watch the whole of the first soccer match between China and England. When the Chinese team scored a goal he clapped his hands excitedly. He hoped that the Chinese team would ... catch up with the level of experienced international teams. On 2 June he was short of breath all day, running a slight temperature, and could not sleep all night. On 3 June he participated in a meeting at eight o'clock and returned home at noon. His face was ashen and he found it difficult to stay upright. In the afternoon he entered hospital again. Having run a slight temperature for several days, he had breathing problems on 6 June and did not feel comfortable. Therefore he was put on the drip and given oxygen. That day he stubbornly ignored the advice of his doctors, put on his favourite shirt and let his attendants push his wheelchair to the rostrum in the Grand Hall of the People, and persisted in listening to the whole report on the government delivered by Prime Minister Zhao Ziyang [at this session of the National People's Congress]. On returning to the hospital his health continued to deteriorate. On 7 June he was still engaged in ... the problem of the reunification of the motherland. On 8 June he made specific and detailed arrangements for a unit which was to receive an Overseas Chinese who had returned to China, and made suggestions going as far as the choice of the hotel and the people who were to meet him.[63]

Liao continued working on 8 and 9 June when his health took a further turn for the worse. Several family members were at his bedside when Liao died:

Our beloved father has left politics, left our mother, us children and grandchildren, numbering twenty ... At 4.20 his breathing stopped. At 5.22 his heart stopped beating. We who were at his bedside suddenly felt as if heaven and earth had fallen apart. We could control our grief no longer, could not hold back our tears and kept calling loudly 'Daddy, Daddy' ... You can't watch television together with us any more, bite our noses to make us call out 'Dear Grandpa' ...[64]

Notes on Eventide

1. *Yomiuri Shinbun*, 8 (*yukan*) and 22 August 1978.
2. *JTW*, 8 December 1979.
3. *Asahi Evening News*, 1 February 1979.
4. *PD*, 30 October 1978.
5. See for instance Deng Xiaoping's outline of Japan policy on 6 September 1978, (*PD*, 7 September 1978).
6. See reports of Ohira's visit to Peking in December 1979; neither Zhang Xiangshan nor Sun Pinghua figures prominently (*PD*, 6-9 December 1979). Moreover in a report on a meeting between Mrs Ohira and wives of PRC officials Liao's wife Jing Puchun was mentioned in second place after Mrs Deng Xiaoping, but ahead of the wife of Huang Hua (*PD*, 8 December 1979).
7. Deng is said to have proposed sending a large friendship mission by sea to Japan during his Tokyo visit (*Yomiuri shinbun*, 30 August 1978 and *Asahi shinbun*, 4 September 1978). On the twinning of cities, *JTW*, 4 October 1980; 24 October 1981; 13 March 1982; *PD*, 10 May 1979, and *Kakyoho*, 5 July 1983. One may add here the 'adoption' of communes by Japanese (*Kakyoho*, 5 July 1983).
8. For details of the schedule, see *PD*, 8 May 1979.
9. *PD*, 20 May 1979.
10. *Asahi Evening News*, 19 May 1979.
11. *Kakyoho*, 5 July 1983. See also Li Mei, in *Liaogong zai renjian*, p 170, *Guangming ribao*, 25 June 1983, and *Kokusai boeki*, 16 June 1983.
12. See Kusano Shinpei, in *Liaogong zai renjian*, p 149. Stressing Llao's opposition to nepotism Li Mei added that 'when even his own sister could not get on board that ship, how much more useless for his children to think of it' (*Liaogong zai renjian*, p 170).
13. These rumours are well known among Overseas Chinese and Japanese observers of developments in China.
14. It is not chance that changes in Overseas Chinese policy were emphasised in provinces with traditional links with relatives in Taiwan. In 1979 Canton and Fukian issued a circular concerning the advancing of the change of status classification of 'Overseas Chinese landlords and rich households' and at Liao's suggestion decided to remove the labels 'landlord' and 'rich peasant'.
15. See *Nanfang ribao*, 27 June 1983.
16. 'Liao on reunification: We can wait.' *Ta Kung Pao (Weekly Supplement)* 808 (31 December 1981 - 6 January 1982).
17. After the establishment of diplomatic relations between Tokyo and Peking in 1972, and in particular following the break in formal relations between the ROC and the USA, there was a conspicuous intensification of 'united front work' mainly directed towards Overseas Chinese and Hong Kong and Taiwan, aimed at weakening the ROC government at home and abroad. Liao's contacts with American visitors are less well known and not always publicised. A 1978 article revealed that members of the first American youth delegation to break the US blockade in 1957 had talks with Zhou and Liao (*Dagongbao*, 31 August 1978). One of the most important officials involved besides Liao was Luo Qingchang. Liao was also involved in matters concerning Hong Kong; despite frequent reports on activities in these areas it seems doubtful that Liao at this stage played a substantial role in policy formulation (see *Zhongguo shibao*, 11 June 1983). Visits by

Eventide

PRC officials to Japan were sometimes used to strengthen this 'united front' approach among Japanese and Overseas Chinese in Japan, but a detailed survey goes beyond the framework of this study. For reports on the changing approach to Taiwan, see for instance *Yomiuri shinbun*, 6 (*yukan*) and 31 August 1978; *Yomiuri* (English edition), 6 June 1979; *Japan Times*, 25 March 1979; *Sekai nippo*, 22 May 1979; *Zhongguo shibao*, 11 June 1983.

18   See for instance Liao's important speech on Taiwan policy on 28 December 1979, in *Gongfei yuanshi ziliao huibian*, pp 107 ff.
19   Liao met members of the Japanese law delegation under Furui Yoshimi, but it is striking that he was only mentioned once (*PD*, 19 June 1979), and he seems not to have been present at the reception by Deng Xiaoping (*PD*, 20 June 1979).
20   *Liaogong zai renjian*, p 151.
21   Zhuang Xiquan, in *Liaogong zai renjian*, p 80.
22   When I interviewed Hagiwara Teiji on 25 July 1979 he told me that Liao had just left hospital about a week before. Li Xiawen mentions that both Xia Yan and Liao Chengzhi had entered hospital at the time of the NPC session in 1979 (Li Xiawen, in *Liaogong zai renjian*, p 109).
23   *Liaogong zai renjian*, pp 151 and 57.
24   *PD*, 19 June 1983. According to Chang Chuan 'Liao gong de zuihou shike' the name of the operating professor was Dr Harrison of Stanford.
25   *PD*, 19 June 1983.
26   Wu Fanwu, in *PD*, 28 June 1983. According to some sources Liao left for the United States in or before 1979 (*Nihon keizai shinbun*, *Yomiuri shinbun* and *Zhongguo shibao*, 11 June 1983). Both Japanese papers refer to the insertion of a pacemaker. For pictures showing Liao during his stay in the United States, see *Liao Chengzhi de yisheng*, pp 114-5.
27   Jing Puchun, *Liaogong zai renjian*, p 9.
28   *Liaogong zai renjian*, p 151. See also Zhuang Xiquan in *Liaogong zai renjian*, p 80.
29   Jing Puchun, *Liaogong zai renjian*, p 9.
30   Liao Jian, *Guangming ribao*, 25 June 1983.
31   Zhang Xiangshan was the only Japan specialist listed in a report on Deng Xiaoping's departure for Japan (*PD*, 23 October 1978). In 1980 Zhang Xiangshan appeared at a function 'on behalf of Liao' (*PD*, 29 April 1980). See also the reports on Hua's meeting with Nakasone (*PD*, 1 and 15 May 1980).
32   Yet even at that time Liao Chengzhi seems to have been in and out of hospital; see Chen Shunchen, in *Liaogong zai renjian*, p 130, and Ding Cong, in *ibid*, p 48.
33   *Asahi shinbun*, 11 June 1983. Further on Liao's involvement in policy towards Taiwan, see also Xiang Nan, in *Liaogong zai renjian*, p 65, and Cheng Kunwang, in *ibid*, p 133.
34   Ma Bi, *Liaogong zai renjian*, p 74.
35   See for instance, Song Meilin's 'Gei Liao Chengzhi gongkaixin' (*Lianhebao*, 18 August 1982), and *Xintaibao*, 18 August 1982; *Zhongguo shibao*, 24 August 1982; *Zhangwang*, no 495 (August 1982).
36   *JTW*, 9 October 1982 contains a good summary of the affair. See also reports on Suzuki's visit to Peking in *JTW*, 2 October 1982, and *PD*, 29 and 30 September 1982.
37   On the importance of Liao during the crisis, see *Yomiuri shinbun* and *Nihon keizai shinbun*, 11 June 1983.

China's Relations with Japan

38   Liao was in hospital in July 1982 (Wang-Liu, in *Liaogong zai renjian*, p 71). Li Xiawen, in *Liaogong zai renjian*, p 109; *Nihon to Chugoku*, 6-25 (1983). *Kakyoho*, 5 July 1983. See also Wu Fanwu, *PD*, 28 June 1983. He was able to give a speech on 20 August 1982 in Canton at the opening ceremony of the Memorial building for his parents (Miyazaki Seimin, in *Liaogong zai renjian*, p 143). His planned visit to Japan was also related to Liao's plan to hold an annual conference of Chinese and Japanese private citizens, alternately in Japan and Peking (*Kakyoho*, 5 July 1983). *Liao Chengzhi de yisheng*, p 138.

39   *Nihon keizai shinbun*, 11 June 1983.

40   *Zhongguo shibao*, 11 June 1983.

41   See Luo Bing's column 'Beixing fangyu' in *Zhengming* 68 (June 1983), p 7. In the end Wu Lanfu (also a United Front Work figure) was elected to the position of Vice-Premier.

42   *Asahi shinbun*, 11 June 1983 and *JTW*, 7 November 1981.

43   *Nihon keizai shinbun* and *Yomiuri shinbun*, 11 June 1983; Liao was generally regarded as one of the main figures in the talks with Britain on the future of Hong Kong (*International Herald Tribune*, 11 June 1983). On examples for Liao's frequent contacts with people from Hong Kong, see for instance *Liaogong zai renjian*, p 113; Liao Yiyuan, in *ibid*, p 105; Li Mei in *ibid*, p 105. See also Wu Yongming's article in *PD*, 12 June 1983; for a reaction from Hong Kong, for instance Wang Shutao, 'Wei Xianggang zhuquan wenti zhi Liao Chengzhi shu', *Zhanwang* (499).

44   See for instance Lu Zhenji, 'Shei neng baozheng zhonggong de "baozheng"? Cong Liao Chengzhi zhi si kan zhonggong yu Xianggang qiantu' ('Who can guarantee the Chinese Communists' guarantees? The future for Communist China and Hong Kong after Liao Chengzhi').

45   *PD*, June 1983. Ma Haide, in *Liaogong zai renjian*, p 69.

46   Li Xiawen, *Liaogong zai renjian*, p 109.

47   *Jingji ribao*, 24 June 1983.

48   Tang Xiaodan, in *Liaogong zai renjian*, pp 97 ff.

49   *Guangming ribao*, 20 June 1983 and *Yomiuri shinbun*, 11 June 1983.

50   *PD*, 6 October 1982.

51   *Kokusai boeki*, 16 June 1983.

52   *Kakyoho*, 5 July 1983; *Nihon to Chugoku*, 6-25 (1983).

53   *Liao Chengzhi de yisheng*, p 142. The poem without title is dated 23 December 1982.

54   Zhuang Xiquan, in *Liaogong zai renjian*, p 81; *PD*, 24 June 1983.

55   Tong Xiaopeng, in *PD*, 21 June 1983.

56   Tong Xiaopeng, in *PD*, 21 June 1983.

57   Liao Liuwei, in *Liaogong zai renjian*, p 175.

58   *Kokusai boeki*, 16 June 1983. According to *Liao Chengzhi de yisheng*, p 140 Liao (also) met Sakurauchi in September 1982.

59   *Kakyoho*, 25 June 1983.

60   *International Herald Tribune*, 11 June 1983.

61   *Liao Chengzhi de yisheng*, p 159.

62   See also *Guangming ribao*, 25 June 1983.

63   Liao Jian et al, in *Liaogong zai renjian*, pp 152-3.

64   *Liaogong zai renjian*, p 150. There had been widespread rumours that Liao's sudden death had been due to negligence in his medical care, rumours that were refuted by Chang Chuan in his article 'Liao gong de zuihou shike', p 26.

China, Japan and Liao Chengzhi: Conclusions

This study has tried to combine a biography of the PRC's most prominent Japan specialist with a chronological account of the development of the PRC's *political* relations with Japan up to 1983, when Liao died. Despite a number of previous studies on the history of Japan's relations with the PRC it seemed necessary to present an additional account focussing on the political side of PRC Japan policy. Since there are relatively few biographical studies of leading PRC politicians there seems no need to justify the compilation of an up-to-date biography of Liao.

Seventeen years ago Stephen Fitzgerald drew the attention of English speaking readers to Liao's importance in the area of Overseas Chinese policy. As has been shown, there are clear links between foreign policy areas such as Taiwan, Hong Kong, Southeast Asia and Overseas Chinese policy, and the PRC's international united front strategy in general. It is less well known, that, originally, PRC foreign policy towards Japan was also developed within this context, and that this factor continues to shape and influence the PRC's foreign policy approach to Japan.

Liao Chengzhi combined leading offices in all three areas. For extended periods he was nominal, if not actual, head of the PRC's Overseas Chinese policy apparatus. From the early fifties he was consistently regarded as the PRC's main Japan specialist whose special links with Zhou Enlai made him the most authoritative spokesman vis-à-vis Japan, ranking only after Zhou (and Mao Zedong himself), thus bypassing the PRC's formal foreign affairs bureaucracy. Perhaps less known is Liao's deep involvement in international front organisations, mainly during the fifties. In the chronological account presented here the attempt has been made to portray Liao's activities synchronically in such a way that the interaction between these areas becomes clear. Liao's career, his successes and failures, can be understood only against the background of his leading role in all *three* areas.

The lack of diplomatic relations between Japan and the PRC for more than two decades prevented a thorough bureaucratisation and routinisation of PRC Japan policy even after 1972, when diplomatic relations were established. As a result, policy formulation was even more heavily influenced by party committees dealing with various aspects of foreign affairs and *ad hoc* decisions by top PRC leaders.

It seems fairly obvious that the dramatic increase in the PRC's mainly economic links with Japan - both qualitative and quantitative - will make the application of statistical methods in the analysis of PRC-Japan policy more relevant in future. Despite the seemingly greater predictability of future PRC policy towards Japan it would be wrong to ignore political, strategic and military factors which will continue to exert an influence and it is imperative to watch for signs of a change in the perception of Japan in the minds of the successors to the present élite.

Of course for long periods the formation of views on Japan was overshadowed completely by the experience of Japanese aggression. As early as the twenties, and increasingly during the thirties, Japan was China's enemy number one. During that period, however, Liao was not one of the CCP's 'Japan specialists'. It is perhaps surprising to note that his elevation to the position of the PRC's most prominent Japan specialist did not take place until the early fifties.

Throughout the main part of this study speculation about Liao's 'personal' views has been avoided. The main reason for this is that it is virtually impossible to guess to what extent his utterances after 1949 (and, to some extent, also before that date) contain his personal private views since articles, reported speeches and so on were normally issued as public stances of the CCP and the PRC. In the course of many interviews - most of them conducted in Japan - I have been confronted with a wide variety of subjective impressions of Liao. Most, but not all, those interviewed are mentioned in my 'acknowledgements'. As a rule, these interviews were held in the mother tongue of my counterpart, either Chinese or Japanese. I am most grateful for the willingness with which they shared their considerable knowledge both of Liao and of details of events. Sometimes I was given interesting and intriguing information which I was unable to verify or authenticate. Some ideas in the following observations are based on such information.

Compared to most other leading PRC politicians Liao's upbringing was singularly cosmopolitan. He spent a number of his childhood years in Tokyo. Being Chinese, growing up in Japan of course would not automatically imply love and affection for his host country, particularly in the face of occasional discrimination. Throughout his life Liao never left any doubt that his first loyalty was to China, the country of his parents. By all accounts he was able however to act and feel like a Japanese in contacts at personal level. His Japanese was better than near-native. Liao possessed considerable theatrical talent which suggests that he will have enjoyed assuming a different identity, a quality of considerable value for his later functions which demanded flexibility during contacts with people from different countries, cultures and walks of life. By the same token, having grown up bilingual, he intuitively acquired an ability to 'see things in perspective'. During his childhood years Sino-Japanese relations were not characterised by the antagonism and hostility of the twenties and thirties. No wonder that as a boy Liao could dream of becoming a marine, just like his Japanese classmates.

Liao's parents were Chinese, and nationalistic Chinese at that. Yet we can imagine him hearing at an early age that his father was in fact not born in China but in the United States, and he may have wondered what life would have been like had his father stayed there. Quite a number of Liao's relatives lived in the British colony of Hong Kong, and even now numerous direct relatives may be found as far away as the United States and Europe. Liao's father apparently attached great value to his son learning English, and due to his father's background Liao spoke English with an American accent. Despite such influences it is difficult to be specific about his feelings towards 'Western' countries. He saw little of his father, but even so he realised that his father was a Chinese politician of some importance. Liao Zhongkai himself was not a Communist, or even Socialist in a strict sense of the word, but he certainly had some sympathies in that direction. Direct ideological influence may have been limited but, consciously or unconsciously, Liao may have regarded his father as an example to be followed.

China, Japan and Liao Chengzhi

Throughout his childhood Liao's contact with his mother was much closer. It has often been said that she too was highly politically motivated and she was certainly more independent minded and interested in politics than most Chinese wives in those days. And yet, if Liao Zhongkai was a busy politician, He Xiangning was more a sensitive artist. I was repeatedly told of her strong reservations about the deep (and dangerous) political involvement of her children.

Liao Chengzhi was first confronted with Christianity rather than Socialism or Communism. His grandfather had been a Christian and although Liao Zhongkai had grown up in the United States he was very critical of the Christian mission in China whenever this served the interests of foreign powers rather than China. His decision to send his son to Christian schools both in Japan and China need not be seen as an expression of a pro-Christian attitude since such schools were generally regarded as 'centres of excellence' to which élite members would customarily send their children, regardless of their own religious (or political) convictions. Liao repeatedly pointed out the gap observed by him between the ideals and behaviour of Christians. He may not have 'believed' in Christianity in the religious sense of the word, but in my view it is quite likely that he assimilated part of the Christian value system. Some of his sarcastic comments on (un)Christian behaviour may be regarded as an expression of disappointment with Christian practice, and not so much as opposition to those values. At least one can say that from an early age he was quite well acquainted with that part of Western civilisation.

Like other students in those days Liao became actively involved in the anti-foreign (especially anti-British) student movement. He was deeply shocked by the violent suppression of the 'May 30' movement when he was seventeen, an age when radical ideas often appear attractive. Though not a Communist, Liao's father was a member of the so-called 'left-wing' of the KMT which was willing to collaborate with the Soviet Union and the Communists. We can guess that by then Liao had made his first acquaintance with Communists and their ideas but it is doubtful whether he would have believed in fundamentals of Marxism such as the theory of class struggle. During these years in China, and during his stay in Japan in 1927/28, Liao took active part in the students' movement, but to some of his fellow students in Japan he did not appear to be an 'ideological' activist. The assassination of his father must have been traumatic. It may have increased his readiness to accept more radical ideas, though he is not known to have 'changed his life' in order to avenge his father's death. Soon afterwards he formally joined Communist associations, followed by the German and Chinese Communist Parties. It seems that his mother was not happy with her son's participation in this radical movement. Liao's activity shows convincingly that he was firmly committed to nationalist ideas, at the risk of expulsion from Japan. For his father's generation the rapidly modernising Japan had been a source of admiration and inspiration, and Liao may have been saddened by increasing antagonism between an ever more aggressive Japan and a virtually defenceless China.

Liao's departure from Japan in 1928 marked the beginning of more than two decades during which he had virtually no direct link with that country. He visited

China for only a short period before leaving for Europe. There are conflicting reports as to the reason for his departure for Germany, while at the same time, his sister, Liao Mengxing, went to France. Liao Mengxing was a 'revolutionary' in her own right, intelligent and capable. Especially after the PRC's establishment in 1949 she remained in the shadow of her brother but continued active in politics, for instance in PRC liaison with the Soviet Union. Before 1949 she had been an assistant to Mme Sun Yatsen (Song Qingling). Although a portrayal of Liao's relations with his sister is of interest, available information is insufficient even to serve as a basis for speculation.

Liao spent several years in Europe, mainly Germany and Holland, but also the USSR. He joined the German Communist Party and was active in trade union activities among Chinese seamen overseas. There are indications that his activities were guided not only by the CCP and the German Communist Party, but also by the Comintern. It is, of course, not easy to draw a clear distinction between these activities, and due to the secrecy of such operations it is still difficult to give a precise account of his movements in Europe. Of particular interest is his impression of the Soviet Union. After his return to China Liao does not seem to have referred to his sojourn in the Soviet Union or his impressions there even to his Chinese party comrades. One reason for his reticence may have been the secret nature of part of his activities. His presence in the Soviet Union as such was not a secret, and his meeting with Chiang Kaishek's son, Jiang Jingguo, has been well publicised recently. Since he took the trouble to learn Russian one may conclude that his stay in the Soviet Union was meant to involve more than simply visits to conferences. Although he was enrolled at the University of the Far East I have been unable to obtain reliable information about the length of his stay.

Liao's stay in Europe improved his active knowledge of foreign languages, and his ability to communicate in a number of languages may also have meant that, compared to the average Overseas Chinese, his years in Europe affected him more deeply. If nothing else the experience stood him in good stead when he became one of the PRC's most widely travelled politicians, often attending conferences of international front organisations, and meeting some of his former acquaintances in Peking. His personal contacts with Dutch Communists, for instance, may have had additional relevance in view of Dutch links with Indonesian Communists.

On returning to China Liao briefly engaged in clandestine activities in Shanghai before betrayal and arrest. Due to the influence of several persons, his own mother, Song Qingling, Cai Yuanpei and Liu Yazi, a friend of the family, Liao was freed on condition that he refrain from political activity and submit to house arrest. There is evidence that he agreed to a statement declaring his disavowal of Communism. Even if his release was merely the result of the efforts of He Xiangning, Song Qingling and others, his conditional release set him apart from those Communists from 'lesser' families, some of whom never regained their freedom. Liao's family background had perhaps saved his life in Shanghai, it also contributed to his survival after his arrest by Zhang Guotao during the retreat to Yanan, and was certainly vital when he was arrested again by the (Nationalist) government in 1942.

China, Japan and Liao Chengzhi

Not long after his release in Shanghai in 1933 Liao broke the conditions of his release and headed for Communist-held areas. It is not quite clear whether his flight resulted in reprisals for his guarantors, or whether he left of his own volition or on orders from the Communist underground. Soon after he had joined Zhang Guotao's columns he was stripped of his party membership and faced various restrictions on his movements. Most later accounts attribute this to Zhang's 'viciousness' but it may be that the circumstances of his release aroused suspicion concerning his loyalty to the Communist cause. Political considerations may have restrained Zhang from killing Liao prematurely. In addition, Liao turned out to be useful as a painter and graphic designer, a rare asset among the soldiers in Zhang's column. His eventual release has been ascribed to a chance encounter with Zhou Enlai and Zhou's intervention. Certainly Zhou was personally acquainted with Liao Zhongkai and even knew Liao Chengzhi when he was a boy but the rescue action may have been mainly due to Liao's potential usefulness to the Communist cause, rather than emotional and sentimental reasons. Liao's fate was of deep concern to He Xiangning, Song Qingling and their sympathisers engaged in gaining support for a united national front of resistance including the Communists. Due to their continued membership of the KMT - a result of the fact that they were the living heirs of Sun Yatsen and Liao Zhongkai - Song Qingling and He Xiangning formed a valuable link between the Communist rebels and the KMT, with the Communists still hoping for a second period of co-operation with the KMT which would give them respite from government persecution. Liao's death would have estranged not only He Xiangning and Mme Sun but also those members within the KMT not fundamentally opposed to future co-operation with the Communists.

Liao was about thirty when he became involved in the Communist media in Yanan. In addition he took part in other 'cultural activities', proved himself a popular and capable actor and is also said to have written plays; unfortunately I have not been able to trace copies of these. Liao had been one of the most outspoken opponents of Zhang Guotao during Zhang's 'trial' in 1937, but as yet he did not occupy an important position among the party hierarchy in Yanan. There is also no indication that, during these years, he was associated with the CCP's 'Japan specialists' of the time. Soon after the temporary reconciliation between the KMT and the CCP in 1937-38 Liao was sent to Hong Kong to engage in united front work activity and liaison work. Although he became a leading member of the party organisation in Hong Kong his influence within the party as such seems to have been limited. During these years, until his arrest in 1942, he became acquainted with a number of Communist politicians such as Lu Dingyi, Li Weihan and others, who later on, after 1949, rose to positions of prominence within united front organisations. He also co-operated with Deng Fa and Li Kenong, both important figures in the world of CCP intelligence organisations. Liao's personal involvement in intelligence work is a closely guarded secret, but some of his close collaborators such as Luo Qingchang - whose 'special competence' was Taiwan and Overseas Chinese - are known to have played some role in CCP intelligence.

During these years in the South Liao Chengzhi also met politicians like Qu Wu who were later leading figures in organisations for united front work within China such as the *Minge,* one of the so-called 'democratic parties' in the PRC. When Hong Kong fell to the Japanese Liao was arrested soon after his flight towards an area still under government control. When arrested he had become well known through his work in Hong Kong but it would be exaggerating to say that he was a member of the party's central élite. Yet, even before his release in January 1946, Liao was made an alternate member of the CCP Central Committee, only becoming aware of it after his release. The appointment expressed considerable trust in his continued loyalty to the Communist cause. Among possible motives one may mention recognition of his work in Hong Kong and southern China before his arrest. It is tempting to speculate that such an appointment would make it less attractive for Liao to succumb to offers from Chiang Kaishek. In addition it may perhaps have given Liao added protection at a time when the KMT had to consider some form of negotiation with the Communists by the end of the anti-Japanese war.

Very soon after his release Liao became involved in diplomatic talks with the KMT and American observers about the implementation of the truce agreement in the Dongjiang area of Canton province. Although Liao had conducted talks with colonial authorities in Hong Kong in the late thirties and early forties, this was the first time he had engaged in quasi-diplomatic international talks. The next year saw Liao returning to Yanan to take over the leadership of the New China News Agency (NCNA) from Bo Gu, a well known high-ranking CCP veteran. In contrast to his previous association with the CCP news network this appointment carried considerable political weight. Moreover it again put him in touch with numerous members of the PRC's foreign affairs bureaucracy many with a background in pre-1949 media organisations. Yet again, Liao's participation in the media did not last long. When Mao tried to absolve himself from excesses connected with the campaign for land reform and a simultaneous party purge, he criticised Liao personally for shortcomings in the attitude of the media to these campaigns. Most likely because of this criticism Liao left the NCNA soon afterwards.

Although 1945 to 1949 is of great importance to a proper understanding of PRC history it is one of the least researched and understood in the history of 20th century China. Liao's moves in 1948, for instance, are hard to trace. When he reappeared in 1949 he was appointed to a host of positions involving him mainly in two areas, Overseas Chinese policy and international front organisations. Liao apparently had been unable to obtain a powerful post involving domestic affairs, a *sine qua non* for any élite member aspiring to a position of power in the CCP. At that stage there was still no indication that he would become deeply involved in PRC Japan policy. Communist publications dealing with Japan, and published between 1945 and 1949, do not include important contributions signed by Liao.

As I have shown, there is an intimate link between the development of PRC Japan policy and Liao's activities in international front organisations. I would place the beginning of Liao's career in the area of Japan policy somewhere between 1952 and 1953, the time of the Peace Conference for the Asian and Pacific

China, Japan and Liao Chengzhi

Region and Liao's participation in the negotiations on the repatriation of Japanese citizens. One may also assume that this was the period when Liao began playing a more important role in Central Committee sub-committees such as the United Front Work Department, the Foreign Liaison Office and the External Affairs Committee. Until this period Liao had been able to maintain a time-consuming interest in the theatre. He apparently was co-opted into the so-called Japan policy group in 1953 as one of its important members, carrying out his duties under Zhou's personal guidance. Liao's choice was probably not determined by his 'understanding' of Japan or his special competence in that area, but by his coincident competence in a number of areas. Later Liao did occupy offices within the government's foreign affairs bureaucracy. He became Deputy Director of the Office in Charge of Foreign Affairs in 1958, and adviser to the Foreign Ministry in the seventies. His rise to prominence in foreign affairs was only possible because the party determined and co-ordinated foreign policy through its various committees. Liao's career did not take place within a compartmentalised governmental foreign affairs bureaucracy, but was due to a rather flexible organisational approach to foreign affairs discussed and designed by top party leaders with the aid of committees. His work in the government foreign affairs service is therefore a reflection of his role on a number of party committees dealing with particular aspects of foreign affairs.

Until the death of Zhou Enlai Liao frequently acted as 'Zhou Enlai's personal representative' in negotiations with Japanese and, as such, enjoyed higher authority and standing than other Japan specialists like Zhang Xiangshan, Sun Pinghua, Wang Xiaoyun, Xiao Xiangqian or Jin Sucheng. After Zhou's death Liao appears on occasion to have acted in a similar way as 'Deng Xiaoping's representative' in talks with Japanese visitors. By that time - around 1978 - diplomatic relations with Japan had been established, and the increasing size and complexity of relations demanded routinisation and bureaucratisation, limiting Liao's role to a few areas such as the negotiations for a 'Treaty of Peace and Friendship'.

Liao Chengzhi's career was thus extremely dependent on Zhou Enlai's position. It would be of great interest to ascertain to what extent Liao may have been able to influence the views not only of Zhou but also of other members of the CCP hierarchy. Liao's influence would have been greater had he been able completely to dominate PRC and CCP organs dealing with Japan. This was certainly not the case during the seventies when there was a well-known 'split' between adherents of the radicals and their opponents within the PRC embassy in Tokyo (and elsewhere), and similar disunity also characterised the composition of several delegations to Japan. Yet, even during the fifties and sixties, there were several periods when Liao's apparent pre-eminence did not entail monopolisation, as for instance in the first year of the Great Leap Forward (1958). One may also wonder how far Liao competed with Zhang Xiangshan in matters concerning the JCP, widely assumed to be Zhang's particular responsibility. Also, relations with the JCP at times were dominated by ideological questions related to the Sino-Soviet dispute, questions clearly beyond Liao's competence. For a short period in the late fifties Liao himself was involved in discussions with the Soviets on matters of dispute affecting international front organisations, in particular Communist relations with representatives from Asia, Africa and Latin America. It seems unlikely, however, that he contributed actively to policy formulation in that ideologically charged area.

This brings us to a second point. To what extent did Liao develop and maintain personal views on policy towards Japan, and to what extent could he influence Zhou Enlai and other members of the élite? Generally Liao is seen as a 'moderate', a 'soft-liner', whose name is connected with a gradual approach. Proponents of that approach sought to improve and intensify relations with Japan by the gradual build-up of trade and other links to create a momentum that would eventually result in the establishment of formal diplomatic relations. In 1958 Lei Renmin suggested that the existence of domestic hardliners was frustrating the moderate line represented by Liao. In 1966-67 the ascendancy of more radical views accompanied by Liu Ningyi's rise to prominence eclipsed Liao. The relaxation of PRC policy towards Japan in 1971-72 saw Liao's rehabilitation, and his promotion to high office in government and the party after 1978 coincides with the rise of Deng Xiaoping. Liao is also generally regarded as representing a moderate line in the area of Overseas Chinese policy where he also argued for an incremental approach instead of the all-or-nothing policies of the Cultural Revolution.

A systematic study of Liao's published speeches and articles is less revealing than might be thought. Liao seems to have participated in the composition of his speeches and articles to a greater extent than many other PRC politicians, but the need to adhere to the clichés of the day largely conceals his 'personal' views. Of greater interest is the study of copies and summaries of his speeches to Japanese visitors, some of which I have referred to before. The relative lack of set phrases and empty propaganda contrasts markedly with speeches by other PRC politicians delivered on the same occasions. Generally Liao was averse to conforming to the ideological vagaries of the day and more prone to accept a realistic compromise. This alone may have made him enemies among his more doctrinaire colleagues who in addition may have resented his 'bourgeois' family background and lifestyle. He was certainly a 'moderate' as far as *tactics* is concerned. There seems to be no reason to doubt his loyalty to the Communist cause as the only means of bringing about 'national unity', the only way of satisfying nationalist aspirations.

In the area of international front organisations Liao often appeared as a 'radical' and a typical representative of the PRC's policy of 'incitement towards revolution'. There are reports to the effect that, during Mao's talks with Stalin in early 1950, it was agreed to 'concede' to the CCP propaganda towards Asians in international front organisations and to some extent within the Asian Communist movement. There is no doubt that right from the early beginnings of the front organisations - around 1947 - Communist Chinese representatives made use of the opportunity to establish contacts with fellow Asians, later also with Africans and Arabs, independently from Soviet representatives. To all appearances Liao proved himself very able in establishing a good personal rapport with such representatives from Third World countries. From the beginning of the public revelation of the Sino-Soviet split in 1960 Liao was one of the CPSU's harshest critics. His speeches were full of revolutionary rhetoric and form a conspicuous contrast to his moderate attitude in talks with Japanese visitors. A good example of this is to be found in an important speech delivered a few days before Mao's famous article 'Long Live Leninism', anticipating some of the main themes of the article.

Throughout the sixties Liao was a consistent critic of the United States, and many of his activities in the area of Japan policy were designed to drive a wedge between Japan and the USA. For example, Liao called the Ikeda government in 1962 a 'running dog of American imperialism', and claimed that 'there is no way to change and conceal the iron-hard reality that American imperialism is the factual ruler of Japan'. He urged the Japanese to 'strengthen the struggle until US imperialism has been driven from Chinese territory (ie Taiwan) and from Japanese territory (ie Okinawa and American military bases in Japan)'.

At first sight Liao's attitude revealed in such speeches seems to contradict his 'moderate' approach referred to above. It would not be difficult to rationalise this apparent contradiction in terms of the Marxist-Leninist distinction between 'tactics' and 'strategy'. It is also tempting to ascribe the 'radical' part of his utterances to the dictates of the party, an explanation which has to be taken into account in any case. Another relevant factor lies in Liao's apparent sympathy for 'Asianism' (Asian nationalism). 'Asianism' must have seemed attractive to Liao Chengzhi just as it was to numerous Japanese 'Old China hands'. Whatever the differences between Japanese and Chinese nationalism the exclusion of non-Asian powers - the USSR, Great Britain and the USA - was and is an important element of Japanese and Chinese nationalistic currents. Just as Liao had an aversion to textbook Communism of any type, it is not difficult to imagine that he was particularly opposed to Soviet claims of leadership in international Communism. In this context it may be noted briefly that it was not only Mao's own dogmatic claims for sinicised Communism that caused Chinese Communists to refute Soviet claims.

More than any other single PRC politician Liao had direct access to confidential information on Japanese party politics and factional infighting. There is no doubt that Zhou Enlai also relied on independent intelligence reports, but Liao's judgment must have weighed heavily in the CCP's assessment of the Japanese domestic political situation. Liao will have presented his views either consciously or unconsciously in such a way as to influence PRC policy. Although the majority of PRC Japan specialists supported Liao's approach in general they did not constitute an independent power base that would have enabled him to push his ideas against the wishes and will of central party organs. In a nutshell, the strength of Liao's position lay in his personal relations with Zhou and in the fact that his position had become a political symbol of the state of PRC relations with Japan - the better relations with Japan, the safer Liao's position. It is therefore natural to expect that, regardless of his political and personal view of Japanese policy at a given moment, he must have been interested in a gradual approach avoiding unnecessary risks.

Liao's position rose and fell with PRC united front policy. Many close friends, like Song Qingling, Huang Dingchen, Si Mu, and Situ Huimin, were also active in this area. Liao had many acquaintances in other areas: to give one example, his acquaintance with the important propaganda chief Lu Dingyi dates back to the thirties, but it is doubtful to what extent he could be counted as a positive political asset for Liao. He was also often in touch with members of the government foreign affairs bureaucracy like Ji Pengfei, Qiao Guanhua and Wang Guoquan. He does not seem to have been sufficiently powerful to influence the general direction of foreign policy by manipulation of opposing factions within party and government foreign affairs offices. The Cultural Revolution not only brought personal disaster to many members of the élite, it laid the foundation for new intense personal relations and friendships. Liao's ties with He Long's family clearly result from Liao's aid and protection given to He's children early in the Cultural Revolution; such ties weighed particularly heavily from 1977-78 onwards. Liao had previously been acquainted with Wang Jiaxiang, but became his friend only as a result of the Cultural Revolution. Perhaps the most vivid demonstration of the importance of personal ties created during the GPCR was given during the visit to Japan in 1979 of the PRC's friendship liner *Minghua*. The list of participants reads like a list of élite families, united as a result of shared suffering during the GPCR.

It is not surprising, perhaps, that such bonds also found expression in marriage ties such as those between the children of He Long and Liao Chengzhi. Liao's meteoric rise in government and party hierarchy after 1978 - two years after the death of his most vital patron Zhou Enlai - should not only be seen as a sign of a revitalised united front policy, but also an expression of these (new) personal ties.

As a whole Liao's personal influence on the basic line of PRC foreign policy towards Japan was rather limited. This study has shown that he played an important role in advising Zhou Enlai during various phases of formal and informal negotiations, including matters of negotiating tactics, the issuing of invitations to delegations from Japan and the selection of suitable dates for negotiations and talks. Liao's personal ties with numerous high-ranking Japanese made him an important source for intelligence on Japan. Combined with his functions as a kind of 'guarantor' his presence had come to be regarded in Japan as a reliable indicator for a stable PRC policy towards Japan. From the Japanese point of view it therefore seemed valuable to 'cultivate' personal relations with Liao Chengzhi. Such contacts might increase chances for business with the PRC, or improve a Japanese politician's 'image'. It could also be argued that co-operation with Liao would strengthen Liao's position in Peking, which, in turn, might contribute to the stability of PRC Japan policy, particularly in the period before the establishment of formal diplomatic relations. It is an open question whether this 'symbiotic' relationship was more advantageous to the PRC or to individual Japanese politicians and business representatives. Each needed and supplemented the other.

At various times Japanese politicians friendly to Peking attempted to sound out the possibility of improved relations between the PRC and the USA. Offers made to Japanese visitors by Zhou during the fifties concerning the PRC's willingness to abrogate the defence relationship with the Soviet Union if Japan would abandon its defence agreement with the United States were usually regarded as attempts by Communist China to drive a wedge between Japan and the United States. I also suggested a link between US and Japanese negotiations on the repatriation of their respective citizens from the PRC. In the early sixties Takasaki Tatsunosuke and Nakasone Yasuhiro visited the United States before reporting on US attitudes to the PRC in talks with Liao. During the late sixties Soviet sources repeatedly claimed Japanese-PRC-US 'collusion'. Polemics apart, it seems interesting to elucidate further the extent to which Japanese politicians were able - or not - to function as a bridge between the PRC and the USA. Despite recognition by most researchers of the importance of Japan's US links for the history of relations between the PRC and Japan we are still in need of further studies on this topic. Moreover, just as in the past, PRC views on the nature of the relationship between Japan and the United States will continue to exercise great influence on PRC strategic thinking not just on its policy towards Japan, but also on its strategy in general.

Summarising Liao's role in the history of PRC relations with Japan one may say that, during the fifties and sixties, he was one of the main, if not the main, actors in PRC attempts to establish diplomatic and trade links with Japan which, at that time, were widely regarded as attempts to drive a wedge between the USA and Japan. After an interval of about four years - due to the turmoil of the GPCR - Liao reappeared in 1972 as the PRC's most authoritative spokesman on Japan especially in the political realm, ranking only behind top leaders like Zhou Enlai and Deng Xiaoping. However, Liao's independent power base was small. His career was greatly aided by his family background, international experience, knowledge of languages and successful involvement in Overseas Chinese policy and international front organisations. Coupled with his ability to communicate easily with visiting Japanese from all walks of life he was undeniably able to contribute to the development of PRC relations with Japan. His career however was largely dependent on Zhou's personal patronage and suffered immediately at the first sign of a weakening of the PRC's united front approach, as in 1958 (first year of the Great Leap Forward) and 1966-67 (GPCR).

Liao's rise to high office after 1978, in particular his membership of the Politburo in 1982 and nomination for the vice-presidency of the People's Republic of China a few days before his death in 1983, were recognition of the importance attributed to united front policy as well as to his standing in that area, rather than an expression of independent political power. So far nobody among the PRC's Japan specialists has taken over Liao's unique role. It is to be expected that, henceforth, PRC policy towards Japan will become increasingly routinised, and less dependent on the personal ability and initiative of someone like Liao. Despite his undeniable role in international affairs - in particular in relations with Japan - this study does not contradict the common wisdom that the basic line of PRC foreign policy continues to be the undisputed preserve of central policymakers at the very apex of political power in Peking, at least as long as central power is able to maintain itself against growing regional pressure in the wake of political transformations that are sure to accompany the replacement of Peking's present ageing leaders.

Bibliography

H Adomeit and R Boardman, eds *Foreign Policy Making in Communist Countries. A Comparative Approach*, (England: Westmead, 1979).
Ajia keizai junpo, (periodical).
Akahata, (periodical).
Y Akashi, *The Nanyang Chinese National Salvation Movement, 1937-41*, (University of Kansas, 1970).
Akioka Ieshige, *Pekin tokuhain*, (Asahi shinbunsha, 1973).
Akiyama Yoshiaki, *Chugoku sensen no hansen heishi (senso to ningen no kiroku)*, (Gendaishi shuppankai, 1978).
Ando Hikotaro:
    Nitchu kankei no shiten, (Ryukei shosha, 1975).
    Pekindayori, (Tamagawa daigaku shuppanbu, 1979).
'Anpo haiki ga saiko mokuhyo - Chukyo, tai nichi kosaku o sekkyokuka -', *(Sekai shuho*, 14 April 1964).
Arai Takeo, *Shu Onrai no jissen*, (Ushio shuppansha, 1979).
J D Armstrong, *Revolutionary Diplomacy. Chinese Foreign Policy and the United Front Doctrine*, (1977).
Asahi shinbun, (periodical).
Asahi janaru, (periodical).
Asahi shinbunsha, comp *Tenkai suru kakumei gaiko*, (1971).
Balujun zhengzhibu, comp *Junzheng zazhi*.
Banno Masataka and Eto Shinkichi, comp *Chugoku o meguru kokusai seiji*, (1968).
W J Barnds, ed, *China and America. The Search for a New Relationship*, (New York: 1977).
A Doak Barnett:
    China and the Major Powers in East Asia, (Washington, DC: 1977).
    Communist China and Asia, (1960).
    Communist China: the Early Years, (New York: 1964).
Gregor Benton, 'The Second Wang Ming Line (1935-38)', *China Quarterly* no 61 (March 1975):61-94.
Biographic Information, (US Department of State, 3 June 1956).
Bixu zhongshi qiaowu gongzuo, (Hong Kong: Sanlian, 1978).
Robert Boardman, 'Ideology, Organisation and Environment: Sources of Chinese Foreign Policy Making', Adomeit et al, eds, *Foreign Policy Making in Communist Countries*, pp 112-49.
Boeicho buei kenshusho senshishitsu, comp *Hokushi no chiansen* 2 vols, (1968 and 1971).
Bohai ribao, (periodical).
Howard Boorman, ed, *Biographical Dictionary of Republican China*, (New York and London:, vol 1, 1967; vol 2, 1968; vol 3, 1970; vol 4, 1971).
Hugh Borton et al, eds, *Japan Between East and West*, (1957).
J H Boyle, *China and Japan at War, 1937-1945: The Politics of Collaboration* (Stanford UP, 1972).
Philip Bridgham, 'Mao's Cultural Revolution in 1967: The Struggle to Seize Power', *China Quarterly* 34 (April/June 1968): 6-37.
Roger Glenn Brown, 'Chinese Politics and American Policy: A New Look at the Triangle' *Foreign Policy* 23 (Summer 1976):3-23.

Bibliography

Bill Brugger, *Contemporary China*, (London: 1977).
Monte Ray Bullard, 'People's Republic of China Elite Studies: A Review of the Literature' *Asian Survey* XIX(8) (August 1979): pp 789-800.
'Bunka daikakumei to chukyo jinji kankei', *Sekai shuho* 48-6 (7 February 1967).
Bruce Burton, 'Contending Explanations of the 1979 Sino-Vietnamese War', *International Journal* XXXIV(4) (Autumn 1979):699-722.
Les Buszynski, 'Vietnam Confronts China', *Asian Survey* XX(8) (August 1980):829-43.
Cao Guozhi, *He Xiangning xiansheng yu Zhongguo funü yundong*, (Hong Kong: 1941).
Gilbert Chan Fook-lam, *A Chinese Revolutionary: The Career of Liao Chung-k'ai (1878-1925)*, (PhD, Columbia University, 1975; Xerox University Microfilms).
Steve Chan Sui Tak, *Conflict Modelling and Management: Chinese Foreign Policy Behaviour in the Vietnam War, 1963-1965*, (PhD, University of Minnesota, 1976).
Chang Chuan, 'Liao gong de zuihou shike', *Zhengming* 69 (July 1983):26-9.
C Y Chang, 'Overseas Chinese in China's Policy', *China Quarterly* 82 (1980).
Chang Kuo-t'ao, *The Rise of the Chinese Communist Party, 1921-1927*, vol 1, (1971).
Parris H Chang, 'Research Notes on the Changing Loci of Decision Making in the Chinese Communist Party', *China Quarterly* 44 (October-December 1970):169-94.
'Chedi suqing hei [xiuyang] zai Zhongqiaowei de liudu', *Zhonggong wenhua dageming ziliao huibian, di1juan*, (Ding Wang, comp Mingbao yuekan), pp 711-13.
Chen Cisheng, 'Geming muqin He Xiangning xiansheng', *Huiyi yu huainian - jinian geming laoren He Xiangning shishi shi zhounian*, pp 136-49 (reprinted from *Guangxi ribao*, Xihuangyao ed, beg 1945).
King C Chen:
    'Peking's Attitude Toward Taiwan', *Asian Survey* XVII.10 (October 1977) pp 903-18.
    Vietnam and China, 1938-1954, (Princeton UP, 1969).
Chen Fengxi, 'Yi He Xiangning laoren', *Huiyi yu huainian - jinian geming laoren He Xiangning shishi shi zhounian*, pp 222-32.
Jean Chesneaux, *Le mouvement ouvrier Chinoise de 1919 à 1927*, (Paris: La Haye, 1962).
Chen Xianggong, *Qiu Kin nianpy ji zhuanji ziliao*, Zhonghua shuju, (Peking: 1983).
'Chin Gi fukusori to no kaikenki', *Sekai* 244 (March 1966) pp 88-97.
China Handbook 1937-1945, (New York: 1947).
China News Analysis.
China News Service.
'"Chishima wa Nihon e kaesubeki da." Mo shuseki, Shakaito shisetsudan ni kataru', *Sekai shuho*, (11 August 1964).
Chiu Hungdah, ed, *China and the Taiwan Issue*, (New York: 1979).
M Y Cho, *Die Volks-Diplomatie in Ostasien. Entstehung, Theorie, und Praxis*, (Wiesbaden: 1971).
Golan W Choudhury, 'Trends in China: Post Mao Policy in Asia', *Problems of Communism* (July-August 1977), pp 18-29.
Robert C Christopher, 'The US and Japan: A Time for Healing', *Foreign Affairs* (July 1978), pp 857-66.
W L Chu, 'Liao Ch'eng-chih - A Maoist "Liberated" Cadre', *Issues and Studies* (November 1972), pp 86-8.
Chu Hosaku, see Naka Hosaku.
Chugai chusakai, comp, *Chukyo no tainichi kyoei taido no imi*, (1958). [Tokubetsu shiryo.39]

China's Relations with Japan

'Chugoku kyusanto no higohoteki soshiki', *Koan chusa shiryo* (28 March 1953) [Chukyo kakumei ni kansuru shiryo].

Chugoku kyusantushi shiryoshu, vol 2, (Keiso shobo, 1975).

'[Zadankai] Chugoku mondai to Nihon no gaiko', *Sekai* 223 (July 1964).

Chugoku nenkan, 1955, 1959, 1960, 1961.

Chugoku no Kakyo seisaku, Naikaku kanbo, (Naikaku chusashitsu comp April 1974).

Chukyo no tai nichi kyoei taido no imi, see Chugai chusakai, comp.

Chukyo tai nichi juyo genronshu, 1955, 1956, 1958, 1959, 1960, 1961, 1962, 1963, 1964.

Chin O Chung, *P'yongyang between Peking and Moscow*, (University of Alabama Press, 1978).

'Chunichi yuko kyokai honichi daihyodan no ashiato', *Ajia keizai junpo*, (June 1973, chu).

'Chunichi yuko kyokai setsuritsu taikai ni okeru So Tonan, Ryo Shoshi no aisatsu', in *[Sengo shiryo] Nitchu kankei*, pp 323-4.

Chuo koron, (periodical).

Ralph Clough, 'The Taiwan Issue in Sino-American Relations', in Barnds, ed, *China and America*, pp 144-95.

CNA, (*China News Analysis*, periodical).

Jerome A Cohen, ed, *The Dynamics of China's Foreign Relations*, (Harvard University Press, 1970 [Harvard East Asian Monographs.39]).

Communist China 1955, (Union Research Institute (URI), Hong Kong).

Communist China 1958, (URI, Hong Kong: 1959).

Communist China 1961, vol 2, (URI, Hong Kong: 1962).

Cong gongfei tongzhan zuotanhui de fayan kan feiqu zhenxiang, (1957).

Cong wei zhengxie huiyi yanxi feibang neibu maodun, (March 1957).

'A Criticism of Liao Ch'eng-chih's Revisionist Line of "Three Capitulations and One Destruction"', *Issues and Studies* (April 1973), 84-9.

Dagongbao, (periodical).

Daily Summary of the Japanese Press.

'Daisanji Matsumura hochu no seika', *Sekai* 222 (June 1964), pp 207-12.

Dalu qingbao, (periodical).

Dalu qingshi fenxi huibian. 1969 nian, (Taipei: March 1970).

Dalu qingshi zhaiyao huibian (1975 nian 1 yue 8 ri - 5 yue 29 ri, (Taipei: May 1978)).

Dang de shenghuo, (periodical).

Dangzheng zhuanji, (periodical).

Deng Zhongxia, *Zhongguo zhigong yundong jianshi (1919-1926)*, (1953, first edition 1949).

Despatches of John S Service see Esherick, *Lost Chance in China*.

John Despres et al, *Timely Lessons of History: The Manchurian Model for Soviet Strategy*, Rand Corporation (July 1976). [R-1825-NA].

Ding Chuyuan, 'Feidang "shier zhongquanhui" douzheng "eryue niliu" daji fei "zhongqiaowei"', *Feiwei qiaowu jianbao* (1 December 1968).

Ding Chuyuan, 'Mao fei fadong wenge yu feiwei qiaowu gongzuo', *Qiaowu weiyuanhui diqing yanjiushi* (5 April 1969).

Lowell Dittmer:

'Bases of Power in Chinese Politics: A Theory and an Analysis of the Fall of the "Gang of Four"', *World Politics* XXX.1 (October 1978), pp 26-60.

Bibliography

'China in 1980: Modernization and Its Discontents', *Asian Survey* XX.1 (January 1981), pp 31-50.

Dixia douzheng gangling. See *Zhonggong zhongyang zuijin banbu zhi [dixia douzheng gangling].*

Doi Akio:

'Mo Takuto shuseki to no kaidanki', *Tairiku mondai* (December 1956), pp 26-30.

'Shakaito no tai chukyo seisaku', *Tairiku mondai* (June 1957).

Jürgen Domes, *China nach der Kulturrevolution,* (München: 1975).

William F Dorrill, 'Transfer of Legitimacy in the Chinese Communist Party: Origins of the Maoist Myth', *China Quarterly* 36 (October-December 1968), pp 45-60.

Douzheng, (periodical).

Peter F Drucker, 'Japan: The Problems of Success', *Foreign Affairs* (April 1978), pp 564-78.

V P Dutt, *China and the World. An Analysis of Communist China's Foreign Policy,* (Praeger, 1967).

Lilita I Dzirkals, *'Lightning War' in Manchuria: Soviet Military Analysis of the 1945 Far East Campaign,* (Rand Corporation, 1976).

Edi caozong xia de guojixing qunzhong zuzhi gaikuang diaocha, (Taipei: September 1958).

Ekonomisuto, (periodical).

Robert B Ekvall, *Faithful Echo,* (New York: 1960).

Mark Elvin, *The Pattern of the Chinese Past,* (London: 1973).

Endo Saburo, 'Nitchu jugonen senso to watakushi - kokuzoku. aka no shogun to hito wa iu', *Nitchu shorin* (November 1974).

Joseph W Esherick, ed, *Lost Chance in China. The World War II Despatches of John S Service,* (New York: 1974).

Eto Shinkichi:

comp *Chugoku o meguru kokusai seiji.* See Banno Masataka and Eto Shinkichi, comp *Chugoku o meguru kokusai seiji.*

'Chugoku hodo. Nihon to sekai no shinbun', *Bungei shunju* L.4 (April 1972), pp 172-87.

Higashi Ajia seijishi kenkyu, (Tokyo daigaku shuppankai, 1968).

'Post-war Japanese-Chinese Relations', *Survey*, 18.4 (1972):55-65.

Eto Shinkichi and Banno Masataka, *[Chugoku o meguru] Kokusai seiji,* (1968).

Eto Shinkichi and Tatsumi Okabe, 'Content Analysis of Statements in Regard to Japan Made by the People's Republic of China - Source Materials: *The People's Daily* in Two Periods in 1958', *Developing Economies*, 3.1 (March 1965), pp 48-72.

Peggy Falkenheim, 'Eurocommunism in Asia: The Communist Party of Japan and the Soviet Union', *Pacific Affairs* LII.1 (Spring 1979), pp 64-77.

FEER (Far Eastern Economic Review).

Fei dangzheng ganbu. Renshi ziliao huibian, (Taipei: August 1966).

Fei dui Riben de shentou huodong, (October 1964) [Feiqing yanjiu zhuanbao].

Fei qingniangtuan disanci daibiao dahui jueyian fenxi, (Taipei: June 1957).

Fei shengwei shuji Lao Hong, (Taipei: January 1952).

'Fei xin minzhuzhuyi qingniantuan disanjie dahui zhi fenxi yanjiu.' *Renshi diren* VI.5.

Fei zhuwai ge shilingguan renshi diaocha, (Taipei: July 1979).

Feidang zhongyang renshi ziliao, (Taipei: 1 January 1960).

Feidang zuzhi zuijin you he gaibian, (Taipei: December 1950).

Feie dongtai fenxi, (Taipei).

Feiqing cankao ziliao jianbian, (Taipei: 1 January 1973).
Feiqing jiyao, (Taipei: July 1964).
Feiqing yuebao, (periodical).
Feiqu guancha baogao, (periodical).
Feiri maoyi jingwei, (Taipei: July 1964).
Feiri maoyi pouxi, (Taipei: October 1968). [Dalu jingji yanjiu congshu di16 ji].
Feiwei huaqiao jianbao, (periodical).
Feiwei jiben ziliao huibian. waijiao zhuanji, (Taipei: June 1975).
Feiwei qiaowu gongzuo zhi yanjiu, (periodical).
Feiwei qiaowu jianbao, (periodical).
Feiwei renshi ziliao. 1970 nian, (Taipei: December 1970).
Feiwei renshi ziliao huibian. 1962 nian, (Taipei).
Feiwei renshi ziliao huibian. 1964 nian, (Taipei: May 1964).
Feiwei renshi ziliao huibian. renwuzhi.2 (buchong xiuzheng ziliao). Minguo 56 nian ban, (Taipei).
Feiwei renshi ziliao huibian. renwuzhi.5, (Taipei).
Feiwei renshi ziliao huibian. renwuzhi.1956 nian (buchong xiuzheng ziliao, (Taipei: 1961).
Feiwei renshi ziliao huibian. zuzhibiao. 1956 nian, (Taipei: January 1956).
Feiwei renshi ziliao huibian. zuzhibiao. 1968 nian, (Taipei: June 1968).
Feiwei renshi ziliao huibian. zuzhibiao. 1974 nian, (Taipei: October 1974).
Feiwei renshi ziliao huibian. zuzhibiao. 1975 nian, (Taipei: October 1975).
Feiwei renshi ziliao huibian. zuzhibiao. 1978 nian, (Taipei: June 1978).
Feiwei waijiao yu zhuwai renshi diaocha, (Taipei: July 1978).
Feiyou zhongyao jianghua huibian, vol 5 (1981-82).
Feng Wen, 'Liao fei Chengzhi yu feiwei qiaowu gongzuo', *Gongfei huoqiao zhenxiang*, (Taipei: [comp Qiaowu weiyuanhui diqing yanjiushi]).
Stephen Fitzgerald, *China and the Overseas Chinese. A Study of Peking's Changing Policy, 1949-1970*, (London: 1972).
Five Hundred Leading Communists (In the Eastern Hemisphere, excluding the USSR), Supplement IV, Report: The Strategy and Tactics of World Communism. Committee on Foreign Affairs, comp, US Congress, 1948 [National and International Movements].
Foreign Relations of the United States 1946. Vol X: The Far East: China, (Washington: 1972).
Lawrence Freedman, 'The Consequences of Failure in SALT', *Adelphi Papers* 141, pp 35-42.
Edward Friedman, 'On Maoist Conceptualizations of the Capitalist World System', *China Quarterly* (December 1979), pp 806-37.
Fukui Haruhiro:
    'Foreign-policy Making by Improvisation - The Japanese Experience', *International Journal* XXXII.4 (Autumn 1977), pp 791-812.
    'Tanaka Goes to Peking', in *Policy Making in Japan*, ed T J Pempel, chapter III (page numbers are according to a manuscript copy kindly provided by Prof Fukui).
    Party in Power. The Japanese Liberal-Democrats and Policy-making, (Australian National University Press, Canberra: 1970).
E G Furin, '1960 nen kyosanto kaigi no kaisoroku', *Shakaishugi seiji keizai kenkyu kenkyu shiryo* VII-3 (March 1964), pp 24-41.
Furui Yoshimi:

Bibliography

Nitchu juhachinen, (1978).

'Nitchu kokku seijoka no hiwa', *Chuo koron*, (December 1972).

Fuxiaobao, (periodical).

Gao Jie, '"Fan chaoliu" yu dui Mei zhengce', *Zhonghua yuebao* 699 (December 1973), pp 22-3. [Hong Kong]

B G Garth, ed, *China's Changing Role in the World Economy*, (New York: 1975).

John Garver, 'Chinese Foreign Policy in 1970: The Tilt Towards the Soviet Union', *China Quarterly* (June 1980).

Ge Gongzhen, *Zhongguo baoxue shi*, (Peking: 1955).

'Gensuikin taikai ni okeru "Chuso ronso"', *Sekai* 214 (October 1963).

'Gespräch Mao Tse-tungs mit japanischen Sozialisten. (Sowjetische Darstellung)', Heinz Brahm, *Pekings Griff nach der Vormacht. Der chinesisch-sowjetische Konflikt von Juli 1963 bis März 1965*, (Köln: 1966) [Aktuelle Studien, Bd.3], pp 202-3.

Donald G Gillin, *Warlord: Yen Hsi-shan in Shansi Province, 1911-1949*, (1967).

John Gittings:
>'Military Control and Leadership, 1949-1964', *China Quarterly* 26 (April-June 1966), pp 82-101.
>
>*The Sino-Soviet Dispute*, (Oxford: 1964).
>
>*Survey of the Sino-Soviet Dispute*, (London: 1968).

Joachim Glaubitz:
>'Balancing Between Adversaries: Sino-Japanese Relations and Soviet Interference', *Pacific Community* IX.1 (October 1977), pp 31-45.
>
>*Materialien zur Aussen- und Sicherheitspolitik Japans. 4. Folge*, (April 1978).
>
>*Schwerpunkte der Aussenpolitik Japans 1977-78*, (May 1978).
>
>*Schwerpunkte der Aussenpolitik Japans 1978*, (May 1979).

Merle Goldmann, 'China's Anti-Confucian Campaign, 1973-74', *China Quarterly* 63 (September 1975), pp 435-62.

Steven M Goldstein, 'The Chinese Revolution and the Colonial Areas: The View from Yenan, 1937-41', *China Quarterly* 75 (1978), pp 594-622.

Gong Ping [Jiangxisheng zhengfu wenshiguan] 'Xiangqi le Liao Chengzhi de yifu hua', *Liaowang*, (November 1982), p 33.

Gongfei waijiao renyuan, (Taipei).

Gongdang quanguo xingzheng zuzhi. xitongbiao, (Taipei).

Gongfei de haiwai gongzuo, (Taipei: December 1968). [Feiqing yanjiu zhuanbao]

Gongfei de qiaowu huodong, (Taipei: April 1952).

Gongfei dui Ri maoyi gongshi quanmao, (Taipei). [Feiqing jiben xushu congshu].

Gongfei dui Ri xuanchuan zhi fenxi, (Taipei).

Gongfei duiwai wenhua huodong. Gongfei duiwai huodong congshu, (Taipei: April 1962).

Gongfei duiwai wenhua tongzhan zhi fenxi, (Taipei: October 1963).

Gongfei duiwai xuancuan celüe yunyong fangshi ji wo ying cai zhi duice, (Taipei: 1972).

Gongfei dui yafei diqu geguo shentou dianfu huodong gaikuang, (Taipei: March 1969).

Gongfei ganbu jiyao, (Taipei).

Gongfei jinyinianlai zhongda cuoshi jiqi qingkuang zhi fenxi, (Taipei).

Gongfei juxing disici qiaowu huiyi de yinmou fenxi, (Taipei: June 1956).

Gongfei lingdao wenti, (Taipei: May 1948) (reprint).

'Gongfei qingniantuan juxing "disanci quanguo daibiao dahui".' *Renshi diren* VI.8.
Gongfei renshi ziliao huibian, (Taipei).
Gongfei renwuzhi, (Taipei: January 1970).
Gongfei tongzhan gongzuo de celue yu yunyong, (Taipei: January 1960).
Gongfei waijiao renyuan jiqita haiwai wei guan zhi renshi diaocha, (Taipei: July 1966).
Gongfei xianxing waijiao zhengce ji duiwai huodong, (Taipei: April 1960).
Gongfei xuanchuan neimu, (Taipei: 25 November 1947).
Gongfei yu minmeng zhi jian, Zhonglian 1947.
Gongfei zhanli panduanbiao, di 10 ci, (20 January 1948).
Gongfei zhongyao renwu huibian, (Taipei: 1 February 1965).
Diaochaju, comp *Gongfei zhongyao renwu diaocha*, (Taipei: June 1950).
Gongfei zhongyao ziliao huibian, vol 10, (Taipei: August 1952).
Bernard Gordon:
>'Japan, the United States, and Southeast Asia', *Foreign Affairs* (April 1978), pp 579-600.
>'Loose Cannon on a Rolling Deck? Japan's Changing Security Policies', *Orbis* (Winter 1979), pp 967-1005.

Bruce Grant, 'The Security of Southeast Asia', *Adelphi Paper* 142 (Spring 1978).
A Great Trial in Chinese History, (Peking: 1981).
W E Griffith:
>*Albania and the Sino-Soviet Rift*, (Cambridge, Mass: 1963).
>*Sino-Soviet Relations, 1964-1965*, (Cambridge, Mass and London: 1967).

'Guangdong dongjiang yu qiongyai de youjizhan', *Kangri zhanzheng shiqi de Zhongguo renmin jiefangjun*, (Peking: 1953) [Zhongguo xiandaishi ziliao congkan].
'Guangdong diqu', in *Zhonggong suo xuanchuan [neizhan dier zhanchang] zhi yanjiu*, pp 31-9.
Guangdong renmin kangri yuji zhanzheng huiyi, (Huanan renmin chubanshe, 1951).
Guangming ribao, (periodical).
Guofang yanjiuyuan, ed *Dijiuqi yanjiuyuan guowai kaocha baogao*. (Taipei: December 1968).
Guojun 'Feiqing yanjiu' youliang xinde xuanji, vol 24, Dijiuqi yanjiuyuan guowai kaocha baogao, (June 1961).
Gurtov, 'The Foreign Ministry and Foreign Affairs', in Thomas Robinson, ed, *The Cultural Revolution in China*, (University of California Press, 1971), pp 313-66.
Gushima Kensaburo, 'Nitchu senso to Igirisu', *Nitchu senso*, pp 1-16.
Edward P Haley and Harold W Rood, 'China's Major Trading Partner: Japan Dependent', in Garth, *China's Changing Role*, pp 187-212.
A M Halpern, 'China and Japan Since Normalization', in Hsüeh, Chün-tu, ed *Dimensions of China's Foreign Relations*, (Praeger, 1977).
Thomas T Hammond, comp *Soviet Foreign Relations and World Communism*, (Princeton: 1965).
Hanzhan zhongzhi hou de gongfei waijiao huodong, Dijiuqi yanjiuyuan guowai kaocha baogao (February 1957).
Harako Rinjiro, 'Chukyo to no kessen ni sonaeru. Soren, Kita Betonamu to kaidan', *Sekai shuho*, (3 March 1964).
Randall W Hardy, *Chinese Oil*, (1976).
Lillian Craig Harris, 'China's Relations with the PLO', *Journal of Palestine Studies* VII.1 (Autumn 1977), pp 123-54.

Bibliography

Selig S Harrison, *The Widening Gulf. Asian Nationalism and American Policy*, (New York and London: 1978).

Hatanaka Masaharu, 'Chugoku kojujikai daihyo no rainichi o megutte', *Sekai*, (November 1954).

Hayashi Katsunari, 'Chugoku wa kakubuso shinai. Ryo Shoshi wa kataru', *Sekai*, (January 1960), p 179.

Hayashi Shigeru, 'LT boeki daisannendo keiyaku - sono kosho keika to omo na mondaiten', *Ajia keizai junpo* (February 1965, ge), pp 12-15.

He Xiangning, *Huiyi Sun Zhongshan he Liao Zhongkai*, (Beijing: 1957).

He Xiangning, 'Wode huiyi', *PD*, (6 October 1961).

He Xiangning nishi fabiao wei jinian Liao Zhongkai xianlie gao Huangpu junguanshu.

He Yingqin, *Rifei guanxi yu zhonggong yinmou*, (1972).

He Yuwen, 'Gongfei "wenge" duiyu wei qiaowu gongzuo de yingxiang', *Feiwei qiaowu jianbao* (1 June 1968).

Mohamed Hassanein Heikal, *Uit de geheime Cairo documenten*, (1972).

Dieter Heinzig, *Sowjetische Militärberater bei der Kuomintang 1923-1927*, (1978) [Osteuropa und der internationale Kommunismus, Band 1].

Donald C Hellmann, *Japanese Domestic Politics and Foreign Policy: The Peace Agreement with the Soviet Union*, (Berkeley and Los Angeles: University of California Press, 1969).

Harold C Hinton:
    The China Sea: The American Stake in Its Future, (New York: 1980) [Agenda Paper No 12].
    Communist China in World Politics, (1966).

Hirai Hiroji, *Nitchu boeki no kiso chishiki*, (1971).

Hirano Kyotaro, 'Sekai heiwa undo jisshunen to Chugoku', *Ajia keizai junpo*, 398 (June 1959, chu), pp 1-5.

Hirano Minoru, *Gaiko kisha nikki* (jo, ge), (1979).

Hirano Yoshitaro, 'Ka Konei sensei to au no ki', *Ajia keizai junpo* (May 1966, ge).

Hirotsu Kyusuke, 'Chukyo no koritsuka to Nihon kyosanto', *Kyosanken mondai* X.11 (November 1966).

Hisazumi Tadao, 'Chukyo no kakuheiki hoyu - sono jiki wa amari tokunai', *Sekai shuho*, (1961).

Hokushi no chiansen. See Boeicho boei kenshusho senshishitsu, comp.

Hogen Shinsaku, 'Behandlung der zwischen Japan und China bezw. der Sowjetunion anstehenden Probleme', J Glaubitz, *Materialien zur Aussen- und Sicherheitspolitik Japans* (1978), pp 4-8. (trans from *Sekai shuho*, 31 January 1978), pp 4-5.

Hongqi, (periodical).

'Honichi saikai no kawakiri toshite Sohyo taikai ni shusseki suru Chukyo yojin rainichi no igi', *Koan joho* 83, pp 76-7.

Honkon no kakyo, comp Naikaku kanbo, naikaku chosashitsu, (April 1974).

Hoshino Moto, 'Katai Chugoku no "haken hantai" shisei', *Sekai shuho* (1 July 1975), pp 44-7.

Frank S T Hsiao and Lawrence R Sullivan:
    'The Chinese Communist Party and the Status of Taiwan, 1928-1943', *Pacific Affairs* LII.3 (Fall 1979), pp 446-67.
    'The Politics of Reunification: Peiping's Initiative on Taiwan', *Asian Survey* XX.8 (August 1980), pp 789-802.

Gene T Hsiao, 'The Sino-Japanese Rapprochement: A Relationship of Ambivalence', *China Quarterly* 57 (January-March 1974), pp 101-23.

Hsinhua Newsagency, (bulletins).

China's Relations with Japan

Hsüeh Chün-tu:
    ed *Dimensions of China's Foreign Relations*, (Praeger, 1977).
    The Chinese Communist Movement, 1921-1937, (Stanford University, 1960).
C T Hsüeh and R North, 'Peking's Perceptions of Soviet-American Relations', Hsüeh, ed, *Dimensions of China's Foreign Relations*.
Hu Lanqi, 'Huiyi He Xiangning xiansheng', *Huiyi yu huainian - jinian geming laoren He Xiangning shishi shi zhounian*, pp 189-200.
Hua Yingshen, comp *Zhongguo gongchandang lieshi zhuan*, (1949).
Huang Fu-ch'ing, *Chinese Students in Japan in the Late Ch'ing Period*, (1982) (trans K Whitaker).
Huaqiao ribao, (periodical).
Huashengbao, (periodical).
Huazhong tongxun, (periodical).
Huiyi yu huainian - jinian geming laoren He Xiangning shishi shi zhounian, (Peking: 1982).
A Hummel, ed, *Eminent Chinese of the Ch'ing Period (1644-1912)*, 2 vols, (Washington: 1943, 1944).
Alan Hutchinson, *China's African Revolution*, (London: 1975).
Ichikawa Kenjiro, 'Nitchu senso to Tonan Ajia kakyo', in 'Nitcho senso to kokusaiteki taio', special issue of *Kokusai seiji* 47 (December 1972), pp 75-87.
Ikeda Daisaku, *Wasureenu deai*, (1979).
Ikeda Masanosuke, *Nazo no kuni. Chukyo tairiku no jittai*, (1969).
Ikei Masaru and Masuda Hiroshi, 'Sengo nitchu kankei ni okeru Nihon no kosho noryoku', *Kokusai mondai* 199 (October 1976), pp 24-46.
Ilyushechkiî, 'Studencheskoe dvizhenie 9 dekabrya 1935 g v Kitae', *Kratkie soobshcheniya Instituta Vostokovedeniya* VII (1952), pp 3-19.
Inoue (tokuhain), 'Keizai koten de jishin o masu', *Sekai shuho* (27 October 1964), pp 23-7.
Inoue (tokuhain), 'Minzokuteki jisonshin no takamari', *Sekai shuho* (20 October 1964), pp 40 ff.
Inoue (tokuhain), 'Soren seihen to kakujikken de kincho', *Sekai shuho* (10 November 1964).
Irie Akira:
    'Nitchu kankei to Eibei no "miezaru" kyocho', *Nitchu senso*, pp 17-32.
    'The United States in Chinese Foreign Policy', Barnds ed *China and America*, pp 11-49.
'Ishibashi hochu to Jiminto. (Nihon no ushio.2)', *Sekai* 167 (November 1959), pp 259-62.
Ishikawa Tadao:
    Nitchu mondai shiken, (1973), (2nd ed 1974).
    'Tonan Ajia ni okeru chuso no katsudo jokyo (12 gatsu 16 nichi to kyokai kenkyukai ni okeru koen yoshi)', *Kyosanken mondai* VI.2 (February 1962), pp 39-45.
    Watakushi no mita Nihon gaiko, (1976).
Ito Takeo, 'Ryo Shoshi sensei kara no shukushi - Chugoku kenkyusho dai 27 kai sokai no hi ni', *Ajia keizai junpo* 1082 (June 1976, chu), pp 1-3.
Ito Kikuzo and Shibata Minoru, 'The Dilemma of Mao Tse-tung', *China Quarterly* 35 (July-September 1968), pp 58-77.
R K Jain, *China and Japan. 1949-1976*, (London: 1977).
Jiang Tao, 'Zhonggong yu riben guanxi de yanbian - jianlun Hua Guofeng fang Ri zhi yitu', *Feiqing yanjiu* XXIII.1 (15 January 1980), pp 115-21.
Jiang Yihua, *Guomindang zuopai de qizhi - Liao Zhongkai*, (Shanghai: 1985).
Jiefang, (periodical).

Bibliography

Jiefang ribao, (periodical).
Jiefang zazhi, (periodical).
'Jimint nai no "Chugoku ronso"', *Ekonomisuto* (1 October 1966).
Jingji ribao, (periodical).
'Jinian Song Qingling tekan', *Zhongguo jianshe* (August 1981).
Jinnianlai gongfei pohai qiaobao, (1969). [Diqing yanjiu congkan zhi 20].
Jiyuminshuto, comp, *Showa sanjuichinen rokugatsu itsuka kettei: tomen no juten seisaku kaisetsu*, nd.
Jiyuto gaiko chosakai hokokusho, (July 1955).
Chalmers A Johnson, *Peasant Nationalism in China*, (Stanford University Press, 962).
Kakyoho, (periodical).
Kajiya (tokuhain), 'Warera AA no hatsugen', *Asahi janaru* (20 June 1965), pp 51 ff. [rinji sokan].
Kamigaito Kenichi, *Nihon ryugaku to kakumei undo*, (1982).
G Kaminski, *Die Politik der Volksrepublik China und das Völkerrecht*, (1982).
Kangdibao, (periodical).
Kangri zhanzheng shiqi de Zhongguo renmin jiefangjun, (Peking: 1953). [Zhongguo xiandaishi ziliao congkan].
Kangri zhanzheng shiqi jiefangqu gaikuang, (Renmin, Peking: 1953), (reprint 1981). [Zhongguo xiandaishi ziliao congkan].
Karino Yukio, 'Kakyo no seiji ni tsuite', *Ajia keizai junpo* (September 1965, ge).
K S Karol, *La deuxième révolution chinoise*, (Paris: 1973).
Kasama Shigetoshi, *Nitchu koryushi. Dainiji sekai taisen go*, (1961).
Kato Churoku, 'Ho Chimin gun no Nihon-hei', *Bungei shunju* XXXI.10 (July 1953), pp 174-82.
Bernd Kaufmann and G Raube, 'Die Politik der chinesischen Führer in Fragen der Abrüstung', *Deutsche Aussenpolitik* vol 25, no 8 (1980), pp 109-26.
Kazankai publ, *Nitchu kankei kihon shiryoshu*, (1970).
Kihon shiryoshu. See *Nitchu kankei kihon shiryoshu*.
Kikuchi Hideo, 'Ryo Chukai to daiichiji kokkyo gassaku (jo.chu.ge)', *Ajia keizai junpo*, (May, June 1966).
Hong N Kim:
> '"Anti-Hegemonism" and the Politics of the Sino-Japanese Peace Treaty: A Study in the Miki Government's China Policy', *Asia Quarterly* 2 (1977), pp 101-19.
> 'Deradicalization of the Japanese Communist Party under Kenji Miyamoto', *World Politics* XXVIII.2 (January 1976), pp 273-99.

Kimura Hiroshi, 'Japan-Soviet Relations: Framework, Developments, Prospects', *Asian Survey* XX.7 (July 1980), pp 707-25.
Gottfried-Karl Kindermann, 'Washington Between Beijing and Taipei: The Restructured Triangle, 1978-80', *Asian Survey* XX.5 (May 1980), pp 457-76.
Kishimoto Koichi, *Politics in Modern Japan - Development and Organization*, Preface, (1977).
Donald W Klein, *The Chinese Foreign Ministry*, (PhD, Columbia University, 1974).
Donald W Klein and Anne B Clark, *Biographic Dictionary of Chinese Communism, 1921-1965*, (Cambridge, Mass: 1971).
Donald W Klein and Lois B Hager, 'The Ninth Central Committee', *China Quarterly* 45 (January-March 1971), pp 37-56.
Koan chosacho, comp *Kokusai kyosanshugi seiryoku no genjo*, (1962).

Kokusai boeki, (periodical).
Kokusai kyosanshugi seiryoku no genjo, (1966). See Koan chosacho, comp *Kokusai kyosanshugi seiryoku no genjo*.
Kokusai nenpo, (1958, 1959, 1962, 1963-64, 1965-66, 1967, 1972, 1973, 1974, 1975).
Koan chosacho, comp *Kokusai kyosanshugi seiryoku no genjo*, (1966).
Koan chosacho, comp *Nihon kyosanto no genjo*, (1960).
Koan joho, (periodical).
Komatsu Hisamaro, 'Chugoku de mita Nitchu mondai - Kitamura shisetsudan ni zuiko shite', *Ekonomisuto*, (1964) pp 42-25.
Komei shinbun, (periodical).
Komezawa Hideo comp 'Kakyo kenkyu bunken mokuroku', *Ajia keizai junpo*, (September 1965, ge), pp 13-24.
Kondo Tatsuo, 'Kappatsuka suru Chugoku no toitsu sensen kosaku (tokushu. Nitchu seijoka no ichinen [5])', *Ajia rebiyu* (March 1973), pp 40-5.
Anthony Kubek, *The Amerasia Papers*, (1971) (1st ed 1970).
Warren Kuo, *Analytical History of the Chinese Communist Party*, 4 vols, (Taipei: 1968-1971).
Kusano Fumio, *Konichi Shina sokoku no gensei*, (1942).
D Lach and E S Wehrle, *International Politics in East Asia Since World War II*, (New York: 1975).
Jean Lacouture, *Ho Chi Minh*, (Paris: 1967).
F Langdon, *Japan's Foreign Policy*, (Vancouver: 1973).
Paul F Langer, *The JCP Between Moscow and Peking*.
Bruce D Larkin, *China and Africa 1949-1970*, (1971).
B Lazitch and M M Drachkovitch, *Biographical Dictionary of the Comintern*, (Stanford: 1973).
Leng Shao Chuan, *Japan and Communist China*, (1958).
Lee Chae-jin:
> *Japan Faces China. Political and Economic Relations in the Postwar Era*, (Baltimore and London: 1976).
> 'The Japan Socialist Party and China, 1975-1977', *Asian Survey* XVIII.3 (March 1978), pp 275-89.
> 'The Making of the Sino-Japanese Peace and Friendship Treaty', *Pacific Affairs* (Fall 1979), pp 420-45.

Luke T Lee, *China and International Agreements. A Study of Compliance*, (Leyden-Durham: 1969).
Steven I Levine, 'Soviet-American Rivalry in Manchuria and the Cold War', Hsüeh, Chün-tu ed *Dimensions of China's Foreign Relations*, pp 10-43.
Li Chunqing, *Riben wenti gailun*, (Peking) (cited in Yamaguchi Chugoku to Nippon, 177).
Li Fanfu and He Ganzhi, *Zhongri guoli de duili*, (1936).
Li Fuchun et al, *Kangzhan yu jundui zhengzhi gongzuo*, (1938). [Jiuwang congshu zhi 8]
Li Renren, 'Xiangning laoren zai gui liangsan shi', in *Huiyi yu huainian - jinian geming laoren He Xiangning shishi shi zhounian*:168-171 (reprinted from *Guangxi ribao*, 8 November 1962).
Li Tienmin:
> 'Biographies of Chinese Communist Personalities', *Issues and Studies* (January 1977), pp 77-90.
> *Liu Shao-ch'i. Mao's First Heir-Apparent*, (Taipei: 1975).

Li Zhifu, *Taiwan renmin geming douzheng jianshi*, (Canton: 1955).
Liang Shangyuan, 'Zhuiyi Liaogong zai Xianggang de shihou', *Dagongbao* (Hong Kong: 19 July 1983).

Bibliography

Liao Chengzhi. See also under the Japanese form, Ryo Shoshi:
    'Deng Fa', *Zhongguo gongchandang lieshi zhuan*, (Qingnian: 1951), p 237.
    'Deng Fa', *Zhongguo gongchandang lieshi zhuan*, comp Hua Yingshen, (Xin minzhu chubanshe, 1949), pp 190 f.
    'Deng Fa tongzhi', *Wei renmin er si - [siba] xunguo zhulieshi jiniance--*, (1946).
    comp, *Huiyi yu huainian*, (1983). See also Huiyi yu huainian.
    'Pipan "sirenbang" suowei "haiwai guanxi" wenti de fandong miulun', *Bixu zhongshi qiaowu gongzuo*, (Hong Kong: 1978), pp 6-20 (reprinted from *PD*, 4 January 1978).
    'Ruhe yunyong haiwai huaqiao, huaren zuohao dui Tai gongzuo', *Gongfei yuanshi ziliao huibian*, no 15, 'Feiyou zhongyao jianghua ji shelun, pinglun', (30 April 1980).
    'Wang Ni chuzou yihou', *Kangzhan daxue*, di 2 juan, di 4 qi (fukan hao) (10 February 1939, Kueilin).
    'Wode diaoyan', *Zhongguo jianshe. Jinian Song Qingling tekan* (August 1981), p 14.
    'Wode muqin he tade hua', *PD*, (14 February 1979).
    'Yinshui buwang juejingren', *Zhongri youhao guanxi de xin jieduan*, (Renmin, Peking: 1978) (reprinted from *PD*, 28 August 1978).
    'Zenyang shishi yiwu bingyizhi', *Jiefang* vol 1, 18 (2 October 1937).
    'Zhi Jiang Jingguo xiansheng xin', *PD*, (25 July 1982).
'Liao Ch'eng-chih - A Maoist "Liberated" Cadre', *Issues and Studies* (November 1972), pp 86-8.
'Liao Chengzhi - yige weida de aiguozhe gemingjia', *Zhongguo jianshe* (tekan) (September 1983).
'Liao Chengzhi zai shoudu gejie renmin huanying Riben gongchandang guohui yiyuan fanghua daibiao dahui shang de jianghua', *Riben wenti wenjian huibian*, vol 4, pp 27-32.
'Liao Chengzhi zai Zhongqiaowei duoquan douzheng zhong de zuixing', *Zhonggong wenhua dageming ziliao huibian, di1juan*, Ding Wang, comp Mingbao yuekan, pp 706-10 [reprint from *Geming qiaobao*, 9 April 1967].
Liao Mengxing, *Wode muqin He Xiangning*, (Hong Kong: 1973).
Liao Mong-sing, 'My Father Liao Chung-kai', *China Reconstructs* (November 1964), pp 25-9.
'Liao on reunification: We can wait', *Ta Kung Pao (Weekly Supplement)* 808 (31 December 1981-6 January 1982).
Liaogong zai renjian. Zhongguo xinwenshe, comp, (Hong Kong: 1983). This issue has been quoted throughout the present study. The page numbers of a later issue, published by Sanlian shudian (Peking, June 1984) do not coincide.
Liberation Daily. See *Jiefang zazhi*.
Kenneth Lieberthal, *A Research Guide to Central Party and Government Meetings in China, 1949-1975*, (New York: 1976).
Liening shenghuo, (periodical).
Liu Jiaquan, '"Gonghe" dui kangri zhanzheng de zhongyao gongxian - jinian kangri zhanzheng shengli sishi zhounian', *PD*, (1 September 1985).
Liu Jiaquan, '"Gung Ho" and China', *China Reconstructs* (June 1986), pp 56-9.
Liu Jiaquan, 'Song Qingling yu dageming shiqi de fun yundong', *PD*, (5 May 1985).
Liu Jiaquan and Shang Mingxuan, see Shang Mingxuan and Liu Jiaquan. 'Song Qingling yu dierci guogong hezuo de shixian', *PD*, (24 January 1983).
Liu Jiaquan and Xiao Xing, 'Liao Chengzhi yu Kangri minzu tongyi zhanxian', *Renmin ribao* (27 May 1984), p 5.

China's Relations with Japan

Liu Jiaquan and Gan Yongmei, 'Song Qingling yu baowei Zhongguo tongmeng', *PD*, (25 May 1986).
Liu Mao, '"Changzheng" yu "tongzhan".' *Feiqing yuebao* XX.12, pp 60-5.
Liu Tiansu, 'Liangshi, cimu. - huiyi zai He Xiangning xiansheng bian de rizi', *Huiyi yu huainian - jinian geming laoren He Xiangning shishi shi zhounian*, pp 172-88.
Long Fei, '[pingxi] Zhonggong shezhi guwen zhidu zhi yitu', *Feiqing yanjiu* XXIV.2 (15 February 1981), pp 104-14.
'LT boeki dai 3ji kyogi jiko', in *[Sengo shiryo] Nitchu kankei*, p 365.
'LT boeki no shinten - gekido suru josei to Nitchu boeki no mitoshi', *Ajia keizai junpo* (November 1964, jo), pp 1-12.
Lu Xuezhi et al comp, *Liao Chengzhi de yisheng*, (Xinhua: 1984) (distributor: Kodansha). See also [Shashinshu] *Ryo Shoshi no shogai*.
Lu Zhenji, 'Feiwei qiaoweihui zhuxi Liao Chengzhi beikou zhi mi.' *Feiwei qiaowu jianbao* (1 May 1968).
Lu Zhenji, *Gongfei zhengsu wei qiaowei toumu de fenxi*, (Taipei: 5 March 1969). [Diqing yanjiu congkan zhi 16]
Lu Zhenji, 'Gongfei xianjieduan huoqiao yinmou de dongxiang', *Gongfei huoqiao zhenxiang* (Taipei: February 1968).
Lu Zhenji, 'Feiwei qiaoweihui zhuxi Liao Chengzhi beikou zhi mi', *Feiwei qiaowu jianbao* (1 May 1968).
Luo Bing, 'Li Xiannian yu Xianggang shiwu. - Shei jiren Liao Chengzhi zai qiaoban gangao ban de zhiwu?', *Zhengming* 70 (August 1983), pp 9-10. ['Beixing fangyu']
Luo Chun, 'Huanan renmin wuzhuang baohu gongshangjie liyi de shishi banfa', xerox copy from an unidentified book, pp 46-8.
J G Lutz, *China and the Christian Colleges, 1850-1950*, (Ithaca: 1971).
Luzhongqu dangwei xuanchuanbu, comp *Jianjue shixing tudi gaige. lingdao qunzhong chedi fanshen - qugan zhibu tudi zhengce jiaocai*, (15 September 1946). [Dangnei duwu, bianhao 1191].
Ma Chaojun, *Zhongguo laodong yundong shi*, (Taipei: 1959).
Roderick MacFarquhar, 'Communist China's Twenty Years: A Periodization', *China Quarterly* 39 (July-September 1969), pp 55-63.
Mainichi shinbun, (periodical).
Mantetsu Shanhai jimusho chosashitsu, comp *Kakyo chosa iho*, vol 1, (Dairen, 1940).
'Mao Zhuxi Lin fu zhuxi Zhou zongli guanhuai jiuguo qiaobao', *Qiaowubao* (8-9), (1966).
Masuda Hiroshi, ed, *Sh Nihonshugi: Ishibashi Tanzan gaiko ronshu, 1913-1967*, (Soshisha, 1984).
Matsuki Koichiro, 'LT boeki daiyonendo kosho o meguru mondaiten', *Ajia keizai junpo* (October 1965, chu), pp 1-9.
Matsumoto Shigeharu, *Shanhai jidai*, (1977).
Matsumura Kenzo, 'Nitchu kankei no shindankai', *Chuo koron* (November 1962).
Matsumura Kenzo and Kazemi Akira, 'Chugoku wa ikaga deshita ka', *Chuo koron* 75-2 (February 1960), pp 178-88.
'Matsumura Kenzo. Ryo Shoshi goi memo', *[Sengo shiryo] Nitchu kankei*, p 364.
Stewart Menaul, 'Japan's Defence Policy', *Conflict Studies* 107 (May 1979).
Kay Miller, 'The Thai Communist Movement and China-Vietnam Competition in Southeast Asia', *Berichte des Bundesinstituts für ostwissenschaftliche und internationale Studien*, 28 (1981).
Minami Michiaki, 'Jinmin Chugoku jinmyaku fudoki', *Chuo koron* (December 1975), pp 126-35.

Bibliography

Minshengbao, (periodical).
Minzu husheng, Zhongguo waijiao yanjiusuo (comp, ed), (1946) (first edition).
Miyoshi Osamu and Eto Shinkichi, *Chugoku hodo no henko o tsuku*, (1972).
'Mo Takuto. Shu Onrai kaikenki', *Sekai*, 184 (April 1961), pp 140-51.
J W Morley, *Soviet and Communist Chinese Policies Toward Japan, 1950-1957*, (New York: 1958).
J J Morris, 'Japan and the Moscow Negotiations with the Soviet Union', *The World Today*, XII (November 1956), pp 438-47.
David Mozingo, *Chinese Policy Toward Indonesia, 1949-1967*, (Ithaca and London: 1976).
Mu Xin, *Nanxian xunhui*, (Sanlian: 1951) (2nd printing 1953).
Murata Shiro, *Konmei Shina no zenbo*, (1937).
NS See *Nihon Chukyo koryu nenshi*.
Nagafuchi Kiyotoshi, 'Ishoku no "Pekin hokoku" - naze shinjitsu wa tsutawaranai ka?', *Sekai shuho*, (6 September 1966).
Nagai Michio and Matsumura Kenzo, 'Ajia no heiwa to Nihon no tachiba', *Sekai* 220 (April 1964), pp 97-106.
Naigai shakai undoshi nenpu, Naigai chosakai comp 1965.
Naka Hosaku, *[kaitei zoho] Saikin Shina kyosantoshi*, (1944) (first ed 1940).
M Nakata, *Soren gaiko no kosho gijutsu*, 1980, [Soren gaiko, kosho gijutsu chosa kenkyu iinkai hokokusho].
'Nan Kanshin no yonjunichi. tasai na sekkin no seika o toru', *Ekonomisuto* (2 June 1964).
Nanfang ribao, (periodical).
Nanxian xunhui. See Mu Xin, *Nanxian xunhui*.
Nan yue yinglie zhuan, Di1ji, (Guangdong renmin chubanshe, 1983).
Andrew J Nathan:
    'A Factionalism Model for CCP Politics', *China Quarterly* 53 (January-March 1973), pp 34-66.
    'Policy Oscillations in the People's Republic of China: A Critique', *China Quarterly* 68 (December 1976), pp 720-33.
NCNA, (Bulletins issued by New China News Agency).
Neuhauser, *China and the Afro-Asian People's Solidarity Organisation, 1957-1967*, (Harvard University Press, 1968).
Nieh Yu-hsi, 'Die Hintergründe des Chinesisch-Japanischen Inselstreits', *China aktuell* (May 1978), pp 279-82.
Nihon Chugoku yuko kyokai (seito) chuo honbu, comp *Nitchu yuko undoshi*, (1975).
Nihon Chukyo koryu nenshi, Jinminshugi kenshukai, comp, (Tokyo: annual, 1949-1970). [Microfilm prepared by the Diet Library, Tokyo].
Nihon keizai shinbun, (periodical).
Nihon kokusai seiji gakkai, comp 'Nitchu senso to kokusaiteki tai', *Kokusai seiji* 47 (December 1972).
Nihon to Chugoku, (periodical).
Nippon Times, (periodical).
Nishihara Masashi, 'Wie lange hält die Yoshida Doktrin noch?', *Europa Archiv* XXX.14 (25 July 1978), pp 441-52.
'Nisso daketsugo no nitchu kankei', *Ajia keizai junpo* 305 (November 1956, cho).
Nitchu boeki sokushin giin renmei, comp *[zoho kaiteiban] Nitchu kankei shiryoshu*, (1961).
Nitchu boeki sokushin giin renmei, comp *Nitchu kankei shiryoshu, 1945-1966 nen*, (1967).

Nitchu boeki sokushinkai, comp *Nitchu boeki sokushinkai yuko daihyodan hochu hokokusho*, (1966).
Nitchu kankei kihon shiryoshu, (Kazankai publ, 1970).
[zoho kaiteiban] Nitchu kankei shiryoshu. See Nitchu boeki sokushin giin renmei, comp *[zoho kaiteiban] Nitchu kankei shiryoshu*, (1961).
Nitchu kankei shiryoshu (1967), see Nitchu boeki sokushin giin renmei, comp *Nitchu kankei shiryoshu (1945-1966 nen)*, (1967).
Nitchu kokko kaifuku. kankei shiryoshu, Nitchu kokko kaifuku sokushin giin renmei, comp, (1972).
Nitchu kokko kaifuku sokushin giin renmei, comp *Nitchu kokko kaifuku kankei shiryoshu*, (1972).
Nitchu oboegaki no 11 nen, Nitchu keizai kyokai ed, (1975).
Nitchu oboegaki no 11 nen. Hokokusho fuzoku shiryo - komiyunike. seimei. shasetsu nado -, Nitchu keizai kyokai ed, (1975).
'Nitchu senso', see below.
'Nitchu senso to kokusaiteki taio', see Nihon kokusai seiji gakkai, comp 'Nitchu senso to kokusaiteki taio'.
'Nitchu shuno kaidan ni omou - ryokokumin no yuko no tame ni', *Sekai* (November 1972), pp 69-93.
'Nitchu soho no shinbun kisha kokan ni kansuru Takasaki Tatsunosuke jimusho to Ryo Shoshi jimusho no kaidan memo', *[Sengo shiryo] Nitchu kankei*, p 364.
'Nitchu yuko undo o shido suru nikkyo no hoshin', *Koan joho*, 10, pp 60 ff.
Nitchu yoko undoshi. See Nihon Chugoku yuko kyokai (seio) chuo honbu, comp *Nitchu yuko undoshi*, (1975).
Ogata Sadako, 'The Business Community and Japanese Foreign Policy: Normalization of Relations with the People's Republic of China', *The Foreign Policy of Modern Japan*, R A Scalapino, ed, (1977), pp 175-203.
Ogawa Heishiro, 'Chugoku zaikin o oboete', *Keizai to gaiko* 665 (October 1977), pp 2-4.
Ogawa Heishiro, *Pekin no yonen*, (1977).
A Ogunsanwo, *China's Policy in Africa*.
Ogura Kazuo, 'How the "Inscrutables" Negotiate with the "Inscrutables": Chinese Negotiating Tactics Vis-à-vis the Japanese', *China Quarterly* 79 (September 1979), pp 529-52.
Ohara Shinichiro, 'Ashibumi jotai o dasshita Nitchu kankei', *Sekai shuho* (7-14 May 1974), pp 14-17.
'Ohira hochu koku kyotei no zenshin o kakunin', *Sekai shuho*, (April 1974).
Okabe Tatsumi, 'Content Analysis'. See Eto Shinkichi and Tatsumi Okabe, 'Content Analysis of Statements in Regard to Japan Made by the People's Republic of China - Source Materials: *The People's Daily* in Two Periods in 1958'.
Okamoto Saburo, *Nitchu boekiron*, (1971).
Okazaki Kaheita:
Chugoku mondai e no michi, (1971).
'Chugoku ni kaketa waga hansei no ki', *Chuo koron* (October 1972), pp 92-101.
Watakushi no kiroku, (1979).
Michel Oksenberg:
'China Policy for the 1980s', *Foreign Affairs* (1980-1981), pp 304-22.
'The Institutionalization of the Chinese Communist Revolution: The Ladder of Success on the Eve of the Cultural Revolution', *China Quarterly* 36 (October-December 1968), pp 61-92.
'Methods of Communication Within the Chinese Bureaucracy', *China Quarterly* 57 (January-March 1974), pp 1-39.

Bibliography

'Policy Making Under Mao Tse-tung, 1949-1968', *Comparative Politics* III.3 (April 1971).

Ookubo Yasushi, *Chugoku kyosantoshi.* 2 vols, (1971, 1972).

Oomagari Tadashi, *Asanuma Inejiro. Sono hito, sono shogai*, (1961).

Osteuropa, (periodical).

Ouzhou shibao, (periodical).

Ozawa Masamoto, *Uchiyama Kanzo den*, (1972).

'Pan Hannian jianjie.' *Zhengming* (1983.4), p 72.

Yung H Park:

'The "Anti-hegemony" Controversy in Sino-Japanese Relations', *Pacific Affairs* 49 no 3 (Fall 1976), pp 476-90.

'Japan's Perspectives and Expectations Regarding America's Role in Korea', *Orbis* XX.3 (Fall 1976), pp 761-84.

PD, People's Daily (in Chinese, *Renmin ribao*).

Peking Review, (periodical).

T J Pempel:

'Japanese Foreign Economic Policy: The Domestic Bases for International Behaviour', *International Organization* XXXI.4 (Autumn 1977), pp 723-74.

Policymaking in Contemporary Japan, (Ithaca: Cornell UP, 1977).

D Petrov, 'Japan and the Mao Group's Foreign Policy', *International Affairs* (Moscow: December 1968), pp 30-7.

Michael Pillsbury:

'Strategic Acupuncture', *Foreign Policy* (Winter 1980-81), pp 44-61.

'US-Chinese Military Ties', *Foreign Policy* 20 (Fall 1975), pp 50-64.

Manfred Pohl:

'Die Kommunistische Partei Japans 1974-1977', *Berichte* 27 (1978).

'Der Senkaku-Zwischenfall und seine Auswirkungen auf die japanische Innenpolitik', *China aktuell*, (June 1978), pp 339-43.

Jonathan D Pollack, 'China's Potential as a World Power', *International Journal* XXXV.3 (Summer 1980), pp 580-95.

'Prinz Kinkazu Saiondschi. Japans private Peking Botschaft', *China Analysen* (October 1970), p 30.

Qiaowubao, (periodical).

Qiqibao, (periodical).

Qunzhong, (periodical).

Qunzhong yundong jiangshou dagang, np, nd.

K W Radtke, 'Negotiations Between the PRC and Japan on the Return of Japanese Civilians and the Repatriation of Prisoners of War', *Leyden Studies in Sinology*, (Leiden: 1981), pp 191-213.

Renmin shouce, (Peking: 1951).

Renmin Zhongguo, (periodical).

'Renraku jimusho no sogo setchi narabi ni daihyo no sogo haken ni kansuru Takasaki Tatsunosuke jimusho to Ryo Shoshi jimusho no kaidan memo', *[Sengo shiryo] Nitchu kankei*, p 364.

Renshi diren, (periodical).

Renwu zhuanjid, (periodical).

[Renzhong] Renwuzhi, (Taipei).

Renwuzhi, (Taipei: 1959).

David Rees, 'The Two Koreas in Conflict', *Conflict Studies* 94 (April 1978).
Renmin ribao, (periodical). See also *PD*.
'Riben jiu junren daibiaotuan fangwen feiqu zhi jianwen', *Feiqing guancha baogao*, vol 2, (January 1957), pp 33-54.
Riben touxiang hou de Zhongguo gongchandang, (December 1947).
Riben wenti wenjian huibian, vol 1, (Peking: 1955).
Robert B Rigg, *Red China's Fighting Hordes*, (1971) (reprint of 1951 edition).
Ruci tuanjie, (July 1940).
'Ryo daihyodan. Nihon taizai no ikkagetsu'.
Ryo Shoshi. See also under the Chinese form, Liao Chengzhi:
  'Chugoku no tai nichi seisaku to gaiko seisaku', *Ajia keizai junpo* 872 (August 1972, chu).
  'Sekai heiwa o mamoru tadashii michi', *Ajia keizai junpo* (December 1963, chu).
  'Soren ni taisuru ninshiki ni tsuite', *Ajia keizai junpo* 906 (July 1973,ge), pp 17-20.
  '"Taiwan" de juyo hatsugen', *Ajia keizai junpo* (October 1972, ge).
  'Tomen no kokusai josei ni taisuru Chugoku no kenkai oyobi "yoningumi" iko no Chugoku no hoko', *Ajia keizai junpo* 1042 (May 1977, jo).
'Ryo Shoshi honichidan no ashiato', *Sekai* (July 1973), pp 186-9.
'Ryo Shoshi kaich "Taiwan" de juyo hatsugen', *Ajia keizai junpo* (October 1972, ge).
'Ryo Shoshi kara Ishibashi shi ate shokan', *[Sengo shiryo Nitchu kankei]*, p 129.
[Shashinshu] Ryo Shoshi no shugai, (Tokyo: Xinhuashe, 1984).
'Saikin no Nitchu kankei', *Keizai to gaiko* 665 (October 1977), pp 5-10.
Saionji Kinkazu:
  'Itsu made mo matsu Chugoku', *Sekai* 240 (November 1965).
  'Pekin kara mita anpo keitei to Nitchu kankei', *Sekai* 172 (April 1960).
Saito Takeshi, *Shina - kiko to jinbutsu*, (1937).
L J Samelson, *Soviet and Chinese Negotiating Behaviour: The Western View*, (London: 1976).
Saneto Keishu, *Chugokujin Nihon ryugakushi*, (1970).
Sannianlai gongfei paichu yu yaojin gezhong daibiatuan diaocha, (1961).
Sase Masamori, 'Erneute Diskussion über die japanisch-amerikanische Sicherheitsgarantie', *Glaubitz*, comp *Materialien zur: Aussen- und Sicherheitspolitik Japans*, (1978), trans from *Sankei shinbun*, (Seiron, 2 February 1978).
Sayoku dantai jiten, comp Shakai undo chosakai, (Kyokuto shuppansha, 1968).
Robert A Scalapino, *Elites in the People's Republic of China*, (London and Seattle: 1972).
J Schiebel, 'The Soviet Union and the Sino-American Relationship', *Orbis* (Spring 1977), pp 77-94.
Stuart R Schram, 'Mao Tse-tung as a Charismatic Leader', *Asian Survey* VII.6 (June 1967), pp 383-7.
Sekai nippo, (periodical).
Sekai shuho, (periodical).
Sengo shiryo nitchu kankei, comp Ishikawa Tadao et al, Nippon hyoronsha, (1970).
Shang Mingxuan and Liu Jiaquan, 'Song Qingling yu dierci guogong hezuo de shixian', *PD*, (24 January 1983).
Shei ti gongfei wenxuan kailu? - feibang xinwen tongzhan gongzuo jingji -, (October 1973) [Feiqing yanjiu zhuanbao].
Gerald Segal, 'The PLA and Chinese Foreign Policy Making', *International Affairs* (Summer 1981), pp 449-66.

Bibliography

Shakai mondai shiryo kenkyukai, comp *Kominterun no senryaku senjutsu no hensen - shutoshite Nihon ni okeru kyosanshugi undo to no kanren -*, (1975). [Shiso kenkyu shiryo tokushu, 89]

'Shakaito hochu to kokumin gaiko. (Nihon no ushio.1)', *Sekai* 161 (May 1959), pp 44-7.

Shao Kuo-kang 'Chou En-lai's Diplomatic Approach to Non-aligned States in Asia: 1953-60', *China Quarterly* 78 (June 1979).

Shen Jixie, *Zhonggong waijiao juece guocheng zhong bianshu zhi yanjiu* (January 1981). [Guoli zhengzhi daxue dongya yanjiusuo yanshi lunwen].

Shi Shu, 'Mao (Zedong), He (Long) chuanqixing zhi andou', *Gongdang wenti yanjiu* 12.8 (15 August 1986), pp 42-50.

Ito Kikuzo and Shibata Minoru, 'The Dilemma of Mao Tse-tung', *China Quarterly* 35 (July-September 1968), pp 58-77.

Shibauchi Tadashi, 'Haken mondai to tsunahiki sareru Nihon', *Chuo koron* (July 1975), pp 153-71.

Shijie heping yundong wenxian 1949-1954, Shijie zhishi, 1955.

Shijie zhishi, (periodical).

Shimakura Tamio, *Pekin nikki*, (1972).

Shimazu Tadatsugu, 'Kikoku kosho no omoide', *Nitchu yuko undoshi*, pp 214-19.

Shin Chugoku nenkan, (1962).

Shinano mainichi shinbun, (periodical).

Shiso, (periodical).

[*Shiso josei shisatsu hokokushu. Sono 1*] *Chugoku kyosanto no tai nichi sakubo ni tsuite*, (1975). [Shakai mondai shiryo sosho, I.43].

Shin Chugoku shiryo shusei, Nihon kokusai mondai kenkyusho, Chugoku bukai comp, (1964-1971).

'Shu Chugoku shusho no Afurika homon', *Sekai* 220 (April 1964), pp 162-5.

'Sho Onrai Afurika rekiho no sai no kyodo komiyunike', *Kyosanken mondai* VIII.4 (April 1964).

'Sho Onrai kokusai josei ni kansuru himitsu enzetsu', *Chuo koron* (November 1976), pp 161-74.

'Sho Onrai o mukaeru Afurika shokoku', *Sekai* 218 (February 1964), pp 19-23.

'Sho Onrai wa do kotaeta ka?', *Sekai* 119 (November 1955), pp 82-9.

Sidiwei xuanchanbu, comp *Zenyang fadong qunzhong*.

Sheldon W Simon, *The Broken Triangle, Peking, Djakarta and the PKI* (Baltimore: 1969).

Sinianlai fei Su goujie zhi zongjie yanjiu, (Taipei: December 1953). [Gongfei junshi congshu, di3ji].

E Snow, *Random Notes on Red China, 1936-1945*, (Cambridge, Mass: 1968).

Helen F Snow, *Women in Modern China*, (The Hague: 1967).

Sodai seikatsu, (1953).

Song Feiru, *Riben zhanshi waijiao neimu*, (Chungking: 1940).

Song Qingling et al, *Shang Jiang zongcai shu*, (12 January 1942).

'A Study of "On Policy"', *Peking Review* (27 August 1978).

Su'e tongjian, nd.

Rodger Swearingen, *The Soviet Union and Postwar Japan*, (Stanford: 1978).

Witold S Sworakowski, ed, *World Communism. A Handbook, 1918-1965*. (1973).

Christopher Szymanski, *Bureaucratic Development in the People's Republic of China: A Case Study of the Foreign Affairs System, 1949-1973*, (Thesis, Brown University, 1975).

Tadokoro Takehiko, 'Ichinen no kiseki to kongo no mondai (tokushu. Nitchu seijoka no ichinen [1])', *Ajia rebiyu* (March 1973), pp 8-15.

Tagawa Goro, *Chugoku arinomama hokoku*, (1980).

China's Relations with Japan

Tagawa Seiichi, 'Hori kanjicho no seii o tou', *Ekonomisuto* (28 March 1972).
Tagawa Seiichi:
> '[Nisshi] Matsumura Kenzo no sogi zengo', *Sekai* (March 1972), pp 202-12.
> *Matsumura Kenzo to Chugoku*, (1972).
> *Nitchu kosho hiroku. Tagawa nikki - 14nen no shogen*, (1973).

Tai kakyo no doko, Naikaku kanbo. naikaku chosashitsu, comp (April 1974).
Taigong jianshi, (November 1958).
Taigong shengwei, comp *1951 nian gongzuo zongjie*, (1951).
'Tairiku ni mada Nihonjin nokotte iru!', *Bungei shunju* 35.3 (March 1957), pp 186-99.
Takano Yuichi, 'The Japan-China Joint Communiqué and the Termination of War', *The Japanese Annual of International Law* 17 (1973), pp 76-9.
Takasaki Tatsunosuke, 'Shu Onrai to kaidan shite', *Chuo koron* (February 1961).
Tan Juezhen:
> 'Ryo Shoshi o kataru', *Yokohama West Rotary Weekly* p 847.
> 'Ryo Shoshi o kataru', *Ekonomisuto* (28 March 1953), pp 28-9.

Tanaka Kyoko, 'Mao and Liu in the 1947 Land Reform: Allies or Disputants?', *China Quarterly* 75 (1978), pp 566-93.
Tang Tsou and Ping-ti Ho, eds, *China in Crisis*, (Chicago: 1968).
Jay Taylor, *China and Southeast Asia. Peking's Relations With Revolutionary Movements*, (Praeger, 1974), [Praeger Special Studies in International Politics and Government].
Frederick Teiwes:
> 'The Origins of Rectification: Inner-Party Purges and Education Before Liberation', *China Quarterly* 65 (March 1976), pp 15-53.
> 'The Uses and Limits of Elite Studies: The Chinese Case', *China Quarterly* 58 (April-June 1974), pp 363-72.

Gregory J Terry, 'The "Debate" on Military Affairs in China: 1957-1959', *Asian Survey* XVI.8 (August 1976), pp 788-813.
Ralph Thaxton, 'On Peasant Revolution and National Resistance: Toward a Theory of Peasant Mobilization and Revolutionary War with Special Reference to Modern China', *World Politics* XXX.1 (October 1977), pp 29-37.
The Au Duong, *Berichte des Bundesinstituts für ostwissenschaftliche und internationale Studien* 30 (1979).
Tokyo shinbun, (periodical)
James C Tomson Jr, 'Communist Policy and the United Front in China 1935-36', *Papers on China*, vol II, (Cambridge, Mass: 1957). [East Asia Regional Studies].
'Tongdiao Liao Chengzhi tongzhi', *Shijie zhishi* 4 (1983).
William T Tow, 'The Janzus Option: A Key to Asian/Pacific Security', *Asian Survey* XVIII.12 (December 1978).
James R Townsend, *Politics in China*, (Boston: 1980).
Daniel Tretiak:
> 'Political Movements and Institutional Continuity in the Chinese Ministry of Foreign Affairs, 1966-1979', *Asian Survey* XX.9 (September 1980), pp 943-63.
> 'The Sino-Japanese Treaty of 1978: The Senkaku Incident Prelude', *Asian Survey* XVIII.12 (December 1978), pp 1237-49.

Bibliography

'Who Makes Chinese Foreign Policy Today (Late 1980)', *The Australian Journal of Chinese Affairs* 5 (1981), pp 137-57.

Harry S Truman:
> *The Memoirs of Harry S Truman, Year of Decisions, 1945*, (1955).
> *Years of Trial and Hope, 1946-1953.*

Uchida Hisashi, 'Legal Aspects of Japan-China Trade Between 1949 and 1975'.

Uchida Kenzo:
> 'Matsumura. Takasaki hochu no seika to haikei - hoshuto no tai Chugoku seisaku o miru', *Sekai* 205 (January 1963).
> '[zadankai] Nihon gaiko ni chumon suru - Nitchu kankei ni sokushite', *Sekai* 210 (June 1963).

Uemura Shinichi, *Chugoku nashiyonarizumu.*

'Unite the People, Defeat the Enemy - A Study of "On Policy"', *Peking Review* 35 (27 August 1971).

URI 1959.

URS Biographical Service, (Union Research Service), Hong Kong.

Utsunomiya Tokuma, 'Seifu no [seikan seisaku] ni hantai suru', *Chuo koron* 74-16 (November 1959), pp 44-50.

Peter Van Ness, *Revolution and Chinese Foreign Policy*, (Berkeley, Los Angeles, London: 1970).

Lyman P Van Slyke, *Enemies and Friends. The United Front in Chinese Communist History*, (Stanford: 1967).

E and Näth Von Gröling, M-L *Die Aussenpolitik Chinas*, (München-Wien: 1975).

Waga seishun no Nippon - Chugoku chishikijin no Nippon kaiso, (1982).

F Wakeman, 'The Use and Abuse of Ideology in the Study of Contemporary China', *China Quarterly* 61 (March 1975), pp 127-52.

Nym Wales, *Red Dust. Autobiographies of Chinese Communists as Told to Nym Wales*, (Stanford: 1952).

R L Walker, 'China's Post-Mao Foreign Policy', *Problems of Communism* (March-April 1977), pp 71-5.

Wang Chi-wu, 'Military Preparedness and Security Needs: Perceptions From the Republic of China on Taiwan', *Asian Survey* XXI.6 (June 1981), pp 651-63.

Wang Jun, 'Zhonggong dui waiguo shiwu ji guoji guanxi', *Feiqing yanjiu* XXIV.5 (15 May 1981).

Wang Ruofei Ye Ting Qin Bangxian Deng Fa rongailu, Yu, Er (comp), Xinli, (Hong Kong: 1946).

Wang Shuyao, 'Gongfei dui huaqiao de qipian jieduo yu pohai', *Feiwei qiaowu jianbao.*

Wang Song, *Rigong yu zhonggong guanxi zhi yanjiu (1940-1972).*

Wang Zuoyao, *Dongzong yiye,* (Canton: 1983).

Watanabe Akio:
> 'Foreign Policy Making, Japanese Style', *International Affairs* (Chatham House) (January 1978), pp 75-88.
> 'Seron to gaiko seisaku', *Kokusai mondai* 145 (April 1972), pp 40-53.

Oskar Weggel, 'Die Volksbefreiungsarmee: Fraktionsstreitigkeiten, Krise des Selbstverständnisses und Heilungsversuche zu ihrer Ueberwindung', *China aktuell* (March 1981), pp 181-91.

Wei guomindang geming weiyuanhui chengli yilai zhi huodong gaikuang, (1 December 1948).

Wei zhengxie sanjie shouci huiyi zhi fenxi, (Taipei: May 1959).

Franklin Weinstein, ed, *US-Japan Relations and the Security of East Asia*, (Boulder, Colorado: 1978).

Pierre Weiss, 'La république populaire de Chine et le Proche-Orient', *Politique étrangère* XLIII.2 (1978), pp 181-98.

China's Relations with Japan

Wenhuibao, (periodical).

Allen S Whiting:
    'China and the Superpowers: Toward the Year 2000', *Daedalus* (Fall 1980), pp 97-114.
    The Chinese Calculus of Deterrence, (Ann Arbor: 1975).
    'New Light on Mao: 3. Quemoy 1958: Mao's Miscalculations', *China Quarterly* (June 1975), pp 263-70.

Richard Wich, 'The Tenth Party Congress: The Power Structure and the Succession Question', *China Quarterly* 58 (April-June 1974), pp 231-48.

C M Wilbur, 'Japan and the Rise of Communist China', *Japan Between East and West*, Borton, H ed.

Alexander Woodside, 'Nationalism and Poverty in the Breakdown of Sino-Vietnamese Relations', *Pacific Affairs* LII.3 (Fall 1979), pp 381-409.

'Wo suo zhidao guanyu fuqin de jijianshi', *Xinhua ribao* (Chongqing: 1944) 8.20.

Wu Wenshou, 'Qingliangshan huaijiu jinian xinhua tongxun jianshe wushi zhounian', *PD* (5 November 1981).

Wu Zhenyan, *Gongfei qiaowu bumen de duoquan douzheng. Feiwei qiaowu jianbao*, (1 August 1968).

Wu Zhenyan, 'Gongfei "wenge" hou de qiaowu bumen gaikuang', *Feiwei qiaowu jianbao* (1 August 1968).

Xia Yan:
    'Jinian Pan Hannian tongzhi', *Zhengming* (1983.4), pp 71-2.
    'Jinian Pan Hannian tongzhi', *Renmin ribao* (23 November 1982).

Xiang Cheng and Dai Bailang, *Zhonggong qiaowu yinmou de xin dongxiang*, (March 1958). [Haiwai feiqing yanjiu congshu zhi 1]

Xianghebao, (periodical).

Xin changcheng, (periodical).

'Xin zhengzhi xieshang huiyi choubeihui gedangpai getuanti wei jinian [qiqi] kangri zhanzheng shier zhounian xuanyan', *Renmin ribao*, (7 July 1949). (Japanese translation in *Shin Chugoku shiryo shusei*, vol 2, pp 536-8.

Xin Zhonghua bao, (periodical).

Xingdao ribao, (periodical).

Xingqibao, (periodical).

Xinhua ribao, (periodical).

Xu Dixin, 'Pan Hannian zai Xianggang', *Zhengming*, (1983.4), pp 69-71.

Xu Songling, *Zhongguo kangri dazhan ji*, (Canton: 1947).

Xuefengbao, (periodical).

Michael Yahuda, 'Chinese Foreign Policy After 1963', *China Quarterly* 36 (1968).

Yamaguchi Ichiro, *Chugoku to Nippon*, (1976).

'Yamamoto Kumaichi Nihon keizai yuko shisetsudan dancho to Ryo Shoshi Chugoku Ajia.Afurika iinkai shuseki to no kaidan ni okeru Ryo Shoshi danwa (1961.2.25)', in *[Sengo shiryo] Nitchu kankei*, pp 195-6.

Yamato shinbun, (periodical).

Alexander Ching-an Yang, *The Policy-Making Process in Japan's Policy toward the People's Republic of China: the Making of the Liao-Takasaki Trade Agreement of November 1962*, (PhD dissertation, Columbia University, 1969) [University Microfilms International, 1978].

Yang Chin, comp, *1949nian renmin shouce*.

Bibliography

Dennis T Yasutomo, 'Sato's China Policy, 1964-1966', *Asian Survey* XVII.6 (June 1977), pp 530-44.

Yantai ribao, (periodical).

Yazhou ji taipingyang quyu heping huiyi choubei huiyi, Zhongguo renmin baowei shijie heping weiyuan hui (comp), Shijie zhishi, (1952).

'Yazhou ji Taipingyang quyu heping huiyi guanyu Riben wenti de jueyi', in *Riben wenti wenjian huibian*, vol 1, pp 284-5.

Yazhou ji taipingyang quyu heping huiyi zhongyao baogao ji jueyi, Renmin, (Peking: 1952).

Yi Wen (pseud), 'Jingguo Chengzhi', (ie Jiang Jingguo and Liao Chengzhi) *Zhanwang* (Hong Kong) 493, pp 6-7.

Yijiuwuliunian feiwei zhongyao huiyi dongtai huibian, (Taipei: 6 May 1957).

Yijiuqiwunian feiwei zhongyao huiyi huibian, (Taipei: March 1958).

Yijiuwuqinian gongfei paichu yu yaojin gezhong daibiaotuan diaocha, (Taipei: January 1958).

Yin Ch'ing-yao:
    'Peiping-Hanoi Conflict: Origins and Development', *Issues and Studies* (October 1978), pp 19-41.
    'The Washington-Moscow-Peiping Strategic Triangle: An Overall View', *Issues and Studies* (February 1979), pp 11-35.

Yinianlai gongfei dui Taiwan yinmou huodong jiqi jinhou dongxiang, (Taipei: May 1958).

Yinianlai gongfei paichu yu yaojin gezhong daibiaotuan diaocha, (Taipei: February 1957). [Zhuanti yanjiu zhengzhi bulei zhi er]

Yinianlai de haiwai feiqing jiqi dongxiang, (Taipei: 16 January 1960).

Yinianlai (sanshiwunian) zhi zhonggong dangpai gongzuo, vol 7, (March 1947).

Yokota Minoru, 'Shu Onrai kaikenki', *Sekai*, 119 (November 1955), pp 92-4.

Yomiuri shinbun, (periodical).

Yoji Akashi, *The Nanyang Chinese National Salvation Movement 1937-41* (University of Kansas, 1970).

John Young, *Checklist of Microfilm Reproductions of Selected Archives of the Japanese Army, Navy, and other Government Agencies, 1868-1945*, (1959).

Kenneth T Young, *Negotiating with the Chinese Communists: the United States Experience, 1953-1967*, (New York: 1968).

Y Chukun, 'Kakyo no shin doko to yakuwari', *Ajia rebiyu* (March 1972), pp 58-63.

Yu Feng, 'He Xiangning Zhongguohua yizuo zhanlan suibi', *Huiyi yu huainian - jinian geming laoren He Xiangning shishi shi zhounian* pp 247-54 (reprinted from *Wenhuibao*, 15 March 1979).

Yu Zhi, 'Mao Zedong sihou zhonggong de waijiao gongzuo', *Zhonggong yanjiu* 123, pp 33-46.

Yu Zhi, 'Xianjieduan zhonggong yu Ri Su de sanjiao guanxi', *Zhonggong yanjiu* 126, pp 72-82.

Yu Zhi, 'Zhonggong qiaowu gongzuo xin dongxiang', *Feiqing yanjiu* XXIII.5 (25 May 1980), pp 44-56.

M Yuriev, 'Ye Ting, Organiser of a Revolutionary Army', *Far Eastern Affairs* (Moscow) 4 (1979), pp 176-84.

Frank C Zagare, 'The Geneva Conference of 1954. A Case of Tacit Deception', *International Studies Quarterly* XXII.3 (September 1973), pp 390-411.

Zagoria, *The Sino-Soviet Conflict, 1956-1961*, (Princeton University Press, 1962).

Zai laoqu banlaoqu zenyang jinxing tudi gaige, (Jinan xinhua shudian nd).

Zai Zhu Mao fei shiyuan zhidao xia de Riben gongchandang, nd.

Zeng Sheng, 'Jianchi huanan zhanchang kangzhan de yimian qizhi. - huiyi dongjiang zongdui de zhandou licheng', *PD*, (23 November 1983).

Zeng Zhenan, *Riben tianzhong neige yu zhonggong 'guanxi zhengchanghua' yanjiu*, (Taipei: June 1975). [Zhengda yanshi lunwen]

Zeng Zijing, *Xin Zhongguo renwuji*, (Hong Kong:Nanqiao, 1949).

Zhang Tianxing, 'Wei wujie renda changweihui fuweiyuanzhang Liao Chengzhi', *Feiqing yuebao* XXI.3, pp 77-80.

Zhang Xizhe, *Gongfei dui haiwai huaqiao de tongzhan gongzuo ji dui qiaoshe he qiaojudi de shentou dianfu huodong*, (Taipei: 30 June 1971).

Zhao Yuanhao, 'Gemingzhe, gemingzhe de muqin', *Huiyi yu huainian - jinian geming laoren He Xiangning shishi shi zhounian* pp 233-6 (reprinted from Guomin (Guangzhou, 5 March 1946).

Zheng Senyu, *Riben heping yundong*, (Peking: Shijie zhishi, 1954).

Zhi Xing, 'Zhonggong xin dangquanpai zhi duiwai tongzhan huodong', *Feiqing yuebao* 21.2, pp 45 ff.

Zhong San, 'Wo suo renshi de Liao Chengzhi', *Renwu* (Hong Kong)11 (15 February 1968), pp 23-4.

Zhonggong dixia douzheng luxian gangling.

Zhonggong diaocha tongjiju. *Kangzhan sannianlai zhi Zhongguo gongchandang.*

Zhonggong dui huaqiao de tongzhan yu jingji lüeduo, np, nd.

Zhonggong ganbu jiyao.

Zhongguo gongchandang lieshi zhuan. See *Zhongguo gongchandang lieshi zhuan*, comp Hua Yingshen, Xin minzhe chubanshe.

Zhonggong Guangdong shengwei, comp *Ershige yue kangzhan huode le sheme?* (9 August 1939).

Zhonggong Guangdong shengwei, comp *Guangdong zhengzhi baogao*, (9 August 1939).

Zhonggong Guangdong shengwei, comp *Guanyu dangde zuzhi baogao dagang*, (9 August 1939).

Zhonggong renwuzhi, Dagong shudian, (Hong Kong, nd, 1951?).

Zhonggong shouyao shilüe huibian, (Taipei).

'Zhonggong tuli yong qiaobao jinxing tongzhan', *Zhongyang ribao*, (22 February 1969).

Zhonggong wenhua da geming ziliao huibian, Ding Wang, comp 2 vols, (Hong Kong: 1967).

Zhonggong zhongyang dongnan fenju xuanchuanbu, comp *Dang de xin zhengce taolun dagang*.

Zhonggong zhongyang zuijin banbu zhi [dixia douzheng gangling], (Zhonglian chubanshe, April 1947).

Zhongguo baoxue shi, see Ge Gongzhen, *Zhongguo baoxue shi*.

Zhongguo gongchandang zuzhi xianzhuang yilan.

Zhongguo gongren, (periodical).

Zhongguo nongmin bao, (periodical).

Zhongguo qingnian, (periodical).

Zhongguo qingnianbao, (periodical).

Zhongguo shibao, (periodical).

Zhongyang diaocha tongjiju, comp *Xinsijun gaikuang kuayao*.

Zhongyang ribao, (periodical).

Zhongyao renwu diaocha, (June 1950).

Index

Aviation agreement, 203, 208-212, 215-218, 221, 224

Canton Christian College, 30-36, 67
Chiang Kaishek, 5, 35, 38, 40-44, 67, 72, 75, 138, 144, 159, 258, 260
Cultural Revolution, 167, 169-182, 192, 194, 197, 201, 204, 216, 226, 244, 262, 264

Deng Xiaoping, 121, 146, 201, 205, 216-228, 243-248, 261-265

Gang of Four, 167, 170, 175-177, 180, 181, 194, 200, 216, 219, 247
Great Leap Forward, 123, 124, 128, 134, 137, 140, 261, 265
Guo Moruo, 99, 101, 108, 131, 144, 172, 194

Hegemony/ism, 200, 219, 223
He Long, 17, 175, 176, 216, 244, 264
Hong Kong, 5, 6, 11, 18, 19, 23-26, 31, 32, 35, 51, 63-75, 80-82, 93-96, 166, 167, 181, 192, 195, 199, 207, 216, 243, 245, 248, 255, 256, 259
Hu Hanmin, 25, 26, 30, 32, 34-36

Ishibashi Tanzan, 99, 106, 107, 121-123, 125, 127-131, 135, 202

Japan Communist Party (JCP), 100, 103, 117, 125-127, 130, 132, 133, 139, 140, 144-146, 159-162, 164, 168, 171, 173, 197, 205, 213, 214, 261
Japan Socialist Party (JSP), 118, 119, 122, 123, 126, 127, 132-135, 139-141, 145, 146, 158-168, 171, 174, 193, 195, 202-206, 214, 218, 222
Jiang Jingguo, 12, 13, 35, 42, 72, 247, 258
Jing Puchun, 8, 19, 42-45, 63, 71, 80, 175-178, 244

Kuomintang (KMT), 5, 8, 20, 32-37, 47, 49, 64-68, 71, 75-78, 82, 97, 248, 257, 259

L-T trade, 129, 133, 138, 141, 146, 147, 159-169, 172-174, 182, 194, 208
Liao Mengxing, 23-26, 31, 34-37, 65, 74-77, 170, 249, 258
Liao Zhongkai, 5, 8, 9, 12, 23-27, 30-37, 40, 41, 45, 47, 66, 67, 71-75, 95, 248, 249, 256-259
Liberal Democratic Party (LDP), 96, 119, 123, 126-144, 159-167, 172, 174, 194-199, 209, 211, 213, 218, 222, 226
Lin Biao, 6, 7, 166, 170-175, 178, 180-183, 192, 200, 216, 219, 221
Liu Yazi, 43, 45, 65, 71

Majiazhou, 72-74
Matsumura Kenzo, 123, 125, 127-131, 133-136, 141-145, 161, 168-170, 174, 182, 194, 203
Memorandum Trade (M-T), 93, 174, 182, 192-194, 198
Miyamoto Kenji, 125, 133, 164, 168, 171, 197, 213
Miyazaki Seimin, 126, 223

Nan Hanchen, 99, 102, 103, 161-168, 173
New China News Agency (NCNA), 68, 78-80

Overseas Chinese Affairs Commission (OCAC), 4, 92, 93, 108, 125, 131, 170, 173, 192, 228

Pan Hannian, 63-65, 69, 250
Peace Conference of the Asian and Pacific Region, 99, 101
People's diplomacy, 94, 95, 104, 105, 196, 198-201, 204, 209, 212, 215, 219, 222, 243, 247
People's Liberation Army (PLA), 97

Revolutionary Alliance, 25

Republic of China (ROC), 12, 35, 98, 104, 106, 117-120, 136-144, 159-163, 194, 198-201, 205, 207-210

Sato, 141, 161-165, 168, 170-172, 174, 182, 183, 192-195, 197
Situ Huimin, 33, 37, 64, 67, 68, 71
SOHYO, 101, 126, 131, 133, 146, 173, 206, 218
Song Qingling, 5-8, 16, 36, 40-44, 47, 49, 65-67, 81, 99, 101, 117, 160, 170-173, 248, 258, 259, 263
Sun Yatsen, 5-8, 12, 23-28, 30-32, 36, 38, 40, 44, 66, 170, 172, 216, 249, 259

Taiwan, 6, 8, 12, 13, 81, 98-102, 117, 118, 124-129, 136-142, 146, 174, 192-194, 196, 199-203, 206-212, 215-219, 221-224, 244-248, 255, 259, 263
Takasaki Tatsunosuke, 107, 108, 127, 133-137, 141-146, 265
The Bandung Conference, 106-108, 137, 164
The Long March, 45-50, 79
Tokyo Special Branch, 38, 39
Tongmenghui, 25
Treaty of Peace and Friendship (TPF), 200, 208, 219-228, 243, 261

United Nations, 142, 143, 163, 183, 193, 218

Yan Xishan, 97
Yanan, 6, 48-50, 63, 64, 67, 73, 76-80, 95

Zhang Guotao, 6, 46-49, 173, 258